—500—
ALL-TIME
GREAT
RECIPES

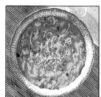

—500—
ALL-TIME
GREAT
RECIPES

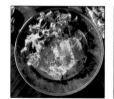

HERMES HOUSE

This edition published by Hermes House in 2001

Hermes House is an imprint of
Anness Publishing Limited
Hermes House
88–89 Blackfriars Road
London SE1 8HA

A CIP catalogue record for this book is available from the British Library.

Publisher: Joanna Lorenz
Managing Editor: Linda Fraser
Designer: Sian Keogh
Photographers: Karl Adamson, Edward Allwright, Steve Baxter, James Duncan, Michelle Garrett,
Amanda Heywood, Don Last, Patrick McLeavy, Michael Michaels
Additional photography: Sopexa UK
Recipes: Carla Capalbo, Maxine Clark, Frances Cleary, Carole Clements, Roz Denny, Christine France,
Sarah Gates, Shirley Gill, Rosamund Grant, Sue Maggs, Annie Nichols, Jenny Stacey, Liz Trigg,
Hilaire Walden, Laura Washburn, Steven Wheeler, Elizabeth Wolf-Cohen
Food for photography: Joanne Craig, Wendy Lee, Jenny Shapter, Jane Stevenson, Elizabeth Wolf-Cohen
Home Economists: Carla Capalbo, Jenny Shapter
Stylists: Madeleine Brehaut, Carla Capalbo, Michelle Garrett, Hilary Guy, Amanda Haywood,
Blake Minton, Kirsty Rawlings, Rebecca Sturrock, Fiona Tillett

Previously published as *Practical Handbook 500 Best Ever Recipes*

Printed and bound in China

1 3 5 7 9 10 8 6 4 2

NOTES

For all recipes, quantities are given in both metric and imperial measures and,
where appropriate, measures are also given in standard cups and spoons. Follow
one set, but not a mixture, because they are not interchangeable.

Standard spoon and cup measures are level.
1 tsp = 5ml, 1 tbsp = 15ml, 1 cup = 250ml/8fl oz

Australian standard tablespoons are 20ml. Australian readers should use 3 tsp
in place of 1 tbsp for measuring small quantities of gelatine, cornflour, salt, etc.

Medium eggs are used unless otherwise stated.

CONTENTS

   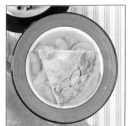

  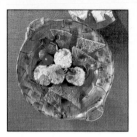 

Introduction

In the modern world's quest for innovation and new taste sensations, it's often easy to forget just how delicious and fulfilling a classic recipe can be. This volume contains a definitive selection of best-ever recipes which will serve as an essential reference point for beginners and as a timely reminder to the experienced cook when planning the perfect meal.

These cosmopolitan creations have gained world-wide status through their harmonious balance of fresh ingredients, herbs and spices. Stemming from justified popularity in their homelands, they have attained universal appeal as part of the international chef's repertoire. Even more appealing is the fact that many traditional recipes are based on a natural nutritional equilibrium which was taken for granted before the days of "fast food" and a high intake of saturated fats. Many of these dishes excel when analyzed in the light of today's vogue for healthy eating. Others are unashamedly sinful (chocoholics, beware!).

The dishes presented in this book are tailored to every season and every event: you can mix and match cooking styles and influences to suit the mood and the occasion, not to mention your pocket. There is a fine selection of hearty soups such as Red Pepper Soup with Lime, which are satisfying enough for a light meal yet attractive enough to serve as an impressive dinner party appetizer. Sophisticated appetizers include Smoked Salmon and Dill Blinis or Chicken Liver Pâté with Marsala, Avocados with Tangy Topping or Pears and Stilton.

Fish and shellfish are increasingly popular in today's health-conscious society. Flavoursome taste sensations such as Smoked Trout with Cucumber or Grilled Fresh Sardines are classic

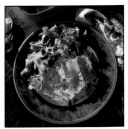

dishes that will always provide a light, fresh main course to tantalize your tastebuds.

Present directions in menu planning may point away from a truly carnivorous way of life, yet there are many occasions when a mouth-watering meat course will win the day. This volume will arm you with the confidence and conviction needed to present a perfect Roast Beef with Yorkshire Pudding or a melting Cottage Pie. Also included is a variety of more unusual dishes such as Duck with Chestnut Sauce, a simple yet impressive dinner party presentation, and economical yet nutritious main courses that will appeal to adults and children alike, such as Sausage and Bean Ragoût. Whether we choose western fare such as Tuna Fishcake Bites or an exotic Kashmir Coconut Fish Curry, these recipes are characterized by a distinctive depth of flavour created by a judicious blend of herbs and spices.

The vegetable dishes in this book are mouth-watering concoctions that can be prepared at short notice for an accompaniment or for a complete, well-balanced meal. Some are long-standing favourites of vegetarian fare, such as Chick-pea Stew; others are innovative versions of world-famous dishes, such as a Chunky Vegetable Paella which combines a colourful appearance with satisfying texture and harmonious flavours.

To finish, the moment that many have been waiting for: the dessert course. These dishes range from light, fluffy mousses and cool, super-smooth sherbets to the richest trifles, and dream puddings made from fruit, cream and chocolate.

This collection of recipes has been drawn together from the combined talents of some of the world's most respected cooks and food writers. With the help of this authoritative guide, your cooking will not only withstand the scrutiny of your most demanding critic – be it yourself or a fierce rival – but will win them over in style.

Carrot and Coriander Soup

Use a good home-made stock for this soup – it adds a far greater depth of flavour than stock made from cubes.

Serves 4

50g/2oz/4 tbsp butter
2 leeks, sliced
450g/1lb carrots, sliced
15ml/1 tbsp ground
   coriander
1.2 litres/2 pints/5 cups
   chicken stock

150ml/¼ pint/⅔ cup
   Greek-style yogurt
salt and ground black
   pepper
30–45ml/2–3 tbsp
   chopped fresh
   coriander, to garnish

1 Melt the butter in a large saucepan. Add the leeks and carrots and stir well, coating the vegetables with the butter. Cover with a tight-fitting lid and cook for about 10 minutes, until the vegetables are beginning to soften but not colour.

2 Stir in the ground coriander and cook for about 1 minute. Pour in the stock and season to taste with salt and pepper. Bring to the boil, cover and simmer for about 20 minutes, until the leeks and carrots are tender.

3 Leave to cool slightly, then purée the soup in a blender until smooth. Return the soup to the pan and add about 30ml/2 tbsp of the yogurt, then taste the soup and adjust the seasoning again to taste. Reheat gently but do not boil.

4 Ladle the soup into bowls and put a spoonful of the remaining yogurt in the centre of each. Scatter over the coriander and serve immediately.

Leek, Potato and Rocket Soup

Rocket, with its distinctive peppery taste, is wonderful in this filling soup. Serve it hot with ciabatta croûtons.

Serves 4–6

50g/2oz/4 tbsp butter
1 onion, chopped
3 leeks, chopped
2 potatoes, diced
900ml/1½ pints/3¾ cups
   light chicken stock
2 large handfuls rocket,
   roughly chopped

150ml/¼ pint/⅔ cup
   double cream
salt and ground black
   pepper
garlic-flavoured ciabatta
   croûtons, to serve

1 Melt the butter in a large heavy-based saucepan, add the onion, leeks and potatoes and stir until all the vegetable pieces are coated in butter.

2 Cover with a tight-fitting lid and leave the vegetables to sweat for about 15 minutes. Pour in the stock, cover once again with the lid, then simmer for a further 20 minutes, until the vegetables are tender.

3 Press the soup through a sieve or food mill and return to the rinsed-out pan. (When puréeing the soup, don't use a blender or food processor, as these will give the soup a gluey texture.) Add the chopped rocket, stir in and cook gently for about 5 minutes.

4 Stir in the cream, then season to taste with salt and pepper. Reheat gently. Ladle the soup into warmed soup bowls, then serve with a few ciabatta croûtons in each.

Cook's Tip

To make the croûtons, cut the bread into 1cm/½ in cubes, without the crust if you wish, and either fry or bake in a roasting tin in oil until golden and crunchy.

Tomato and Basil Soup

In the summer, when tomatoes are both plentiful and cheap to buy, this is a lovely soup to make.

Serves 4

30ml/2 tbsp olive oil	4 fresh basil leaves,
1 onion, chopped	roughly torn
2.5ml/½ tsp caster sugar	300ml/½ pint/1¼ cups
1 carrot, finely chopped	light chicken or
1 potato, finely chopped	vegetable stock
1 garlic clove, crushed	2–3 pieces sun-dried
675g/1½lb ripe tomatoes,	tomatoes in oil
roughly chopped	30ml/2 tbsp shredded
5ml/1 tsp tomato purée	fresh basil leaves
1 bay leaf	salt and ground black
1 thyme sprig	pepper
1 oregano sprig	

1 Heat the oil in a large saucepan, add the onion and sprinkle with the caster sugar. Cook gently for 5 minutes.

2 Add the chopped carrot and potato, cover the pan and cook over a low heat for a further 10 minutes, without browning the vegetables.

3 Stir in the garlic, tomatoes, tomato purée, herbs and stock, and season to taste with salt and pepper. Cover the pan with a tight-fitting lid and cook gently for about 25–30 minutes, or until the vegetables are tender.

4 Remove the pan from the heat and press the soup through a sieve or food mill to extract all the skins and pips. Season again with salt and pepper to taste.

5 Reheat the soup gently, then ladle into four warmed soup bowls. Finely chop the sun-dried tomatoes and mix with a little oil from the jar. Add a spoonful to each serving, then scatter the shredded basil over the top.

Corn and Shellfish Chowder

Chowder comes from the French word *chaudron*, meaning a large pot in which the soup is cooked.

Serves 4

25g/1oz/2 tbsp butter	175g/6oz can white
1 small onion, chopped	crabmeat, drained and
350g/12oz can	flaked
sweetcorn, drained	150ml/¼ pint/⅔ cup
600ml/1 pint/2½ cups	single cream
milk	pinch of cayenne pepper
2 spring onions, finely	salt and ground black
chopped	pepper
115g/4oz/1 cup peeled,	4 whole prawns in the
cooked prawns	shell, to garnish

1 Melt the butter in a large saucepan and gently fry the onion for 4–5 minutes, until softened.

2 Reserve 30ml/2 tbsp of the sweetcorn for the garnish and add the remainder to the pan, along with the milk. Bring the soup to the boil, then reduce the heat, cover the pan with a tight-fitting lid and simmer over a low heat for 5 minutes.

3 Pour the soup, in batches if necessary, into a blender or food processor. Process until smooth.

4 Return the soup to the pan and stir in the spring onions, crabmeat, prawns, cream and cayenne pepper. Reheat gently over a low heat.

5 Meanwhile, place the reserved sweetcorn kernels in a small frying pan without oil and dry-fry over a moderate heat until golden and toasted.

6 Season to taste with salt and pepper and serve each bowl of soup garnished with a few of the toasted sweetcorn kernels and a whole prawn.

Spiced Parsnip Soup

This pale, creamy-textured soup is given a special touch with an aromatic garlic and mustard seed garnish.

Serves 4–6
40g/1½oz/3 tbsp butter
1 onion, chopped
675g/1½lb parsnips, diced
5ml/1 tsp ground
  coriander
2.5ml/½ tsp ground
  cumin
2.5ml/½ tsp ground
  turmeric
1.5ml/¼ tsp chilli
  powder
1.2 litres/2 pints/5 cups
  chicken stock
150ml/¼ pint/⅔ cup
  single cream
15ml/1 tbsp sunflower oil
1 garlic clove, cut into
  julienne strips
10ml/2 tsp yellow
  mustard seeds
salt and ground black
  pepper

1 Melt the butter in a large saucepan and fry the onion and parsnips gently for about 3 minutes.

2 Stir in the spices and cook for 1 minute more. Add the stock, season to taste with salt and pepper and bring to the boil, then reduce the heat. Cover with a tight-fitting lid and simmer for about 45 minutes, until the parsnips are tender.

3 Cool slightly, then place in a blender and purée until smooth. Return the soup to the pan, add the cream and heat through gently over a low heat.

4 Heat the oil in a small pan, add the julienne strips of garlic and yellow mustard seeds and fry quickly until the garlic is beginning to brown and the mustard seeds start to pop and splutter. Remove the pan from the heat.

5 Ladle the soup into warmed soup bowls and pour a little of the hot spice mixture over each. Serve at once.

Cook's Tip
Crushed coriander seeds may be substituted for the mustard seeds in the garnish.

Pumpkin Soup

The flavour of this soup will develop and improve if it is made a day in advance.

Serves 4–6
900g/2lb pumpkin
45ml/3 tbsp olive oil
2 onions, chopped
2 celery sticks, chopped
450g/1lb tomatoes,
  chopped
1.5 litres/2½ pints/6¼
  cups vegetable stock
30ml/2 tbsp tomato purée
1 bouquet garni
2–3 rashers streaky
  bacon, crisply fried
  and crumbled
30ml/2 tbsp chopped
  fresh parsley
salt and ground black
  pepper

1 With a sharp knife cut the pumpkin into thin slices, discarding the skin and seeds.

2 Heat the oil in a large saucepan and fry the onions and celery for about 5 minutes. Add the pumpkin and tomatoes and cook for a further 5 minutes.

3 Add the vegetable stock, tomato purée and bouquet garni to the pan. Season with salt and pepper. Bring the soup to the boil, then reduce the heat, cover and simmer for 45 minutes.

4 Allow the soup to cool slightly, remove the bouquet garni, then purée (in two batches, if necessary) in a food processor or blender.

5 Press the soup through a sieve, then return it to the pan. Reheat gently and season again. Ladle the soup into warmed soup bowls. Sprinkle with the crispy bacon and parsley and serve at once.

Jerusalem Artichoke Soup

Topped with saffron cream, this soup is wonderful to serve on a chilly winter's day.

Serves 4

50g/2oz/4 tbsp butter
1 onion, chopped
450g/1lb Jerusalem
    artichokes, peeled and
    cut into chunks
900ml/1½ pints/3¾ cups
    chicken stock
150ml/¼ pint/⅔ cup milk

150ml/¼ pint/⅔ cup
    double cream
large pinch of saffron
    powder
salt and ground black
    pepper
snipped fresh chives, to
    garnish

1 Melt the butter in a large heavy-based saucepan and cook the onion for 5–8 minutes, until soft but not browned, stirring occasionally.

2 Add the artichokes to the pan and stir until coated in the butter. Cover with a tight-fitting lid and cook gently for 10–15 minutes; do not allow the artichokes to brown. Pour in the stock and milk, then cover again and simmer for about 15 minutes. Cool slightly, then process in a food processor or blender until smooth.

3 Strain the soup back into the pan. Add half the cream, season to taste with salt and pepper, and reheat gently. Lightly whip the remaining cream and saffron powder. Ladle the soup into warmed soup bowls and put a spoonful of saffron cream in the centre of each. Scatter over the snipped chives and serve at once.

Broccoli and Stilton Soup

A really easy, but rich, soup – choose something simple to follow, such as plainly grilled meat, poultry or fish.

Serves 4

350g/12oz/3 cups
    broccoli florets
25g/1oz/2 tbsp butter
1 onion, chopped
1 leek, white part only,
    chopped
1 small potato, diced
600ml/1 pint/2½ cups
    hot chicken stock

300ml/½ pint/1¼ cups
    milk
45ml/3 tbsp double cream
115g/4oz Stilton cheese,
    rind removed,
    crumbled
salt and ground black
    pepper

1 Discard any tough stems from the broccoli florets. Set aside two small florets for the garnish.

2 Melt the butter in a large saucepan and cook the onion and leek until soft but not coloured. Add the broccoli and potato, then pour in the stock. Cover with a tight-fitting lid and simmer for 15–20 minutes, until the vegetables are tender.

3 Cool slightly, then purée in a food processor or blender. Strain through a sieve back into the pan.

4 Add the milk, cream and seasoning to the pan and reheat gently. At the last minute add the cheese, stirring until it just melts. Do not boil.

5 Meanwhile, blanch the reserved broccoli florets and cut them vertically into thin slices. Ladle the soup into warmed bowls and garnish with the broccoli florets and a generous grinding of black pepper.

Cook's Tip
Be very careful not to boil the soup once the cheese has been added.

Minestrone with Pesto

This hearty, Italian mixed vegetable soup is a great way to use up any leftover vegetables you may have.

Serves 4

30ml/2 tbsp olive oil
2 garlic cloves, crushed
1 onion, sliced
225g/8oz/2 cups diced
  lean bacon
2 small courgettes,
  quartered and sliced
50g/2oz/1½ cups French
  beans, chopped
2 small carrots, diced
2 celery sticks, finely
  chopped
bouquet garni
50g/2oz/½ cup short cut
  macaroni
50g/2oz/½ cup frozen
  peas

200g/7oz can red kidney
  beans, drained and
  rinsed
50g/2oz/1 cup shredded
  green cabbage
4 tomatoes, skinned and
  seeded
salt and ground black
  pepper

For the toasts

8 slices French bread
15ml/1 tbsp ready-made
  pesto sauce
15ml/1 tbsp grated
  Parmesan cheese

1 Heat the oil in a large saucepan and gently fry the garlic and onions for 5 minutes, until just softened. Add the bacon, courgettes, French beans, carrots and celery to the pan and stir-fry for a further 3 minutes.

2 Pour 1.2 litres/2 pints/5 cups of cold water over the vegetables and add the bouquet garni. Cover the pan with a tight-fitting lid and simmer for 25 minutes.

3 Add the macaroni, peas and kidney beans and cook for 8 minutes more. Then add the cabbage and tomatoes and cook for an additional 5 minutes.

4 To make the toasts, spread the bread slices with the pesto, sprinkle a little Parmesan over each one and gently brown under a hot grill. Remove the bouquet garni from the soup, season to taste and serve with the toasts.

French Onion Soup

Onion soup comes in many different guises, from smooth and creamy to this – the absolute classic from France.

Serves 4

25g/1oz/2 tbsp butter
15ml/1 tbsp oil
3 large onions, thinly
  sliced
5ml/1 tsp soft brown
  sugar
15g/½oz/1 tbsp plain
  flour
2 x 300g/10oz cans
  condensed beef
  consommé
30ml/2 tbsp medium
  sherry

10ml/2 tsp
  Worcestershire sauce
8 slices French bread
15ml/1 tbsp French
  coarse-grained
  mustard
75g/3oz/1 cup grated
  Gruyère cheese
salt and ground black
  pepper
15ml/1 tbsp chopped
  fresh parsley, to
  garnish

1 Heat the butter and oil in a large saucepan and cook the onions and brown sugar gently for about 20 minutes, stirring occasionally until the onions start to turn golden brown.

2 Stir in the flour and cook for a further 2 minutes. Pour in the consommé plus two cans of water, then add the sherry and Worcestershire sauce. Season with salt and pepper, cover and simmer gently for a further 25–30 minutes.

3 Preheat the grill and, just before serving, toast the bread lightly on both sides. Spread one side of each slice with the mustard and top with the grated cheese. Grill the toasts until bubbling and golden.

4 Ladle the soup into bowls. Pop two croûtons on top of each bowl of soup and garnish with chopped fresh parsley. Serve at once.

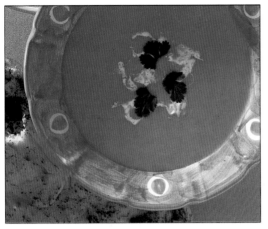

Curried Parsnip Soup

The spices in this soup impart a delicious, mild curry flavour which brings back memories of the Raj.

Serves 4

25g/1oz/2 tbsp butter
1 garlic clove, crushed
1 onion, chopped
5ml/1 tsp ground cumin
5ml/1 tsp ground coriander
450g/1lb (about 4) parsnips, sliced
10ml/2 tsp medium curry paste
450ml/¾ pint/scant 2 cups chicken or vegetable stock
450ml/¾ pint/scant 2 cups milk
60ml/4 tbsp soured cream
good squeeze of lemon juice
salt and ground black pepper
fresh coriander sprigs, to garnish
ready-made garlic and coriander naan bread, to serve

1 Heat the butter in a large saucepan and fry the garlic and onion for 4–5 minutes, until lightly golden. Stir in the spices and cook for a further 1–2 minutes.

2 Add the parsnips and stir until well coated with the butter, then stir in the curry paste, followed by the stock. Cover the pan with a tight-fitting lid and simmer for 15 minutes, until the parsnips are tender.

3 Ladle the soup into a blender or food processor and blend until smooth. Return to the pan and stir in the milk. Heat gently for 2–3 minutes, then add 30ml/2 tbsp of the soured cream and the lemon juice. Season well with salt and pepper.

4 Serve in bowls topped with spoonfuls of the remaining soured cream and the fresh coriander accompanied by the warmed, spicy naan bread.

Cook's Tip
For the best flavour, use home-made chicken or vegetable stock in this soup.

Red Pepper Soup with Lime

The beautiful rich red colour of this soup makes it a very attractive starter or light lunch.

Serves 4–6

4 fresh red peppers, seeded and chopped
1 large onion, chopped
5ml/1 tsp olive oil
1 garlic clove, crushed
1 small red chilli, sliced
45ml/3 tbsp tomato purée
juice of 1 lime
900ml/1½ pints/3¾ cups chicken stock
salt and ground black pepper
finely grated rind and shreds of lime rind, to garnish

1 Cook the onion and peppers gently in the oil in a saucepan covered with a tight-fitting lid for about 5 minutes, shaking the pan occasionally, until softened.

2 Stir in the garlic, then add the chilli with the tomato purée. Stir in half the stock, then bring to the boil. Cover the pan and simmer for 10 minutes.

3 Cool slightly, then purée in a food processor or blender. Return to the pan, then add the remaining stock, the lime rind and juice and seasoning.

4 Bring the soup back to the boil, then serve at once with a few shreds of lime rind scattered into each bowl.

Thai-style Sweetcorn Soup

This is a very quick and easy soup. If you are using frozen prawns, defrost them before adding to the soup.

Serves 4

2.5ml/½ tsp sesame or sunflower oil
2 spring onions, thinly sliced
1 garlic clove, crushed
600ml/1 pint/2½ cups chicken stock
425g/15oz can cream-style sweetcorn

225g/8oz/2 cups peeled, cooked prawns
5ml/1 tsp green chilli paste or chilli sauce (optional)
salt and ground black pepper
fresh coriander leaves, to garnish

Heat the oil in a large heavy-based saucepan and sauté the onions and garlic over a moderate heat for 1 minute, until softened but not browned. Stir in the chicken stock, cream-style sweetcorn, prawns and chilli paste or sauce, if using. Bring the soup to the boil, stirring occasionally. Season to taste with salt and pepper, then serve at once, sprinkled with fresh coriander leaves to garnish.

Haddock and Broccoli Chowder

This hearty soup makes a meal in itself when served with crusty, country-style bread.

Serves 4

4 spring onions, sliced
450g/1lb new potatoes, diced
300ml/½ pint/1¼ cups home-made fish stock or water
300ml/½ pint/1¼ cups skimmed milk
1 bay leaf

225g/8oz/2 cups broccoli florets, sliced
450g/1lb smoked haddock fillets, skinned
200g/7oz can sweetcorn, drained
ground black pepper
chopped spring onions, to garnish

Place the spring onions and potatoes in a pan and add the stock, milk and bay leaf. Bring to the boil, reduce the heat, cover and simmer for 10 minutes. Add the broccoli. Cut the fish into bite-size chunks; add to the pan with the sweetcorn. Season well with black pepper, then cover again and simmer until the fish is cooked through. Remove the bay leaf, scatter over the chopped spring onions and serve immediately.

Cock-a-leekie Soup

This healthy main course soup is given a sweet touch by the inclusion of prunes.

Serves 4–6

Gently cook 1.2 litres/2 pints/5 cups chicken stock and bouquet garni for 40 minutes. Cut 4 leeks into 2.5cm/1in slices, add to the pan along with 8–12 soaked prunes and cook gently for 20 minutes. Discard the bouquet garni. Remove the chicken, discard the skin and bones and chop the flesh. Return the chicken to the pan and season to taste. Heat the soup, then serve with soft buttered rolls.

Green Pea and Mint Soup

This soup is equally delicious lightly chilled. Stir in the swirl of cream just before serving.

Serves 4

50g/2oz/4 tbsp butter
4 spring onions, chopped
450g/1lb/4 cups fresh or frozen peas
600ml/1 pint/2½ cups chicken or vegetable stock
2 large fresh mint sprigs
600ml/1 pint/2½ cups milk
pinch of sugar (optional)
salt and ground black pepper
single cream, to serve
small fresh mint sprigs, to garnish

1 Heat the butter in a large saucepan and gently fry the spring onions until just softened but not coloured.

2 Stir the peas into the pan, add the stock and mint and bring to the boil. Cover and simmer very gently for about 30 minutes for fresh peas or 15 minutes if you are using frozen peas, until the peas are very tender. Remove about 45ml/3 tbsp of the peas using a slotted spoon, and reserve for the garnish.

3 Pour the soup into a food processor or blender, add the milk and purée until smooth. Then return the soup to the pan and reheat gently. Season to taste with salt and pepper, adding a pinch of sugar if you wish.

4 Pour the soup into bowls. Swirl a little cream into each, then garnish with mint and the reserved peas.

Cook's Tip
Fresh peas are increasingly available during the summer months from greengrocers and supermarkets. The effort of podding them is well worthwhile, as they impart a unique flavour to this delicious, vibrant soup.

Beetroot and Apricot Swirl

This soup is most attractive if you swirl together the two coloured purées, but mix them together if you prefer.

Serves 4

4 large cooked beetroot, roughly chopped
1 small onion, roughly chopped
600ml/1 pint/2½ cups chicken stock
200g/7oz ready-to-eat dried apricots
250ml/8fl oz/1 cup orange juice
salt and ground black pepper

1 Place the beetroot and half of the onion in a saucepan with the stock. Bring to the boil, then reduce the heat, cover with a tight-fitting lid and simmer for about 10 minutes. Purée in a food processor or blender.

2 Place the rest of the onion in a pan with the apricots and orange juice, cover and simmer gently for about 15 minutes until tender. Purée in a food processor or blender.

3 Return the two mixtures to the saucepans and reheat. Season to taste with salt and pepper, then swirl the mixtures together in individual soup bowls to create a marbled effect.

Cook's Tip
Beetroot are available ready cooked. To cook your own, simply place in a saucepan with enough water to cover, bring to the boil, then cover and cook for 1 hour. Drain, then peel the beetroot with your fingers when cool enough to handle.

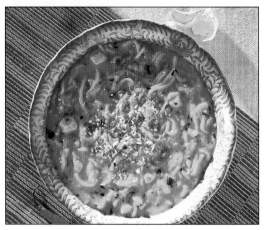

Thai-style Chicken Soup

New England Pumpkin Soup

Omit the red chilli from the garnish if you prefer a milder flavour in this soup.

For a smooth-textured soup, process all the mixture in a food processor or blender.

Serves 4

15ml/1 tbsp vegetable oil
1 garlic clove, finely
    chopped
2 x 175g/6oz boned
    chicken breasts,
    skinned and chopped
2.5ml/½ tsp ground
    turmeric
1.5ml/¼ tsp hot chilli
    powder
75g/3oz creamed coconut
900ml/1½ pints/3¾ cups
    hot chicken stock
30ml/2 tbsp lemon or lime
    juice

30ml/2 tbsp crunchy
    peanut butter
50g/2oz/1 cup thread egg
    noodles, broken into
    small pieces
15ml/1 tbsp spring
    onions, finely chopped
15ml/1 tbsp chopped fresh
    coriander
salt and ground black
    pepper
30ml/2 tbsp desiccated
    coconut and ½ red
    chilli, seeded and finely
    chopped, to garnish

1 Heat the oil in a large saucepan and fry the garlic for 1 minute until lightly golden. Add the chicken and spices and stir-fry for a further 3–4 minutes. Crumble the creamed coconut into the stock and stir until dissolved. Pour on to the chicken and add the lemon juice, peanut butter and egg noodles. Cover and simmer for 15 minutes. Add the spring onions and coriander, season to taste with salt and pepper and cook for a further 5 minutes.

2 Fry the coconut and chilli for 2–3 minutes, stirring until the coconut is lightly browned. Use as a garnish for the soup.

Serves 4

25g/1oz/2 tbsp butter
1 onion, finely chopped
1 garlic clove, crushed
15g/½ oz/1 tbsp plain
    flour
pinch of grated nutmeg
2.5ml/½ tsp ground
    cinnamon
350g/12oz pumpkin,
    seeded, peeled and diced
600ml/1 pint/2½ cups
    chicken stock

150ml/¼ pint/⅔ cup
    orange juice
5ml/1 tsp brown sugar

For the croûtons

15ml/1 tbsp vegetable oil
2 slices granary bread,
    without the crusts
30ml/2 tbsp sunflower
    seeds
salt and ground black
    pepper

1 Melt the butter in a large saucepan and gently fry the onions and garlic for 4–5 minutes, until softened.

2 Stir in the flour, spices and pumpkin, then cover and cook gently for 6 minutes, stirring occasionally.

3 Add the chicken stock, orange juice and brown sugar. Cover again, and bring to the boil, then simmer for 20 minutes until the pumpkin has softened.

4 Process half the mixture in a blender or food processor. Return the soup to the pan with the remaining chunky mixture, stirring constantly. Season to taste and heat through.

5 To make the croûtons, heat the oil in a frying pan, cut the bread into cubes and gently fry until just beginning to brown. Add the sunflower seeds and fry for 1–2 minutes. Drain the croûtons on kitchen paper. Serve the soup hot, garnished with a few of the croûtons scattered over the top, and serve the remaining croûtons separately.

Split Pea and Courgette Soup

Rich and satisfying, this tasty and nutritious soup is ideal to serve on a chilly winter's day.

Serves 4

175g/6oz/1 cup yellow
  split peas
5ml/1 tsp sunflower oil
1 large onion, finely
  chopped
2 courgettes, finely diced

900ml/1½ pints/3¾ cups
  chicken stock
2.5ml/½ tsp ground
  turmeric
salt and ground black
  pepper

1 Place the split peas in a bowl, cover with cold water and leave to soak for several hours or overnight. Drain, rinse in cold water and drain again.

2 Heat the oil in a saucepan. Add the onion, cover with a tight-fitting lid and cook until soft. Reserve a handful of diced courgettes and add the rest to the pan. Cook, stirring constantly, for 2–3 minutes.

3 Add the stock and turmeric to the pan and bring to the boil. Reduce the heat, then cover and simmer for about 30–40 minutes, or until the split peas are tender. Add seasoning to taste.

4 When the soup is almost ready, bring a large saucepan of water to the boil, add the reserved diced courgettes and cook for 1 minute, then drain and add to the soup before serving hot with warm crusty bread.

Cook's Tip
For a quicker alternative, use split red lentils for this soup. They do not require presoaking and cook very quickly. Adjust the amount of chicken stock used, if you need to.

Mediterranean Tomato Soup

Children will love this soup – especially if you use fancy pasta such as alphabet or animal shapes.

Serves 4

675g/1½lb ripe plum
  tomatoes
1 onion, quartered
1 celery stick
1 garlic clove
15ml/1 tbsp olive oil
450ml/¾ pint/scant
  2 cups chicken stock

15ml/2 tbsp tomato purée
50g/2oz/½ cup small
  pasta shapes
salt and ground black
  pepper
fresh coriander or parsley
  sprigs, to garnish

1 Place the tomatoes, onion, celery and garlic in a saucepan with the oil. Cover with a tight-fitting lid and cook over a gentle heat for 40–45 minutes, shaking the pan occasionally, until the vegetables become very soft.

2 Spoon the vegetables into a food processor or blender and process until smooth. Press through a sieve to remove the tomato pips, then return to the pan.

3 Stir in the stock and tomato purée and bring to the boil. Add the pasta and simmer gently for about 8 minutes, or until the pasta is tender. Add salt and pepper to taste, then sprinkle with coriander or parsley to garnish and serve hot.

White Bean Soup

Small white lima beans or pinto beans work well in this soup, or try butter beans for a change.

Serves 6

350g/12oz/1½ cups dried
   cannellini or other
   white beans
1 bay leaf
75ml/5 tbsp olive oil
1 onion, finely chopped
1 carrot, finely chopped
1 celery stick, finely
   chopped
3 tomatoes, peeled and
   finely chopped

2 garlic cloves, finely
   chopped
5ml/1 tsp fresh thyme
   leaves or 2.5ml/½ tsp
   dried thyme
750ml/1¼ pints/3⅔ cups
   boiling water
salt and ground black
   pepper
extra virgin olive oil, to
   serve

1 Pick over the beans carefully, discarding any stones or other particles. Soak the beans in a large bowl of cold water overnight. Drain. Place the beans in a large saucepan of water, bring to the boil, and cook for 20 minutes. Drain. Return the beans to the pan, cover with cold water, and bring to the boil again. Add the bay leaf, and cook 1–2 hours until the beans are tender. Drain again. Remove the bay leaf.

2 Purée about three-quarters of the beans in a food processor or blender. Alternatively, pass through a food mill, adding a little water if needed.

3 Heat the oil in a large saucepan and cook the onion until softened but not browned. Add the carrot and celery, and cook for a further 5 minutes.

4 Stir in the tomatoes, garlic and fresh or dried thyme. Cook for 6–8 minutes more, stirring often.

5 Pour in the boiling water. Stir in the beans and the bean purée. Season to taste with salt and pepper. Simmer for about 10–15 minutes. Serve in individual soup bowls, sprinkled with a little extra virgin olive oil.

Fish Soup

For extra flavour use some smoked fish in this soup and rub the bread with a garlic clove before toasting.

Serves 6

900g/2¼ lb mixed fish
   fillets such as coley,
   dogfish, whiting, red
   mullet or cod
90ml/6 tbsp olive oil,
   plus extra to serve
1 onion, finely chopped
1 celery stick, chopped
1 carrot, chopped
60ml/4 tbsp chopped
   fresh parsley

175ml/6 fl oz/¾ cup dry
   white wine
3 tomatoes, peeled and
   chopped
2 garlic cloves, finely
   chopped
1.5 litres/2½ pints/
   6¼ cups boiling water
salt and ground black
   pepper
French bread, to serve

1 Scale and clean the fish, discarding all innards but leaving the heads on. Cut into large pieces. Rinse well in cool water.

2 Heat the oil in a large saucepan and cook the onion over a low to moderate heat until just softened. Stir in the celery and carrot and cook for 5 minutes more. Add the parsley.

3 Pour in the wine, raise the heat and cook until it reduces by about half. Stir in the tomatoes and garlic. Cook for 3–4 minutes, stirring occasionally. Pour in the boiling water and bring back to the boil. Cook for 15 minutes.

4 Stir in the fish and simmer for 10–15 minutes, or until the fish are tender. Season to taste with salt and pepper.

5 Remove the fish from the soup with a slotted spoon. Discard any bones. Place in a food processor and purée until smooth. Taste again for seasoning. If the soup is too thick, add a little more water.

6 To serve, heat the soup to simmering. Toast the rounds of bread and sprinkle with olive oil. Place two or three in each soup plate before pouring over the soup.

Barley and Vegetable Soup

This soup comes from the Alto Adige region, in Italy's mountainous north. It is thick, nourishing and warming.

Serves 6–8

225g/8oz/1 cup pearl
    barley, preferably
    organic
2 litres/3½ pints/9 cups
    meat stock or water, or
    a combination of both
45ml/3 tbsp olive oil
2 carrots, finely chopped
2 celery sticks, finely
    chopped
1 leek, thinly sliced
1 large potato, finely
    chopped

115g/4oz/½ cup diced
    ham
1 bay leaf
45ml/3 tbsp chopped
    fresh parsley
1 small fresh rosemary
    sprig
salt and ground black
    pepper
freshly grated Parmesan
    cheese, to serve

1 Pick over the barley and discard any stones or other particles. Wash the barley in cold water and soak it in cold water for at least 3 hours.

2 Drain the barley and place it in a large saucepan with the stock or water. Bring to the boil, lower the heat and simmer for 1 hour. Skim off any scum.

3 Stir in the oil, all the vegetables and the ham. Add the herbs. If necessary add more water; the ingredients should be covered by at least 2.5cm/1in. Simmer for 1–1½ hours, or until the vegetables and barley are very tender.

4 Season to taste with salt and pepper. Serve hot with grated Parmesan cheese, if desired.

Pasta and Dried Bean Soup

In Italy this soup is made with dried or fresh beans and served hot or at room temperature.

Serves 4–6

300g/11oz/1¼ cups dried
    borlotti or cannellini
    beans
400g/14oz can plum
    tomatoes, chopped,
    with their juice
3 garlic cloves, crushed
2 bay leaves
coarsely ground black
    pepper
90ml/6 tbsp olive oil,
    plus extra to serve

750ml/1¼ pints/3½ cups
    water
10ml/2 tsp salt
200g/7oz/scant 2 cups
    ditalini or other small
    pasta
45ml/3 tbsp chopped
    fresh parsley
freshly grated Parmesan
    cheese, to serve

1 Soak the beans in water overnight. Rinse and drain well. Place them in a large saucepan and cover with water. Bring to the boil and cook for 10 minutes. Rinse and drain again.

2 Return the beans to the pan. Add enough water to cover them by 2.5cm/1in. Stir in the coarsely chopped tomatoes with their juice, the garlic, bay leaves, black pepper and the oil. Simmer for 1½–2 hours, or until the beans are tender. Add more water if necessary.

3 Remove the bay leaves. Pass about half of the bean mixture through a food mill, or purée in a food processor. Stir into the pan with the remaining bean mixture. Add the water and bring the soup to the boil.

4 Add the salt and the pasta. Stir, then cook until the pasta is just done. Stir in the parsley. Allow the dish to stand for at least 10 minutes, then serve with extra olive oil and grated Parmesan cheese.

Pasta and Lentil Soup

Small brown lentils are usually used in this wholesome soup, but green lentils may be substituted.

Serves 4–6

225g/8oz/1 cup dried green or brown lentils
90ml/6 tbsp olive oil
50g/2oz/¼ cup ham or salt pork, finely diced
1 onion, finely chopped
1 celery stick, finely chopped
1 carrot, finely chopped
2 litres/3½ pints/9 cups chicken stock or water
1 fresh sage leaf
1 fresh thyme sprig or 1.5ml/¼ tsp dried thyme
salt and ground black pepper
175g/6oz/2½ cups ditalini or other small soup pasta

1   Carefully check the lentils for small stones. Place them in a bowl, cover with cold water and soak for 2–3 hours. Rinse and drain well through a colander.

2   Heat the oil in a large saucepan and sauté the ham or salt pork for 2–3 minutes. Add the onion and cook gently until it softens but does not brown.

3   Stir in the celery and carrot and cook for 5 minutes more, stirring frequently. Add the lentils and stir to coat them evenly in the cooking fats.

4   Pour in the stock or water and the herbs and bring the soup to the boil. Cook over a moderate heat for about 1 hour or until the lentils are tender. Season to taste.

5   Stir in the pasta, and cook until it is just done. Allow the soup to stand for a few minutes before serving.

Pasta and Chick-pea Soup

The addition of a fresh rosemary sprig creates a typically Mediterranean flavour in this soup.

Serves 4–6

200g/7oz/generous 1 cup dried chick-peas
3 garlic cloves, peeled
1 bay leaf
90ml/6 tbsp olive oil
pinch of ground black pepper
50g/2oz/¼ cup diced salt pork, pancetta or bacon
1 fresh rosemary sprig
600ml/1 pint/2½ cups water
150g/5oz/generous 1 cup ditalini or other short hollow pasta
pinch of salt
freshly grated Parmesan cheese, to serve (optional)

1   Soak the chick-peas in water overnight. Rinse well and drain. Place in a large saucepan with water to cover. Boil for 15 minutes. Rinse and drain.

2   Return the chick-peas to the pan. Add water to cover, one garlic clove, the bay leaf, half of the oil and the pinch of pepper.

3   Simmer about 2 hours until tender, adding more water as necessary. Remove the bay leaf. Pass about half the chick-peas through a food mill or purée in a food processor with a little cooking liquid. Return the purée to the pan with the rest of the chick-peas and the remaining cooking water.

4   Sauté the diced pork, pancetta or bacon gently in the remaining oil with the rosemary and two garlic cloves until just golden. Discard the rosemary and garlic.

5   Stir the meat with its oils into the chick-pea mixture.

6   Add the water to the chick-peas, and bring to the boil. Adjust the seasoning if necessary. Stir in the pasta, and cook until just *al dente*. Serve with Parmesan cheese, if you wish.

Leek and Potato Soup

Scotch Broth

If you prefer a smoother textured soup, press the mixture through a sieve or purée it in a food mill.

Sustaining and warming, this traditional Scottish soup makes a delicious winter soup anywhere in the world.

Serves 4

50g/2oz/4 tbsp butter
2 leeks, chopped
1 small onion, finely
  chopped
350g/12oz potatoes,
  chopped

900ml/1½ pints/3¾ cups
  chicken or vegetable
  stock
salt and ground black
  pepper

Serves 6–8

900g/2lb lean neck of
  lamb, cut into large
  even-size chunks
1.75 litres/3 pints/
  7½ cups water
1 large onion, chopped
50g/2oz/¼ cup pearl
  barley
bouquet garni

1 large carrot, chopped
1 turnip, chopped
3 leeks, chopped
½ small white cabbage,
  shredded
salt and ground black
  pepper
chopped fresh parsley, to
  garnish

1 Heat 25g/1oz/2 tbsp of the butter in a large saucepan and gently cook the leeks and onions for about 7 minutes, stirring occasionally until softened but not browned.

2 Add the chopped potatoes to the pan and cook for 2–3 minutes, stirring occasionally, then add the chicken or vegetable stock and bring to the boil. Cover the pan with a tight-fitting lid and simmer gently for 30–35 minutes, until all the vegetables are very tender.

3 Season to taste with salt and pepper. Remove the pan from the heat and stir in the remaining butter in small pieces until completely melted. Serve the soup hot with warm crusty bread and butter, if you wish.

Cook's Tip
Never use a food processor or blender to purée potatoes as the starch in the vegetable will be broken down and will create an unpleasant gluey consistency.

1 Put the lamb and water into a large saucepan and bring to the boil. Skim off the scum, then stir in the onion, barley and bouquet garni.

2 Bring the soup back to the boil, then partly cover the saucepan and simmer gently for 1 hour. Add the remaining vegetables and season to taste with salt and pepper. Bring to the boil, partly cover again and simmer for about 35 minutes until the vegetables are tender.

3 Remove any surplus fat from the top of the soup, then serve hot, sprinkled with chopped parsley.

Country Vegetable Soup

To ring the changes, vary the vegetables according to what you like and what is in season.

Serves 4

50g/2oz/4 tbsp butter	bouquet garni
1 onion, chopped	115g/4oz/1 cup green
2 leeks, sliced	beans, chopped
2 celery sticks, sliced	salt and ground black
2 carrots, sliced	pepper
2 small turnips, chopped	chopped fresh herbs such
4 ripe tomatoes, skinned	as tarragon, thyme,
and chopped	chives and parsley, to
1 litre/1¾ pints/4 cups	garnish
chicken or vegetable	
stock	

1 Heat the butter in a large saucepan and cook the onion and leeks gently until soft but not coloured.

2 Add the celery, carrots and turnips and cook them for about 3–4 minutes, stirring occasionally. Stir in the tomatoes and stock, add the bouquet garni and simmer the vegetables gently for about 20 minutes.

3 Add the beans to the soup and continue to cook until all the vegetables are tender. Season to taste with salt and pepper and serve garnished with chopped herbs.

Split Pea and Bacon Soup

This soup is also called "London Particular", because of the city's smog. The fogs in turn were named "pea-soupers".

Serves 4

15g/½oz/1 tbsp butter	1.2 litres/2 pints/5 cups
115g/4oz smoked back	chicken stock
bacon, chopped	2 thick slices firm bread,
1 large onion, chopped	buttered and without
1 carrot, chopped	crusts
1 celery stick, chopped	2 slices streaky bacon
75g/3oz/scant ½ cup	salt and ground black
split peas	pepper

1 Heat the butter in a saucepan and cook the back bacon until the fat runs. Stir in the onion, carrot and celery and cook for 2–3 minutes.

2 Add the split peas, followed by the stock. Bring to the boil, stirring occasionally, then cover with a tight-fitting lid and simmer for 45–60 minutes.

3 Meanwhile, preheat the oven to 180°C/350°F/Gas 4. Bake the bread for about 20 minutes, until crisp and brown, then cut into dice.

4 Grill the streaky bacon until very crisp, then chop finely.

5 When the soup is ready, season to taste and serve hot with the chopped bacon and croûtons scattered on each portion.

Smoked Haddock and Potato Soup

This soup's traditional name is "cullen skink". A "cullen" is a town's port district and "skink" means stock or broth.

Serves 6

1 Finnan haddock (about 350g/12oz)
1 onion, chopped
bouquet garni
900ml/1½ pints/3¾ cups water
500g/1¼lb potatoes, quartered
600ml/1 pint/2½ cups milk
40g/1½ oz/3 tbsp butter
salt and ground black pepper
snipped fresh chives, to garnish

1 Put the haddock, onion, bouquet garni and water into a large saucepan and bring to the boil. Skim the scum from the surface, then cover the pan with a tight-fitting lid. Reduce the heat and poach for about 10–15 minutes, or until the haddock flakes easily.

2 Lift the poached fish from the pan using a fish slice and remove the skin and bones. Flake the flesh and reserve. Return the skin and bones to the pan and simmer, uncovered, for 30 minutes.

3 Strain the fish stock and return to the pan, then add the potatoes and simmer for about 25 minutes or until tender. Remove the potatoes from the pan using a slotted spoon. Add the milk to the pan and bring to the boil.

4 Meanwhile, mash the potatoes with the butter, then whisk into the milk in the pan until thick and creamy. Add the flaked fish to the pan and adjust the seasoning. Sprinkle with chives and serve at once with crusty bread, if you wish.

Cook's Tip
If Finnan haddock is not available, ordinary smoked haddock may be substituted.

Mulligatawny Soup

Choose red split lentils for the best colour, although green or brown lentils could also be used.

Serves 4

50g/2oz/4 tbsp butter or 60ml/4 tbsp oil
2 large chicken joints (about 35g/12oz each)
1 onion, chopped
1 carrot, chopped
1 small turnip, chopped
about 15ml/1 tbsp curry powder, to taste
4 cloves
6 black peppercorns, lightly crushed
50g/2oz/¼ cup lentils
900ml/1½ pints/3¾ cups chicken stock
40g/1½oz/¼ cup sultanas
salt and ground black pepper

1 Heat the butter or oil in a large saucepan and brown the chicken over a brisk heat. Transfer the chicken to a plate.

2 Add the onion, carrot and turnip to the pan and cook, stirring occasionally, until lightly coloured. Stir in the curry powder, cloves and peppercorns and cook for 1–2 minutes, then add the lentils.

3 Pour the stock into the pan, bring to the boil, then add the sultanas and chicken and any juices from the plate. Cover and simmer gently for about 1¼ hours.

4 Remove the chicken from the pan and discard the skin and bones. Chop the flesh into bite-size chunks, return to the soup and reheat. Season to taste with salt and pepper before serving the soup piping hot.

Smoked Haddock Pâté

This easily-prepared pâté is made with Arbroath Smokies, small haddock which have been salted and hot-smoked.

Serves 6

3 large Arbroath Smokies (about 225g/8oz each)
275g/10oz/1¼ cups medium-fat soft cheese
3 eggs, beaten
30–45ml/2–3 tbsp lemon juice

pinch of freshly ground black pepper
fresh chervil sprigs, to garnish
lemon wedges and lettuce leaves, to serve

1 Preheat the oven to 160°C/325°F/Gas 3. Generously butter six individual ramekin dishes.

2 Lay the smokies in a baking dish and heat through in the oven for 10 minutes. Carefully remove the skin and bones from the smokies, then flake the flesh into a bowl.

3 Mash the fish with a fork and work in the cheese, then the eggs. Add the lemon juice and season with pepper to taste.

4 Divide the fish mixture among the six ramekins and place in a roasting tin. Pour hot water into the roasting tin to come halfway up the dishes. Bake for 30 minutes, until just set.

5 Allow to cool for 2–3 minutes, then run a knife point around the edge of each dish and invert on to a warmed plate. Garnish with fresh chervil sprigs and serve with the lemon wedges and lettuce.

Spinach, Bacon and Prawn Salad

Serve this hot salad with plenty of crusty bread to mop up the delicious juices.

Serves 4

105ml/7 tbsp olive oil
30ml/2 tbsp sherry vinegar
2 garlic cloves, finely chopped
5ml/1 tsp Dijon mustard
12 cooked king prawns, in the shell

115g/4oz rindless streaky bacon, cut into strips
115g/4oz/1 cup fresh young spinach leaves
½ head oak leaf lettuce, roughly torn
salt and ground black pepper

1 To make the dressing, whisk together 90ml/6 tbsp of the olive oil with the vinegar, garlic, mustard and seasoning in a small saucepan. Heat gently until thickened slightly, then keep warm.

2 Carefully peel the king prawns, leaving their tails intact. Set aside until needed.

3 Heat the remaining oil in a frying pan and fry the bacon until golden and crisp, stirring occasionally. Add the prawns and stir-fry for a few minutes until warmed through.

4 While the bacon and prawns are cooking, arrange the spinach and torn oak leaf lettuce leaves on four individual serving plates.

5 Spoon the bacon and prawns on to the leaves, then pour over the hot dressing. Serve at once.

Cook's Tip
Sherry vinegar lends its pungent flavour to this delicious salad. It is readily available in large supermarkets or delicatessens. However, red or white wine vinegar could be substituted if you prefer.

Hot Tomato and Mozzarella Salad

A quick, easy starter with a Mediterranean flavour. It can be prepared in advance, then grilled just before serving.

Serves 4

450g/1lb plum tomatoes,
  sliced
225g/8oz mozzarella
  cheese
1 red onion, chopped
4 – 6 pieces sun-dried
  tomatoes in oil,
  drained and chopped
60ml/4 tbsp olive oil
5ml/1 tsp red wine
  vinegar

2.5ml/½ tsp Dijon
  mustard
60ml/4 tbsp mixed
  chopped fresh herbs
  such as basil, parsley,
  oregano and chives
salt and ground black
  pepper
fresh herb sprigs, to
  garnish (optional)

1 Arrange the sliced tomatoes and mozzarella in circles in four shallow flameproof dishes. Scatter over the onion and sun-dried tomatoes. Whisk together the olive oil, vinegar, mustard, chopped herbs and seasoning. Pour over the salads.

2 Place the salads under a hot grill for 4 – 5 minutes, until the mozzarella starts to melt. Grind over plenty of black pepper and serve garnished with fresh herb sprigs, if you wish.

Asparagus with Tarragon Butter

Eating fresh asparagus with your fingers is correct but messy, so serve this dish with finger bowls.

Serves 4

500g/1¼lb fresh
  asparagus
115g/4oz/½ cup butter
30ml/2 tbsp chopped
  fresh tarragon

15ml/1 tbsp chopped
  fresh parsley
grated rind of ½ lemon
15ml/1 tbsp lemon juice
salt and black pepper

1 Trim the woody ends from the asparagus spears, then tie them into four equal bundles.

2 Place the bundles of asparagus in a large frying pan with about 2.5cm/1in boiling water. Cover with a lid and cook for about 6 – 8 minutes, until the asparagus is tender but still firm. Drain well and discard the strings.

3 Arrange the asparagus spears on four warmed serving plates. Make the tarragon butter by creaming together the remaining ingredients; heat it gently and pour it over the asparagus. Serve at once.

Devilled Kidneys

This tangy dish makes an impressive starter, although it is sometimes served as an English breakfast dish.

Serves 4

Mix 10ml/2 tbsp Worcestershire sauce, 15ml/1 tbsp each English mustard, lemon juice and tomato purée. Season with cayenne pepper and salt. Melt 40g/1½oz/3 tbsp butter, add 1 chopped shallot; cook until softened. Stir in 8 prepared lambs' kidneys; cook for 3 minutes on each side. Coat with the sauce; serve sprinkled with chopped parsley.

Egg and Tomato Salad with Crab

You could also adjust the quantities in this tasty salad to make a quick, light and healthy weekday meal.

Serves 4

1 round lettuce
2 x 200g/7oz cans
  crabmeat, drained
4 hard-boiled eggs, sliced
16 cherry tomatoes,
  halved
½ green pepper, seeded
  and thinly sliced
6 stoned black olives,
  sliced

250g/8fl oz/1 cup
  mayonnaise
10ml/2 tsp fresh lemon
  juice
½ green pepper, seeded
  and finely chopped
5ml/1 tsp prepared
  horseradish
5ml/1 tsp Worcestershire
  sauce

For the dressing
45ml/3 tbsp chilli sauce

1 To make the dressing, place all the ingredients in a bowl and mix well. Set aside in a cool place.

2 Line four plates with the lettuce leaves. Mound the crabmeat in the centre. Arrange the eggs around the outside with the tomatoes on top.

3 Spoon some of the dressing over the crabmeat. Arrange the green pepper slices on top and sprinkle with the olives. Serve immediately with the remaining dressing.

Stuffed Mushrooms

These flavoursome mushrooms may also be served as an accompaniment to a main course.

Serves 4

275g/10oz spinach, stalks
  removed
400g/14oz medium cap
  mushrooms
25g/1oz/2 tbsp butter,
  plus extra for
  brushing
25g/1oz bacon, chopped
½ small onion, chopped

75g/5 tbsp double cream
about 60ml/4 tbsp grated
  Cheddar cheese
30ml/2 tbsp fresh
  breadcrumbs
salt and ground black
  pepper
fresh parsley sprigs, to
  garnish

1 Preheat the oven to 190°C/375°F/Gas 5. Butter a baking dish. Wash but do not dry the spinach. Place it in a saucepan and cook, stirring occasionally, until wilted.

2 Place the spinach in a colander and squeeze out as much liquid as possible. Chop finely. Snap the stalks from the mushrooms and chop the stalks finely.

3 Melt the butter in a pan and cook the bacon, onion and mushroom stalks for about 5 minutes. Stir in the spinach, cook for a moment or two, then remove the pan from the heat, stir in the cream and season to taste with salt and pepper.

4 Brush the mushroom caps with melted butter, then place, gills uppermost, in a single layer in the baking dish.

5 Divide the spinach mixture among the mushrooms. Mix together the cheese and breadcrumbs, sprinkle over the mushrooms, then bake for about 20 minutes until the mushrooms are tender. Serve warm, garnished with parsley.

Cook's Tip
Squeeze out all the excess water from the cooked
spinach, otherwise the stuffing will be too soggy.

Pears and Stilton

Stilton is the classic British blue cheese, but you could use blue Cheshire instead, or even Gorgonzola.

Serves 4

4 ripe pears
75g/3oz blue Stilton
   cheese
50g/2oz/3 tbsp curd
   cheese
pinch of ground black
   pepper
fresh watercress sprigs,
   to garnish

For the dressing
45ml/3 tbsp light olive oil
15ml/1 tbsp lemon juice
10ml/½ tbsp toasted
   poppy seeds
salt and ground black
   pepper

1 First make the dressing. Place the olive oil, lemon juice, poppy seeds and seasoning in a screw-topped jar and shake together until emulsified.

2 Cut the pears in half lengthways, then scoop out the cores and cut away the calyx from the rounded end.

3 Beat together the Stilton, curd cheese and a little pepper. Divide this mixture among the cavities in the pears.

4 Shake the dressing to mix it again, then spoon it over the pears. Serve garnished with watercress.

Cook's Tip
The pears should be lightly chilled in the fridge before they are used in this dish.

Potted Shrimps

The brown shrimps traditionally used for potting are very fiddly to peel. Use peeled cooked prawns if you prefer.

Serves 4

225g/8oz/2 cups shelled
   shrimps
225g/8oz/1 cup butter
pinch of ground mace
salt and cayenne pepper

fresh dill sprigs, to
   garnish
lemon wedges and thin
   slices of brown bread
   and butter, to serve

1 Chop a quarter of the shrimps. Melt half of the butter slowly, carefully skimming off any foam that rises to the surface.

2 Stir all the shrimps, the mace, salt and cayenne pepper into the saucepan and heat gently without boiling. Pour the shrimp and butter mixture into four individual pots and leave it aside to cool.

3 Heat the remaining butter in a clean small pan, then carefully spoon the clear butter over the shrimps, leaving behind the sediment.

4 Leave until the butter is almost set, then place a dill sprig in the centre of each pot. Leave to set completely, then cover and chill in the fridge.

5 Transfer the shrimps to room temperature 30 minutes before serving with lemon wedges and thin slices of brown bread and butter.

Leek Terrine with Deli Meats

This attractive starter is simple yet looks spectacular. It can be made a day ahead.

Serves 6

20–24 small young leeks
about 225g/8oz mixed
  sliced meats, such as
  Parma ham, coppa
  and pancetta
50g/2oz/½ cup walnuts,
  toasted and chopped

For the dressing
60ml/4 tbsp walnut oil
60ml/4 tbsp olive oil
30ml/2 tbsp white wine
  vinegar
5ml/1 tsp wholegrain
  mustard
salt and ground black
  pepper

1 Cut off the roots and most of the green part from the leeks. Wash them thoroughly under cold running water.

2 Bring a large saucepan of salted water to the boil. Add the leeks, bring the water back to the boil, then simmer for 6–8 minutes, until the leeks are just tender. Drain well.

3 Fill a 450g/1lb loaf tin with the leeks, placing them alternately head to tail and sprinkling each layer as you go with salt and pepper.

4 Put another loaf tin inside the first and gently press down on the leeks. Carefully invert both tins and let any water drain out. Place one or two weights on top of the tins and chill the terrine for at least 4 hours, or overnight.

5 To make the dressing, whisk together the walnut and olive oils, vinegar and mustard in a small bowl. Season to taste.

6 Carefully turn out the terrine on to a board and cut into slices using a large sharp knife. Lay the slices of leek terrine on serving plates and arrange the slices of meat alongside.

7 Spoon the dressing over the slices of terrine and scatter the chopped walnuts over the top. Serve at once.

Garlic Prawns in Filo Tartlets

Tartlets made with crisp layers of filo pastry and filled with garlic prawns make a tempting and unusual starter.

Serves 4
For the tartlets
50g/2oz/4 tbsp butter,
  melted
2–3 large sheets filo
  pastry

For the filling
115g/4oz/½ cup butter
2–3 garlic cloves,
  crushed

1 fresh red chilli, seeded
  and chopped
350g/12oz/3 cups peeled,
  cooked prawns
30ml/2 tbsp chopped
  fresh parsley or
  snipped fresh chives
salt and ground black
  pepper

1 Preheat the oven to 200°C/400°F/Gas 6. Brush four individual 7.5cm/3in flan tins with melted butter.

2 Cut the filo pastry into twelve 10cm/4in squares and brush with the melted butter.

3 Place three squares inside each tin, overlapping them at slight angles and carefully frilling the edges and points while forming a good hollow in each centre. Bake the pastry for 10–15 minutes, until crisp and golden. Cool slightly and remove from the tins.

4 To make the filling, melt the butter in a large frying pan, fry the garlic, chilli and prawns for 1–2 minutes to warm through. Stir in the parsley or chives and season to taste with salt and pepper.

5 Spoon the prawn filling into the tartlets and serve at once.

Cook's Tip
Use fresh filo pastry rather than frozen, then simply wrap and freeze any leftover sheets.

Smoked Salmon and Dill Blinis

Celeriac Fritters with Mustard Dip

Blinis, small pancakes of Russian origin, are so easy to make, yet they make a sophisticated dinner party starter.

The combination of the hot, crispy fritters and the cold mustard dip is extremely tasty.

Serves 4

115g/4oz/1 cup buckwheat flour	15ml/1 tbsp melted butter, plus extra for shallow-frying
115g/4oz/1 cup plain flour	150ml/¼ pint/⅔ cup crème fraîche
pinch of salt	45ml/3 tbsp chopped fresh dill
15ml/1 tbsp easy-blend dried yeast	225g/8oz smoked salmon, thinly sliced
2 eggs	fresh dill sprigs, to garnish
350ml/12fl oz/1½ cups warm milk	

1 Mix together the buckwheat and plain flours in a large bowl with the salt. Sprinkle in the yeast and mix well. Separate one of the eggs. Whisk together the whole egg and the yolk, the warm milk and the melted butter.

2 Pour the egg mixture on to the flour mixture. Beat well to form a smooth batter. Cover with clear film and leave to rise in a warm place for 1–2 hours.

3 Whisk the remaining egg white in a large bowl until stiff peaks form, then gently fold into the batter.

4 Preheat a heavy-based frying pan or griddle and brush with melted butter. Drop tablespoons of the batter on to the pan, spacing them well apart. Cook for about 40 seconds, until bubbles appear on the surface.

5 Flip over the blinis and cook for 30 seconds on the other side. Wrap in foil and keep warm in a low oven. Repeat with the remaining mixture, buttering the pan each time.

6 Combine the crème fraîche and dill. Serve the blinis topped with the salmon and cream. Garnish with dill sprigs.

Serves 4

	For the mustard dip
1 egg	150ml/¼ pint/⅔ cup soured cream
115g/4oz/1 cup ground almonds	15–30ml/1–2 tbsp wholegrain mustard
45ml/3 tbsp freshly grated Parmesan cheese	salt and ground black pepper
45ml/3 tbsp chopped fresh parsley	sea salt flakes, for sprinkling
1 celeriac (about 450g/1lb)	
squeeze of lemon juice	
oil, for deep-frying	

1 Beat the egg well and pour into a shallow dish. Mix together the almonds, grated Parmesan and parsley in a separate dish. Season to taste, then set aside.

2 Peel and cut the celeriac into strips about 1cm/½in wide and 5cm/2in long. Drop them immediately into a bowl of water with a little lemon juice added to prevent them from becoming discoloured.

3 Heat the oil in a deep-fat fryer to 180°C/350°F. Drain and then pat dry half the celeriac chips. Dip them into the beaten egg, then into the ground almond mixture, making sure that the pieces are coated completely and evenly.

4 Deep-fry the celeriac fritters, a few at a time, for about 2–3 minutes until golden. Drain on kitchen paper and keep warm while you cook the remainder.

5 To make the mustard dip, mix together the soured cream, mustard and sea salt to taste. Spoon into a small serving bowl.

6 Heap the celeriac fritters on to warmed individual serving plates. Sprinkle with sea salt flakes and serve at once with the mustard dip.

Chicken Liver Pâté with Marsala

This is a really quick and simple pâté to make, yet it has a delicious – and quite sophisticated – flavour.

Serves 4

350g/12oz chicken livers, defrosted if frozen
225g/8oz/1 cup butter
2 garlic cloves, crushed
15ml/1 tbsp Marsala
5ml/1 tsp chopped sage
salt and ground black pepper
8 fresh sage leaves, to garnish
Melba toast, to serve

1 Pick over the chicken livers, then rinse and dry with kitchen paper. Melt 25g/1oz/2 tbsp of the butter in a frying pan and fry the chicken livers with the garlic over a moderate heat for about 5 minutes, or until they are firm but still pink in their centres.

2 Transfer the livers to a food processor or blender using a slotted spoon. Add the Marsala and chopped sage.

3 Melt 150g/5oz/generous ½ cup of the remaining butter in the frying pan, stirring to loosen any sediment, then pour into the food processor or blender and process until smooth. Season well with salt and pepper.

4 Spoon the pâté into four individual pots and smooth the surface. Melt the remaining butter in a separate pan and pour over the pâtés. Garnish with sage leaves and chill in the fridge until set. Serve with triangles of Melba toast.

Cook's Tip
This delicious pâté contains Marsala, a dark, sweet, pungent dessert wine made in Sicily. If this is not available, you could substitute either brandy or a medium-dry sherry.

Salmon Rillettes

A variation on the traditional pork rillette, this starter is much easier to make.

Serves 6

350g/12oz salmon fillets
175g/6oz/¾ cup butter
1 celery stick, finely chopped
1 leek, white part only, finely chopped
1 bay leaf
150ml/¼ pint/⅔ cup dry white wine
115g/4oz smoked salmon trimmings
large pinch of ground mace
60ml/4 tbsp fromage frais
salt and ground black pepper
salad leaves, to serve

1 Lightly season the salmon with salt and pepper. Melt 25g/1oz/2 tbsp of the butter in a frying pan and cook the celery and leek for about 5 minutes. Add the salmon and bay leaf and pour over the wine. Cover with a tight-fitting lid and cook for about 15 minutes until the fish is tender.

2 Strain the cooking liquid into a saucepan and boil until reduced to 30ml/2 tbsp. Cool. Melt 50g/2oz/4 tbsp of the remaining butter and gently cook the smoked salmon until it turns pale pink. Leave to cool.

3 Remove the skin and any bones from the salmon fillets. Flake the flesh into a bowl and add the cooking liquid.

4 Beat in the remaining butter, the mace and fromage frais. Break up the smoked salmon trimmings and fold into the mixture with the pan juices. Taste and adjust the seasoning.

5 Spoon the salmon mixture into a dish or terrine and smooth the top level. Cover and chill in the fridge.

6 To serve the salmon rillettes, shape the mixture into oval quenelles using two dessert spoons and arrange on individual plates with the salad leaves. Accompany with brown bread or oatcakes, if you wish.

Mexican Dip with Chips

Omit the fresh chilli and the chilli powder if you prefer a
dip to have a mild flavour.

Serves 4

2 medium-ripe avocados
juice of 1 lime
½ small onion, finely
    chopped
½ red chilli, seeded and
    finely chopped
3 tomatoes, skinned,
    seeded and finely
    diced
30ml/2 tbsp chopped
    fresh coriander
30ml/2 tbsp soured
    cream
salt and ground black
    pepper

15 ml/1 tbsp soured
    cream and a pinch of
    cayenne pepper, to
    garnish

For the chips
150g/5oz bag tortilla
    chips
30ml/2 tbsp finely grated
    mature Cheddar
    cheese
1.5ml/¼ tsp chilli powder
10ml/2 tsp chopped fresh
    parsley

1 Halve and stone the avocados and remove the flesh with a
spoon, scraping the shells well.

2 Place the flesh in a blender or food processor with the
remaining ingredients, reserving the soured cream and
cayenne pepper. Process until fairly smooth. Transfer to a
bowl, cover and chill in the fridge until required.

3 To make the chips, preheat the grill, then scatter the tortilla
chips over a baking sheet. Mix the grated cheese with the
chilli powder, sprinkle over the chips and grill for about
1–2 minutes, until the cheese has melted.

4 Remove the avocado dip from the fridge, top with the
soured cream and sprinkle with cayenne pepper. Serve the
bowl on a plate surrounded by the tortilla chips, garnished
with the chopped fresh parsley.

French Goat's Cheese Salad

The deep, tangy flavours of this salad would also make it
satisfying enough for a light meal, if you wished.

Serves 4

200g/7oz bag prepared
    mixed salad leaves
4 rashers rindless back
    bacon
16 thin slices French
    bread
115g/4oz/½ cup full-fat
    goat's cheese

For the dressing
60ml/4 tbsp olive oil
15ml/1 tbsp tarragon
    vinegar
10ml/2 tsp walnut oil
5ml/1 tsp Dijon mustard
5ml/1 tsp wholegrain
    mustard

1 Preheat the grill to a moderate heat. Rinse and dry the
salad leaves, then arrange in four individual bowls. Place the
ingredients for the dressing in a screw-top jar, shake together
well and reserve.

2 Lay the bacon rashers on a board, then stretch with the
back of a knife and cut each into four. Roll each piece up and
grill for about 2–3 minutes.

3 Meanwhile, slice the goat's cheese into eight and halve
each slice. Top each slice of bread with a piece of goat's cheese
and pop under the grill. Turn over the bacon and continue
cooking with the goat's cheese toasts until the cheese is
golden and bubbling.

4 Arrange the bacon rolls and toasts on top of the prepared
salad leaves, shake the dressing well and pour a little of the
dressing over each one.

Chinese Garlic Mushrooms

High in protein and low in fat, marinated tofu makes an unusual stuffing for these mushrooms.

Serves 4

8 large open mushrooms
3 spring onions, sliced
1 garlic clove, crushed
30ml/2 tbsp oyster sauce
5g/10oz packet marinated
   tofu, diced

200g/7oz can sweetcorn,
   drained
10ml/2 tsp sesame oil
salt and ground black
   pepper

1 Preheat the oven to 200°C/400°F/Gas 6. Finely chop the mushroom stalks and mix with the next three ingredients.

2 Stir in the diced marinated tofu and sweetcorn, season well, then spoon the filling into the mushrooms.

3 Brush the edges of the mushrooms with the sesame oil. Arrange them in a baking dish and bake for 12–15 minutes, until the mushrooms are just tender, then serve at once.

Tomato Cheese Tarts

These crisp little tartlets are easier to make than they look and are best eaten fresh from the oven.

Serves 4

2 sheets filo pastry
1 egg white
115g/4oz/ ½ cup
   skimmed milk soft
   cheese

handful of fresh basil
   leaves
3 small tomatoes, sliced
salt and ground black
   pepper

1 Preheat the oven to 200°C/400°F/Gas 5. Brush the sheets of filo pastry lightly with egg white and cut into sixteen 10cm/4in squares.

2 Layer the squares in twos, in eight patty tins. Spoon the cheese into the pastry cases. Season with salt and ground black pepper and top with basil leaves.

3 Arrange the tomato slices on the tarts, add seasoning and bake for 10–12 minutes, until golden. Serve warm.

Ricotta and Borlotti Bean Pâté

A lovely light yet full-flavoured pâté that can be enjoyed by vegetarians.

Serves 4

Process 400g/14oz borlotti beans, 175g/6oz/¾ cup Ricotta cheese, 1 garlic clove, 60ml/4 tbsp melted butter, juice of ½ lemon and seasoning. Add 30ml/2 tbsp chopped fresh parsley and 15ml/1 tbsp fresh thyme or dill; blend. Spoon into one serving dish or four lightly-oiled and base-lined ramekins. Chill. Garnish with salad leaves and serve with warm crusty bread or toast. If serving the pâté individually, turn each one out of its ramekin on to a plate, then remove the paper. Top the pâté with radish slices and sprigs of dill.

Avocados with Tangy Topping

Lightly grilled with a tasty topping of red onions and cheese, this dish makes a delightful starter.

Serves 4

15ml/1 tbsp sunflower oil
1 small red onion, sliced
1 garlic clove, crushed
dash of Worcestershire
 sauce
2 ripe avocados, stoned
 and halved
2 small tomatoes, sliced

15ml/1 tbsp chopped
 fresh basil, marjoram
 or parsley
50g/2oz Lancashire or
 mozzarella cheese,
 sliced
salt and ground black
 pepper

1 Heat the oil in a frying pan and gently fry the onion and garlic for about 5 minutes until just softened. Shake in a little Worcestershire sauce.

2 Preheat a grill. Place the avocado halves on the grill pan and spoon the onions into the centre.

3 Divide the tomato slices and fresh herbs between the four halves and top each one with the cheese.

4 Season well with salt and pepper and grill until the cheese melts and starts to brown.

Bruschetta with Goat's Cheese

Simple to prepare in advance, this appetising dish can be served as a starter or at a finger buffet.

Serves 4–6

For the tapenade
400g/14oz can black
 olives, stoned and
 finely chopped
50g/2oz sun-dried
 tomatoes in oil,
 chopped
30ml/2 tbsp capers,
 chopped
15ml/1 tbsp green
 peppercorns, in brine,
 crushed
2 garlic cloves, crushed
45ml/3 tbsp chopped
 fresh basil or 5ml/
 1 tsp dried basil

45–60ml/3–4 tbsp olive
 oil
salt and ground black
 pepper

For the bases
12 slices ciabatta or other
 crusty bread
olive oil, for brushing
2 garlic cloves, halved
115g/4oz/½ cup soft
 goat's cheese or other
 full-fat soft cheese
mixed fresh herb sprigs,
 to garnish

1 To make the tapenade, mix all the tapenade ingredients together and check the seasoning. It should not need too much. Allow to marinate overnight, if possible.

2 To make the bruschetta, grill both sides of the bread lightly until golden. Brush one side with oil and then rub with a cut clove of garlic. Set aside until ready to serve.

3 Spread the bruschetta with the cheese, roughing it up with a fork, and spoon the tapenade on top. Garnish with sprigs of mixed fresh herbs.

Cook's Tip
Grill the bruschetta on a barbecue for a delicious smoky flavour if you are making this starter in the summer.

Grilled Garlic Mussels

Use a combination of fresh herbs, such as oregano, basil and flat-leaf parsley.

Serves 4

1.5kg/3 – 3½lb live
  mussels
120ml/4fl oz/½ cup dry
  white wine
50g/2oz/4 tbsp butter
2 shallots, finely chopped
2 garlic cloves, crushed
50g/2oz/1 cup dried
  white breadcrumbs

60ml/4 tbsp mixed
  chopped fresh herbs
30ml/2 tbsp freshly
  grated Parmesan
  cheese
salt and ground black
  pepper
fresh basil leaves, to
  garnish

1 Scrub the mussels well under cold running water. Remove the beards and discard any mussels that are open. Place in a large saucepan with the wine. Cover and cook over a high heat, shaking the pan occasionally for 5–8 minutes, until the mussels have opened.

2 Strain the mussels and reserve the cooking liquid. Discard any mussels that remain closed. Allow them to cool slightly, then remove and discard the top half of each shell.

3 Melt the butter in a pan and fry the shallots until softened. Add the garlic and cook for 1–2 minutes. Stir in the dried breadcrumbs and cook, stirring until lightly browned. Remove the pan from the heat and stir in the herbs. Moisten with a little of the reserved mussel liquid, then season to taste with salt and pepper.

4 Spoon the breadcrumb mixture over the mussels and arrange on baking sheets. Sprinkle with the grated Parmesan.

5 Cook the mussels under a hot grill in batches for about 2 minutes, until the topping is crisp and golden. Keep the cooked mussels warm in a low oven while grilling the remainder. Garnish with fresh basil leaves and serve hot.

Nut Patties with Mango Relish

These spicy patties can be made in advance, if you wish, and reheated just before serving.

Serves 4–6

175g/6oz/1½ cups finely
  chopped roasted and
  salted cashew nuts
175g/6oz/1½ cups finely
  chopped walnuts
1 small onion, finely
  chopped
1 garlic clove, crushed
1 green chilli, seeded and
  chopped
5ml/1 tsp ground cumin
10ml/2 tsp ground
  coriander
2 carrots, coarsely grated
50g/2oz/1 cup fresh
  white breadcrumbs
30ml/2 tbsp chopped
  fresh coriander

15ml/1 tbsp lemon juice
1–2 eggs, beaten
salt and ground black
  pepper
fresh coriander sprigs, to
  garnish

For the relish

1 large ripe mango, cut
  into small dice
1 small onion, cut into
  slivers
5ml/1 tsp grated fresh
  root ginger
pinch of salt
15ml/1 tbsp sesame oil
5ml/1 tsp black mustard
  seeds

1 Preheat the oven to 180°C/350°F/Gas 4. In a bowl, mix together the nuts, onion, garlic, chilli, spices, breadcrumbs, carrots, chopped coriander and seasoning.

2 Sprinkle the lemon juice over the mixture and add enough of the beaten egg to bind the mixture together. Shape the mixture into twelve balls, then flatten slightly into round patties. Place them on a lightly greased baking sheet and bake for about 25 minutes, until golden brown.

3 To make the relish, mix together the mango, onion, fresh root ginger and salt. Heat the oil in a small frying pan and fry the mustard seeds for a few seconds until they pop, then stir into the mango mixture. Serve with the nut patties, garnished with coriander.

Dim Sum

A popular Chinese snack, these tiny dumplings are now fashionable in many specialist restaurants.

Serves 4

For the dough

150g/5oz/1¼ cups plain flour
50ml/2fl oz/¼ cup boiling water
25ml/1fl oz/⅛ cup cold water
7.5ml/1½ tbsp vegetable oil

For the filling

75g/3oz minced pork

45ml/3 tbsp chopped canned bamboo shoots
7.5ml/½ tbsp light soy sauce
5ml/1 tsp dry sherry
5ml/1 tsp demerara sugar
2.5ml/½ tsp sesame oil
5ml/1 tsp cornflour
mixed fresh lettuce leaves such as iceberg, frisée or Webbs

1 To make the dough, sift the flour into a bowl. Stir in the boiling water, then the cold water together with the oil. Mix to form a ball and knead until smooth. Divide the mixture into sixteen equal pieces and shape into circles.

2 For the filling, mix together the pork, bamboo shoots, soy sauce, sherry, sugar and oil. Then stir in the cornflour.

3 Place a little of the filling in the centre of each dim sum circle. Carefully pinch the edges of the dough together to form little "purses".

4 Line a steamer with a damp dish towel. Place the dim sum in the steamer and steam for 5–10 minutes. Serve on a bed of lettuce with soy sauce, spring onion curls, sliced red chilli and prawn crackers, if you wish.

Cook's Tip

As an alternative filling, substitute the pork with cooked, peeled prawns.

Sesame Prawn Toasts

Serve about four of these delicious toasts per person with a soy sauce for dipping.

Serves 6

175g/6oz/1½ cups peeled, cooked prawns
2 spring onions, finely chopped
2.5cm/1in piece fresh root ginger, peeled and grated
2 garlic cloves, crushed
30ml/2 tbsp cornflour

10ml/2 tsp soy sauce, plus extra for dipping
6 slices stale bread from a small loaf, without crusts
40g/1½ oz sesame seeds
about 600ml/1 pint/2½ cups vegetable oil, for deep-frying

1 Place the prawns, spring onions, ginger and garlic cloves into a food processor fitted with a metal blade. Add the cornflour and soy sauce and work the mixture into a paste.

2 Spread the bread slices evenly with the paste and cut into triangles. Sprinkle with the sesame seeds, making sure they stick to the bread. Chill in the fridge for 30 minutes.

3 Heat the oil for deep-frying in a large heavy-based saucepan until it reaches a temperature of 190°C/375°F. Using a slotted spoon, lower the toasts into the oil, sesame-seed side down, and fry for 2–3 minutes, turning over for the last minute. Drain on absorbent kitchen paper. Keep the toasts warm whilst frying the remainder.

4 Serve the toasts with soy sauce for dipping.

English Ploughman's Pâté

This is a thoroughly modern interpretation of a traditional ploughman's lunch.

Serves 4

50g/2oz/3 tbsp full-fat soft
  cheese
50g/2oz/½ cup grated
  Caerphilly cheese
50g/2oz/½ cup grated
  Double Gloucester
  cheese
4 pickled silverskin
  onions, drained and
  finely chopped

15ml/1 tbsp apricot
  chutney
30ml/2 tbsp butter, melted
30ml/2 tbsp snipped fresh
  chives
4 slices soft-grain bread
salt and ground black
  pepper
watercress and cherry
  tomatoes, to serve

1 Mix together the soft cheese, grated cheeses, onions, chutney and butter in a bowl and season lightly with salt and ground black pepper.

2 Spoon the mixture on to a sheet of greaseproof paper and roll up into a cylinder, smoothing the mixture into a roll with your hands. Scrunch the ends of the paper together and twist them to seal. Place in the freezer for about 30 minutes, until the parcel is just firm.

3 Spread the chives on a plate, then unwrap the chilled cheese pâté. Roll in the chives until evenly coated. Wrap in clear film and chill for 10 minutes in the fridge.

4 Preheat the grill. To make Melba toast, lightly toast the bread on both sides. Cut off the crusts and slice each piece in half horizontally. Cut each half into two triangles. Grill, untoasted side up, until golden and curled at the edges.

5 Slice the pâté into rounds with a sharp knife and serve three or four rounds per person with the Melba toast, watercress and cherry tomatoes.

Golden Cheese Puffs

Serve these deep-fried puffs – called *aigrettes* in France – with a fruity chutney and salad.

Makes 8

50g/2oz/½ cup plain
  flour
15g/½oz/1 tbsp butter
1 egg plus 1 egg yolk
50g/2oz/½ cup finely
  grated mature
  Cheddar cheese
15ml/1 tbsp grated
  Parmesan cheese

2.5ml/½ tsp mustard
  powder
pinch of cayenne pepper
oil, for deep-frying
salt and ground black
  pepper
mango chutney and
  green salad, to serve

1 Sift the flour on to a square of greaseproof paper and set aside. Place the butter and 150ml/⅔ pint/⅔ cup water in a saucepan and heat gently until the butter has melted.

2 Bring the liquid to the boil and tip in the flour all at once. Remove from the heat and stir well with a wooden spoon until the mixture begins to leave the sides of the pan and forms a ball. Allow to cool slightly.

3 Beat the egg and egg yolk together in a bowl with a fork and then gradually add to the mixture in the pan, beating well after each addition.

4 Stir the cheeses, mustard powder and cayenne pepper into the mixture and season to taste with salt and pepper.

5 Heat the oil in a large pan to 190°C/375°F or until a cube of bread dropped into the pan browns in 30 seconds. Drop four spoonfuls of the cheese mixture into the oil at a time and deep-fry for 2–3 minutes until golden. Drain on kitchen paper and keep hot in the oven while cooking the remaining mixture. Serve two puffs per person with a spoonful of mango chutney and green salad.

Kansas City Fritters

Crispy bacon and vegetable fritters are served with a spicy tomato salsa.

Makes 8

200g/7oz/1¼ cups
   canned sweetcorn,
   drained well
2 eggs, separated
75g/3oz /¾ cup plain
   flour
75ml/5 tbsp milk
1 small courgette, grated
2 rashers rindless back
   bacon, diced
2 spring onions, finely
   chopped
large pinch of cayenne
   pepper
45ml/3 tbsp sunflower oil

salt and ground black
   pepper
fresh coriander sprigs, to
   garnish

For the salsa
3 tomatoes, skinned,
   seeded and diced
½ small red pepper,
   seeded and diced
½ small onion, diced
15ml/1 tbsp lemon juice
15ml/1 tbsp chopped
   fresh coriander
dash of Tabasco sauce

1 To make the salsa, mix all the ingredients together and season to taste. Cover and chill until required.

2 Empty the sweetcorn into a bowl and mix in the egg yolks. Add the flour and blend in with a wooden spoon. When the mixture thickens, gradually blend in the milk.

3 Stir in the courgette, bacon, spring onions, cayenne pepper and seasoning and set aside. Whisk the egg whites until stiff peaks form. Gently fold into the sweetcorn batter mixture.

4 Heat the oil in a large frying pan and place four large spoonfuls of the mixture into the oil. Fry over a moderate heat for 2–3 minutes on each side until golden. Drain on kitchen paper and keep warm in the oven while frying the remaining four fritters.

5 Serve two fritters each, garnished with coriander sprigs and a spoonful of the chilled tomato salsa.

Spinach and Cheese Dumplings

These tasty little dumplings are known as *gnocchi* in Italy, where they are very popular.

Serves 4

175g/6oz cold mashed
   potato
75g/3oz/½ cup semolina
115g/4oz/1 cup frozen
   leaf spinach, defrosted,
   squeezed and chopped
115g/4oz/½ cup ricotta
   cheese
75ml/5 tbsp freshly
   grated Parmesan
   cheese
30ml/2 tbsp beaten egg
2.5ml/½ tsp salt
large pinch of grated
   nutmeg

pinch of ground black
   pepper
30ml/2 tbsp freshly
   grated Parmesan
   cheese
fresh basil sprigs, to
   garnish

For the butter
75g/3oz/6 tbsp butter
5ml/1 tsp grated lemon
   rind
15ml/1 tbsp lemon juice
15ml/1 tbsp chopped
   fresh basil

1 Place all the gnocchi ingredients except the 30ml/2 tbsp Parmesan and the basil in a bowl and mix well. Take walnut-size pieces of the mixture and roll each one back and forth along the prongs of a fork until ridged. Make 28 gnocchi in this way.

2 Bring a large pan of water to the boil, reduce to a simmer and drop in the gnocchi. They will sink at first, but as they cook they will rise to the surface; this procedure will take about 2 minutes, then simmer for 1 minute. Transfer the gnocchi to a lightly-greased and warmed ovenproof dish.

3 Sprinkle the gnocchi with the Parmesan cheese and grill under a high heat for 2 minutes, or until lightly browned. Meanwhile, heat the butter in a pan and stir in the lemon rind, lemon juice and basil. Season to taste. Pour some of this butter over each portion of gnocchi and serve hot, garnished with the chopped fresh basil.

Tricolor Salad

This can be a simple starter if served on individual salad plates, or part of a light buffet meal laid out on a platter.

Serves 4–6

1 small red onion, thinly
  sliced
6 large full-flavoured
  tomatoes
extra virgin olive oil, to
  sprinkle
50g/2oz rocket or
  watercress, chopped

175g/6oz mozzarella
  cheese, thinly sliced
salt and ground black
  pepper
30ml/2 tbsp pine nuts
  (optional), to garnish

1 Soak the onion slices in a bowl of cold water for about 30 minutes, then drain and pat dry. Skin the tomatoes by slashing and dipping briefly in boiling water. Remove the cores and slice the flesh.

2 Arrange half the sliced tomatoes on a large platter or divide them among small plates.

3 Sprinkle liberally with olive oil, then layer with the chopped rocket or watercress and soaked onion slices, seasoning well with salt and pepper. Add the cheese, then sprinkle over more oil and seasoning.

4 Repeat with the remaining tomato slices, salad leaves, cheese and oil.

5 Season well to finish and complete with some oil and a good scattering of pine nuts, if using. Cover the salad and chill in the fridge for at least 2 hours before serving.

Cook's Tip
When lightly salted, tomatoes make their own dressing with their natural juices. The sharpness of the rocket or watercress offsets them wonderfully.

Minted Melon Salad

Use two different varieties of melon in this salad, such as a Charentais and a Galia.

Serves 4

2 ripe melons
fresh mint sprigs, to
  decorate

For the dressing
30ml/2 tbsp roughly
  chopped fresh mint

5ml/1 tsp caster sugar
30ml/2 tbsp raspberry
  vinegar
90ml/6 tbsp extra virgin
  olive oil
salt and ground black
  pepper

1 Halve the melons, then scoop out the seeds using a dessertspoon. Cut the melons into thin wedges using a large sharp knife and remove the skins.

2 Arrange the two different varieties of melon wedges alternately among four individual serving plates.

3 To make the dressing, whisk together the mint, sugar, vinegar, oil and seasoning in a small bowl, or put them in a screw-top jar and shake until blended.

4 Spoon the mint dressing over the melon wedges and decorate with mint sprigs. Serve very lightly chilled.

Cook's Tip
You could also try an orange-fleshed Cantaloupe with a pale green Ogen, or choose a small white-fleshed Honeydew for a different variation.

Garlic Mushrooms

Serve these on toast for a quick, tasty starter or pop them into ramekins and serve with slices of warm crusty bread.

Serves 4

450g/1lb button
    mushrooms, sliced if
    large
45ml/3 tbsp olive oil
45ml/3 tbsp stock or water
30ml/2 tbsp dry sherry
    (optional)
3 garlic cloves, crushed

115g/4oz/½ cup low-fat
    soft cheese
30ml/2 tbsp chopped fresh
    parsley
15ml/1 tbsp snipped fresh
    chives
salt and ground black
    pepper

1 Put the mushrooms into a large saucepan with the olive oil, stock or water and sherry, if using. Heat until bubbling, then cover the pan with a tight-fitting lid and simmer gently for about 5 minutes.

2 Add the crushed garlic and stir well to mix. Cook for a further 2 minutes. Remove the mushrooms with a slotted spoon and set them aside. Cook the liquor until it reduces down to 30ml/2 tbsp. Remove from the heat and stir in the soft cheese, parsley and chives.

3 Stir the mixture well until the cheese has completely melted, then return the mushrooms to the pan so that they become coated with the cheesy mixture. Season to taste with salt and pepper.

4 Pile the mushrooms on to thick slabs of hot toast. Alternatively, spoon them into four ramekins and serve accompanied by slices of crusty bread.

Cook's Tip
Use a mixture of different types of mushrooms for this dish, if you prefer. Shiitake mushrooms will give this starter a particularly rich flavour, if you can find them.

Vegetables with Tahini

This colourful starter is easily prepared in advance. For an *al fresco* **meal, grill the vegetables on a barbecue.**

Serves 4

2 red, green or yellow
    peppers, seeded and
    quartered
2 courgettes, halved
    lengthways
2 small aubergines,
    degorged and halved
    lengthways
1 fennel bulb, quartered
dash of olive oil
115g/4oz Green
    Halloumi cheese,
    sliced

salt and ground black
    pepper

For the tahini cream
225g/8oz tahini paste
1 garlic clove, crushed
30ml/2 tbsp olive oil
30ml/2 tbsp fresh lemon
    juice
120ml/4fl oz/½ cup cold
    water
warm pitta or naan
    bread, to serve

1 Preheat the grill or barbecue until hot. Brush the vegetables with the oil and grill until just browned, turning once. (If the peppers blacken, don't worry. The skins can be peeled off when cool enough to handle.) Cook the vegetables until just softened.

2 Place all the vegetables in a shallow dish and season to taste with salt and pepper. Allow to cool. Meanwhile, brush the cheese slices with olive oil and grill these on both sides until they are just charred. Remove them from the grill pan with a palette knife.

3 To make the tahini cream, place all the ingredients, except the water, in a food processor or blender. Process for a few seconds to mix, then, with the motor still running, pour in the water and blend until smooth.

4 Place the vegetables and grilled cheese slices on a platter and trickle over the tahini cream. Serve with plenty of warm pitta or naan bread.

Haddock with Parsley Sauce

The parsley sauce is enriched with cream and an egg yolk in this simple supper dish.

Serves 4

4 haddock fillets (about 175g/6oz each)
50g/2oz/4 tbsp butter
150ml/¼ pint/⅔ cup milk
150ml/¼ pint/⅔ cup fish stock
1 bay leaf

20ml/4 tsp plain flour
60ml/4 tbsp cream
1 egg yolk
45ml/3 tbsp chopped fresh parsley
grated rind and juice of ½ lemon
salt and ground black pepper

1 Place the fish in a frying pan and heat half the butter, the milk, fish stock, bay leaf and seasoning, and heat over a moderately low heat to simmering point. Lower the heat, cover the pan with a tight-fitting lid and poach the fish for 10–15 minutes, depending on the thickness of the fillets, until the fish is tender and the flesh just begins to flake.

2 Transfer the fish to a warmed serving plate with a slotted spoon, cover the fish and keep warm while you make the sauce. Return the cooking liquid to the heat and bring to the boil, stirring. Simmer for about 4 minutes, then remove and discard the bay leaf.

3 Melt the remaining butter in a saucepan and add the flour, stirring continuously for 1 minute. Remove from the heat and gradually stir in the fish cooking liquid. Return to the heat and bring to the boil, stirring. Simmer for about 4 minutes, stirring frequently.

4 Remove the pan from the heat, blend the cream into the egg yolk, then stir into the sauce with the parsley. Reheat gently, stirring for a few minutes; do not allow to boil. Remove from the heat, add the lemon juice and rind, and season to taste with salt and pepper. Pour into a warmed sauceboat and serve with the fish.

Pickled Herrings

A good basic pickled herring dish which is enhanced by the grainy mustard vinaigrette.

Serves 4

4 fresh herrings
160ml/5fl oz/⅔ cup white wine vinegar
2 tsp salt
12 black peppercorns
2 bay leaves
4 whole cloves
2 small onions, sliced

For the dressing
1 tsp coarse grain mustard
3 tbsp olive oil
1 tbsp white wine vinegar
salt and ground black pepper

1 Pre-heat the oven to 160C°/325°F/Gas 3. Clean and bone the fish. Cut each fish into two fillets.

2 Roll up the fillets tightly and place them closely packed together in an ovenproof dish so that they can't unroll.

3 Pour the vinegar over the fish and add just enough water to cover them.

4 Add the spices and onion, cover and cook for 1 hour. Leave to cool with the liquid. To make the dressing, combine all the ingredients and shake well; serve with the fish.

Herrings in Oatmeal with Mustard

In this delicious dish, crunchy-coated herrings are served with a piquant mayonnaise sauce.

Serves 4

about 15ml/1 tbsp Dijon
   mustard
about 7.5ml/1½ tsp
   tarragon vinegar
175ml/6fl oz/¾ cup thick
   mayonnaise

4 herrings (about
   225g/8oz each)
1 lemon, halved
115g/4oz/1 cup medium
   oatmeal
salt and ground black
   pepper

1 Beat the mustard and vinegar to taste into the mayonnaise. Chill lightly in the fridge.

2 Place one fish at a time on a board, cut-side down and opened out. Press gently along the backbone with your thumbs. Turn over the fish and carefully lift away the backbone and discard.

3 Squeeze lemon juice over both sides of the fish, then season with salt and ground black pepper. Fold the fish in half, skin-side outwards.

4 Preheat a grill until fairly hot. Place the oatmeal on a plate, then coat each herring evenly in the oatmeal, pressing it on gently with your fingers.

5 Place the herrings on a grill rack and grill the fish for about 3 – 4 minutes on each side, until the skin is golden brown and crisp and the flesh flakes easily. Serve hot with the mustard sauce, served separately.

Fish and Chips

The traditional British combination of battered fish and thick-cut chips is served with lemon wedges.

Serves 4

115g/4oz/1 cup
   self-raising flour
150ml/¼ pint/⅔ cup
   water
675g/1½ lb potatoes

675g/1½ lb piece skinned
   cod fillet, cut into four
oil, for deep-frying
salt and ground black
   pepper
lemon wedges, to serve

1 Stir the flour and salt together in a bowl, then form a well in the centre. Gradually pour in the water, whisking in the flour to make a smooth batter. Leave for 30 minutes.

2 Cut the potatoes into strips about 1cm/½in wide and 5cm/2in long, using a sharp knife. Place the potatoes in a colander, rinse in cold water, then drain and dry them well.

3 Heat the oil in a deep-fat fryer or large heavy-based saucepan to 150°C/300°F. Using the wire basket, lower the potatoes in batches into the oil and cook for 5 – 6 minutes, shaking the basket occasionally until the potatoes are soft but not browned. Remove the chips from the oil and drain them thoroughly on kitchen paper.

4 Heat the oil in the fryer to 190°C/375°F. Season the fish. Stir the batter, then dip the pieces of fish in turn into it, allowing the excess to drain off.

5 Working in two batches if necessary, lower the fish into the oil and fry for 6 – 8 minutes, until crisp and brown. Drain the fish on kitchen paper and keep warm.

6 Add the chips in batches to the oil and cook them for about 2 – 3 minutes, until brown and crisp. Keep hot until ready to serve, then sprinkle with salt and serve with the fish, accompanied by lemon wedges.

Trout with Hazelnuts

The hazelnuts in this recipe make an interesting change from the almonds that are more often used.

Serves 4

50g/2oz/⅓ cup hazelnuts, chopped	30ml/2 tbsp lemon juice
65g/2½oz/5 tbsp butter	salt and ground black pepper
4 trout (about 275g/ 10oz each)	lemon slices and flat-leaf parsley sprigs, to serve

1 Preheat the grill. Toast the nuts in a single layer, stirring frequently, until the skins split. Then tip the nuts on to a clean dish towel and rub to remove the skins. Leave the nuts to cool, then chop them coarsely.

2 Heat 50g/2oz/4 tbsp of the butter in a large frying pan. Season the trout inside and out, then fry two at a time for 12–15 minutes, turning once, until the trout are brown and the flesh flakes easily when tested with the point of a sharp kitchen knife.

3 Drain the cooked trout on kitchen paper, then transfer to a warm serving plate and keep warm while frying the remaining trout in the same way. (If your frying pan is large enough, you could, of course, cook the trout in one batch.)

4 Add the remaining butter to the frying pan and fry the hazelnuts until evenly browned. Stir the lemon juice into the pan and mix well, then quickly pour the buttery sauce over the trout and serve at once, garnished with slices of lemon and flat-leaf parsley sprigs.

Cook's Tip
You can use a microwave to prepare the nuts instead of the grill. Spread them out in a shallow microwave dish and leave uncovered. Cook on full power until the skins split, then remove the skins using a dish towel as described above.

Trout Wrapped in a Blanket

The "blanket" of bacon bastes the fish during cooking, keeping it moist and adding flavour at the same time.

Serves 4

juice of ½ lemon	salt and ground black pepper
4 trout (about 275g/ 10oz each)	chopped fresh parsley and thyme sprigs, to garnish
4 fresh thyme sprigs	
8 thin slices rindless streaky bacon	lemon wedges, to serve

1 Preheat the oven to 200°C/400°F/Gas 6. Squeeze lemon juice over the skin and in the cavity of each fish, season all over with salt and ground black pepper, then put a thyme sprig in each cavity.

2 Stretch each bacon slice using the back of a knife, then wind two slices around each fish. Place the fish in a lightly greased shallow baking dish, with the loose ends of bacon tucked underneath to prevent them unwinding.

3 Bake in the oven for 15–20 minutes, until the trout flesh flakes easily when tested with the point of a sharp knife and the bacon is crisp and beginning to brown.

4 Serve garnished with chopped parsley, sprigs of thyme and accompanied by lemon wedges.

Cook's Tip
Smoked streaky bacon will impart a stronger flavour to the fish. If you prefer, use fresh chopped coriander in place of the parsley for the garnish.

Smoked Trout Salad

Horseradish goes as well with smoked trout. It combines
well with yogurt to make a lovely dressing.

Serves 4

1 oakleaf or other red
  lettuce, such as lollo
  rosso
225g/8oz small ripe
  tomatoes, cut into thin
  wedges
½ cucumber, peeled and
  thinly sliced
4 smoked trout fillets,
  about 200g/7oz each,
  skinned and flaked
  coarsely

For the dressing
pinch of English mustard
  powder
15–20ml/3–4 tsp white
  wine vinegar
30ml/2 tbsp light olive oil
100ml/3½fl oz/scant ½
  cup natural yogurt
about 30ml/2 tbsp grated
  fresh or bottled
  horseradish
pinch of caster sugar

1 To make the dressing, mix together the mustard powder
and vinegar, then gradually whisk in the oil, yogurt,
horseradish and sugar. Set aside for 30 minutes.

2 Place the lettuce leaves in a large bowl. Stir the dressing
again, then pour half of it over the leaves and toss lightly
using two spoons.

3 Arrange the lettuce on four individual plates with the
tomatoes, cucumber and trout. Spoon over the remaining
dressing and serve at once.

Cook's Tip
*The addition of salt to the horseradish salad dressing
should not be necessary because of the saltiness of the
smoked trout fillets.*

Moroccan Fish Tagine

Tagine is the name of the large cooking pot used for this
type of cooking in Morocco.

Serves 4

2 garlic cloves, crushed
30ml/2 tbsp ground
  cumin
30ml/2 tbsp paprika
1 small fresh red chilli
  (optional)
30ml/2 tbsp tomato purée
60ml/4 tbsp lemon juice
4 whiting or cod cutlets
  (about 175g/6oz each)

350g/12oz tomatoes,
  sliced
2 green peppers, seeded
  and thinly sliced
salt and ground black
  pepper
chopped fresh coriander,
  to garnish

1 Mix together the garlic, cumin, paprika, chilli, tomato
purée and lemon juice. Spread this mixture over the fish, then
cover and chill in the fridge for about 30 minutes to let the
flavours penetrate.

2 Preheat the oven to 200°C/400°F/Gas 6. Arrange half of
the tomatoes and peppers in a baking dish.

3 Cover with the fish, then arrange the remaining tomatoes
and peppers on top. Cover the baking dish with foil and bake
for about 45 minutes, until the fish is tender. Sprinkle with
chopped coriander or parsley to serve.

Cook's Tip
*Try different white fish in this dish, such as hoki or
pollack. If you are preparing this dish for a dinner
party, it can be assembled completely and stored in the
fridge until you are ready to cook it.*

Prawn and Mint Salad

Green prawns make all the difference to this salad, as the flavours marinate well into the prawns before cooking.

Serves 4

12 large green prawns	5ml/1 tsp caster sugar
15g/½oz/1 tbsp unsalted	1 garlic clove, crushed
butter	2 fresh red chillies, seeded
15ml/1 tbsp fish sauce	and finely chopped
juice of 1 lime	30ml/2 tbsp fresh mint
45ml/3 tbsp thin coconut	leaves
milk	ground black pepper
2.5cm/1in piece of root	225g/8oz light green
ginger, peeled and	lettuce leaves, such as
grated	butterhead, to serve

1 Peel the prawns, leaving the tails intact.

2 Melt the butter in a large frying pan and toss in the green prawns until they turn pink.

3 Mix the fish sauce, lime juice, coconut milk, ginger, sugar, garlic, chillies and pepper together.

4 Toss the warm prawns into the sauce with the mint leaves. Serve the prawn mixture on a bed of green lettuce leaves.

Cook's Tip
For a really tropical touch, garnish this flavoursome salad with some shavings of fresh coconut made using a potato peeler.

Mackerel with Tomatoes and Pesto

This rich and oily fish needs the sharp tomato sauce. The aromatic pesto is excellent drizzled over the fish.

Serves 4

For the pesto sauce	salt and ground black
50g/2oz/½ cup pine nuts	pepper
30ml/2 tbsp fresh basil	
leaves	**For the fish**
2 garlic cloves, crushed	4 mackerel, gutted
30ml/2 tbsp freshly	30ml/2 tbsp olive oil
grated Parmesan	115g/4oz onion, roughly
cheese	chopped
150ml/¼ pint/⅔ cup	450g/1lb tomatoes,
extra virgin olive oil	roughly chopped

1 To make the pesto sauce, place the pine nuts, basil and garlic cloves in a food processor fitted with a metal blade. Process until the mixture forms a rough paste. Add the Parmesan cheese and, with the machine running, gradually add the oil. Set aside until required.

2 Heat the grill until very hot. Season the mackerel well with salt and pepper and cook for 10 minutes on either side.

3 Meanwhile, heat the oil in a large heavy-based saucepan and sauté the onions until soft.

4 Stir in the tomatoes and cook for 5 minutes. Serve the warm fish on top of the tomato mixture and top with a dollop of pesto sauce.

Cook's Tip
The pesto sauce can be made ahead and stored in the fridge until needed. Soften it again before using. For red pesto sauce, add some puréed sun-dried tomatoes after the oil.

Mackerel with Mustard and Lemon

Mackerel must be really fresh to be enjoyed. Look for bright, firm-fleshed fish.

Serves 4

4 fresh mackerel (about
    275g/10oz each),
    gutted and cleaned
175–225g/6–8oz/
    1½–2 cups spinach

30ml/2 tbsp wholegrain
    mustard
grated rind of 1 lemon
30ml/2 tbsp lemon juice
45ml/3 tbsp chopped
    fresh parsley
salt and ground black
    pepper

For the mustard and
lemon butter

115g/4oz/½ cup butter,
    melted

1 To prepare each mackerel, use a sharp knife to cut off the head just behind the gills, then cut along the belly so that the fish can be opened out flat.

2 Place the fish on a board, skin-side up, and, with the heel of your hand, press along the backbone to loosen it.

3 Turn the fish the right way up and pull the bone away from the flesh. Remove the tail and cut each fish in half lengthways. Wash and pat dry with kitchen paper.

4 Score the skin three or four times, then season the fish. To make the mustard and lemon butter, mix together the melted butter, mustard, lemon rind and juice and parsley. Season with salt and pepper. Place the mackerel on a grill rack. Brush a little of the butter over the mackerel and grill for 5 minutes each side, basting occasionally until cooked through.

5 Arrange the spinach leaves in the centre of four large plates. Place the mackerel on top. Heat the remaining butter in a small saucepan until sizzling and pour over the mackerel. Serve immediately.

Whitebait with Herb Sandwiches

Whitebait are the tiny fry of sprats or herring and are served whole. Cayenne pepper makes them spicy hot.

Serves 4

unsalted butter, for
    spreading
6 slices granary bread
90ml/6 tbsp mixed
    chopped fresh herbs,
    such as parsley,
    chervil and chives
450g/1lb whitebait,
    defrosted if frozen

65g/2½oz/scant ¾ cup
    plain flour
15ml/1 tbsp chopped
    fresh parsley
salt and cayenne pepper
groundnut oil,
    for deep-frying
lemon slices, to garnish

1 Butter the bread slices. Sprinkle the herbs over three of the slices, then top with the remaining slices of bread. Remove the crusts and cut each sandwich into eight triangles. Cover with clear film and set aside.

2 Rinse the whitebait thoroughly. Drain and then pat dry on kitchen paper.

3 Put the flour, chopped parsley, salt and cayenne pepper in a large plastic bag and shake to mix. Add the whitebait and toss gently in the seasoned flour until lightly coated. Heat the oil in a deep-fat fryer to 180°C/350°F.

4 Fry the fish in batches for 2–3 minutes, until golden and crisp. Lift out of the oil and drain on kitchen paper. Keep warm in the oven until all the fish are cooked.

5 Sprinkle the whitebait with salt and more cayenne pepper, if liked, and garnish with the lemon slices. Serve at once with the herb sandwiches.

Sole Goujons with Lime Mayonnaise

This simple dish can be rustled up very quickly. It makes an excellent light lunch or supper.

Serves 4

*675g/1½lb sole fillets,
  skinned
2 eggs, beaten
115g/4oz/2 cups fresh
  white breadcrumbs
oil, for deep-frying
salt and ground black
  pepper
lime wedges, to serve*

*1 small garlic clove,
  crushed
10ml/2 tsp capers, rinsed
  and chopped
10ml/2 tsp chopped
  gherkins
finely grated rind
  of ½ lime
10ml/2 tsp lime juice
15ml/1 tbsp chopped
  fresh coriander*

For the mayonnaise

*200ml/7fl oz/scant 1 cup
  mayonnaise*

1 To make the lime mayonnaise, mix together the mayonnaise, garlic, capers, gherkins, lime rind and juice and chopped coriander. Season to taste with salt and pepper. Transfer to a serving bowl and chill until required.

2 Cut the sole fillets into finger-length strips. Dip into the beaten egg, then into the breadcrumbs.

3 Heat the oil in a deep-fat fryer to 180°C/350°F. Add the fish in batches and fry until golden brown and crisp. Drain well on kitchen paper.

4 Pile the goujons on to warmed serving plates and serve with the lime wedges for squeezing over. Hand the lime mayonnaise round separately.

Cook's Tip

Make sure you use good quality mayonnaise for the sauce, or – better still – make your own. But remember that some people, including pregnant women, should not eat raw egg.

Spicy Fish Rösti

Serve these delicious fish cakes crisp and hot for lunch or supper with a mixed green salad.

Serves 4

*350g/12oz large, firm
  waxy potatoes
350g/12oz salmon or cod
  fillet, skinned and
  boned
3–4 spring onions,
  finely chopped
5ml/1 tsp grated fresh
  root ginger*

*30ml/2 tbsp chopped
  fresh coriander
10ml/2 tsp lemon juice
30–45ml/2–3 tbsp
  sunflower oil
salt and cayenne pepper
lemon wedges, to serve
fresh coriander sprigs, to
  garnish*

1 Bring a saucepan of water to the boil and cook the potatoes with their skins on for about 10 minutes. Drain and leave to cool for a few minutes.

2 Meanwhile, finely chop the salmon or cod fillet and place in a bowl. Stir in the chopped spring onions, grated root ginger, chopped coriander and lemon juice. Season to taste with salt and cayenne pepper.

3 When the potatoes are cool enough to handle, peel off the skins and grate the potatoes coarsely. Gently stir the grated potato into the fish mixture.

4 Form the fish mixture into 12 cakes, pressing the mixture together but leaving the edges slightly rough.

5 Heat the oil in a large frying pan, and, when hot, fry the fish cakes a few at a time for 3 minutes on each side, until golden brown and crisp. Drain on kitchen paper. Serve hot with lemon wedges for squeezing over. Garnish with sprigs of fresh coriander.

Mediterranean Plaice Rolls

Sun-dried tomatoes, pine nuts and anchovies make a flavoursome combination for the stuffing mixture.

Serves 4

4 plaice fillets (about
225g/8oz each),
skinned
75g/3oz/6 tbsp butter
1 small onion, chopped
1 celery stick, finely
chopped
115g/4oz/2 cups fresh
white breadcrumbs
45ml/3 tbsp chopped
fresh parsley

30ml/2 tbsp pine nuts,
toasted
3–4 pieces sun-dried
tomatoes in oil,
drained and chopped
50g/2oz can anchovy
fillets, drained and
chopped
75ml/5 tbsp fish stock
pinch of black pepper

1 Preheat the oven to 180°C/350°F/Gas 4. Using a sharp knife, cut the plaice fillets in half lengthways to make eight smaller fillets.

2 Melt the butter in a pan and cook the onion and celery. Cover with a tight-fitting lid and cook over a low heat for about 15 minutes until softened. Do not allow to brown.

3 Mix together the breadcrumbs, parsley, pine nuts, sun-dried tomatoes and anchovies. Stir in the softened vegetables with the buttery juices and season to taste with pepper.

4 Divide the stuffing into eight portions. Taking one portion at a time, form the stuffing into balls, then roll up each one inside a plaice fillet. Secure each roll with a cocktail stick.

5 Place the rolled-up fillets in a buttered ovenproof dish. Pour over the stock and cover the dish with buttered foil. Bake for about 20 minutes, or until the fish flakes easily. Remove the cocktail sticks, then serve with a little of the cooking juices drizzled over.

Salmon with Watercress Sauce

Adding the watercress right at the end of cooking retains much of its flavour and colour.

Serves 4

300ml/½ pint/1¼ cups
crème fraîche
30ml/2 tbsp chopped
fresh tarragon
25g/1oz/2 tbsp butter
15ml/1 tbsp sunflower oil
4 salmon fillets, skinned
and boned

1 garlic clove, crushed
120ml/4fl oz/½ cup dry
white wine
1 bunch watercress
salt and ground black
pepper

1 Gently heat the crème fraîche in a small saucepan until just beginning to boil. Remove the pan from the heat and stir in half the tarragon. Leave the herb cream to infuse while cooking the fish.

2 Heat the butter and oil in a frying pan and fry the salmon fillets for 3–5 minutes on each side. Remove from the pan and keep warm.

3 Add the garlic and fry for a further 1 minute, then pour in the wine and let it bubble until reduced to about 15ml/1 tbsp.

4 Meanwhile, strip the leaves off the watercress stalks and chop finely. Discard any damaged leaves. (Save the watercress stalks for soup, if you wish.)

5 Strain the herb cream into the pan and cook for a few minutes, stirring until the sauce has thickened. Stir in the remaining tarragon and watercress, then cook for a few minutes, until wilted but still bright green. Season to taste with salt and pepper and serve at once, spooned over the salmon. The dish can be accompanied by a mixed lettuce salad if you wish.

Warm Salmon Salad

This light salad is perfect in summer. Serve immediately, or the salad leaves will lose their colour.

Serves 4

450g/1lb salmon fillet,
  skinned
30ml/2 tbsp sesame oil
grated rind of ½ orange
juice of 1 orange
5ml/1 tsp Dijon mustard
15ml/1 tbsp chopped
  fresh tarragon
45ml/3 tbsp groundnut
  oil

115g/4oz fine green
  beans, trimmed
175g/6oz mixed salad
  leaves, such as young
  spinach leaves,
  radicchio and frisée
15ml/1 tbsp toasted
  sesame seeds
salt and ground black
  pepper

1 Cut the salmon into bite-size pieces, then make the dressing. Mix together the sesame oil, orange rind and juice, mustard, chopped tarragon and season to taste with salt and ground black pepper. Set aside.

2 Heat the groundnut oil in a frying pan and fry the salmon pieces for 3–4 minutes, or until lightly browned but still tender on the inside.

3 While the salmon is cooking, blanch the green beans in boiling salted water for about 5–6 minutes, until tender yet still slightly crisp.

4 Add the dressing to the salmon, toss together gently and cook for 30 seconds. Remove the pan from the heat.

5 Arrange the salad leaves on serving plates. Drain the beans and toss over the leaves. Spoon over the salmon and cooking juices and serve immediately, sprinkled with the toasted sesame seeds.

Red Mullet with Fennel

Ask the fishmonger to gut the mullet but not to discard the liver, as this is a delicacy and provides much of the flavour.

Serves 4

3 small fennel bulbs
60ml/4 tbsp olive oil
2 small onions, sliced
2–4 fresh basil leaves
4 small or 2 large red
  mullet, cleaned

grated rind of ½ lemon
150ml/¼ pint/⅔ cup fish
  stock
50g/2oz/4 tbsp butter
juice of 1 lemon

1 Snip off the feathery fronds from the fennel bulbs, finely chop and reserve for the garnish. Cut the fennel into wedges, being careful to leave the layers attached at the root ends so the pieces stay intact.

2 Heat the oil in a frying pan large enough to take the fish in a single layer and cook the wedges of fennel and onions for about 10–15 minutes, until softened and lightly browned.

3 Tuck a basil leaf inside each mullet, then place on top of the vegetables. Sprinkle the lemon rind on top. Pour in the stock and bring just to the boil. Cover with a tight-fitting lid and cook gently for 15–20 minutes, until the fish is tender.

4 Melt the butter in a small saucepan and, when it starts to sizzle and colour slightly, add the lemon juice. Pour over the mullet, sprinkle with the reserved fennel fronds and serve.

Cook's Tip
Grey mullet can also be cooked in this way. Look for fish with bright, convex eyes and firm, gleaming flesh and red gills.

Tuna with Pan-fried Tomatoes

Meaty and filling tuna steaks are served here with juicy tomatoes and black olives.

Serves 2
2 tuna steaks (about
   175g/6oz each)
90ml/6 tbsp olive oil
30ml/2 tbsp lemon juice
2 garlic cloves, chopped
5ml/1 tsp chopped fresh
   thyme
4 canned anchovy fillets,
   drained and chopped

225g/8oz plum tomatoes,
   halved
30ml/2 tbsp chopped
   fresh parsley
4 – 6 black olives, stoned
   and chopped
pinch of ground black
   pepper
crusty bread, to serve

1 Place the tuna steaks in a shallow non-metallic dish. Mix 60ml/4 tbsp of the oil with the lemon juice, garlic, thyme, anchovies and pepper. Pour this mixture over the tuna and leave to marinate for at least 1 hour.

2 Lift the tuna from the marinade and place on a grill rack. Grill for 4 minutes on each side, or until the tuna feels firm to touch, basting with the marinade. Take care not to overcook.

3 Meanwhile, heat the remaining oil in a frying pan and fry the tomatoes for a maximum of 2 minutes on each side.

4 Divide the tomatoes equally between two serving plates and scatter the chopped parsley and olives over them. Top each with a tuna steak.

5 Add the remaining marinade to the pan juices and warm through. Pour over the tomatoes and tuna steaks and serve at once with crusty bread for mopping up the juices.

Cook's Tip
If you are unable to find fresh tuna steaks, you could replace them with salmon fillets, if you wish – just grill them for one or two minutes more on each side.

Sautéed Salmon with Cucumber

Cucumber is the classic accompaniment to salmon. Here it is served hot, but be careful not to overcook it.

Serves 4
450g/1lb salmon fillet,
   skinned
40g/1½oz/3 tbsp butter
2 spring onions, chopped
½ cucumber, seeded and
   cut into strips
60ml/4 tbsp dry white
   wine

120ml/4fl oz/½ cup
   crème fraîche
30ml/2 tbsp snipped
   fresh chives
2 tomatoes, peeled, seeded
   and diced
salt and ground black
   pepper

1 Cut the salmon into about 12 thin slices, then cut across into strips.

2 Melt the butter in a large frying pan and sauté the salmon for 1 – 2 minutes. Remove the salmon strips using a slotted spoon and set aside.

3 Add the spring onions to the pan and cook for 2 minutes. Stir in the cucumber and sauté for 1 – 2 minutes, until hot. Remove the cucumber and keep warm with the salmon.

4 Add the wine to the pan and let it bubble until well reduced. Stir in the cucumber, crème fraîche, half of the chives and season to taste with salt and pepper. Return the salmon to the pan and warm through gently. Sprinkle the tomatoes and remaining chives over the top. Serve at once.

Crunchy-topped Cod

It's easy to forget just how tasty and satisfying a simple, classic dish can be.

Serves 4

4 pieces cod fillet (about
    115g/4oz each)
    skinned
2 tomatoes, sliced
50g/2oz/1 cup fresh
    wholemeal
    breadcrumbs

30ml/2 tbsp chopped
    fresh parsley
finely grated rind and
    juice of ½ lemon
5ml/1 tsp sunflower oil
salt and ground black
    pepper

1 Preheat the oven to 200°C/400°F/Gas 6. Arrange the cod fillets in a wide, ovenproof dish.

2 Arrange the tomato slices on top. Mix together the breadcrumbs, fresh parsley, lemon rind and juice and the oil with seasoning to taste.

3 Spoon the crumb mixture evenly over the fish, then bake for 15–20 minutes. Serve hot.

Fish Balls in Tomato Sauce

This quick meal is a good choice for young children, as you can guarantee there are no bones.

Serves 4

450g/1lb hoki or other
    white fish fillets,
    skinned
60ml/4 tbsp fresh
    wholemeal
    breadcrumbs
30ml/2 tbsp snipped
    chives or spring onion

400g/14oz can chopped
    tomatoes
50g/2oz button
    mushrooms, sliced
salt and ground black
    pepper

1 Cut the fish fillets into chunks; place in a food processor. Add the breadcrumbs, chives or spring onion. Season and process until the fish is chopped, but still with some texture. Divide the fish mixture into about 16 even-sized pieces, then mould them into balls with your hands.

2 Place the tomatoes and mushrooms in a saucepan; cook over a medium heat until boiling. Add the fish balls, cover and simmer for about 10 minutes until cooked. Serve hot.

Tuna and Corn Fish Cakes

These economical tuna fish cakes are quick to make. Use either fresh mashed potatoes or instant mash.

Serves 4

Place 300g/11oz/1½ cups mashed potato in a bowl; stir in 200g/7oz tuna fish, 115g/4oz/¼ cup canned sweetcorn and 30ml/2 tbsp chopped parsley. Season to taste with salt and black pepper, then shape into eight patties. Press the fish cakes into 50g/2oz/1 cup fresh breadcrumbs to coat them lightly, then place on a baking sheet. Cook under a moderate grill until crisp and golden, turning once. Serve hot with lemon wedges and fresh vegetables.

Cod Creole

Inspired by the cuisine of the Caribbean, this fish dish is both colourful and delicious.

Serves 4

450g/1lb cod fillets, skinned
15ml/1 tbsp lime or lemon juice
10ml/2 tsp olive oil
1 onion, finely chopped
1 green pepper, seeded and sliced

2.5ml/½ tsp cayenne pepper
2.5ml/½ tsp garlic salt
500g/14oz can chopped tomatoes
boiled rice or potatoes, to serve

1 Cut the cod fillets into bite-size chunks and sprinkle with the lime or lemon juice.

2 Heat the oil in a large, non-stick frying pan and fry the onion and pepper gently until softened. Add the cayenne pepper and garlic salt.

3 Stir in the cod and the chopped tomatoes. Bring to the boil, then cover and simmer for about 5 minutes, or until the fish flakes easily. Serve with boiled rice or potatoes.

Cook's Tip

This flavoursome dish is surprisingly light in calories, so if you are worried about your waistline, this is the meal for you.

Salmon Pasta with Parsley Sauce

The parsley sauce is added at the last moment to the salmon mixture and does not have to be cooked separately.

Serves 4

450g/1lb salmon fillet, skinned
225g/8oz/2 cups pasta, such as penne
175g/6oz cherry tomatoes, halved
150ml/¼ pint/⅔ cup low-fat crème fraîche

45ml/3 tbsp finely chopped parsley
finely grated rind of ½ orange
salt and ground black pepper

1 Cut the salmon into bite-size pieces, arrange on a heatproof plate and cover with foil.

2 Bring a large saucepan of salted water to the boil, add the pasta and return to the boil. Place the plate of salmon on top and simmer for 10–12 minutes, until the pasta and salmon are cooked.

3 Drain the pasta and toss with the tomatoes and salmon. Mix together the crème fraîche, parsley, orange rind and pepper to taste, then toss into the salmon and pasta and serve hot or leave to cool to room temperature.

Cook's Tip

The grated orange rind in the sauce complements the salmon beautifully in this recipe. For an alternative, try trout fillets and substitute grated lemon rind.

Monkfish with Mexican Salsa

Seafood Pancakes

Remove the pinkish-grey membrane from the tail before cooking, or the fish will be tough.

The combination of fresh and smoked haddock imparts a wonderful flavour to the pancake filling.

Serves 4

675g/1½lb monkfish tail
45ml/3 tbsp olive oil
30ml/2 tbsp lime juice
1 garlic clove, crushed
15ml/1 tbsp fresh
  coriander, chopped
salt and ground black
  pepper
fresh coriander sprigs
  and lime slices, to
  garnish

For the salsa
4 tomatoes, seeded, peeled
  and diced
1 avocado, stoned, peeled
  and diced
½ red onion, chopped
1 green chilli, seeded and
  chopped
30ml/2 tbsp chopped
  fresh coriander
30ml/2 tbsp olive oil
15ml/1 tbsp lime juice

Serves 4–6

12 ready-made pancakes

For the filling
225g/8oz smoked haddock
  fillet
225g/8oz fresh haddock
  fillet
300ml/½ pint/1¼ cups
  milk
150ml/¼ pint/⅔ cup
  single cream
40g/1½oz/3 tbsp butter

40g/1½oz/3 tbsp plain
  flour
pinch of freshly grated
  nutmeg
2 hard-boiled eggs,
  shelled and chopped
salt and ground black
  pepper
sprinkling of Gruyère
  cheese
curly salad leaves, to
  serve

1 To make the salsa, mix the salsa ingredients and leave at room temperature for about 40 minutes.

2 Prepare the monkfish. Using a sharp knife, remove the pinkish-grey membrane. Cut the fillets from either side of the backbone, then cut each fillet in half to give four steaks.

3 Mix together the oil, lime juice, garlic, coriander and seasoning in a shallow non-metallic dish. Turn the monkfish several times to coat with the marinade, then cover the dish and leave to marinate at cool room temperature, or in the fridge, for 30 minutes.

4 Remove the monkfish from the marinade and grill for 10–12 minutes, turning once and brushing regularly with the marinade until cooked through.

5 Serve the monkfish garnished with coriander sprigs and lime slices and accompanied by the salsa.

1 To make the filling, put the haddock fillets in a large pan. Add the milk and poach for 6–8 minutes, until just tender. Lift out the fish using a draining spoon and, when cool enough to handle, remove skin and bones. Reserve the milk. Measure the single cream into a jug, then strain enough milk into the jug to make it up to 450ml/¾ pint/scant 2 cups.

2 Melt the butter in a pan, stir in the flour and cook gently for 1 minute. Gradually mix in the milk mixture, stirring continuously to make a smooth sauce. Cook for 2–3 minutes. Season to taste with salt, pepper and nutmeg. Flake the haddock and fold into the sauce with the eggs. Leave to cool.

3 Preheat the oven to 180°C/350°F/Gas 4. Divide the filling among the pancakes. Fold the sides of each pancake into the centre, then roll them up to enclose the filling completely. Butter four or six individual ovenproof dishes and arrange two or three filled pancakes in each, or butter one large dish for all the pancakes. Brush with melted butter and cook for 15 minutes. Sprinkle over the Gruyère and cook for a further 5 minutes, until warmed through. Serve hot with a few curly salad leaves, if you wish.

Herby Plaice Croquettes

Deep-fry with clean oil every time as the fish will flavour the oil and taint any other foods fried in the oil.

Serves 4

450g/1lb plaice fillets
300ml/½ pint/1¼ cups milk
450g/1lb cooked potatoes
1 bulb fennel, finely chopped
1 garlic clove, finely chopped
45ml/3 tbsp chopped fresh parsley
2 eggs
15g/½oz/1 tbsp unsalted butter
225g/8oz/2 cups white breadcrumbs
30ml/2 tbsp sesame seeds
oil, for deep-frying
salt and ground black pepper

1 Poach the fish fillets in the milk for about 15 minutes until the fish flakes. Drain the fillets and reserve the milk.

2 Peel the skin off the fish and remove any bones. Process the fish, potatoes, fennel, garlic, parsley, eggs and butter in a food processor fitted with a metal blade.

3 Add 30ml/2 tbsp of the reserved cooking milk and season to taste with salt and pepper.

4 Chill in the fridge for about 30 minutes, then shape into 20 croquettes with your hands.

5 Mix together the breadcrumbs and sesame seeds.

6 Roll the croquettes in the mixture to form a good coating. Heat the oil in a large heavy-based saucepan and deep-fry in batches for about 4 minutes until golden brown. Drain well on kitchen paper and serve hot.

Mixed Smoked Fish Kedgeree

An ideal breakfast dish on a cold morning. Garnish with quartered hard-boiled eggs and season well.

Serves 6

450g/1lb mixed smoked fish such as smoked cod, smoked haddock, smoked mussels or oysters, if available
300ml/½ pint/1¼ cups milk
175g/6oz/1 cup long grain rice
1 slice of lemon
50g/2oz/4 tbsp butter
5ml/1 tsp medium-hot curry powder
2.5ml/½ tsp freshly grated nutmeg
15ml/1 tbsp chopped fresh parsley
salt and ground black pepper
2 hard-boiled eggs, to garnish

1 Poach the uncooked smoked fish in milk for 10 minutes or until it flakes. Drain off the milk and flake the fish. Mix with the other smoked fish.

2 Cook the rice in boiling water together with a slice of lemon for 10 minutes, or according to the instructions on the packet, until just cooked. Drain well.

3 Melt the butter in a large saucepan and add the rice and fish. Shake the pan to mix all the ingredients together well.

4 Stir in the curry powder, nutmeg, parsley and seasoning. Serve immediately, garnished with quartered eggs.

Cook's Tip
When flaking the fish, keep the pieces fairly large to give this dish a chunky consistency.

Spanish-style Hake

Cod and haddock cutlets will work just as well as hake in this tasty fish dish.

Serves 4

30ml/2 tbsp olive oil
25g/1oz/2 tbsp butter
1 onion, chopped
3 garlic cloves, crushed
15g/½oz/1 tbsp plain
  flour
2.5ml/½ tsp paprika
4 hake cutlets (about
  175g/6oz each)
250g/8oz fine green
  beans, cut into
  2.5cm/1in lengths

350ml/12fl oz/1½ cups
  fresh fish stock
150ml/¼ pint/generous
  ½ cup dry white wine
30ml/2 tbsp dry sherry
15–20 live mussels in
  the shell, cleaned
45ml/3 tbsp chopped
  fresh parsley
salt and ground black
  pepper
crusty bread, to serve

1 Heat the oil and butter in a sauté or frying pan and cook the onion for 5 minutes, until softened but not browned. Add the crushed garlic and cook for 1 minute more.

2 Mix together the plain flour and paprika, then lightly dust over the hake cutlets. Push the sautéed onion and garlic to one side of the pan.

3 Add the hake cutlets to the pan and fry until golden on both sides. Stir in the beans, stock, wine, sherry and season to taste with salt and pepper. Bring to the boil and cook for about 2 minutes.

4 Add the mussels and parsley, cover the pan with a tight-fitting lid and cook for 5–8 minutes, until the mussels have opened. Discard any that do not open.

5 Serve the hake in warmed, shallow soup bowls with crusty bread to mop up the juices.

Fish Goujons

Any white fish fillets can be used for the goujons – you could try a mixture of haddock and cod for a change.

Serves 4

60ml/4 tbsp mayonnaise
30ml/2 tbsp natural
  yogurt
grated rind of ½ lemon
squeeze of lemon juice
15ml/1 tbsp chopped
  fresh parsley
15ml/1 tbsp capers,
  chopped
2 x 175g/6oz sole fillets,
  skinned

2 x 175g/6oz plaice
  fillets, skinned
1 egg, lightly beaten
115g/4oz/2 cups fresh
  white breadcrumbs
15ml/1 tbsp sesame seeds
pinch of paprika
oil, for frying
salt and ground black
  pepper
4 lemon wedges, to serve

1 To make the lemon mayonnaise, mix the mayonnaise, yogurt, lemon rind and juice, parsley and capers in a bowl. Cover and chill.

2 Cut the fish fillets into thin strips. Place the beaten egg in one shallow bowl. Mix together the breadcrumbs, sesame seeds, paprika and seasoning in another bowl. Dip the fish strips, one at a time, into the beaten egg, then into the breadcrumb mixture and toss until coated evenly. Lay on a clean plate.

3 Heat about 2.5cm/1in of oil in a frying pan until a cube of bread browns in 30 seconds. Deep-fry the strips in batches for 2-3 minutes, until lightly golden.

4 Remove with a slotted spoon, drain on kitchen paper and keep warm in the oven while frying the remainder. Garnish with watercress and serve hot with lemon wedges and the chilled lemon mayonnaise.

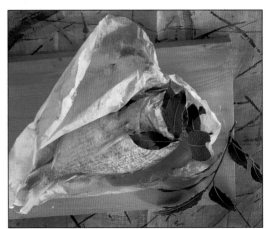

Pan-fried Garlic Sardines

Lightly fry a sliced garlic clove to garnish the fish. This dish could also be made with sprats or fresh anchovies.

Serves 4

1.1kg/2½ lb fresh
  sardines
30ml/2 tbsp olive oil
4 garlic cloves
finely grated rind of
  2 lemons
30ml/2 tbsp chopped
  fresh parsley

salt and ground black
  pepper

For the tomato bread
8 slices crusty bread,
  toasted
2 large ripe beefsteak
  tomatoes

1 Gut and clean the sardines thoroughly.

2 Heat the oil in a frying pan and cook the garlic cloves until they are softened.

3 Add the sardines and fry for 4–5 minutes. Sprinkle the lemon rind, parsley and seasoning over the top.

4 Cut the tomatoes in half and rub them on to the toast. Discard the skins. Serve the sardines with the tomato toast.

Cook's Tip
Make sure you use very ripe beefsteak tomatoes for this dish so they will rub on to the toast easily.

Sea Bass en Papillote

Bring the unopened parcels to the table and let your guests unfold their own fish to release the delicious aroma.

Serves 4

4 small sea bass, gutted
130g/4½oz/generous ½
  cup butter
450g/1lb spinach
3 shallots, finely chopped
60ml/4 tbsp white wine

4 bay leaves
salt and ground black
  pepper
new potatoes and glazed
  carrots, to serve

1 Preheat the oven to 180°C/350°F/Gas 4. Season both the inside and outside of the fish with salt and pepper. Melt 50g/2oz/4 tbsp of the butter in a large heavy-based saucepan and add the spinach. Cook gently until the spinach has broken down into a smooth purée. Set aside to cool.

2 Melt another 50g/2oz/4 tbsp of the butter in a clean pan and add the shallots. Gently sauté for 5 minutes until soft. Add to the spinach and leave to cool.

3 Stuff the insides of the fish with the spinach filling.

4 For each fish, fold a large sheet of greaseproof paper in half and cut around the fish laid on one half, to make a heart shape when unfolded. It should be at least 5cm/2in larger than the fish. Melt the remaining butter and brush a little on to the paper. Set the fish on one side of the paper.

5 Add a little wine and a bay leaf to each package.

6 Fold the other side of the paper over the fish and make small pleats to seal the two edges, starting at the curve of the heart. Brush the outsides with butter. Transfer the packages to a baking sheet and bake for 20–25 minutes until the packages are brown. Serve with new potatoes and glazed carrots.

Chilli Prawns

This delightful, spicy combination makes a lovely light main course for a casual supper.

Serves 3–4

45ml/3 tbsp olive oil
2 shallots, chopped
2 garlic cloves, chopped
1 fresh red chilli, chopped
450g/1lb ripe tomatoes, peeled, seeded and chopped
15ml/1 tbsp tomato purée
1 bay leaf

1 fresh thyme sprig
90ml/6 tbsp dry white wine
450g/1lb/4 cups peeled, cooked large prawns
salt and ground black pepper
roughly torn fresh basil leaves, to garnish

1 Heat the oil in a saucepan and fry the shallots, garlic and chilli until the garlic starts to brown.

2 Add the tomatoes, tomato purée, bay leaf, thyme, wine and seasoning. Bring to the boil, then reduce the heat and cook gently for about 10 minutes, stirring occasionally until the sauce has thickened. Discard the herbs.

3 Stir the prawns into the sauce and heat through for a few minutes. Taste and adjust the seasoning. Scatter the basil leaves over the top and serve at once.

Scallops with Ginger

Scallops are at their best in winter. Rich and creamy, this dish is very simple to make and quite delicious.

Serves 4

8 – 12 shelled scallops
40g/1½ oz/3 tbsp butter
2.5cm/1in piece fresh root ginger, finely chopped
1 bunch spring onions, diagonally sliced
60ml/4 tbsp white vermouth

250ml/8fl oz/1 cup crème fraîche
salt and ground black pepper
chopped fresh parsley, to garnish

1 Remove the tough muscle opposite the coral on each scallop. Separate the coral and cut the white part of the scallop in half horizontally.

2 Melt the butter in a frying pan. Add the scallops, including the corals, and sauté for about 2 minutes until lightly browned. Take care not to overcook the scallops as this will toughen them.

3 Lift out the scallops with a draining spoon and transfer to a warmed serving dish. Keep warm.

4 Add the ginger and spring onions to the pan and stir-fry for 2 minutes. Pour in the vermouth and allow to bubble until it has almost evaporated. Stir in the crème fraîche and cook for a few minutes until the sauce has thickened. Season to taste with salt and pepper.

5 Pour the sauce over the scallops, sprinkle with parsley and serve at once.

Smoked Trout Pilaff

Smoked trout might seem an unusual partner for rice, but this is a winning combination.

Serves 4

225g/8oz/1¼ cups white
  basmati rice
40g/1½oz/3 tbsp butter
2 onions, sliced into
  rings
1 garlic clove, crushed
2 bay leaves
2 whole cloves
2 green cardamom pods
2 cinnamon sticks
5ml/1 tsp cumin seeds

4 smoked trout fillets,
  skinned
50g/2oz/½ cup slivered
  almonds, toasted
50g/2oz/generous ½ cup
  seedless raisins
30ml/2 tbsp chopped
  fresh parsley
mango chutney and
  poppadoms, to serve

1 Wash the rice thoroughly in several changes of water and drain well. Set aside. Melt the butter in a large frying pan and fry the onions until well browned, stirring frequently.

2 Add the garlic, bay leaves, cloves, cardamom pods, cinnamon and cumin seeds, and stir-fry for 1 minute.

3 Stir in the rice, then add 600ml/1 pint/2½ cups boiling water. Bring to the boil. Cover the pan with a tight-fitting lid, reduce the heat and cook very gently for 20–25 minutes, until the water has been absorbed and the rice is tender.

4 Flake the smoked trout and add to the pan with the almonds and raisins. Fork through gently. Re-cover the pan and allow the smoked trout to warm in the rice for a few minutes. Scatter the parsley over the top and serve with mango chutney and poppadoms.

Cod with Spiced Red Lentils

This is a very tasty and filling dish, yet it is a healthy option at the same time.

Serves 4

175g/6oz/¾ cup red
  lentils
1.25ml/¼ tsp ground
  turmeric
600ml/1 pint/2½ cups
  fish stock
30ml/2 tbsp vegetable oil
7.5ml/1½ tsp cumin
  seeds
15ml/1 tbsp grated fresh
  root ginger

2.5ml/½ tsp cayenne
  pepper
15ml/1 tbsp lemon juice
30ml/2 tbsp chopped
  fresh coriander
450g/1lb cod fillets,
  skinned and cut into
  large chunks
pinch of salt, to taste
fresh coriander leaves
  and lemon wedges,
  to garnish

1 Put the lentils in a saucepan with the turmeric and stock. Bring to the boil, cover with a tight-fitting lid and simmer for 20–25 minutes, until the lentils are just tender. Remove from the heat and add salt.

2 Heat the oil in a small frying pan. Add the cumin seeds and, when they begin to pop, add the ginger and cayenne pepper. Stir-fry the spices for a few seconds, then pour on to the lentils. Add the lemon juice and the coriander and stir them gently into the mixture.

3 Lay the pieces of cod on top of the lentils, cover the pan and then cook gently over a low heat for 10–15 minutes, or until the fish is tender.

4 Transfer the lentils and cod to warmed serving plates with a fish slice. Sprinkle over the coriander leaves and garnish each serving with one or two lemon wedges. Serve hot.

Mediterranean Fish Stew

Use any combination of fish you wish in this stew, which is served with an authentic rouille sauce.

Serves 4

*225g/8oz/2 cups cooked
    prawns in the shell
450g/1lb mixed white
    fish, skinned and
    chopped (reserve skins
    for the stock)
45ml/3 tbsp olive oil
1 onion, chopped
1 leek, sliced
1 carrot, diced
1 garlic clove, chopped
2.5ml/½ tsp ground
    turmeric
150ml/¼ pint/⅔ cup dry
    white wine or cider
400g/14oz can chopped
    tomatoes
sprig of fresh parsley,
    thyme and fennel
1 bay leaf*

*small piece of orange peel
1 prepared squid, body
    cut into rings and
    tentacles chopped
12 mussels in the shell
salt and ground black
    pepper
30–45ml/2–3 tbsp fresh
    Parmesan cheese
    shavings and fresh
    parsley, to garnish*

For the rouille sauce
*2 slices white bread,
    without crusts
2 garlic cloves, crushed
½ fresh red chilli
15ml/1 tbsp tomato purée
45–60ml/3–4 tbsp
    olive oil*

1 Peel the prawns, leaving the tails. Make stock with the prawn and fish skins and 450ml/¾ pint/1¾ cups water. Fry the onion, leek, carrot and garlic in the oil for about 6–7 minutes; stir in the turmeric. Add the wine, tomatoes, the reserved fish stock, herbs and orange peel. Bring to the boil, cover and simmer for 20 minutes.

2 To make the rouille sauce, purée all the sauce ingredients in a food processor or blender.

3 Add the fish and seafood to the pan and simmer for about 5–6 minutes, until the mussels open. Remove the bay leaf and peel; season to taste. Serve with a spoonful of the rouille, garnished with Parmesan cheese and parsley.

Salmon with Herb Butter

Other fresh herbs could be used to flavour the butter – try mint, fennel, parsley or oregano.

Serves 4

*50g/2oz/4 tbsp butter,
    softened
finely grated rind of ½
    small lemon
15ml/1 tbsp lemon juice
15ml/1 tbsp chopped
    fresh dill*

*4 salmon steaks
2 lemon slices, halved
4 fresh dill sprigs
salt and ground black
    pepper*

1 Place the butter, lemon rind, lemon juice, chopped dill and seasoning in a small bowl and mix together with a fork until thoroughly blended.

2 Spoon the butter on to a piece of greaseproof paper and roll up, smoothing with your hands into a sausage shape. Twist the ends tightly, wrap in clear film and place in the freezer for 20 minutes until firm.

3 Meanwhile, preheat the oven to 190°C/375°F/Gas 5. Cut out four squares of foil big enough to encase the salmon steaks and grease lightly. Place a salmon steak in the centre of each square.

4 Remove the butter from the freezer and slice into eight rounds. Place two rounds on top of each salmon steak with a halved lemon slice in the centre and a sprig of dill on top. Lift up the edges of the foil and crinkle them together until they are well sealed.

5 Lift the parcels on to a baking sheet and bake for about 20 minutes. Remove from the oven and place the unopened parcels on warmed plates. Open the parcels and slide the contents on to the plates with the juices.

Spanish Seafood Paella

Use monkfish instead of the cod, if you wish, and add a red mullet cut into chunks.

Serves 4

60ml/4 tbsp olive oil
225g/8oz cod, skinned and
  cut into chunks
3 prepared baby squid,
  body cut into rings and
  tentacles chopped
1 onion, chopped
3 garlic cloves, finely
  chopped
1 red pepper, seeded and
  sliced
4 tomatoes, skinned and
  chopped
225g/8oz/1¼ cups arborio
  rice
450ml/¾ pint/scant 2
  cups fish stock
150ml/¼ pint/⅔ cup
  white wine
75g/3oz/¼ cup frozen peas
4–5 saffron strands,
  soaked in 30ml/2 tbsp
  hot water
115g/4oz/1 cup peeled,
  cooked prawns
8 fresh mussels in the
  shell, scrubbed
salt and ground black
  pepper
15ml/1 tbsp chopped fresh
  parsley, to garnish
lemon wedges, to serve

1 Heat 30ml/2 tbsp of the oil in a frying pan and stir-fry the cod and the squid for 2 minutes. Transfer to a bowl.

2 Heat the remaining oil in the pan and fry the onion, garlic and pepper for 6–7 minutes, stirring until softened.

3 Stir in the tomatoes and fry for a further 2 minutes, then add the rice, stirring to coat the grains with oil, and cook for 2–3 minutes more. Pour on the stock and wine and add the peas, saffron and water. Season to taste.

4 Gently stir in the reserved cooked fish with all the juices, followed by the prawns, and then push the mussels into the rice. Cover with a tight-fitting lid and cook over a gentle heat for about 30 minutes, or until the stock has been absorbed. Remove from the heat, keep covered and leave to stand for 5 minutes. Sprinkle with parsley; serve with lemon wedges.

Spaghetti with Seafood Sauce

The Italian name for this tomato-based sauce is *marinara*. It is very popular in coastal regions.

Serves 4

45ml/3 tbsp olive oil
1 onion, chopped
225g/8oz spaghetti
600ml/1 pint/2½ cups
  passata
15ml/1 tbsp tomato purée
5ml/1 tsp dried oregano
1 bay leaf
5ml/1 tsp sugar
115g/4oz/1 cup peeled,
  cooked shrimps
115g/4oz/1 cup peeled,
  cooked prawns
175g/6oz cooked clam or
  cockle meat (rinsed
  well if canned or
  bottled)
15ml/1 tbsp lemon juice
45ml/3 tbsp chopped
  fresh parsley
25g/1oz/2 tbsp butter
salt and ground black
  pepper
4 cooked prawns, to
  garnish

1 Heat the oil in a saucepan and fry the onion and garlic for 6–7 minutes until softened. Meanwhile, cook the spaghetti in a large pan of boiling salted water for 10–12 minutes or according to the instructions on the packet, until *al dente*.

2 Stir the passata, tomato purée, oregano, bay leaf and sugar into the onions and season to taste with salt and pepper. Bring to the boil, then simmer for 2–3 minutes.

3 Add the shellfish, lemon juice and 30ml/2 tbsp of the parsley. Stir well, then cover and cook for 6–7 minutes more.

4 Drain the spaghetti and add the butter to the pan. Return the drained spaghetti to the pan and toss in the butter. Season well.

5 Divide the spaghetti among four warmed plates and top with the seafood sauce. Sprinkle with the remaining parsley, garnish with whole prawns and serve immediately.

Garlic Chilli Prawns

In Spain *gambas al ajillo* are traditionally cooked in small earthenware dishes, but a frying pan is just as suitable.

Serves 4

60ml/4 tbsp olive oil
2–3 garlic cloves, finely chopped
1/2 –1 fresh red chilli, seeded and chopped
16 cooked whole Mediterranean prawns

15ml/1 tbsp chopped fresh parsley
salt and ground black pepper
lemon wedges and French bread, to serve

1 Heat the oil in a large frying pan and stir-fry the garlic and chilli for 1 minute, until the garlic begins to turn brown.

2 Add the Mediterranean prawns and stir-fry for about 3–4 minutes, coating them well with the flavoured oil.

3 Add the parsley, remove from the heat and serve four prawns per person in heated bowls, with the flavoured oil spooned over them. Serve with lemon wedges for squeezing and French bread to mop up the juices.

Deep-fried Spicy Whitebait

This is a delicious British dish – serve these tiny fish very hot and crisp.

Serves 4

450g/1lb whitebait
40g/1½oz/3 tbsp plain flour
5ml/1 tsp paprika
pinch of cayenne pepper
12 fresh parsley sprigs

vegetable oil, for deep-frying
salt and ground black pepper
4 lemon wedges, to garnish

1 If using frozen whitebait, defrost in the bag, then drain off any water. Spread the fish on kitchen paper and pat dry.

2 Place the flour, paprika, cayenne and seasoning in a large plastic bag. Add the whitebait and shake gently until all the fish are lightly coated with the flour. Transfer to a plate.

3 Heat about 5cm/2in of oil in a saucepan or deep-fat fryer to 190°C/375°F, or until a cube of bread dropped into the oil browns in about 30 seconds.

4 Add the whitebait in batches and deep-fry in the hot oil for 2–3 minutes, until the coating is lightly golden and crispy. Remove, drain on kitchen paper and keep warm in the oven while frying the remainder.

5 When all the whitebait is cooked, drop the sprigs of parsley into the hot oil (don't worry if the oil spits a bit) and fry for a few seconds until crisp. Drain on kitchen paper. Serve the whitebait garnished with the deep-fried parsley sprigs and lemon wedges.

Baked Fish Creole-style

Fish fillets cooked in a colourful pepper and tomato sauce are topped with a cheesy crust.

Serves 4

15ml/1 tbsp oil
25g/1oz/2 tbsp butter
1 onion, thinly sliced
1 garlic clove, chopped
1 red pepper, seeded,
    halved and sliced
1 green pepper, seeded,
    halved and sliced
400g/14oz can chopped
    tomatoes with basil
15ml/1 tbsp tomato purée
30ml/2 tbsp capers,
    chopped
3–4 drops Tabasco sauce

4 tail end pieces cod or
    haddock fillets (about
    175g/6oz each),
    skinned
6 basil leaves, shredded
45ml/3 tbsp fresh
    breadcrumbs
25g/1oz/¼ cup grated
    Cheddar cheese
10ml/2 tsp chopped fresh
    parsley
salt and ground black
    pepper
fresh basil sprigs,
    to garnish

1 Preheat the oven to 230°C/450°F/Gas 8. Heat the oil and half of the butter in a saucepan, and fry the sliced onion for about 6–7 minutes until softened. Add the garlic, peppers, chopped tomatoes, tomato purée, capers and Tabasco and season to taste. Cover and cook for 15 minutes, then uncover and simmer gently for 5 minutes to reduce slightly.

2 Place the fish fillets in a buttered ovenproof dish, dot with the remaining butter and season lightly. Spoon the tomato and pepper sauce over the top and sprinkle with the shredded basil. Bake in the oven for about 10 minutes.

3 Meanwhile, mix together the breadcrumbs, cheese and parsley in a bowl. Remove the fish from the oven and scatter the cheese mixture over the top. Return to the oven and bake for about another 10 minutes. Let the fish stand for about a minute, then, using a fish slice, carefully transfer each topped fillet to warmed plates. Garnish with sprigs of fresh basil and serve while still hot.

Tuna Fishcake Bites

An updated version of a traditional British tea-time dish, these little cakes would also make an elegant starter.

Serves 4

675g/1½lb potatoes
knob of butter
2 hard-boiled eggs,
    chopped
3 spring onions, chopped
grated rind of ½ lemon
5ml/1 tsp lemon juice
30ml/2 tbsp chopped
    fresh parsley
200g/7oz can tuna in oil,
    drained
10ml/2 tsp capers,
    chopped
2 eggs, lightly beaten
115g/4oz/2 cups fresh
    white breadcrumbs

sunflower oil, for
    shallow-frying
salt and ground black
    pepper
green salad, to serve

For the tartare sauce

60ml/4 tbsp mayonnaise
15ml/1 tbsp natural
    yogurt
15ml/1 tbsp finely
    chopped gherkins
15ml/1 tbsp capers,
    chopped
15ml/1 tbsp chopped
    fresh parsley

1 Boil the potatoes. Drain and mash with the butter.

2 Mix the hard-boiled eggs, spring onions, lemon rind and juice, parsley, tuna, capers and 15ml/1 tbsp of the beaten egg into the cooled potato. Season to taste, cover and chill.

3 Mix all the sauce ingredients together. Chill in the fridge.

4 Roll the fishcake mixture into about 24 balls. Dip these into the egg and then roll gently in the breadcrumbs until evenly coated. Transfer to a plate.

5 Heat 90ml/6 tbsp of the oil in a frying pan and fry the balls over a moderate heat, in batches, for about 4 minutes, turning two or three times until browned all over. Drain on kitchen paper and keep warm in the oven while frying the remainder. Serve with the tartare sauce and a salad.

Kashmir Coconut Fish Curry

The combination of spices in this dish give an interesting depth of flavour to the creamy curry sauce.

Serves 4

30ml/2 tbsp vegetable oil
2 onions, sliced
1 green pepper, seeded and sliced
1 garlic clove, crushed
1 dried chilli, seeded and chopped
5ml/1 tsp ground coriander
4ml/1 tsp ground cumin
2.5ml/½ tsp ground turmeric
2.5ml/½ tsp hot chilli powder
2.5ml/½ tsp garam masala

15g/½oz/1 tbsp plain flour
115g/4oz creamed coconut, chopped
675g/1½lb haddock fillet, skinned and chopped
4 tomatoes, skinned, seeded and chopped
15ml/1 tbsp lemon juice
30ml/2 tbsp ground almonds
30ml/2 tbsp double cream
fresh coriander sprigs, to garnish
naan bread and boiled rice, to serve

1 Heat the oil in a large saucepan and add the onions, pepper and garlic. Cook for 6–7 minutes, until the onions and peppers have softened. Stir in the chopped dried chilli, all the ground spices, the chilli powder, garam masala and flour, and cook for 1 minute.

2 Dissolve the coconut in 600ml/1 pint/2½ cups boiling water and stir into the spicy vegetable mixture. Bring to the boil, cover and then simmer gently for 6 minutes.

3 Add the fish and tomatoes and cook for 5–6 minutes, or until the fish has turned opaque. Uncover and gently stir in the lemon juice, ground almonds and cream. Season well, garnish with coriander and serve with naan bread and rice.

Mussels with Wine and Garlic

This famous French dish is traditionally known as *moules marinière,* **and can be served as a starter or a main course.**

Serves 4

1.75kg/4lb live mussels
15ml/1 tbsp oil
25g/1oz/2 tbsp butter
1 small onion or 2 shallots, finely chopped
2 garlic cloves, finely chopped

150ml/¼ pint/⅔ cup dry white wine or cider
fresh parsley sprigs
ground black pepper
30ml/2 tbsp chopped fresh parsley, to garnish
French bread, to serve

1 Check that the mussels are closed. (Throw away any that are cracked or won't close when tapped.) Scrape the shells under cold running water and pull off the hairy beard attached to the hinge of the shell. Rinse well in two or three changes of water.

2 Heat the oil and butter in a large pan and fry the onions and garlic for 3–4 minutes.

3 Pour on the wine or cider and add the parsley sprigs, stir well, bring to the boil, then add the mussels. Cover with a tight-fitting lid and cook for about 5–7 minutes, shaking the pan once or twice until the shells open (throw away any that have not opened).

4 Serve the mussels and their juices sprinkled with the chopped parsley and some ground black pepper. Accompany with hot French bread.

Thai Prawn Salad

This salad has the distinctive flavour of lemon grass, the bulbous grass used widely in South-East Asian cooking.

Serves 2

250g/9oz/2¼ cups peeled, cooked, extra large tiger prawns
15ml/1 tbsp oriental fish sauce
30ml/2 tbsp lime juice
7.5ml/½ tbsp soft light brown sugar
1 small fresh red chilli, finely chopped
1 spring onion, finely chopped

1 small garlic clove, crushed
2.5cm/1in piece fresh lemon grass, finely chopped
30ml/2 tbsp chopped fresh coriander
45ml/3 tbsp dry white wine
8 – 12 Little Gem lettuce leaves, to serve
fresh coriander sprigs, to garnish

1 Place the tiger prawns in a bowl and add all the remaining ingredients. Stir well, cover and leave to marinate in the fridge for 2 – 3 hours, mixing and turning the prawns from time to time.

2 Arrange two or three of the lettuce leaves on each of four individual serving plates.

3 Spoon the prawn salad into the lettuce leaves. Garnish with fresh coriander and serve at once.

Cajun Spiced Fish

Fillets of fish are coated with an aromatic blend of herbs and spices and pan-fried in butter.

Serves 4

5ml/1 tsp dried thyme
5ml/1 tsp dried oregano
5ml/1 tsp ground black pepper
1.25ml/¼ tsp cayenne pepper
10ml/2 tsp paprika
2.5ml/½ tsp garlic salt
75g/3oz/6 tbsp butter

4 x tail end pieces of cod fillet (about 175g/6oz each)
½ fresh red pepper, sliced
½ green pepper, sliced
fresh thyme sprigs, to garnish
grilled tomatoes and sweet potato purée, to serve

1 Place all the herbs and spices in a bowl and mix well. Dip the fish fillets in the spice mixture until lightly coated.

2 Heat 25g/1oz/2 tbsp of the butter in a large frying pan, add the peppers and fry for 4 – 5 minutes, until softened. Remove the peppers and keep warm.

3 Add the remaining butter to the pan and heat until sizzling. Add the cod fillets and fry over a moderate heat for about 3 – 4 minutes on each side, until browned and cooked.

4 Transfer the fish to a warmed serving dish, surround with the peppers and garnish with thyme. Serve the spiced fish with some grilled tomatoes and sweet potato purée.

63

Golden Fish Pie

This lovely light pie with a crumpled filo pastry topping makes a delicious lunch or supper dish.

Serves 4–6

675g/1½lb white fish
  fillets
300ml/½ pint/1¼ cups
  milk
flavouring ingredients
  such as onion slices,
  bay leaf and black
  peppercorns
115g/4oz/1 cup peeled,
  cooked prawns,
  defrosted if frozen
115g/4oz/½ cup butter

50g/2oz/½ cup plain
  flour
300ml/½ pint/1¼ cups
  single cream
75g/3oz/¾ cup grated
  Gruyère cheese
1 bunch watercress,
  leaves only, chopped
5ml/1 tsp mustard
5 sheets filo pastry
salt and ground black
  pepper

1 Place the fish in a saucepan, pour over the milk and add the flavouring ingredients. Bring to the boil, cover with a lid and simmer for 10–12 minutes, until the fish is almost tender. Skin and bone the fish, then roughly flake into a shallow ovenproof dish. Scatter the prawns over the fish. Strain the milk and reserve.

2 Melt 50g/2oz/4 tbsp of the butter in a pan. Stir in the flour; cook for 1 minute. Stir in the milk and cream. Bring to the boil, stirring, then simmer for 2–3 minutes, until thickened. Remove from the heat and stir in the Gruyère, watercress, mustard, and season. Pour the mixture over the fish and leave to cool.

3 Preheat the oven to 190°C/375°F/Gas 5, then melt the remaining butter. Brush one sheet of filo pastry with a little butter, then crumple up loosely and place on top of the filling. Repeat with the remaining filo sheets and butter until they are all used up and the pie is completely covered.

4 Bake in the oven for 25–30 minutes, until the pastry is golden and crisp. Serve immediately.

Special Fish Pie

This fish pie is colourful, healthy and best of all, it is very simple to make.

Serves 4

350g/12oz haddock fillet,
  skinned
30ml/2 tbsp cornflour
115g/4oz/1 cup peeled,
  cooked prawns
200g/7oz can sweetcorn,
  drained
75g/3oz/scant 1 cup
  frozen peas
150ml/¼ pint/⅔ cup
  skimmed milk

150ml/¼ pint/⅔ cup
  low-fat fromage frais
75g/3oz/1½ cups fresh
  wholemeal
  breadcrumbs
40g/1½oz/generous
  ¼ cup grated reduced-
  fat Cheddar cheese
salt and ground black
  pepper

1 Preheat the oven to 190°C/375°F/Gas 5. Cut the haddock into bite-size pieces and toss in cornflour to coat evenly.

2 Place the fish, prawns, sweetcorn and peas in an ovenproof dish. Beat together the milk, fromage frais and seasoning, then pour into the dish.

3 Mix together the breadcrumbs and grated cheese, then spoon evenly over the top. Bake for 25–30 minutes, or until golden brown. Serve hot with fresh vegetables.

Cook's Tip

For a more economical version of this dish, omit the prawns and replace with more fish fillet.

Smoked Trout with Cucumber

Smoked trout provides an easy and delicious first course or light meal. Serve at room temperature for the best flavour.

Serves 4

1 large cucumber	*4 smoked trout fillets*
60ml/4 tbsp crème	*salt and ground black*
fraîche or Greek-style	*pepper*
yogurt	*dill sprigs, to garnish*
15ml/1 tbsp chopped	*crusty wholemeal bread,*
fresh dill	*to serve*

1 Peel the cucumber, cut in half lengthways and scoop out the seeds using a teaspoon. Cut into tiny dice.

2 Put the cucumber in a colander set over a plate and sprinkle with salt. Leave to drain for at least 1 hour to draw out the excess moisture.

3 Rinse the cucumber well, then pat dry on kitchen paper. Transfer the diced cucumber to a bowl and stir in the crème fraîche or yogurt, chopped dill and some freshly ground pepper. Chill the cucumber salad for about 30 minutes.

4 Arrange the trout fillets on individual plates. Spoon the cucumber and dill salad on one side and grind over a little black pepper. Garnish the dish with dill sprigs and serve with crusty bread.

Fish Cakes

Home-made fish cakes are an underrated food which bear little resemblance to the shop-bought type.

Serves 4

450g/1lb cooked, mashed	*1 egg, separated*
potatoes	*1 egg, beaten*
450g/1lb cooled mixed	*fine breadcrumbs made*
white and smoked fish	*with stale bread (about*
such as haddock or	*50g/2oz/1 cup)*
cod, flaked	*pinch of pepper*
25g/1oz/2 tbsp butter,	*vegetable oil, for*
cubed	*shallow frying*
45ml/3 tbsp chopped	
fresh parsley	

1 Place the potatoes in a bowl and beat in the fish, butter, parsley and egg yolk. Season to taste with pepper.

2 Divide the fish mixture into eight equal portions, then, with floured hands, form each into a flat cake.

3 Beat the remaining egg white with the whole egg. Dip each fish cake in the beaten egg, then in breadcrumbs.

4 Heat the oil in a frying pan and fry the fish cakes for about 3–5 minutes on each side, until crisp and golden. Drain on kitchen paper and serve hot with a crisp salad.

Cook's Tip
Make smaller fish cakes to serve as a starter with a salad garnish. For an extra special version, make them with cooked fresh salmon or drained, canned red or pink salmon.

Stuffed Plaice Rolls

Plaice fillets are a good choice for families because they are economical, easy to cook and free of bones.

Serves 4

1 courgette, grated
2 carrots, grated
60ml/4 tbsp fresh
*   wholemeal*
*   breadcrumbs*

15ml/1 tbsp lime or
*   lemon juice*
4 plaice fillets
salt and ground black
*   pepper*

1 Preheat the oven to 200°C/400°F/Gas 6. Mix together the carrots and courgettes. Stir in the breadcrumbs, lime juice and season with salt and pepper.

2 Lay the fish fillets skin-side up and divide the stuffing between them, spreading it evenly.

3 Roll up to enclose the stuffing and place in an ovenproof dish. Cover and bake for about 30 minutes, or until the fish flakes easily. Serve hot with new potatoes.

Mackerel Kebabs with Parsley

Oily fish such as mackerel are ideal for grilling as they cook quickly and need no extra oil.

Serves 4

450g/1lb mackerel fillets
finely grated rind and
*   juice of 1 lemon*
45ml/3 tbsp chopped
*   fresh parsley*

12 cherry tomatoes
8 stoned black olives
salt and ground black
*   pepper*

1 Cut the fish into 4cm/1½in chunks and place in a bowl with half the lemon rind and juice, half of the parsley and some seasoning. Cover the bowl and leave to marinate for about 30 minutes.

2 Thread the chunks of fish on to eight long wooden or metal skewers, alternating them with the cherry tomatoes and olives. Cook the kebabs under a hot grill for 3–4 minutes, turning the kebabs occasionally until the fish is cooked.

3 Mix the remaining lemon rind and juice with the remaining parsley in a small bowl, then season to taste with salt and pepper. Spoon the dressing over the kebabs. Serve hot with plain boiled rice or noodles and a leafy green salad.

Grilled Salmon Steaks with Fennel

Fennel grows wild all over the south of Italy. Its mild aniseed flavour goes well with fish.

Serves 4

juice of 1 lemon
45ml/3 tbsp chopped
  fresh fennel, or the
  green fronds from the
  top of a fennel bulb
5ml/1 tsp fennel seeds
45ml/3 tbsp olive oil

4 salmon steaks of the
  same thickness (about
  700g/1½lb)
salt and ground black
  pepper
lemon wedges, to garnish

1 Combine the lemon juice, chopped fennel and fennel seeds with the olive oil in a bowl. Add the salmon steaks, turning them to coat them with the marinade. Sprinkle with salt and ground black pepper. Cover and place in the fridge. Allow to stand for about 2 hours.

2 Preheat the grill. Arrange the fish in one layer on a grill pan or shallow baking tray. Grill about 10cm/4in from the heat source for 3–4 minutes.

3 Turn the steaks over and spoon on the remaining marinade. Grill for 3–4 minutes, or until the edges begin to brown. Serve hot, garnished with lemon wedges.

Cook's Tip
If you wish, remove the skin from the salmon steaks before serving. Simply insert the prongs of a fork between the flesh and the skin at one end and roll the skin around the prongs in a fluent action.

Seafood Pilaff

This one-pan dish makes a satisfying meal. For a special occasion, use dry white wine instead of orange juice.

Serves 4

10ml/2 tsp olive oil
250g/9oz/1½ cups long
  grain rice
5ml/1 tsp ground
  turmeric
1 fresh red pepper, seeded
  and diced
1 small onion, finely
  chopped
2 courgettes, sliced
150g/5oz button
  mushrooms, wiped
  and halved

350ml/12fl oz/1½ cups
  fish or chicken stock
150ml/¼ pint/⅔ cup
  orange juice
350g/12oz white fish
  fillets
12 live mussels (or
  cooked shelled
  mussels)
salt and ground black
  pepper
grated rind of 1 orange,
  to garnish

1 Heat the oil in a large non-stick frying pan and fry the rice and turmeric over a gentle heat for about 1 minute.

2 Add the pepper, onion, courgettes and mushrooms. Stir in the stock and orange juice. Bring to the boil.

3 Reduce the heat and add the fish. Cover with a tight-fitting lid and simmer gently for about 15 minutes, until the rice is tender and the liquid absorbed. Stir in the mussels and heat thoroughly. Adjust the seasoning, sprinkle with orange rind and serve hot.

Cook's Tip
If you wish, bring the pan to the table, rather than transferring the pilaff to a serving dish, and let everyone help themselves.

Grilled Fresh Sardines

Fresh sardines are flavoursome, firm-fleshed and rather different in taste and consistency from those canned in oil.

Serves 4–6

900kg/2lb very heavy fresh sardines, gutted and with heads removed
olive oil, for brushing

salt and ground black pepper
45ml/3 tbsp chopped fresh parsley, to serve
lemon wedges, to garnish

1 Preheat the grill. Rinse the sardines in water. Pat dry with kitchen paper.

2 Brush the sardines lightly with olive oil and sprinkle generously with salt and pepper. Place the sardines in one layer in a grill pan. Grill for about 3–4 minutes.

3 Turn, and cook for 3–4 minutes more, or until the skin begins to brown. Serve immediately, sprinkled with parsley and garnished with lemon wedges.

Cook's Tip
Frozen sardines are now available in supermarkets and will keep well in the freezer for 6 weeks. Thaw them in the fridge overnight, then use a sharp pointed knife to slit the belly, remove the innards and cut the heads off. For a fuller flavour, you might like to leave them whole, as they do in some Mediterranean countries.

Red Mullet with Tomatoes

Red mullet is a popular fish in Italy, and in this recipe both its flavour and colour are accentuated.

Serves 4

4 red mullet (about 175–200g/6–7oz each)
450g/1lb tomatoes, peeled, or 400g/14oz can plum tomatoes
60ml/4 tbsp olive oil
60ml/4 tbsp finely chopped fresh parsley

2 cloves garlic, finely chopped
120ml/4fl oz/½ cup dry white wine
4 thin lemon slices, cut in half
salt and ground black pepper

1 Scale and clean the fish without removing the liver. Wash and pat dry with kitchen paper.

2 Finely chop the tomatoes. Heat the oil in a saucepan or casserole large enough to hold the fish in one layer. Add the parsley and garlic, and sauté for 1 minute. Stir in the tomatoes and cook over a moderate heat for 15–20 minutes. Season to taste with salt and pepper.

3 Add the red mullets to the tomato sauce and cook over a moderate to high heat for 5 minutes. Add the wine and the lemon slices. Bring the sauce back to the boil, and cook for about 5 minutes more. Turn the fish over and continue to cook for 4–5 minutes more. Remove the fish to a warmed serving platter and keep warm until needed.

4 Boil the sauce for 3–4 minutes to reduce it slightly, then spoon it over the fish and serve immediately.

Cook's Tip
To peel fresh tomatoes, use a sharp knife to make a slit in their bases, plunge into boiling water for 30 seconds, or until the skins split, and then plunge into cold water. The skins should then slip off easily.

Middle Eastern Sea Bream

Buy the smallest sea bream you can find to cook whole, allowing one for two people.

Serves 4

1.75kg/4lb sea bream or 2 smaller sea bream
30ml/2 tbsp olive oil
75g/3oz/¾ cup pine nuts
1 large onion, finely chopped
450g/1lb ripe tomatoes, roughly chopped
75g/3oz/½ cup raisins
1.5ml/¼ tsp ground cinnamon
1.5ml/¼ tsp mixed spice
45ml/3 tbsp chopped fresh mint
225g/8oz/1¼ cups long grain rice
3 lemon slices
300ml/½ pint/1¼ cups fish stock

1 Trim, gut and scale the sea bream. Meanwhile, preheat the oven to 175°C/350°F/Gas 4.

2 Heat the oil in a large heavy-based saucepan and stir-fry the pine nuts for 1 minute. Add the onions and continue to stir-fry until softened but not coloured.

3 Add the tomatoes and simmer for 10 minutes, then stir in the raisins, cinnamon, mixed spice and mint.

4 Add the rice and lemon slices. Transfer to a large roasting tin and pour the fish stock over the top.

5 Place the fish on top and cut several slashes in the skin. Sprinkle over a little salt, mixed spice and cinnamon and bake in the preheated oven for 30–35 minutes for large fish or 20–25 minutes for smaller fish.

Cook's Tip
If you prefer, use almonds instead of pine nuts. Use the same quantity of blanched almonds and split them in half before stir-frying.

Salmon with Spicy Pesto

This pesto uses sunflower seeds and chilli as its flavouring rather than the classic basil and pine nuts.

Serves 4

4 x 225g/8oz salmon steaks
30ml/2 tbsp sunflower oil
finely grated rind and juice of 1 lime
pinch of salt

For the pesto
6 mild fresh red chillies
2 garlic cloves
30ml/2 tbsp pumpkin or sunflower seeds
freshly grated rind and juice of 1 lime
75ml/5 tbsp olive oil
salt and ground black pepper

1 Insert a very sharp knife close to the top of the salmon's backbone. Working closely to the bone, cut your way to the end of the steak so one side of the steak has been released and one side is still attached. Repeat with the other side. Pull out any extra visible bones with a pair of tweezers.

2 Sprinkle a little salt on the surface and take hold of the end of the salmon, skin-side down. Insert a small sharp knife under the skin and, working away from you, cut off the skin keeping as close to the skin as possible. Repeat with the three remaining pieces of fish.

3 Rub the sunflower oil into the boneless fish rounds. Add the lime juice and rind and marinate in the fridge for 2 hours.

4 To make the pesto, seed the chillies and place them together with the garlic cloves, pumpkin or sunflower seeds, lime juice, rind and seasoning in a food processor or blender. Process until well mixed. Pour the olive oil gradually over the moving blades until the sauce has thickened and emulsified. Drain the salmon from its marinade. Grill the fish steaks for about 5 minutes on either side and serve with the spicy pesto.

Roast Chicken with Celeriac

Celeriac and brown breadcrumbs give the stuffing an unusual and delicious twist.

Serves 4

1.6kg/3½lb chicken
15g/½ oz/1 tbsp butter

For the stuffing
450g/1lb celeriac, chopped
25g/1oz/2 tbsp butter
3 slices bacon, chopped
1 onion, finely chopped
leaves from 1 fresh thyme sprig, chopped

leaves from 1 fresh small tarragon sprig, chopped
30ml/2 tbsp chopped fresh parsley
75g/3oz/1½ cups fresh brown breadcrumbs
dash of Worcestershire sauce
1 egg
salt and ground black pepper

1 To make the stuffing, cook the celeriac in boiling water until tender. Drain well and chop finely. Heat the butter in a saucepan and gently cook the bacon and onion until the onion is soft. Stir in the celeriac and herbs and cook, stirring occasionally, for 2–3 minutes. Meanwhile, preheat the oven to 200°C/400°F/Gas 6.

2 Remove the pan from the heat and stir in the fresh breadcrumbs, Worcestershire sauce, sufficient egg to bind the mixture, and season it with salt and pepper. Use this mixture to stuff the neck end of the chicken. Season the bird's skin, then rub it with the butter.

3 Roast the chicken, basting occasionally with the juices, for 1¼–1½ hours, until the juices run clear when the thickest part of the leg is pierced. Turn off the oven, prop the door open slightly and allow the chicken to rest for about 10 minutes before carving.

Chicken with Lemon and Herbs

The herbs can be changed according to what is available; for example, parsley or thyme could be used.

Serves 2

50g/2oz/4 tbsp butter
2 spring onions, white part only, finely chopped
15ml/1 tbsp chopped fresh tarragon

15ml/1 tbsp chopped fresh fennel
juice of 1 lemon
4 chicken thighs
salt and ground black pepper
lemon slices and herb sprigs, to garnish

1 Preheat the grill to moderate. In a small saucepan, melt the butter, then add the spring onions, herbs, lemon juice and season with salt and pepper.

2 Brush the chicken thighs generously with the herb mixture, then grill for 10–12 minutes, basting frequently with the herb mixture.

3 Turn the chicken over and baste again, then cook for a further 10–12 minutes or until the chicken juices run clear.

4 Serve the chicken garnished with lemon slices and herb sprigs, and accompanied by any remaining herb mixture.

Chicken with Peppers

This colourful dish comes from the south of Italy, where sweet peppers are plentiful.

Serves 4

1.5kg/3lb chicken, cut into serving pieces
3 large fresh peppers, red, yellow or green
90ml/6 tbsp olive oil
2 red onions, finely sliced
2 garlic cloves, finely chopped
small piece of dried chilli, crumbled (optional)

120ml/4fl oz/½ cup dry white wine
2 tomatoes, fresh or canned, peeled and chopped
45g/3 tbsp chopped fresh parsley
salt and ground black pepper

1 Trim any fat off the chicken and remove all excess skin. Wash the peppers. Prepare by cutting them in half, scooping out the seeds, and cutting away the stem. Slice into strips.

2 Heat half the oil in a large heavy saucepan or casserole and cook the onion over a gentle heat until soft. Remove to a side dish. Add the remaining oil to the pan, raise the heat to moderate, add the chicken pieces and brown them on all sides, 6–8 minutes. Return the onions to the pan, and add the garlic and dried chilli, if using.

3 Pour in the wine and cook until it has reduced by half. Add the peppers and stir well to coat. Season to taste. After 3–4 minutes, stir in the tomatoes. Lower the heat, cover the pan with a tight-fitting lid, and cook for about 25–30 minutes, until the peppers are soft and the chicken is cooked. Stir occasionally. Stir in the parsley and serve.

Cook's Tip

For a more elegant version of this dish to serve at a dinner party, use skinless, boneless chicken breasts. Substitute the fresh parsley with different chopped fresh herbs, such as coriander, tarragon, rosemary, chervil or marjoram.

Golden Parmesan Chicken

Served cold with the garlic mayonnaise, these morsels of chicken make good picnic food.

Serves 4

4 chicken breast fillets, skinned
75g/3oz/1½ cups fresh white breadcrumbs
40g/1½oz/½ cup Parmesan cheese, finely grated
30ml/2 tbsp chopped fresh parsley
2 eggs, beaten
50g/2oz/4 tbsp butter, melted

salt and ground black pepper

For the garlic mayonnaise
120ml/4fl oz/½ cup good quality mayonnaise
120ml/4fl oz/½ cup fromage frais
1–2 garlic cloves, crushed

1 Cut each chicken fillet into four or five large chunks. Mix together the breadcrumbs, Parmesan cheese, parsley and salt and pepper in a shallow dish.

2 Dip the chicken pieces in the beaten egg, then into the breadcrumb mixture. Place in a single layer on a baking sheet and chill in the fridge for at least 30 minutes.

3 Meanwhile, to make the garlic mayonnaise, mix the mayonnaise, fromage frais, garlic and pepper to taste. Spoon the mayonnaise into a small serving bowl. Chill in the fridge until ready to serve.

4 Preheat the oven to 180°C/350°F/Gas 4. Drizzle the melted butter over the chicken pieces and cook for about 20 minutes, until crisp and golden. Serve the chicken immediately with a crisp green salad and the garlic mayonnaise for dipping.

Chicken in Green Sauce

Slow, gentle cooking makes the chicken in this dish very succulent and tender.

Serves 4

25g/1oz/2 tbsp butter
15ml/1 tbsp olive oil
4 chicken portions (legs,
   breasts or quarters)
1 small onion, finely
   chopped
150ml/¼ pint/⅔ cup
   medium-bodied dry
   white wine
150ml/¼ pint/⅔ cup
   chicken stock

leaves from 2 fresh thyme
   sprigs and 2 fresh
   tarragon sprigs
175g/6oz watercress,
   leaves removed
150ml/¼ pint/⅔ cup
   double cream
salt and ground black
   pepper
watercress leaves, to
   garnish

1 Heat the butter and oil in a frying pan and brown the chicken evenly. Transfer the chicken to a plate using a slotted spoon and keep warm in the oven.

2 Add the onion to the cooking juices in the pan and cook until softened but not coloured. Stir in the wine, then boil for 2–3 minutes. Add the stock and bring to the boil. Return the chicken to the pan, cover with a tight-fitting lid and cook very gently for about 30 minutes, until the chicken juices run clear when pierced with the point of a knife. Then transfer the chicken to a warm dish, cover and keep warm.

3 Boil the cooking juices hard until they are reduced to about 60ml/4 tbsp. Remove the leaves from the herbs and add to the pan with the watercress leaves and cream. Simmer over a moderate heat until slightly thickened.

4 Return the chicken to the casserole, season to taste with salt and pepper and heat through for a few minutes. Garnish with watercress leaves to serve.

Spatchcocked Devilled Poussin

"Spatchcock" refers to birds that have been split and skewered flat. This shortens the cooking time considerably.

Serves 4

15ml/1 tbsp English
   mustard powder
15ml/1 tbsp paprika
15ml/1 tbsp ground
   cumin
20ml/4 tsp tomato
   ketchup

15ml/1 tbsp lemon juice
65g/2½ oz/5 tbsp butter,
   melted
4 poussins (about
   450g/1lb each)
pinch of salt

1 Mix together the mustard, paprika, cumin, ketchup, lemon juice and salt until smooth, then gradually stir in the butter.

2 Using game shears or strong kitchen scissors, split each poussin along one side of the backbone, then cut down the other side of the backbone to remove it.

3 Open out a poussin, skin-side uppermost, then press down firmly with the heel of your hand. Pass a long skewer through one leg and out through the other to secure the bird open and flat. Repeat with the remaining birds.

4 Spread the mustard mixture evenly over the skin of the birds. Cover loosely and leave in a cool place for at least 2 hours to marinate. Preheat the grill.

5 Place the birds, skin-side uppermost, under the grill and cook for about 12 minutes. Turn the birds over, baste with any juices in the pan, and cook for a further 7 minutes, until the juices run clear when pierced with the point of a knife.

Cook's Tip
For an al fresco meal in the summer, these spatchcocked poussins may be cooked on a barbecue.

Stoved Chicken

"Stoved" is derived from the French *étouffer*, meaning to cook in a covered pot.

Serves 4

1kg/2lb potatoes, cut into
    5mm/¼ in slices
2 large onions, thinly
    sliced
15ml/1 tbsp chopped
    fresh thyme
25g/1oz/2 tbsp butter
15ml/1 tbsp sunflower oil

2 large slices bacon,
    chopped
4 large chicken joints,
    halved
1 bay leaf
600ml/1 pint/2½ cups
    chicken stock
salt and ground black
    pepper

1 Preheat the oven to 150°C/300°F/Gas 2. Make a thick layer of half the potato slices in a large heavy-based casserole, then cover with half the onion. Sprinkle with half of the thyme and the seasoning.

2 Heat the butter and oil in a large frying pan and brown the bacon and chicken. Using a draining spoon, transfer the chicken and bacon to the casserole. Reserve the fat in the pan. Sprinkle the remaining thyme and some seasoning over the chicken. Cover with the remaining onion, followed by a neat layer of overlapping potato slices. Sprinkle with seasoning.

3 Pour the stock into the casserole, brush the potatoes with the reserved fat, then cover with a tight-fitting lid and cook in the oven for about 2 hours, until the chicken is tender.

4 Preheat the grill. Uncover the casserole and place under the grill. Cook until the slices of potatoes are beginning to brown and crisp. Serve hot.

Cook's Tip
Instead of using large chicken joints, use thighs or drumsticks, or a mixture of the two.

Chicken with Red Cabbage

Crushed juniper berries provide a distinctive flavour in this unusual casserole.

Serves 4

50g/oz/4 tbsp butter
4 large chicken joints,
    halved
1 onion, chopped
500g/1¼lb/8¼ cups red
    cabbage, shredded
    finely

4 juniper berries, crushed
12 cooked chestnuts
120ml/4fl oz/½ cup
    full-bodied red wine
salt and ground black
    pepper

1 Heat the butter in a heavy-based flameproof casserole and lightly brown the chicken pieces. Transfer to a plate.

2 Add the onion to the casserole and fry gently until soft and light golden brown. Stir the cabbage and juniper berries into the casserole, season and cook over a moderate heat for about 6–7 minutes, stirring once or twice.

3 Stir the chestnuts into the casserole, then tuck the chicken pieces under the cabbage so they are on the base of the casserole. Pour in the red wine.

4 Cover and cook gently for about 40 minutes until the chicken juices run clear and the cabbage is very tender. Adjust the seasoning to taste and serve immediately.

Italian Chicken

Use chicken legs, breasts or quarters in this colourful dish, and a different type of pasta if you prefer.

Serves 4

25g/1oz/2 tbsp plain
  flour
4 chicken portions
30ml/2 tbsp olive oil
1 onion, chopped
2 garlic cloves, chopped
1 fresh red pepper, seeded
  and chopped
400g/14oz can chopped
  tomatoes
30ml/2 tbsp red pesto
  sauce

4 sun-dried tomatoes in
  oil, chopped
150ml/¼ pint/⅔ cup
  chicken stock
5ml/1 tsp dried oregano
8 black olives, stoned
salt and ground black
  pepper
chopped fresh basil and
  whole basil leaves, to
  garnish
tagliatelle, to serve

1 Place the flour and seasoning in a plastic bag. Add the chicken pieces and shake well until coated. Heat the oil in a flameproof casserole and brown the chicken quickly. Remove with a slotted spoon and set aside.

2 Lower the heat and add the onion, garlic and pepper and cook for 5 minutes. Stir in the remaining ingredients, except the olives, and bring to the boil.

3 Return the sautéed chicken portions to the casserole, season lightly, cover with a tight-fitting lid and simmer for 30–35 minutes, or until the chicken is cooked.

4 Add the black olives and simmer for a further 5 minutes. Transfer to a warmed serving dish, sprinkle with the chopped basil and garnish with basil leaves. Serve with hot tagliatelle.

Cook's Tip
If you do not have red pesto sauce, use green pesto instead. Finely chop then purée two sun-dried tomato pieces in a blender or food processor and add with the other ingredients.

Honey and Orange Glazed Chicken

This dish is popular in the United States and Australia and is ideal for an easy meal served with baked potatoes.

Serves 4

4 x 175g/6oz boneless
  chicken breasts
15ml/1 tbsp sunflower oil
4 spring onions, chopped
1 garlic clove, crushed
45ml/3 tbsp clear honey
60ml/4 tbsp fresh orange
  juice

1 orange, peeled and
  segmented
30ml/2 tbsp soy sauce
fresh lemon balm or flat-
  leaf parsley, to garnish
baked potatoes and mixed
  salad, to serve

1 Preheat the oven to 190°C/375°F/Gas 5. Place the chicken breasts, with skins on, in a single layer in a shallow roasting tin and set aside.

2 Heat the sunflower oil in a small saucepan, and gently fry the spring onions and garlic for about 2 minutes until softened but not browned. Add the honey, orange juice, orange segments and soy sauce to the pan, stirring well, and cook until the honey has completely dissolved.

3 Pour the sauce over the chicken and bake, uncovered, for about 45 minutes, basting once or twice until the chicken is cooked. Check by piercing with the point of a knife; the juices should run clear. Garnish with lemon balm or flat leaf parsley and serve with baked potatoes and a salad.

Cook's Tip
For a slightly spicier version, look out for mustard that has been flavoured with honey to add to this dish instead of the clear honey. Use the same amount.

Cajun Chicken Jambalaya

Wonderfully spicy Cajun cooking was developed by the French-speaking immigrants in Louisiana, USA.

Serves 4

1.2kg/2½lb fresh chicken
1½ onions
1 bay leaf
4 black peppercorns
30ml/2 tbsp vegetable oil
2 garlic cloves, chopped
1 green pepper, seeded
   and chopped
1 celery stick, chopped
225g/8oz/1¼ cups long
   grain rice
115g/4oz chorizo
   sausage, sliced
115g/4oz/1 cup chopped,
   cooked ham

400g/14oz can chopped
   tomatoes
2.5ml/½ tsp hot chilli
   powder
2.5ml/½ tsp cumin seeds
2.5ml/½ tsp ground
   cumin
5ml/1 tsp dried thyme
115g/4oz/1 cup peeled,
   cooked prawns
dash of Tabasco sauce
salt and ground black
   pepper
chopped fresh parsley, to
   garnish

1 Place the chicken in a flameproof casserole and pour over 600ml/1 pint/2½ cups water. Add half an onion, the bay leaf and peppercorns and bring to the boil. Cover and simmer for 1½ hours. Then lift the chicken out of the pan. Skin, bone and chop the meat. Strain the stock and reserve.

2 Chop the remaining whole onion. Heat the oil in a large frying pan and fry the onion, garlic, green pepper and celery for 5 minutes. Stir in the rice. Add the sausage, ham and chicken and fry for 2–3 minutes, stirring frequently.

3 Pour in the tomatoes and 300ml/½ pint/1¼ cups of the reserved stock and add the chilli, cumin and thyme. Bring to the boil, cover and simmer gently for 20 minutes, or until the rice is tender and the liquid absorbed.

4 Stir in the prawns and Tabasco. Cook for 5 minutes more, then season to taste with salt and ground black pepper. Serve hot, garnished with chopped fresh parsley.

Moroccan Chicken Couscous

The combination of sweet and spicy flavours in the sauce and couscous makes this dish irresistible.

Serves 4

15g/½oz/1 tbsp butter
15ml/1 tbsp sunflower oil
4 chicken portions
2 onions, finely chopped
2 garlic cloves, crushed
2.5ml/½ tsp ground
   cinnamon
1.5ml/¼ tsp ground
   ginger
1.5ml/¼ tsp ground
   turmeric
30ml/2 tbsp orange juice
10ml/2 tsp clear honey
pinch of salt
fresh mint sprigs,
   to garnish

For the couscous
350g/12oz/2¼ cups
   couscous
5ml/1 tsp salt
10ml/2 tsp caster sugar
15ml/1 tbsp sunflower oil
2.5ml/½ tsp ground
   cinnamon
pinch of grated nutmeg
15ml/1 tbsp orange
   blossom water
30ml/2 tbsp sultanas
50g/2oz/½ cup chopped
   toasted almonds
45ml/3 tbsp chopped
   pistachios

1 Fry the chicken portions, skin-side down in the butter and oil until golden. Turn them over. Add the onions, garlic, spices, a pinch of salt, the orange juice and 300ml/½ pint/1¼ cups water. Cover and bring to the boil, then simmer for about 30 minutes.

2 Mix the couscous with the salt and 350ml/12fl oz/1½ cups water. Leave for 5 minutes. Add the rest of the ingredients for the couscous.

3 Line a steamer with greaseproof paper and spoon in the couscous. Set over the chicken and steam for 10 minutes.

4 Remove the steamer and keep covered. Stir the honey into the chicken liquid and boil rapidly for 3–4 minutes. Serve the chicken on a bed of couscous with some sauce spooned over. Garnish with fresh mint and serve with the remaining sauce.

Rabbit with Mustard

Rabbit is increasingly available in larger supermarkets, ready prepared and jointed.

Serves 4

*15g/½oz/1 tbsp plain
  flour
15ml/1 tbsp English
  mustard powder
4 large rabbit joints
25g/1oz/2 tbsp butter
30ml/2 tbsp oil
1 onion, finely chopped
150ml/¼ pint/⅔ cup beer
300ml/½ pint/1¼ cups
  chicken or veal stock
15ml/1 tbsp tarragon
  vinegar
25g/1oz/2 tbsp dark
  brown sugar*

*10–15ml/2–3 tsp
  prepared English
  mustard
salt and ground black
  pepper*

To finish

*50g/2oz/4 tbsp butter
30ml/2 tbsp oil
50g/2oz/1 cup fresh
  breadcrumbs
15ml/1 tbsp snipped
  fresh chives
15ml/1 tbsp chopped
  fresh tarragon*

1 Preheat the oven to 160°C/325°F/Gas 3. Mix the flour and mustard powder together, then put on a plate. Dip the rabbit joints in the flour mixture; reserve the excess flour. Heat the butter and oil in a heavy flameproof casserole and brown the rabbit. Transfer to a plate. Stir in the onion and cook until soft.

2 Stir any reserved flour mixture into the casserole, cook for 1 minute, then stir in the beer, stock and vinegar. Bring to the boil and add the sugar and pepper. Simmer for 2 minutes. Return the rabbit and any juices that have collected on the plate to the casserole, cover with a tight-fitting lid and cook in the oven for 1 hour. Stir the mustard and salt to taste into the casserole, cover again and cook for a further 15 minutes.

3 To finish, heat together the butter and oil in a frying pan and fry the breadcrumbs, stirring frequently, until golden, then stir in the herbs. Transfer the rabbit to a warmed serving dish and sprinkle the breadcrumb mixture over the top.

Turkey Hot-pot

Turkey and sausages combine well with kidney beans and other vegetables in this hearty stew.

Serves 4

*115g/4oz/scant ½ cup
  kidney beans, soaked
  overnight, drained
  and rinsed
40g/1½oz/3 tbsp butter
2 herby pork sausages
450g/1lb turkey casserole
  meat
3 leeks, sliced*

*2 carrots, finely chopped
4 tomatoes, chopped
10–15ml/2–3 tsp
  tomato purée
bouquet garni
400ml/14fl oz/1½ cups
  chicken stock
salt and ground black
  pepper*

1 Cook the kidney beans in unsalted boiling water for 40 minutes, then drain well.

2 Meanwhile, heat the butter in a flameproof casserole, then cook the sausages until browned and the fat runs. Drain on kitchen paper, stir the turkey into the casserole and cook until lightly browned all over, then transfer to a bowl using a slotted spoon. Stir the leeks and carrot into the casserole and brown them lightly, stirring occasionally.

3 Add the chopped tomatoes and tomato purée and simmer gently for about 5 minutes.

4 Chop the sausages and return to the casserole with the beans, turkey, bouquet garni, stock and seasoning. Cover with a tight-fitting lid and cook gently for about 1¼ hours, until the beans are tender and there is very little liquid.

Duck with Cumberland Sauce

A sophisticated dish: the sauce contains both port and brandy, making it very rich.

Serves 4

4 duck portions	60ml/4 tbsp port
grated rind and juice of	pinch of ground mace or
1 lemon	ginger
grated rind and juice of	15ml/1 tbsp brandy
1 large orange	salt and ground black
60ml/4 tbsp redcurrant	pepper
jelly	orange slices, to garnish

1 Preheat the oven to 190°C/375°F/Gas 5. Place a rack in a roasting tin. Prick the duck portions all over, sprinkle with salt and pepper. Place on the rack and cook in the oven for 45–50 minutes, until the duck skin is crisp and the juices run clear when pricked with the point of a knife.

2 Meanwhile, simmer the lemon and orange rinds and juices together in a saucepan for 5 minutes.

3 Add the redcurrant jelly and stir until melted, then stir in the port. Bring to the boil and add mace or ginger and salt and pepper, to taste.

4 Transfer the duck to a serving plate; keep warm. Pour the fat from the roasting tin, leaving the cooking juices. With the tin over a gentle heat, stir in the brandy, dislodge the sediment and bring to the boil. Stir in the port sauce and serve with the duck, garnished with orange slices.

Coronation Chicken

A cold chicken dish with a mild, curry-flavoured sauce, ideal for summer lunch parties.

Serves 8

½ lemon	15ml/1 tbsp tomato purée
2.25kg/5lb chicken	120ml/4fl oz/½ cup red
1 onion, quartered	wine
1 carrot, quartered	1 bay leaf
large bouquet garni	juice of ½ lemon, or more
8 black peppercorns,	to taste
crushed	10–15ml/2 – 3 tsp apricot
pinch of salt	jam
fresh watercress sprigs,	300ml/½ pint/1¼ cups
to garnish	mayonnaise
	120ml/4fl oz/½ cup
For the sauce	whipping cream,
1 small onion, chopped	whipped
15g/½oz/1 tbsp butter	salt and ground black
15ml/1 tbsp curry paste	pepper

1 Put the lemon half in the chicken cavity, then place the chicken in a saucepan that it just fits. Add the vegetables, bouquet garni, peppercorns and salt.

2 Add sufficient water to come two-thirds of the way up the chicken, bring to the boil, then cover and cook gently for about 1½ hours, until the chicken juices run clear.

3 Transfer the chicken to a large bowl, pour the cooking liquid over and leave to cool. When cool, skin and bone the chicken, then chop.

4 To make the sauce, cook the onion in the butter until soft. Add the curry paste, tomato purée, wine, bay leaf and lemon juice, then cook for 10 minutes. Add the jam; sieve and cool.

5 Beat the sauce mixture into the mayonnaise. Fold in the cream, season to taste with salt and pepper and add the lemon juice, then stir in with the chicken.

Tandoori Chicken Kebabs

Chinese Chicken with Cashew Nuts

This popular dish originates from the Punjab, where it is traditionally cooked in clay ovens known as *tandoors*.

The cashew nuts give this oriental dish a delightful crunchy texture that contrasts well with the noodles.

Serves 4

4 boneless chicken breasts
(about 175g/6oz each),
skinned
15ml/1 tbsp lemon juice
45ml/3 tbsp tandoori
paste
45ml/3 tbsp natural
yogurt
1 garlic clove, crushed
30ml/2 tbsp chopped
fresh coriander

1 small onion, cut into
wedges and separated
into layers
a little oil, for brushing
salt and ground black
pepper
fresh coriander sprigs, to
garnish
pilau rice and naan
bread, to serve

1 Chop the chicken breasts into 2.5cm/1in dice, place in a bowl and add the lemon juice, tandoori paste, yogurt, garlic, coriander and seasoning. Cover and leave to marinate in the fridge for 2–3 hours.

2 Preheat the grill. Thread alternate pieces of marinated chicken and onion on to four skewers.

3 Brush the onions with a little oil, lay on a grill rack and cook under a high heat for 10–12 minutes, turning once. Garnish the kebabs with fresh coriander and serve at once with pilau rice and naan bread.

Cook's Tip
If you are using wooden skewers, soak them first in cold water to prevent them catching fire under the grill. For an economical alternative, use chicken thighs instead of breasts.

Serves 4

4 boneless chicken breasts
(about 175g/6oz each),
skinned
3 garlic cloves, crushed
60ml/4 tbsp soy sauce
30ml/2 tbsp cornflour
225g/8oz/4 cups dried
egg noodles
45ml/3 tbsp peanut or
sunflower oil

15ml/1 tbsp sesame oil
115g/4oz/1 cup roasted
cashew nuts
6 spring onions, cut into
5cm/2in pieces and
halved lengthways
spring onion curls and a
little chopped fresh red
chilli, to garnish

1 Slice the chicken into strips, then combine with the garlic, soy sauce and cornflour. Cover and chill in the fridge for about 30 minutes.

2 Meanwhile, bring a saucepan of water to the boil and add the egg noodles. Turn off the heat and leave to stand for 5 minutes. Drain well and reserve.

3 Heat the oils in a large frying pan or wok and stir-fry the chilled chicken and marinade juices over a high heat for about 3–4 minutes, or until golden brown.

4 Add the cashew nuts and spring onions to the pan or wok and stir-fry for a further 2–3 minutes.

5 Add the drained noodles and stir-fry for 2 minutes more. Toss the noodles well and serve immediately, garnished with the spring onion curls and chopped chilli.

Cook's Tip
For a milder garnish, seed the red chilli before chopping or finely dice some red pepper instead and use with the spring onion curls.

Chinese-style Chicken Salad

For a variation and to add more colour, add some cooked, peeled prawns to this lovely salad.

Serves 4

*4 boneless chicken breasts
(about 175g/6oz each)
60ml/4 tbsp dark soy
sauce
pinch of Chinese
five-spice powder
squeeze of lemon juice
½ cucumber, peeled and
cut into matchsticks
5ml/1 tsp salt
45ml/3 tbsp sunflower oil
30ml/2 tbsp sesame oil
15ml/1 tbsp sesame seeds
30ml/2 tbsp dry sherry*

*2 carrots, cut into
matchsticks
8 spring onions, shredded
75g/3oz/1 cup
beansprouts*

For the sauce
*60ml/4 tbsp crunchy
peanut butter
10ml/2 tsp lemon juice
10ml/2 tsp sesame oil
1.5ml/¼ tsp hot chilli
powder
1 spring onion, finely
chopped*

1 Put the chicken into a saucepan and cover with water. Add 15ml/1 tbsp of the soy sauce, the Chinese five-spice powder and lemon juice. Cover, bring to the boil, then simmer for 20 minutes. Then skin and slice into thin strips.

2 Sprinkle the cucumber matchsticks with salt, leave for 30 minutes, then rinse and pat dry.

3 Fry the sesame seeds in the oils for 30 seconds, then stir in the remaining soy sauce and the sherry. Add the carrots and stir-fry for 2 minutes, then remove from the heat.

4 Mix together the cucumber, spring onions, beansprouts, carrots, pan juices and chicken. Transfer to a shallow dish. Cover and chill for 1 hour.

5 For the sauce, cream the first four ingredients together, then stir in the spring onion. Serve the chicken with the sauce.

Duck, Avocado and Berry Salad

Duck breasts are roasted until crisp with a honey and soy glaze to serve warm with fresh raspberries and avocado.

Serves 4

*4 small or 2 large duck
breasts, halved if large
15ml/1 tbsp clear honey
15ml/1 tbsp dark soy
sauce
mixed chopped fresh
salad leaves such as
lamb's lettuce, red
chicory or frisée
2 avocados, stoned,
peeled and cut into
chunks
115g/4oz/1 cup
raspberries*

*salt and ground black
pepper*

For the dressing
*60ml/4 tbsp olive oil
15ml/1 tbsp raspberry
vinegar
15ml/1 tbsp redcurrant
jelly
salt and ground black
pepper*

1 Preheat the oven to 200°C/425°F/Gas 7. Prick the skin of each duck breast with a fork. Blend the honey and soy sauce together in a small bowl, then brush all over the skin.

2 Place the duck breasts on a rack set over a roasting tin and season with salt and pepper. Roast in the oven for about 15–20 minutes, until the skins are crisp and the meat cooked.

3 Meanwhile, to make the dressing, put the oil, vinegar, redcurrant jelly and seasoning in a small bowl and whisk well until evenly blended.

4 Slice the duck breasts diagonally and arrange among four individual plates with the salad leaves, avocados and raspberries. Spoon the dressing over the top and serve.

Cook's Tip
Small avocados contain the most flavour and have a good texture. They should be ripe but not too soft, so avoid any whose skins are turning black.

Crumbed Turkey Steaks

The authentic Austrian dish, *wiener schnitzel*, uses veal escalopes, but turkey breasts make a tasty alternative.

Serves 4

4 turkey breast steaks
  (about 150g/5oz each)
40g/1½oz/3 tbsp plain
  flour, seasoned
1 egg, lightly beaten
75g/3oz/1½ cups fresh
  breadcrumbs

75ml/5 tbsp finely grated
  Parmesan cheese
25g/1oz/2 tbsp butter
45ml/3 tbsp sunflower oil
fresh parsley sprigs, to
  garnish
4 lemon wedges, to serve

1 Lay the turkey steaks between two sheets of clear film. Hit each one with a rolling pin until flattened. Snip the edges of the steaks with scissors a few times to prevent them from curling during cooking.

2 Place the seasoned flour on one plate, the egg in a shallow bowl and the breadcrumbs and Parmesan mixed together on another plate.

3 Dip each side of the steaks into the flour and shake off any excess. Next, dip them into the egg and then gently press each side into the breadcrumbs and cheese until evenly coated.

4 Heat the butter and oil in a large frying pan and fry the turkey steaks over a moderate heat for 2–3 minutes on each side, until golden. Garnish with the fresh parsley sprigs and serve with lemon wedges.

Country Cider Hot-pot

Rabbit meat is regaining popularity in Britain and is a healthy, low-fat option, as is all game.

Serves 4

25g/1oz/2 tbsp plain
  flour
4 boneless rabbit portions
25g/1oz/2 tbsp butter
15ml/1 tbsp vegetable oil
15 baby onions
4 rashers streaky bacon,
  chopped
10ml/2 tsp mustard

450ml/¾ pint/1¾ cups
  dry cider
3 carrots, chopped
2 parsnips, chopped
12 ready-to-eat dried
  prunes, stoned
1 fresh rosemary sprig
1 bay leaf
salt and ground black
  pepper

1 Preheat the oven to 160°C/325°F/Gas 3. Place the flour and seasoning in a plastic bag, add the rabbit portions and shake until coated. Set aside.

2 Heat the butter and oil in a flameproof casserole and add the onions and bacon. Fry for 4 minutes, until the onions have softened. Remove with a slotted spoon and reserve.

3 Fry the seasoned rabbit portions in the oil left in the flameproof casserole until they are browned all over, then spread a little of the mustard over the top of each portion.

4 Return the onions and bacon to the pan. Pour on the cider and add the carrots, parsnips, prunes, rosemary and bay leaf. Season well. Bring to the boil, then cover with a tight-fitting lid and transfer to the oven. Cook for about 1½ hours until the meat and vegetables are tender.

5 Remove the rosemary sprig and bay leaf and serve the rabbit hot with creamy mashed potatoes, if you wish.

Turkey Pastitsio

A traditional Greek pastitsio is a rich, high fat dish made with beef mince, but this lighter version is just as tasty.

Serves 4–6

450g/1lb lean minced turkey
1 large onion, finely chopped
60ml/4 tbsp tomato purée
250ml/8fl oz/1 cup red wine or stock
5ml/1 tsp ground cinnamon
300g/11oz/2½ cups macaroni
300ml/½ pint/1¼ cups skimmed milk

25g/1oz/2 tbsp sunflower margarine
25g/1oz/2 tbsp plain flour
5ml/1 tsp grated nutmeg
2 tomatoes, sliced
60ml/4 tbsp wholemeal breadcrumbs
salt and ground black pepper
green salad, to serve

1 Preheat the oven to 220°C/425°F/Gas 7. Fry the turkey and onion in a non-stick frying pan without fat, stirring until lightly browned.

2 Stir in the tomato purée, red wine or stock and cinnamon. Season with salt and pepper, then cover with a tight-fitting lid and simmer for 5 minutes.

3 Cook the macaroni in boiling salted water until just tender, then drain. Layer with the meat mixture in a wide ovenproof dish.

4 Place the milk, margarine and flour in a saucepan and whisk over a moderate heat until thickened and smooth. Add the nutmeg, and salt and pepper to taste.

5 Pour the sauce evenly over the pasta and meat. Arrange the tomato slices on top and sprinkle lines of breadcrumbs over the surface. Bake for 30–35 minutes, or until golden brown and bubbling. Serve hot with a green salad.

Tuscan Chicken

A simple peasant casserole with all the flavours of Tuscan ingredients. The wine can be replaced by chicken stock.

Serves 4

5ml/1 tsp olive oil
8 chicken thighs, skinned
1 onion, thinly sliced
2 fresh red peppers, seeded and sliced
1 garlic clove, crushed
300ml/½ pint/1¼ cups passata
150ml/¼ pint/⅔ cup dry white wine

large fresh oregano sprig, or 5ml/1 tsp dried oregano
400g/14oz can cannellini beans, drained
45ml/3 tbsp fresh breadcrumbs
salt and ground black pepper

1 Heat the oil in a non-stick or heavy saucepan and fry the chicken until golden brown. Remove and keep hot. Add the onion and peppers to the pan and gently sauté until softened, but not brown. Stir in the garlic.

2 Add the chicken, passata, wine and oregano. Season well with salt and pepper, bring to the boil, then cover the pan with a tight lid.

3 Lower the heat and simmer gently, stirring occasionally for 30–35 minutes or until the chicken is tender and the juices run clear, not pink, when pierced with the point of a knife.

4 Stir in the cannellini beans and simmer for a further 5 minutes until heated through. Sprinkle with the breadcrumbs and cook under a hot grill until golden brown.

Poussins with Grapes in Vermouth

This sauce could also be served with roast chicken, but poussins have the stronger flavour.

Serves 4

4 oven-ready poussins (about 450g/1lb each)
50g/2oz/4 tbsp butter, softened
2 shallots, chopped
60ml/4 tbsp chopped fresh parsley
225g/8oz/2 cups white grapes, preferably Muscatel, halved and seeded

150ml/¼ pint/⅔ cup white vermouth
5ml/1 tsp cornflour
60ml/4 tbsp double cream
30ml/2 tbsp pine nuts, toasted
salt and ground black pepper
watercress sprigs, to garnish

1 Preheat the oven to 200°C/400°F/Gas 6. Wash and dry the poussins. Spread the softened butter all over the poussins and put a hazelnut-sized piece in the cavity of each bird.

2 Mix together the shallots and parsley and place a quarter of the mixture inside each poussin. Put the poussins side by side in a large roasting tin and roast for 40–50 minutes, or until the juices run clear when the thickest part of the flesh is pierced with a skewer. Transfer the poussins to a warmed serving plate. Cover and keep warm.

3 Skim off most of the fat from the roasting tin, then add the grapes and vermouth. Place the tin directly over a low heat for a few minutes to warm and slightly soften the grapes.

4 Lift the grapes out of the tin using a slotted spoon and scatter them around the poussin. Keep covered. Stir the cornflour into the cream, then add to the tin juices. Cook gently for a few minutes, stirring, until the sauce has thickened. Season to taste with salt and pepper. Pour the sauce around the poussins. Sprinkle with the toasted pine nuts and garnish with watercress sprigs.

Chicken Parcels with Herb Butter

These delightful, individual filo pastry parcels contain a wonderfully moist and herby filling.

Serves 4

4 chicken breast fillets, skinned
150g/5oz/generous ½ cup butter, softened
90ml/6 tbsp mixed chopped fresh herbs such as thyme, parsley, oregano and rosemary

5ml/1 tsp lemon juice
5 large sheets filo pastry, defrosted if frozen
1 egg, beaten
30ml/2 tbsp freshly grated Parmesan cheese
salt and ground black pepper

1 Season the chicken fillets. Melt 25g/1oz/2 tbsp of the butter in a frying pan and fry the chicken fillets to seal and brown lightly. Allow to cool.

2 Preheat the oven to 190°C/375°F/Gas 5. Put the remaining butter, the herbs, lemon juice and seasoning in a food processor or blender and process until smooth. Melt half of this herb butter.

3 Take one sheet of filo pastry and brush with melted herb butter. Keep the other sheets covered with a damp dish towel. Fold the filo pastry sheet in half and brush again with butter. Place a chicken fillet about 2.5cm/1in from the top end.

4 Dot the chicken with a quarter of the remaining unmelted herb butter. Fold in the sides of the pastry, then roll up to enclose it completely. Place seam-side down on a lightly greased baking sheet. Repeat with the other chicken fillets.

5 Brush the filo parcels with beaten egg. Cut the last sheet of filo into strips, then scrunch and arrange on top. Brush the parcels once again with the egg glaze, then sprinkle with Parmesan cheese. Bake for about 35–50 minutes, until golden brown. Serve hot.

Pot-roast of Venison

The venison is marinated for 24 hours before preparation to give this rich dish an even fuller flavour.

Serves 4–5

1.75kg/4–4½lb boned joint of venison
75ml/5 tbsp oil
4 cloves
8 black peppercorns, lightly crushed
12 juniper berries, lightly crushed
250ml/8fl oz/1 cup full-bodied red wine
115g/4oz lightly smoked streaky bacon, chopped

2 onions, finely chopped
2 carrots, chopped
150g/5oz large mushrooms, sliced
15g/½oz/1 tbsp plain flour
250ml/8fl oz/1 cup veal stock
30ml/2 tbsp redcurrant jelly
salt and ground black pepper

1 Put the venison in a bowl, add half the oil, the spices and wine, cover and leave in a cool place for 24 hours, turning the meat occasionally.

2 Preheat the oven to 160°C/325°F/Gas 3. Remove the venison from the bowl and pat dry. Reserve the marinade. Heat the remaining oil in a shallow saucepan, then brown the venison evenly. Transfer to a plate.

3 Stir the bacon, onions, carrots and mushrooms into the pan and cook for about 5 minutes. Stir in the flour and cook for 2 minutes, then remove from the heat and stir in the marinade, stock, redcurrant jelly and seasoning. Return to the heat, bring to the boil, stirring, then simmer for 2–3 minutes.

4 Transfer the venison and sauce to a casserole and cover with a tight-fitting lid. Cook in the oven for about 3 hours, turning the joint from time to time, until tender.

Pheasant with Mushrooms

The wine and mushroom sauce in this recipe is given a lift by the inclusion of anchovy fillets.

Serves 4

1 pheasant, jointed
250ml/8fl oz/1 cup red wine
45ml/3 tbsp oil
60ml/4 tbsp Spanish sherry vinegar
1 large onion, chopped
2 rashers smoked bacon
350g/12oz chestnut mushrooms, sliced

3 anchovy fillets, soaked for 10 minutes and drained
350ml/12fl oz/1½ cups game, veal or chicken stock
bouquet garni
salt and ground black pepper

1 Place the pheasant in a dish, add the wine, half the oil and half the vinegar, and scatter over half the onion. Season with salt and pepper, then cover the dish and leave in a cool place for about 8–12 hours, turning the pheasant occasionally.

2 Preheat the oven to 160°C/325°F/Gas 3. Lift the pheasant from the dish and pat dry with kitchen paper. Reserve the marinade for later.

3 Heat the remaining oil in a flameproof casserole, then brown the pheasant joints. Transfer to a plate.

4 Cut the bacon into strips then add with the remaining onion to the casserole and cook until the onion is soft. Stir in the mushrooms and cook for about 3 minutes.

5 Stir in the anchovies and remaining vinegar and boil until reduced. Add the marinade, cook for 2 minutes, then add the stock and bouquet garni. Return the pheasant to the casserole, cover and bake for about 1½ hours. Transfer the pheasant to a serving dish. Boil the cooking juices to reduce. Discard the bouquet garni. Pour over the pheasant and serve at once.

Minty Yogurt Chicken

Marinated, grilled chicken thighs make a tasty light lunch or supper. Use drumsticks if you prefer.

Serves 4

8 chicken thigh portions
15ml/1 tbsp clear honey
30ml/2 tbsp lime juice
30ml/2 tbsp natural
  yogurt

60ml/4 tbsp chopped
  fresh mint
salt and ground black
  pepper

1 Skin the chicken thighs and slash the flesh at intervals with a sharp knife. Place in a bowl. Mix together the honey, lime juice, yogurt, seasoning and half the mint.

2 Spoon the marinade over the chicken and leave to marinate for 30 minutes. Line a grill pan with foil and cook the chicken under a moderately hot grill until thoroughly cooked and golden brown, turning occasionally.

3 Sprinkle with remaining mint and serve with potatoes and tomato salad, if you wish.

Mandarin Sesame Duck

The rind, juice and flesh of sweet mandarin oranges are used in this delightful roast dish.

Serves 4

4 duck leg or boned
  breast portions
30ml/2 tbsp light soy
  sauce
45ml/3 tbsp clear honey

15ml/1 tbsp sesame seeds
4 mandarin oranges
5ml/1 tsp cornflour
salt and ground black
  pepper

1 Preheat the oven to 180°C/350°F/Gas 4. Prick the duck skin all over. Slash the breast skin diagonally at intervals. Roast the duck for 1 hour. Mix 15ml/1 tbsp soy sauce with 30ml/2 tbsp honey and brush over the duck. Sprinkle with sesame seeds. Roast for 15 minutes more.

2 Grate the rind from one mandarin and squeeze the juice from two. Mix in the cornflour, remaining soy sauce and honey. Heat, stirring, until thickened and clear. Season. Peel and slice the remaining mandarins. Serve the duck with the mandarin slices and the sauce.

Sticky Ginger Chicken

For a fuller flavour, marinate the chicken drumsticks in the glaze for 30 minutes before cooking.

Serves 4

Mix 30ml/2 tbsp lemon juice, 25g/1oz light muscovado sugar, 5ml/1 tsp grated fresh ginger root, 10ml/2 tsp soy sauce and ground pepper to taste. Using a sharp knife, slash eight chicken drumsticks about three times through the thickest part of the flesh, then toss the chicken in the glaze. Cook it under a hot grill or on a barbecue, turning occasionally and brushing with the glaze, until it is golden and the juices run clear when pierced. Serve on a bed of lettuce, with crusty bread, if you wish.

Oat-crusted Chicken with Sage

Oats make a good, crunchy coating for savoury foods, and offer a good way to add extra fibre.

Serves 4

45ml/3 tbsp milk
10ml/2 tsp English mustard
40g/1½oz/½ cup rolled oats
45ml/3 tbsp chopped fresh sage leaves
8 chicken thighs or drumsticks, skinned

120ml/4fl oz/½ cup fromage frais
5ml/1 tsp wholegrain mustard
salt and ground black pepper
fresh sage leaves, to garnish

1 Preheat the oven to 200°C/400°F/Gas 6. Mix together the milk and English mustard.

2 Mix the oats with 30ml/2 tbsp of the chopped sage and the seasoning on a plate. Brush the chicken with the milk and press into the oats to coat evenly.

3 Place the chicken on a baking sheet and bake for about 40 minutes, or until the juices run clear, not pink, when pierced through the thickest part.

4 Meanwhile, mix together the fromage frais, wholegrain mustard, remaining sage and seasoning, transfer to a serving dish and serve with the chicken. Garnish the chicken with fresh sage leaves.

Cook's Tip
If fresh sage is not available, choose another fresh herb such as thyme or parsley rather than using a dried alternative. These chicken thighs or drumsticks may be served hot or cold.

Chicken in Creamy Orange Sauce

The brandy adds a rich flavour to the sauce, but omit if you prefer and use orange juice alone.

Serves 4

8 chicken thighs or drumsticks, skinned
45ml/3 tbsp brandy
300ml/½ pint/1¼ cups orange juice

3 spring onions, chopped
10ml/2 tsp cornflour
90ml/6 tbsp fromage frais
salt and ground black pepper

1 Fry the chicken pieces without fat in a non-stick or heavy frying pan, turning until evenly browned.

2 Stir in the brandy, orange juice and spring onions. Bring to the boil, then cover and simmer for 15 minutes, or until the chicken is tender and the juices run clear, not pink, when pierced with the point of a sharp knife.

3 Blend the cornflour with a little water, then mix into the fromage frais. Stir this into a small saucepan and cook over a moderate heat until boiling.

4 Adjust the seasoning to taste and serve with boiled rice or pasta and green salad, if you wish.

Cook's Tip
For a healthy version of this dish, suitable for those who are watching their weight, use low-fat fromage frais which is virtually fat-free. The sauce will still be beautifully creamy.

Normandy Roast Chicken

The chicken is turned over halfway through roasting so that it cooks evenly and stays wonderfully moist.

Serves 4

*50g/2oz/4 tbsp butter,
   softened
30ml/2 tbsp chopped
   fresh tarragon
1 small garlic clove,
   crushed
1.5kg/3lb fresh chicken
5ml/1 tsp plain flour*

*150ml/¼ pint/⅔ cup
   single cream
squeeze of lemon juice
salt and ground black
   pepper
fresh tarragon and lemon
   slices, to garnish*

1 Preheat the oven to 200°C/400°F/Gas 6. Mix together the butter, 15ml/1 tbsp of the chopped tarragon, the garlic and seasoning in a bowl. Spoon half the butter mixture into the cavity of the chicken.

2 Carefully lift the skin at the neck end of the bird from the breast flesh on each side, then gently push a little of the butter mixture into each pocket and smooth it down over the breasts with your fingers.

3 Season the bird and lay it, breast-side down, in a roasting tin. Roast in the oven for 45 minutes, then turn the chicken over and baste with the juices. Cook for a further 45 minutes.

4 When the chicken is cooked, lift it to drain out any juices from the cavity into the tin, then transfer the bird to a warmed platter and keep warm.

5 Place the roasting tin on the hob and heat until sizzling. Stir in the flour and cook for 1 minute, then stir in the cream, the remaining tarragon, 150ml/ ¼ pint/⅔ cup water, the lemon juice and seasoning. Boil and stir for 2–3 minutes, until thickened. Garnish the chicken with tarragon and lemon slices and serve with the sauce.

Duck Breasts with Orange Sauce

A simple variation on the classic French whole roast duck, which makes for a more elegant presentation.

Serves 4

*4 duck breasts
15ml/1 tbsp sunflower oil
2 oranges
150ml/¼ pint/⅔cup
   fresh orange juice
15ml/1 tbsp port*

*30ml/2 tbsp Seville
   orange marmalade
15g/½oz/1 tbsp butter
5ml/1 tsp cornflour
salt and ground black
   pepper*

1 Season the duck breast skin. Heat the oil in a frying pan over a moderate heat and add the duck breasts, skin-side down. Cover and cook for 3–4 minutes, until just lightly browned. Turn the breasts over, lower the heat slightly and cook uncovered for 5–6 minutes.

2 Peel the skin and pith from the oranges. Working over a bowl to catch any juice, slice either side of the membranes to release the orange segments, then set aside with the juice.

3 Remove the duck breasts from the pan with a slotted spoon, drain on kitchen paper and keep warm in the oven while making the sauce.

4 Drain off the fat from the frying pan. Add the segmented oranges, all but 30ml/2 tbsp of the orange juice, the port and the orange marmalade. Bring to the boil and then reduce the heat slightly. Whisk small knobs of the butter into the sauce and season with salt and pepper.

5 Blend the cornflour with the reserved orange juice, pour into the pan and stir until slightly thickened. Add the duck breasts and cook gently for about 3 minutes. To serve, arrange the sliced breasts on plates with the sauce.

Pot-roast Poussin

This dish is inspired by the French method of cooking these birds. Pot-roasting keeps them moist and succulent.

Serves 4

15ml/1 tbsp olive oil
1 onion, sliced
1 large garlic clove, sliced
50g/2oz/½ cup diced
   smoked bacon
2 fresh poussins (about
   450g/1lb each)
30ml/2 tbsp melted
   butter
2 baby celery hearts, each
   cut into 4 pieces
8 baby carrots
2 small courgettes, cut
   into chunks
8 small new potatoes

600ml/1 pint/2½ cups
   chicken stock
150ml/¼ pint/⅔ cup dry
   white wine
1 bay leaf
2 fresh thyme sprigs
2 fresh rosemary sprigs
15ml/1 tbsp butter,
   softened
15g/1½oz/1 tbsp plain
   flour
salt and ground black
   pepper
fresh herbs, to garnish

1 Preheat the oven to 190°C/375°F/Gas 5. Heat the olive oil in a large flameproof casserole and sauté the onions, garlic and bacon for 5–6 minutes until the onions have softened. Brush the poussins with half the melted butter and season. Add to the casserole with the vegetables. Pour in the stock and wine and add the herbs. Cover and bake for 20 minutes.

2 Remove the lid and brush the birds with the remaining butter. Bake for 25–30 minutes more until golden. Transfer the poussins to a warmed serving platter and cut each in half with poultry shears or scissors. Remove the vegetables with a slotted spoon and arrange them round the birds. Cover with foil and keep warm.

3 Discard the herbs from the casserole. Mix the butter and flour to a paste. Bring the cooking liquid to the boil then whisk in spoonfuls of paste until thickened. Season and serve with the poussins and vegetables, garnished with herbs.

Coq au Vin

Chicken is flamed in brandy, then braised in red wine with bacon, mushrooms and onions in this classic dish.

Serves 4

50g/2oz/½ cup plain
   flour
1.5kg/3lb chicken, cut
   into 8 joints
15ml/1 tbsp olive oil
65g/2½oz/5 tbsp butter
20 baby onions
75g/3oz rindless streaky
   bacon, diced
about 20 button
   mushrooms

30ml/2 tbsp brandy
75cl bottle red Burgundy
bouquet garni
3 garlic cloves
5ml/1 tsp soft light
   brown sugar
salt and ground black
   pepper
15ml/1 tbsp chopped
   fresh parsley and
   croûtons, to garnish

1 Place 40g/1½oz/3 tbsp of the flour and seasoning in a large plastic bag and coat the chicken joints. Heat the oil and 50g/2oz/4 tbsp of the butter in a large flameproof casserole and sauté the onions and bacon until the onions have browned lightly. Add the mushrooms and fry for 2 minutes more. Remove with a slotted spoon and reserve.

2 Add the chicken pieces to the hot oil and cook for about 5–6 minutes until browned. Add the brandy and, standing well back, light it with a match, then shake the casserole gently until the flames subside.

3 Add the wine, bouquet garni, garlic and sugar, and season. Bring to the boil, cover and simmer for 1 hour, stirring from time to time. Add the onions, bacon and mushrooms, cover and cook for 30 minutes. Transfer the chicken, vegetables and bacon to a warmed dish.

4 Remove the bouquet garni; boil the liquid for 2 minutes. Cream the remaining butter and flour. Whisk in spoonfuls of the mixture to thicken the liquid. Pour the sauce over the chicken and serve garnished with parsley and croûtons.

Moroccan Spiced Roast Poussin

The poussins are stuffed with an aromatic rice mixture and glazed with spiced yogurt in this flavoursome dish.

Serves 4

75g/3oz/1 cup cooked long grain rice
1 small onion, chopped
finely grated rind and juice of 1 lemon
30ml/2 tbsp chopped fresh mint
45ml/3 tbsp chopped dried apricots
30ml/2 tbsp natural yogurt
10ml/2 tsp ground turmeric
10ml/2 tsp ground cumin
2 x 450g/1lb poussin
salt and ground black pepper
lemon slices and fresh mint sprigs, to garnish

1 Preheat the oven to 200°C/400°F/Gas 6. Mix together the rice, onion, lemon rind, mint and apricots. Stir in half each of the lemon juice, yogurt, turmeric, cumin, and salt and pepper.

2 Stuff the poussins with the rice mixture at the neck end only. The spare stuffing can be served separately. Place the poussins on a rack in a roasting tin.

3 Mix together the remaining lemon juice, yogurt, turmeric and cumin, then brush this over the poussins. Cover loosely with foil and cook in the oven for 30 minutes.

4 Remove the foil and roast for a further 15 minutes, or until golden brown and the juices run clear, not pink, when the thickest part of the flesh is pierced with a skewer.

5 Cut both the poussins in half with a sharp knife or poultry shears, and serve with the reserved rice. Garnish with slices of lemon and fresh mint sprigs.

Chilli Chicken Couscous

Couscous is a very easy alternative to rice and makes a good base for all kinds of ingredients.

Serves 4

225g/8oz/2 cups couscous
1 litre/1¼ pints/4 cups boiling water
5ml/1 tsp olive oil
400g/14oz boneless, skinless chicken, diced
1 yellow pepper, seeded and sliced
2 large courgettes, sliced thickly
1 small green chilli, thinly sliced, or 5ml/1 tsp chilli sauce
1 large tomato, diced
425g/15oz can chick-peas, drained
salt and ground black pepper
fresh coriander or parsley sprigs, to garnish

1 Place couscous in a large bowl and pour the boiling water over. Cover and leave to stand for 30 minutes.

2 Heat the oil in a large non-stick frying pan and stir-fry the chicken quickly to seal, then reduce the heat.

3 Stir in the pepper, courgettes and chilli or chilli sauce and cook for 10 minutes, until the vegetables are softened.

4 Stir in the tomato and chick-peas, then add the couscous. Adjust the seasoning and stir over a moderate heat until hot. Serve garnished with sprigs of fresh coriander or parsley.

Cook's Tip
If you prefer, use dried chick-peas in this recipe. Soak them overnight, then drain, place in a saucepan and add water to cover. Bring to the boil, then cook until tender, 45–60 minutes.

Mediterranean Turkey Skewers

These skewers are easy to assemble, and can be cooked under a grill or on a charcoal barbecue.

Serves 4

90ml/6 tbsp olive oil
45ml/3 tbsp lemon juice
1 garlic clove, finely
  chopped
30ml/2 tbsp chopped
  fresh basil
2 courgettes
1 long thin aubergine

300g/11oz boned turkey,
  cut into 5cm/2in cubes
12 – 16 pickled onions
1 red or yellow pepper,
  cut into 5cm/2in
  squares
salt and ground black
  pepper

1 Mix the oil with the lemon juice, garlic and basil in a small bowl. Season with salt and pepper.

2 Slice the courgettes and aubergine lengthways into strips 5mm/¼in thick. Cut them crossways about two-thirds of the way along their length. Discard the shorter length. Wrap half the turkey pieces with the courgette slices, and the other half with the aubergine slices.

3 Prepare the skewers by alternating the turkey, onions and pepper pieces. If you are using wooden skewers, soak them in water for several minutes. This will prevent them from charring during grilling. Lay the prepared skewers on a platter and sprinkle with the flavoured oil. Then leave them to marinate for at least 30 minutes. Preheat the grill or light the coals to prepare a barbecue.

4 Grill or barbecue for 10 minutes, until the vegetables are tender, turning occasionally. Serve hot.

Duck with Chestnut Sauce

This autumnal dish makes use of the sweet chestnuts that are gathered in Italian woods.

Serves 4–5

1 fresh rosemary sprig
1 garlic clove, sliced
30ml/2 tbsp olive oil
4 boned duck breasts,
  fat removed

For the sauce
450g/1lb/4 cups
  chestnuts
5ml/1 tsp oil

350ml/12fl oz/1½ cups
  milk
1 small onion, finely
  chopped
1 carrot, finely chopped
1 small bay leaf
salt and ground black
  pepper
30ml/2 tbsp cream,
  warmed

1 Pull the leaves from the sprig of rosemary. Combine them with the garlic and oil in a shallow bowl. Pat the duck breasts dry with kitchen paper. Brush them with the marinade and allow to stand for at least 2 hours before cooking.

2 Preheat the oven to 180°C/350°F/Gas 4. Cut a cross in the flat side of each chestnut with a sharp knife. Place the chestnuts on a baking sheet with the oil and shake the sheet until they are coated with oil. Bake for 20 minutes, then peel.

3 Place the peeled chestnuts in a heavy saucepan with the milk, onion, carrot and bay leaf. Cook slowly for about 10–15 minutes until the chestnuts are tender, then season. Discard the bay leaf. Press the mixture through a sieve.

4 Return the sauce to the pan. Heat gently while the duck breasts are cooking. Just before serving, stir in the cream. If the sauce is too thick, add a little more cream. Preheat the grill, or prepare a barbecue.

5 Grill the duck breasts until medium-rare, for about 6–8 minutes. They should be pink inside. Slice into rounds and arrange on warmed plates. Serve with the heated sauce.

Turkey Spirals

These little spirals may look difficult, but they're so easy to make, and a very good way to pep up plain turkey.

Serves 4

4 thinly sliced turkey breast steaks (about 90g/3½oz each)	25g/1oz/2 tbsp wholemeal flour
20ml/4 tsp tomato purée	salt and ground black pepper
15g/½oz large fresh basil leaves	passata or fresh tomato sauce and pasta with fresh basil, to serve
1 garlic clove, crushed	
15ml/1 tbsp skimmed milk	

1 Place the turkey steaks on a board. If too thick, flatten them slightly by beating with a rolling pin.

2 Spread each turkey breast steak with tomato purée, then top with a few leaves of basil, a little crushed garlic, and salt and pepper.

3 Roll up firmly around the filling and secure with a cocktail stick. Brush with milk and sprinkle with flour to coat lightly.

4 Place the spirals on a foil-lined grill pan. Cook under a moderately hot grill for 15–20 minutes, turning them occasionally, until thoroughly cooked. Serve hot, sliced with a spoonful or two of passata or fresh tomato sauce and pasta, sprinkled with fresh basil.

Caribbean Chicken Kebabs

These kebabs have a rich, sunshine Caribbean flavour and the marinade keeps them moist without the need for oil.

Serves 4

500g/1¼lb boned chicken breasts, skinned	15g/½oz/1 tbsp light muscovado sugar
finely grated rind of 1 lime	5ml/1 tsp ground cinnamon
30ml/2 tbsp lime juice	2 mangoes, peeled and diced
15ml/1 tbsp rum or sherry	rice and salad, to serve

1 Cut the chicken into bite-size chunks and place in a bowl with the lime rind and juice, rum, sugar and cinnamon. Toss well, cover and leave to stand for 1 hour.

2 Save the juices and thread the chicken on to four wooden skewers, alternating with the mango cubes.

3 Cook the skewers under a hot grill or on a barbecue for about 8-10 minutes, turning occasionally and basting with the juices until the chicken is tender and golden brown. Serve at once with rice and salad.

Cook's Tip
These kebabs may be served with a colourful salad and rice. The rum or sherry adds a lovely rich flavour but it is optional, so leave it out if you prefer.

Autumn Pheasant

Pheasant is worth buying as it is low in fat, full of flavour and never dry when cooked in this way.

Serves 4

1 oven-ready pheasant
2 small onions, quartered
3 celery sticks, thickly
 sliced
2 red eating apples,
 thickly sliced
120ml/4fl oz/½ cup stock
15ml/1 tbsp clear honey
30ml/2 tbsp
 Worcestershire sauce
pinch of freshly grated
 nutmeg
30ml/2 tbsp toasted
 hazelnuts
salt and ground black
 pepper

1 Preheat the oven to 180°C/350°F/Gas 4. Fry the pheasant without fat in a non-stick frying pan, turning occasionally until golden. Remove and keep hot.

2 Fry the onions and celery in the pan to brown lightly. Spoon into a casserole and place the pheasant on top. Tuck the apple slices around it.

3 Spoon over the stock, honey and Worcestershire sauce. Sprinkle with nutmeg, salt and pepper, cover with a tight-fitting lid and bake for 1¼–1½ hours or until tender. Sprinkle with nuts and serve hot.

Cook's Tip
Pheasant should be hung by the neck to develop their distinctive flavour for 7–14 days, according to the degree of gaminess preferred. If you are buying the bird ready-prepared, make sure all the tendons have been removed from the legs. This recipe provides an excellent method of cooking older, cock birds which tend to be rather tough and dry if plain roasted.

Chicken Stroganoff

This dish is based on the classic Russian dish, which is made with fillet of beef, and it is just as good.

Serves 4

4 boneless, skinless
 chicken breasts
45ml/3 tbsp olive oil
1 large onion, thinly
 sliced
225g/8oz mushrooms,
 sliced
300ml/½ pint/1¼ cups
 soured cream
salt and ground black
 pepper
15ml/1 tbsp chopped
 fresh parsley, to
 garnish

1 Divide the chicken breasts into two natural fillets, place between two sheets of clear film and flatten each to a thickness of 5mm/¼in with a rolling pin.

2 Cut into 2.5cm/1in strips diagonally across the fillets.

3 Heat 30ml/2 tbsp oil in a large frying pan and cook the sliced onion slowly until soft but not coloured.

4 Add the mushrooms and cook until golden brown. Remove and keep warm.

5 Increase the heat, add the remaining oil and fry the chicken very quickly, in small batches, for 3–4 minutes until lightly coloured. Remove and keep warm while frying the rest of the chicken.

6 Return all the chicken, onions and mushrooms to the pan and season with salt and pepper. Stir in the soured cream and bring to the boil. Sprinkle with fresh parsley and serve immediately.

Chicken Tikka

The red food colourings give this dish its traditional bright colour. Serve with lemon wedges and a crisp mixed salad.

Serves 4

175kg/3½ lb chicken
mixed fresh salad leaves
  such as frisée, oakleaf
  lettuce or radiccio,
  to serve

5ml/1 tsp ground paprika
10ml/2 tsp grated fresh
  root ginger
1 garlic clove, crushed
10ml/2 tsp garam masala
2.5ml/½ tsp salt
red food colouring
  (optional)
juice of 1 lemon

For the marinade

150ml/¼ pint/⅔ cup
  natural low-fat yogurt

1 Joint the chicken and cut it into eight even-size pieces, using a sharp knife.

2 Mix all the marinade ingredients in a large dish, add the chicken pieces to coat and chill for 4 hours or overnight to allow the flavours to penetrate the flesh.

3 Preheat the oven to 200°C/400°F/Gas 6. Remove the chicken pieces from the marinade and arrange them in a single layer in a large ovenproof dish. Bake for 30–40 minutes or until tender.

4 Baste with a little of the marinade while cooking. Arrange on a bed of salad leaves and serve hot or cold.

Cook's Tip

This dish would also make an excellent starter. Joint the chicken into smaller pieces and reduce the cooking time slightly, then serve with lemon wedges and just a simple salad garnish.

Simple Chicken Curry

Curry powder can be bought in three different strengths – mild, medium and hot. Use your own preferred type.

Serves 4

8 chicken legs, each piece
  including thigh and
  drumstick
30ml/2 tbsp olive oil
1 onion, thinly sliced
1 garlic clove, crushed
15ml/1 tbsp medium
  curry powder
25g/1oz/1 tbsp plain
  flour

450ml/¾ pint/1¾ cups
  chicken stock
1 beefsteak tomato
15ml/1 tbsp mango
  chutney
15ml/1 tbsp lemon juice
salt and ground black
  pepper
350g/12oz/2½ cups
  boiled rice, to serve

1 Cut the chicken legs in half. Heat the olive oil in a large flameproof casserole and brown the chicken pieces on both sides. Remove and keep warm.

2 Add the onion and garlic clove to the casserole and cook them until tender. Add the curry powder and cook gently for a further 2 minutes.

3 Add the flour and gradually blend in the chicken stock and seasoning.

4 Bring to the boil, replace the chicken pieces, cover and simmer for 20–30 minutes or until tender.

5 Skin the beefsteak tomato by blanching in boiling water for about 15 seconds, then running it under cold water to loosen the skin. Peel and cut into small dice.

6 Add to the chicken with the mango chutney and lemon juice. Heat through gently and adjust the seasoning to taste. Serve with boiled rice and Indian accompaniments.

Chicken Biryani

A *biryani* – from the Urdu – is a dish mixed with rice which resembles a risotto. It provides a one-pan meal.

Serves 4

275g/10oz/1½ cups
    basmati rice, rinsed
2.5ml/½ tsp salt
5 whole cardamom pods
2–3 whole cloves
1 cinnamon stick
45ml/3 tbsp vegetable oil
3 onions, sliced
675g/1½lb boneless,
    skinless, diced chicken
1.5ml/¼ tsp ground
    cloves
5 cardamom pods, seeds
    removed and ground
1.5ml/¼ tsp hot chilli
    powder
5ml/1 tsp ground cumin
5ml/1 tsp ground
    coriander

2.5ml/½ tsp freshly
    ground black pepper
3 garlic cloves, finely
    chopped
5ml/1 tsp finely chopped
    fresh root ginger
juice of 1 lemon
4 tomatoes, sliced
30ml/2 tbsp chopped fresh
    coriander
150ml/¼ pint/⅔ cup
    natural yogurt
2.5ml/½ tsp saffron
    strands soaked in
    10ml/2 tsp hot milk
45ml/3 tbsp toasted flaked
    almonds and fresh
    coriander sprigs, to
    garnish
natural yogurt, to serve

1 Preheat the oven to 190°C/375°F/Gas 5. Boil the rice mixture, salt, cardamom pods, cloves and cinnamon stick for 2 minutes. Then drain, leaving the whole spices in the rice.

2 Brown the onions in the oil. Add the chicken, ground spices, garlic, ginger and lemon juice. Stir-fry for 5 minutes.

3 Transfer to a casserole; top with the tomatoes. In layers, add the coriander, yogurt and rice. Drizzle over the saffron and milk, then 150ml/¼ pint/⅔ cup water.

4 Cover and bake for 1 hour. Transfer to a warmed serving platter and remove the whole spices. Garnish with toasted almonds and coriander and serve with yogurt.

Spatchcock of Poussin

Allow one poussin per person and sharp knives to tackle them. Serve with new potatoes and salad, if wished.

Serves 4

4 poussins
15ml/1 tbsp mixed
    chopped fresh herbs
    such as rosemary and
    parsley, plus extra to
    garnish

15ml/1 tbsp lemon juice
50g/2oz/4 tbsp butter,
    melted
salt and ground black
    pepper
lemon slices, to garnish

1 Remove any trussing strings from the birds, and using a pair of kitchen scissors, cut down on either side of the backbone. Lay the poussins flat and flatten with the help of a rolling pin or mallet, or use the heel of your hand.

2 Thread the legs and wings on to skewers to keep the poussins flat while they are cooking.

3 Brush both sides with melted butter and season with salt and pepper. Sprinkle with lemon juice and herbs.

4 Preheat the grill to moderate heat and cook skin-side first for 6 minutes until golden brown. Turn over, brush with butter and grill for a further 6–8 minutes or until cooked. Garnish with chopped herbs and lemon slices.

Chicken, Leek and Parsley Pie

A filling pie with a two-cheese sauce, this dish is ideal for serving on a cold winter's day.

Serves 4–6

3 boneless chicken breasts
flavourings: carrot,
* onion, peppercorns,*
* bouquet garni*
shortcrust pastry, made
* with 275g/10oz/*
* 2½ cups plain flour*
50g/2oz/4 tbsp butter
2 leeks, thinly sliced
50g/2oz/½ cup grated
* Cheddar cheese*
25g/1 oz/¼ cup grated
* Parmesan cheese*

45ml/3 tbsp chopped
* fresh parsley*
30ml/2 tbsp wholegrain
* mustard*
5ml/1 tsp cornflour
300ml/½ pint/1¼ cups
* double cream*
salt and ground black
* pepper*
beaten egg, to glaze
mixed fresh green salad
* leaves, to serve*

1 Poach the chicken breasts with the flavourings in water to cover, until tender. Cool in the liquid, then cut into strips.

2 Preheat the oven to 200°C/400°F/Gas 6. Divide the pastry into two pieces, one slightly larger than the other. Use the larger piece to line an 18 x 28cm/7 x 11in baking tin. Prick the base, bake for 15 minutes, then leave to cool.

3 Fry the leeks in the butter until soft. Stir in the cheeses and parsley. Spread half the leek mixture over the pastry base, cover with the chicken strips, then top with the remaining leek mixture. Mix the mustard, cornflour and cream. Season and pour into the pie.

4 Moisten the pastry base edges. Use the remaining pastry to cover the pie. Brush with beaten egg and bake for 30–40 minutes until golden and crisp. Serve with salad.

Hampshire Farmhouse Flan

A traditional dish from the south of England, this flan will satisfy the hungriest person.

Serves 4

225g/8oz/2 cups
* wholemeal flour*
50g/2oz/4 tbsp butter,
* cubed*
50g/2oz/4 tbsp lard
5ml/1 tsp caraway seeds
5ml/1 tbsp oil
1 onion, chopped
1 garlic clove, crushed
225g/8oz/2 cups cooked
* chicken, chopped*
75g/3oz watercress
* leaves, chopped*

grated rind of ½ lemon
2 eggs, lightly beaten
175ml/6fl oz/¼ cup
* double cream*
45ml/3 tbsp natural
* yogurt*
large pinch of grated
* nutmeg*
45ml/3 tbsp grated
* Caerphilly cheese*
beaten egg, to glaze
salt and ground black
* pepper*

1 Rub the fats into the flour with a pinch of salt until the mixture resembles breadcrumbs.

2 Stir in the caraway seeds and 45ml/3 tbsp iced water and mix to a firm dough. Knead until smooth, then use to line an 18 x 28cm/7 x 11in loose-based flan tin. Reserve the dough trimmings. Prick the base and chill for 20 minutes. Heat a baking sheet in the oven at 200°C/400°F/Gas 6.

3 Sauté the onion and garlic in the oil until softened. Remove from the heat and cool. Meanwhile, line the pastry case with greaseproof paper and baking beans. Bake for 10 minutes, remove the paper and beans and cook for 5 minutes.

4 Mix the onion, chicken, watercress and lemon rind; spoon into the flan case. Beat the eggs, cream, yogurt, nutmeg, cheese and seasoning; pour over the chicken mixture. Cut the pastry trimmings into 1cm/½in strips. Brush with egg, then twist and lay in a lattice over the flan. Press on the ends. Bake for 35 minutes, until golden.

Chicken Charter Pie

A light pie with a fresh taste; it is versatile enough to use for light meals or informal dinners.

Serves 4

50g/2oz/4 tbsp butter
4 chicken legs
1 onion, finely chopped
150ml/¼ pint/⅔ cup milk
150ml/¼ pint/⅔ cup soured cream
4 spring onions, quartered

20g/¾ oz fresh parsley leaves, finely chopped
225g/8oz ready-made puff pastry
120ml/4fl oz/½ cup double cream
2 eggs, beaten, plus extra for glazing
salt and ground black pepper

1 Melt the butter in a frying pan and brown the chicken legs. Transfer to a plate. Add the chopped onion to the pan and cook until softened but not browned. Stir the milk, soured cream, spring onions, parsley and seasoning into the pan, bring to the boil, then simmer for 2 minutes.

2 Return the chicken to the pan with any juices, cover and cook gently for 30 minutes. Transfer the chicken mixture to a 1.2 litre/2 pint/5 cup pie dish. Leave to cool.

3 Preheat the oven to 220°C/425°F/Gas 7. Place a narrow strip of pastry on the edge of the pie dish. Moisten the strip, then cover the dish with the pastry. Press the edges together. Make a hole in the centre of the pastry and insert a small funnel of foil. Brush the pastry with beaten egg, then bake for 15–20 minutes.

4 Reduce the oven temperature to 180°C/350°F/Gas 4. Mix the cream and eggs, then pour into the pie through the funnel. Shake the pie to distribute the cream, then return to the oven for 5–10 minutes. Leave the pie in a warm place for about 5–10 minutes before serving, or cool completely.

Chicken and Ham Pie

This is a rich pie flavoured with fresh herbs and lightly spiced with mace – ideal for taking on a picnic.

Serves 8

400g/14oz ready-made shortcrust pastry
800g/1¾ lb chicken breast
350g/12oz uncooked gammon
60ml/4 tbsp double cream
6 spring onions, finely chopped
15ml/1 tbsp chopped fresh tarragon

10ml/2 tsp chopped fresh thyme
grated rind and juice of ½ large lemon
5ml/1 tsp freshly ground mace
salt and ground black pepper
beaten egg or milk, to glaze

1 Preheat the oven to 190°C/375°F/Gas 5. Roll out one-third of the pastry and use it to line a 20cm/8in pie tin, 5cm/2in deep. Place on a baking sheet.

2 Mince 115g/4oz of the chicken with the gammon, then mix with the cream, spring onions, herbs, lemon rind and 15ml/1 tbsp of the lemon juice; season lightly. Cut the remaining chicken into 1cm/½in pieces and mix with the remaining lemon juice, the mace and seasoning.

3 Make a layer of one-third of the gammon mixture in the pastry base, cover with half the chopped chicken, then add another layer of one-third of the gammon. Add all the remaining chicken followed by the remaining gammon.

4 Dampen the edges of the pastry base and roll out the remaining pastry to make a lid for the pie. Use the trimmings to make a lattice decoration. Make a small hole in the centre of the pie, brush the top with beaten egg or milk, then bake for 20 minutes. Reduce the temperature to 160°C/325°F/Gas 3 and bake for a further 1–1¼ hours. Transfer the pie to a wire rack and leave to cool.

Venison with Cranberry Sauce

Turkey and Mange-tout Stir-fry

Venison steaks are now readily available. Lean and low in fat, they make a healthy choice for a special occasion.

Have all the ingredients prepared before you start cooking this dish, as it will be ready in minutes.

Serves 4

1 orange	150ml/¼ pint/⅔ cup
1 lemon	ruby port
75g/3oz/¾ cup fresh or	30ml/2 tbsp sunflower oil
frozen unthawed	4 venison steaks
cranberries	2 shallots, finely chopped
5ml/1 tsp grated fresh	salt and ground black
root ginger	pepper
1 fresh thyme sprig	fresh thyme sprigs, to
5ml/1 tsp Dijon mustard	garnish
60ml/4 tbsp redcurrant	mashed potatoes and
jelly	broccoli, to serve

Serves 4

30ml/2 tbsp sesame oil	30ml/2 tbsp groundnut
90ml/6 tbsp lemon juice	oil
1 garlic clove, crushed	50g/2oz/½ cup cashew
1cm/½in piece fresh root	nuts
ginger, peeled and	6 spring onions, cut into
grated	strips
5ml/1 tsp clear honey	225g/8oz can water
450g/1lb turkey fillets,	chestnuts, drained and
cut into strips	thinly sliced
115g/4oz/1 cup	pinch of salt
mange-touts, trimmed	saffron rice, to serve

1 Pare the rind from half the orange and half the lemon using a vegetable peeler, then cut into very fine strips. Blanch the strips in a small saucepan of boiling water for 5 minutes until tender. Drain the strips and refresh under cold water.

2 Squeeze the juice from the citrus fruit and pour into a small pan. Add the cranberries, ginger, thyme, mustard, redcurrant jelly and port. Cook gently until the jelly melts. Bring to the boil, stirring, cover and reduce the heat. Cook for 15 minutes, until the cranberries are just tender.

3 Fry the venison steaks in the oil over a high heat for 2–3 minutes. Turn them over and add the shallots. Cook on the other side for 2–3 minutes, to taste. Just before the end of cooking, pour in the sauce and add the strips of orange and lemon rind. Leave the sauce to bubble for a few seconds to thicken slightly, then remove the thyme sprig and adjust the seasoning to taste.

4 Transfer the venison steaks to warmed plates and spoon over the sauce. Garnish with thyme sprigs and serve accompanied by creamy mashed potatoes and broccoli.

1 Mix together the sesame oil, lemon juice, garlic, ginger and honey in a shallow non-metallic dish. Add the turkey and mix well. Cover and leave to marinate for 3–4 hours.

2 Blanch the mange-touts in boiling salted water for about 1 minute. Drain and refresh under cold running water.

3 Drain the marinade from the turkey strips and reserve the marinade. Heat the groundnut oil in a wok or large frying pan, add the cashew nuts and stir-fry for about 1–2 minutes until golden brown. Remove the cashew nuts from the wok or frying pan using a slotted spoon and set aside.

4 Add the turkey and stir-fry for 3–4 minutes, until golden brown. Add the spring onions, mange-touts, water chestnuts and the reserved marinade. Cook for a few minutes, until the turkey is tender and the sauce is bubbling and hot. Stir in the cashew nuts and serve with saffron rice.

Cook's Tip
This dish could be served on a bed of medium-width egg noodles for a quick meal.

Farmhouse Venison Pie

A simple and satisfying pie; the venison is cooked in a rich gravy, topped with potato and parsnip mash.

Serves 4

45ml/3 tbsp sunflower oil	5ml/1 tsp chopped fresh
1 onion, chopped	thyme
1 garlic clove, crushed	5ml/1 tsp Dijon mustard
3 rashers rindless streaky	15ml/1 tbsp redcurrant
bacon, chopped	jelly
675g/1½ lb minced	675g/1½lb potatoes
venison	450g/1lb parsnips
115g/4oz button	1 egg yolk
mushrooms, chopped	50g/2oz/4 tbsp butter
25g/1oz/2 tbsp plain flour	pinch of freshly grated
450ml/¾ pint/1¾ cups	nutmeg
beef stock	45ml/3 tbsp chopped
150ml/¼ pint/⅔ cup	fresh parsley
ruby port	salt and ground black
2 bay leaves	pepper

1 Heat the oil in a large frying pan and fry the onion, garlic and bacon for 5 minutes. Add the venison and mushrooms and cook for a few minutes, stirring, until browned.

2 Stir in the flour and cook for 1–2 minutes, then add the stock, port, herbs, mustard, redcurrant jelly and seasoning. Bring to the boil, cover with a tight-fitting lid and simmer for 30–40 minutes, until tender. Spoon into a large pie dish or four individual ovenproof dishes.

3 While the venison and mushroom mixture is cooking, preheat the oven to 200°C/400°F/Gas 6. Cut the potatoes and parsnips into large chunks. Cook together in boiling salted water for 20 minutes or until tender. Drain and mash, then beat in the egg yolk, butter, nutmeg, parsley and seasoning.

4 Spread the potato and parsnip mixture over the meat and bake for 30–40 minutes, until piping hot and golden brown. Serve at once with a green vegetable, if you wish.

Normandy Pheasant

Calvados, cider, apples and cream – the produce of Normandy – make this a rich and flavoursome dish.

Serves 4

2 oven-ready pheasants	3 Cox's Pippin apples
15ml/1 tbsp olive oil	150ml/¼ pint/⅔ cup
25g/1oz/2 tbsp butter	double cream
60ml/4 tbsp Calvados	salt and ground black
450ml/¾ pint/1¾ cups	pepper
dry cider	fresh thyme sprigs, to
bouquet garni	garnish

1 Preheat the oven to 160°C/325°F/Gas 3. Joint both the pheasants into four pieces using a large sharp knife. Discard the backbones and knuckles.

2 Heat the oil and butter in a large flameproof casserole. Working in two batches, add the pheasant pieces to the casserole and brown them over a high heat. Return all the pheasant pieces to the casserole.

3 Standing well back, pour over the Calvados and set it alight with a match. Shake the casserole and when the flames have subsided, pour in the cider, then add the bouquet garni and season to taste with salt and pepper. Bring to the boil, cover with a tight-fitting lid and cook for about 50 minutes.

4 Peel, core and thickly slice the apples. Tuck the apple slices around the pheasant. Cover and cook for 5–10 minutes, or until the pheasant is tender. Transfer the pheasant and apples to a warmed serving plate. Keep warm.

5 Remove the bouquet garni, then boil the sauce rapidly to reduce by half to a syrupy consistency. Stir in the double cream and simmer for a further 2–3 minutes until thickened. Taste the sauce and adjust the seasoning if necessary. Spoon the sauce over the pheasant pieces and serve immediately, garnished with fresh thyme sprigs.

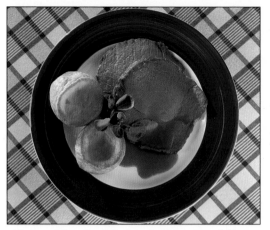

Roast Beef with Yorkshire Pudding

This classic British dish is often served at Sunday lunch, accompanied by potatoes, mustard and horseradish sauce.

Serves 6

1.75kg/4lb joint of beef
30–60ml/2–4 tbsp
  dripping or oil
300ml/½ pint/1¼ cups
  vegetable or veal stock,
  wine or water
salt and ground black
  pepper

For the puddings
50g/2oz/½ cup plain
  flour
1 egg, beaten
150ml/¼ pint/⅔ cup
  water mixed with milk
dripping or oil, for
  cooking

1 Weigh the beef and calculate the cooking time. Allow 15 minutes per 450g/1lb plus 15 minutes for rare meat, 20 minutes plus 20 minutes for medium, and 25–30 minutes plus 25 minutes for well-done.

2 Preheat the oven to 220°C/425°F/Gas 7. Heat the dripping or oil in a roasting tin in the oven. Place the meat on a rack, fat-side uppermost, then place the rack in the roasting tin. Baste the beef with the dripping or oil, and cook for the required time, basting occasionally.

3 To make the Yorkshire puddings, stir the flour, salt and pepper together in a bowl and form a well in the centre. Pour the egg into the well, then slowly pour in the milk, stirring in the flour to give a smooth batter. Stand for 30 minutes.

4 A few minutes before the meat is ready, spoon a little dripping or oil in each of 12 patty tins and place in the oven until very hot. Remove the meat, season, then cover loosely with foil and keep warm. Quickly divide the batter among the patty tins, then bake for 15–20 minutes, until well risen and brown.

5 Spoon off the fat from the roasting tin. Add the stock, wine or water, stirring, and boil for a few minutes. Season to taste, then serve with the beef and Yorkshire puddings.

Beef Olives

So-called because of their shape, these beef rolls contain a delicious filling made with bacon and mushrooms.

Serves 4

25g/1oz/2 tbsp butter
2 rashers bacon, finely
  chopped
115g/4oz mushrooms,
  chopped
15ml/1 tbsp chopped
  fresh parsley
grated rind and juice of
  1 lemon
115g/4oz/2 cups fresh
  breadcrumbs

675g/1½ lb topside of
  beef, cut into 8 thin
  slices
40g/1½ oz/3 tbsp plain
  flour
45ml/3 tbsp oil
2 onions, sliced
450ml/¾ pint/1¾ cups
  brown veal stock
salt and ground black
  pepper

1 Preheat the oven to 160°C/325°F/Gas 3. Melt the butter in a saucepan and fry the bacon and mushrooms for 3 minutes. Mix them with the chopped parsley, lemon rind and juice, breadcrumbs and seasoning.

2 Spread an equal amount of the breadcrumb mixture evenly over the beef slices, leaving a narrow border clear around the edge. Roll up the slices and tie securely with fine string, then dip the beef rolls in the flour to coat lightly, shaking off any excess flour.

3 Heat the oil in a frying pan, then fry the beef rolls until lightly browned. Remove and keep warm. Add the onions and fry until browned. Stir in the remaining flour and cook until lightly browned. Pour in the stock, stirring constantly, bring to the boil, stirring, and simmer for 2–3 minutes.

4 Transfer the rolls to a casserole, pour the sauce over the top, then cover with a tight-fitting lid and cook in the oven for 2 hours. Lift out the "olives" using a slotted spoon and remove the string. Return them to the sauce and serve hot.

Lamb and Spring Vegetable Stew

Known as a *blanquette* in France, this stew may have blanched asparagus spears or French beans added.

Serves 4

65g/2½oz/5 tbsp butter
900g/2lb lean boned
   shoulder of lamb, cut
   into 4cm/1¼ in dice
600ml/1 pint/2½ cups
   lamb stock or water
150ml/¼ pint/⅔ cup dry
   white wine
1 onion, quartered
2 fresh thyme sprigs
1 bay leaf
225g/8oz baby onions,
   halved
225g/8oz young carrots

2 small turnips,
   quartered
175g/6oz/¾ cup shelled
   broad beans
15g/½oz/1 tbsp plain
   flour
1 egg yolk .
45l/3 tbsp double cream
10ml/2 tsp lemon juice
salt and ground black
   pepper
30ml/2 tbsp chopped
   fresh parsley, to
   garnish

1 Sauté the lamb in 25g/1oz/2 tbsp of the butter to seal. Add the stock or water and wine, bring to the boil and skim. Add the quartered onion, thyme and bay leaf. Cover and simmer for 1 hour.

2 Brown the baby onions in 15g/½oz/1 tbsp of the butter. Add to the lamb with the carrots and turnips. Cook for 20 minutes. Add the beans and cook for 10 minutes.

3 Arrange the lamb and vegetables on a serving dish. Cover and keep warm. Discard the onion quarters and herbs. Strain the stock; skim off the fat. Bring to the boil and reduce the stock to 450ml/¾ pint/1¾ cups. Mix the remaining butter and flour to a paste. Whisk into the stock, then simmer briefly.

4 Combine the egg yolk and cream. Add a little hot sauce then stir into the pan. Do not boil. Add the lemon juice, and season. Pour the sauce over the lamb; garnish with parsley.

Beef Paprika with Roasted Peppers

This dish is perfect for family suppers – and roasting the peppers gives an added dimension.

Serves 4

30ml/2 tbsp olive oil
675g/1½lb chuck steak,
   cut into 4cm/1½in
   dice
2 onions, chopped
1 garlic clove, crushed
15g/½oz/1 tbsp plain
   flour
15ml/1 tbsp paprika, plus
   extra to garnish

400g/14oz can chopped
   tomatoes
2 red peppers, seeded and
   halved
150ml/¼ pint/⅔ cup
   crème fraîche
salt and ground black
   pepper
buttered noodles, to serve

1 Preheat the oven to 140°C/275°F/Gas 1. Heat the oil in a large flameproof casserole and brown the diced chuck steak in batches. Remove the meat from the casserole using a slotted spoon and set aside.

2 Add the onions and garlic and fry gently until softened but not browned. Stir in the flour and paprika and continue cooking for a further 1–2 minutes, stirring continuously to prevent sticking.

3 Return the meat and any juices that have collected on the plate to the casserole, then add the chopped tomatoes and salt and ground black pepper. Bring to the boil while stirring continuously, then cover with a tight-fitting lid and cook in the oven for 2½ hours.

4 Meanwhile, place the peppers skin-side up on a grill rack and grill until the skins have blistered and charred. Cool, then peel off the skins. Cut the flesh into strips, then add to the casserole and cook for a further 15–30 minutes, or until the meat is tender.

5 Stir in the crème fraîche and sprinkle with a little paprika. Serve hot with buttered noodles.

Beef in Guinness

Guinness gives this stew a deep, rich flavour. Use Beamish or another stout if you prefer.

Serves 6

*900g/2lb chuck steak, cut
  into 4cm/1½ in dice
plain flour, for coating
45ml/3 tbsp oil
1 large onion, sliced
1 carrot, thinly sliced
2 celery sticks, thinly
  sliced
10ml/2 tsp granulated
  sugar*

*5ml/1 tsp English
  mustard powder
15ml/1 tbsp tomato purée
2.5 x 7.5cm/1 x 3in strip
  orange rind
bouquet garni
600ml/1 pint/2½ cups
  Guinness
salt and ground black
  pepper*

1 Toss the beef in flour to coat. Heat 30ml/2 tbsp of the oil in a large shallow saucepan, then cook the beef in batches until lightly browned. Transfer to a bowl.

2 Add the remaining oil to the pan, then cook the onions until well browned, adding the thinly sliced carrot and celery towards the end.

3 Stir in the sugar, mustard, tomato purée, orange rind, Guinness and seasoning, then add the bouquet garni and bring to the boil. Return the meat, and any juices in the bowl, to the pan; add water, if necessary, so that the meat is covered. Cover the pan with a tight-fitting lid and cook gently for 2–2½ hours, until the meat is very tender.

Cottage Pie

This traditional dish is always a favourite with adults and children alike.

Serves 4

*30ml/2 tbsp oil
1 onion, finely chopped
1 carrot, finely chopped
115g/4oz mushrooms,
  chopped
500g/1¼lb lean chuck
  steak, minced
300ml/½ pint/1¼ cups
  brown veal stock or
  water
15g/½oz/1 tbsp plain
  flour*

*1 bay leaf
10–15ml/2–3 tsp
  Worcestershire sauce
15ml/1 tbsp tomato purée
675g/1½lb potatoes,
  boiled
25g/1oz/2 tbsp butter
45ml/3 tbsp hot milk
15ml/1 tbsp chopped
  fresh tarragon
salt and ground black
  pepper*

1 Heat the oil in a saucepan and cook the onion, carrot and mushrooms, stirring occasionally, until browned. Stir the beef into the pan and cook, stirring to break up the lumps, until lightly browned.

2 Blend a few spoonfuls of the stock or water with the flour, then stir into the pan. Stir in the remaining stock or water and bring to a simmer, stirring. Add the bay leaf, Worcestershire sauce and tomato purée, then cover with a tight-fitting lid and cook very gently for 1 hour, stirring occasionally. Uncover towards the end of cooking to allow any excess liquid to evaporate, if necessary.

3 Preheat the oven to 190°C/375°F/Gas 5. Gently heat the potatoes for a couple of minutes, then mash with the butter, milk and seasoning.

4 Add the tarragon to the mince and season to taste with salt and pepper, then pour into a pie dish. Cover the mince with an even layer of potato and mark the top with the prongs of a fork. Bake for about 25 minutes, until golden brown.

Irish Stew

This wholesome and filling stew is given a slight piquancy by the inclusion of a little anchovy sauce.

Serves 4

4 rashers smoked streaky bacon
2 celery sticks, chopped
2 large onions, sliced
8 middle neck lamb chops (about 1kg/ 2¼lb total weight)
1kg/2¼lb potatoes, sliced

300ml/½ pint/1¼ cups brown veal stock
7.5ml/1½ tsp Worcestershire sauce
5ml/1 tsp anchovy sauce
salt and ground black pepper
fresh parsley, to garnish

1 Preheat the oven to 160°C/325°F/Gas 3. Chop and then fry the bacon for 3–5 minutes until the fat runs, then add the celery and one-third of the onions and continue to cook, stirring occasionally, until browned.

2 Layer the lamb chops, potatoes, vegetables and bacon and remaining onions in a heavy flameproof casserole, seasoning each layer with salt and pepper as you go. Finish with a layer of potatoes.

3 Pour the veal stock, Worcestershire sauce and anchovy sauce into the bacon and vegetable cooking juices in the pan, stir, and bring to the boil. Pour the mixture into the casserole, adding water if necessary so that the liquid comes halfway up the sides of the casserole.

4 Cover the casserole with a tight-fitting lid, then cook in the oven for 3 hours, until the meat and vegetables are tender. Return to the oven for longer if necessary. Serve hot, sprinkled with chopped fresh parsley.

Cook's Tip
This is a good way of cooking cheaper cuts of lamb but for a more elegant dish, use diced lamb or lamb steaks instead of the chops and cook in the oven for 2 hours.

Oatmeal and Herb Rack of Lamb

Ask the butcher to remove the chine bone that runs along the eye of the meat – this will make carving easier.

Serves 6

2 best end necks of lamb (about 900kg/2lb each)
finely grated rind of 1 lemon
60ml/4 tbsp medium oatmeal
50g/2oz/1 cup fresh white breadcrumbs
60ml/4 tbsp chopped fresh parsley

25g/1oz/2 tbsp butter, melted
30ml/2 tbsp clear honey
salt and ground black pepper
roasted baby vegetables and gravy, to serve
fresh herb sprigs, to garnish

1 Preheat the oven to 200°C/400°F/Gas 6. Using a small sharp knife, cut through the skin and meat of both pieces of lamb about 2.5cm/1in from the tips of the bones. Pull off the fatty meat to expose the bones, then scrape around each bone tip until completely clean.

2 Trim all the skin and most of the fat from the meat, then lightly score the remaining fat with a sharp knife. Repeat with the second rack.

3 Mix together the lemon rind, oatmeal, breadcrumbs, the parsley and seasoning, then stir in the melted butter.

4 Brush the fatty side of each rack of lamb with honey, then press the oatmeal mixture evenly over the surface with your fingers until well coated.

5 Place the racks in a roasting tin with the oatmeal sides uppermost. Roast for 40–50 minutes, depending on whether you like rare or medium lamb. Cover loosely with foil if browning too much. To serve, slice each rack into three and accompany with roasted baby vegetables and gravy made with the pan juices. Garnish with herb sprigs.

Beef Wellington

This dish is so-named because of a supposed resemblance of shape and colour to the Duke of Wellington's boot.

Serves 8

1.4kg/3lb fillet of beef
15g/½oz/1 tbsp butter
30ml/2 tbsp oil
½ small onion, finely
    chopped
175g/6oz mushrooms,
    chopped
175g/6oz liver pâté
freshly squeezed lemon
    juice
a few drops of
    Worcestershire sauce
400g/14oz ready-made
    puff pastry
salt and ground black
    pepper
beaten egg, to glaze

1 Preheat the oven to 200°C/425°F/Gas 7. Season the beef with pepper, then tie it at intervals with string.

2 Heat the butter and oil in a roasting tin. Brown the beef over a high heat, then cook in the oven for 20 minutes. Cool and remove the string.

3 Scrape the cooking juices into a pan, add the onion and mushrooms and cook until tender. Cool, then mix with the pâté. Add lemon juice and Worcestershire sauce.

4 Roll out the pastry to a large 5mm/¼in thick rectangle. Spread the pâté mixture on the beef, then place it in the centre of the pastry. Dampen the edges of the pastry, then fold it over the beef to make a neat parcel, tucking in the ends neatly; press to seal.

5 Place the parcel on a baking sheet with the join on the underside and brush with beaten egg. Bake in the oven for 25–45 minutes, depending how well done you like the beef. Serve in generous slices.

Butterflied Cumin and Garlic Lamb

Ground cumin and garlic give the lamb a wonderful Middle-Eastern flavour to this recipe.

Serves 6

1.75kg/4lb leg of lamb
60ml/4 tbsp extra virgin
    olive oil
30ml/2 tbsp ground
    cumin
4–6 garlic cloves,
    crushed
salt and ground black
    pepper
toasted almond and
    raisin rice, to serve
fresh coriander sprigs
    and lemon wedges,
    to garnish

1 To butterfly the lamb, cut away the meat from the bone using a small sharp knife. Remove any excess fat and the thin, parchment-like membrane. Bat out the meat with a rolling pin to an even thickness, then prick the fleshy side of the lamb well with the tip of a knife.

2 In a bowl, mix together the olive oil, cumin and garlic and season with pepper. Spoon the mixture all over the lamb, then rub it well into the crevices. Cover the bowl and leave the lamb to marinate overnight.

3 Preheat the oven to 200°C/400°F/Gas 6. Spread the lamb, skin-side down, on a rack in a roasting tin. Season with salt and roast for 45–60 minutes, until crusty brown on the outside but still pink in the centre.

4 Remove the lamb from the oven and leave it to rest for about 10 minutes. Cut into diagonal slices and serve with the toasted almond and raisin rice. Garnish with the fresh coriander sprigs and lemon wedges.

Cook's Tip
The lamb may be barbecued rather than roasted. Thread it on to two long skewers and barbecue for about 20-25 minutes on each side, until it is cooked to your liking.

Lamb with Mint Sauce

In this flavoursome dish, the classic combination of lamb and mint is given an original twist.

Serves 4

8 lamb noisettes,
  2–2.5cm/³/₄ – 1in
  thick
30ml/2 tbsp oil
45ml/3 tbsp medium-
  bodied dry white wine,
  or vegetable or veal
  stock
salt and ground black
  pepper
fresh mint sprigs, to
  garnish

For the sauce
30ml/2 tbsp boiling
  water
5–10ml/1–2 tsp
  granulated sugar
leaves from a small
  bunch of fresh mint,
  finely chopped
about 30ml/2 tbsp white
  wine vinegar

1 To make the sauce, stir the water and sugar together, then add the mint, vinegar to taste and season with salt and black pepper. Leave for 30 minutes.

2 Season the lamb with pepper. Heat the oil in a large frying pan and fry the lamb, in batches if necessary so that the pan is not crowded, for about 3 minutes on each side for meat that is pink in the middle.

3 Transfer the lamb to a warmed plate and season with salt, then cover and keep warm.

4 Stir the wine or stock into the cooking juices, dislodging the sediment, and bring to the boil. Bubble for a couple of minutes, then pour over the lamb. Garnish the lamb noisettes with small sprigs of mint and serve hot with the mint sauce.

Somerset Pork with Apples

A creamy cider sauce accompanies tender pieces of pork and sliced apples to make a rich supper dish.

Serves 4

25g/1oz/2 tbsp butter
500g/1¼lb pork loin, cut
  into bite-size pieces
12 baby onions, peeled
10ml/2 tsp grated lemon
  rind
300ml/½ pint/1¼ cups
  dry cider
150ml/¼ pint/⅔ cup veal
  stock

2 crisp eating apples such
  as Granny Smith,
  cored and sliced
45ml/3 tbsp chopped
  fresh parsley
100ml/3½fl oz/scant
  ½ cup whipping cream
salt and ground black
  pepper

1 Heat the butter in a large sauté or frying pan and brown the pork in batches. Transfer the pork to a bowl.

2 Add the onions to the pan, brown lightly, then stir in the lemon rind, cider and stock and boil for about 3 minutes. Return all the pork to the pan and cook gently for about 25 minutes, until tender.

3 Add the apples to the pan and continue to cook for a further 5 minutes. Using a slotted spoon, transfer the pork, onions and apples to a warmed serving dish, cover and keep warm. Stir the parsley and cream into the pan and allow to bubble to thicken the sauce slightly. Season, then pour over the pork and serve hot.

Pork with Plums

Plums poached in apple juice are used here to make a delightfully fruity sauce for pork chops.

Serves 4

450g/1lb ripe plums,
  halved and stoned
300ml/½ pint/1¼ cups
  apple juice
40g/1½oz/3 tbsp butter
15ml/1 tbsp oil
4 pork chops (about
  200g/7oz each)

1 onion, finely chopped
pinch of freshly ground
  mace
salt and ground black
  pepper
fresh sage leaves, to
  garnish

1 Simmer the plums in the apple juice until tender. Strain off and reserve the juice, then purée half the plums with a little of the juice.

2 Meanwhile, heat the butter and oil in a large frying pan and fry the chops until brown on both sides, then transfer them to a plate.

3 Add the onion to the pan and cook gently until soft, but not coloured. Return the chops to the pan. Pour over the plum purée and all the juice.

4 Simmer, uncovered, for 10–15 minutes, until the chops are cooked through. Add the remaining plums to the pan, then add the mace and seasoning. Warm the sauce through over a moderate heat and serve garnished with fresh sage leaves.

Lancashire Hot-pot

Browning the lamb and kidneys, plus the extra vegetables and herbs, adds flavour to the traditional basic ingredients.

Serves 4

40g/1½oz/3 tbsp
  dripping, or
  45ml/3 tbsp oil
8 medium neck lamb
  chops (about 900g/2lb
  total weight)
175g/6oz lamb's kidneys,
  cut into large pieces
900g/2lb potatoes, thinly
  sliced
3 carrots, thickly sliced
450g/1lb leeks, sliced

3 celery sticks, sliced
15ml/1 tbsp chopped
  fresh thyme
30ml/2 tbsp chopped
  fresh parsley
small fresh rosemary
  sprig
600ml/1 pint/2½ cups
  veal stock
salt and ground black
  pepper

1 Preheat the oven to 170°C/325°F/Gas 3. Heat the dripping or oil in a frying pan and brown the chops and kidneys in batches, then reserve the fat.

2 In a large casserole, make alternate layers of lamb chops, kidneys, three-quarters of the potatoes and the carrots, leeks and celery, sprinkling the herbs and seasoning over each layer as you go. Tuck the rosemary sprig down the side.

3 Arrange the remaining potatoes on top. Pour over the stock, brush with the reserved fat, then cover the casserole with a tight-fitting lid and bake for 2½ hours. Increase the oven temperature to 220°C/425°F/Gas 7. Uncover and cook for a further 30 minutes.

Pork Loin with Celery

Have a change from a plain Sunday roast and try this whole loin of pork in a celery and cream sauce instead.

Serves 4

15ml/1 tbsp oil
50g/2oz/4 tbsp butter
1kg/2¼lb boned, rolled
  loin of pork, rind
  removed and trimmed
1 onion, chopped
bouquet garni
3 fresh dill sprigs
150ml/¼ pint/⅔ cup dry
  white wine
150ml/¼ pint/⅔ cup
  water

sticks from 1 celery head,
  cut into 2.5cm/1in
  lengths
25g/1oz/2 tbsp plain
  flour
150ml/¼ pint/⅔ cup
  double cream
squeeze of lemon juice
salt and ground black
  pepper
chopped fresh dill, to
  garnish

1 Heat the oil and half the butter in a heavy flameproof casserole just large enough to hold the pork and celery, then brown the pork evenly. Transfer the pork to a plate.

2 Add the onion to the casserole and cook until softened but not browned. Place the bouquet garni and the dill sprigs on the onion, then place the pork on top and add any juices from the plate. Pour the wine and water over the pork, season to taste, cover and simmer gently for 30 minutes.

3 Turn the pork, arrange the celery around it, cover again and cook for 40 minutes, until the pork and celery are tender. Transfer the pork and celery to a serving plate, cover and keep warm. Discard the bouquet garni and dill.

4 Cream the remaining butter and flour, then whisk into the cooking liquid while it is barely simmering. Cook for about 2–3 minutes, stirring occasionally. Stir the cream into the casserole, bring to the boil and add a squeeze of lemon juice.

5 Slice the pork, pour some sauce over the slices and garnish with dill. Serve with remaining sauce separately.

Spiced Lamb with Apricots

Inspired by Middle Eastern cooking, this fruity, spicy casserole is simple to make yet looks impressive.

Serves 4

115g/4oz ready-to-eat
  dried apricots
50g/2oz/scant ½ cup
  seedless raisins
2.5ml/½ tsp saffron
  strands
150ml/¼ pint/⅔ cup
  orange juice
15ml/1 tbsp red wine
  vinegar
30–45ml/2–3 tbsp olive
  oil
1.5kg/3lb leg of lamb,
  boned and diced
1 onion, chopped
2 garlic cloves, crushed
10ml/2 tsp ground
  cumin

1.25ml/¼ tsp ground
  cloves
15ml/1 tbsp ground
  coriander
25g/1oz/2 tbsp plain
  flour
600ml/1 pint/2½ cups
  lamb stock
45ml/3 tbsp chopped
  fresh coriander
salt and ground black
  pepper
saffron rice mixed with
  toasted almonds and
  chopped fresh
  coriander, to serve

1 Mix together the dried apricots, raisins, saffron, orange juice and vinegar. Cover and leave to soak for 2–3 hours.

2 Preheat the oven to 160°C/325°F/Gas 3. Heat 30ml/2 tbsp oil in a large flameproof casserole and brown the lamb in batches. Remove and set aside. Add the onion and garlic with a little more of the remaining oil and cook until softened.

3 Stir in the spices and flour and cook for 1–2 minutes more. Return the meat to the casserole. Stir in the stock, fresh coriander and the soaked fruit with its liquid. Season to taste with salt and pepper, then bring to the boil. Cover the casserole with a tight-fitting lid and cook for 1½ hours (adding extra stock if necessary), or until the lamb is tender. Serve with saffron rice mixed with toasted almonds and fresh coriander.

Beef and Mushroom Burgers

It's worth making your own burgers to cut down on fat – in these the meat is extended with mushrooms for extra fibre.

Serves 4

1 small onion, chopped
150g/5oz/2 cups small
   cup mushrooms
450g/1lb lean minced
   beef
50g/2oz/1 cup fresh
   breadcrumbs

5ml/1 tsp dried mixed
   herbs
15ml/1 tbsp tomato purée
flour, for shaping
salt and black pepper

1 Process the onion and mushrooms until finely chopped. Add the beef, breadcrumbs, herbs, tomato purée and seasoning. Process until the mixture binds but still has some texture. Divide into 8 – 10 pieces and press into burger shapes.

2 Cook the burgers in a non-stick frying pan, or under a hot grill, for 12 – 15 minutes, turning once, until evenly cooked. Serve with relish and salad, in burger buns or pitta bread.

Ruby Bacon Chops

This dish can be prepared with the minimum of effort, yet would still impress at an informal dinner party.

Serves 4

1 ruby grapefruit
4 lean bacon loin chops

45ml/3 tbsp redcurrant
   jelly
ground black pepper

1 Using a sharp knife, cut away all the peel and pith from the grapefruit. Carefully remove the segments, catching the juice in a bowl.

2 Fry the bacon chops in a non-stick frying pan without fat, turning them once, until golden. Add the reserved grapefruit juice and redcurrant jelly to the pan and stir until melted. Add the grapefruit segments, then season with pepper and serve hot with fresh vegetables.

Beef Strips with Orange and Ginger

Stir-frying is a good way of cooking with the minimum of fat. It's also one of the quickest ways to cook.

Serves 4

Place 450g/1 lb beef strips in a bowl; sprinkle over the rind and juice of 1 orange. Leave to marinate for at least 30 minutes. Drain the liquid and set aside, then mix the meat with 15ml/1 tbsp soy sauce, 5ml/1 tbsp cornflour and 2.5cm/1in root ginger. Heat 10ml/2 tsp sesame oil in a wok or large frying pan and add the beef. Stir-fry for 1 minute, add 1 carrot cut into small strips and stir-fry for a further 2 – 3 minutes. Stir in 2 sliced spring onions and the reserved liquid, then boil, stirring, until thickened.

Steak, Kidney and Mushroom Pie

If you prefer, omit the kidneys from this pie and substitute more chuck steak in their place.

Serves 4

30ml/2 tbsp sunflower oil
1 onion, chopped
115g/4oz bacon, finely chopped
500g/1¼lb chuck steak, diced
25g/1oz/2 tbsp plain flour
115g/4oz lamb's kidneys
400ml/14fl oz/1¾ cups beef stock
large bouquet garni
115g/4oz button mushrooms
225g/8oz ready-made puff pastry
beaten egg, to glaze
salt and ground black pepper

1 Preheat the oven to 160°C/325°F/Gas 3. Heat the oil in a heavy-based saucepan and cook the bacon and onion until lightly browned.

2 Toss the steak in the flour. Stir the meat into the pan in batches and cook, stirring, until browned. Toss the kidneys in flour; add to the pan with the bouquet garni. Transfer to a casserole dish then pour in the stock, cover with a tight-fitting lid and cook in the oven for 2 hours. Stir in the mushrooms and seasoning and leave to cool.

3 Preheat the oven to 220°C/425°F/Gas 7. Roll out the pastry to 2cm/¾ in larger than the top of a 1.2 litre/2 pint/5 cup pie dish. Cut off a pastry strip and then fit it around the dampened rim of the dish. Brush the pastry strip with water.

4 Tip the meat mixture into the dish. Lay the pastry over the dish, press the edges together to seal, then knock them up with the back of a knife. Make a small slit in the pastry, brush with beaten egg and bake for 20 minutes. Lower the oven temperature to 180°C/350°F/Gas 4 and bake for a further 20 minutes, until the pastry is risen, golden and crisp.

Lamb Pie with Mustard Thatch

This makes a pleasant change from a classic shepherd's pie – and it is a healthier option, as well.

Serves 4

750g/1½lb old potatoes, diced
30ml/2 tbsp skimmed milk
15ml/1 tbsp wholegrain or French mustard
450g/1lb lean minced lamb
1 onion, chopped
2 celery sticks, sliced
2 carrots, diced
150ml/¼ pint/⅔ cup beef stock
60ml/4 tbsp rolled oats
15ml/1 tbsp Worcestershire sauce
30ml/2 tbsp fresh rosemary, chopped, or 10ml/2 tsp dried rosemary
salt and ground black pepper

1 Cook the potatoes in lightly salted boiling water until tender. Drain and mash until smooth, then stir in the milk and mustard. Meanwhile, preheat the oven to 200°C/400°F/Gas 6.

2 Break up the lamb with a fork and fry without any fat in a non-stick pan until lightly browned. Add the onion, celery and carrots to the saucepan and cook for 2–3 minutes, stirring continuously.

3 Stir in the stock and rolled oats. Bring to the boil, then add the Worcestershire sauce and rosemary and season to taste with salt and pepper.

4 Turn the meat mixture into a 1.75 litre/3 pint/7½ cup ovenproof dish and spread the potato topping evenly over the top, swirling with the edge of a knife. Bake for 30–35 minutes, or until golden. Serve hot with fresh vegetables.

Sausage and Bean Ragoût

An economical and nutritious main course that children will love. Serve with garlic and herb bread, if you wish.

Serves 4

*350g/12oz/2 cups dried
  flageolet beans, soaked
  overnight*
45ml/3 tbsp olive oil
1 onion, finely chopped
2 garlic cloves, crushed
*450g/1lb good-quality
  chunky sausages,
  skinned and thickly
  sliced*
15ml/1 tbsp tomato purée
*30ml/2 tbsp chopped
  fresh parsley*
*15ml/1 tbsp chopped
  fresh thyme*
*400g/14oz can chopped
  tomatoes*
*salt and ground black
  pepper*
*chopped fresh thyme and
  parsley, to garnish*

1 Drain and rinse the soaked beans and place them in a saucepan with enough water to cover. Bring to the boil, cover the pan with a tight-fitting lid and simmer for about 1 hour, or until tender. Drain the beans and set aside.

2 Heat the oil in a frying pan and fry the onion, garlic and sausages until golden.

3 Stir in the tomato purée, tomatoes, chopped parsley and thyme. Season with salt and pepper, then bring to the boil.

4 Add the beans, then cover with a lid and cook gently for about 15 minutes, stirring occasionally, until the sausage slices are cooked through. Garnish with chopped fresh thyme and parsley and serve immediately.

Cook's Tip
*For a spicier version, add some skinned, thinly sliced
chorizo or kabanos sausage along with the flageolet
beans for the last 15 minutes of cooking.*

Peppered Steaks with Madeira

A really easy dish for special occasions. Mixed peppercorns have an excellent flavour, though black pepper will do.

Serves 4

*15ml/1 tbsp mixed dried
  peppercorns (green,
  pink and black)*
*4 fillet or sirloin steaks
  (about 175g/6oz each)*
*15ml/1 tbsp olive oil,
  plus extra oil for
  shallow frying*
1 garlic clove, crushed
60ml/4 tbsp Madeira
*90ml/6 tbsp fresh beef
  stock*
*150ml/¼ pint/⅔ cup
  double cream*
pinch of salt

1 Finely crush the peppercorns using a coffee grinder or pestle and mortar, then press them evenly on to both sides of the sirloin steaks.

2 Place the steaks in a shallow non-metallic dish, then add the olive oil, garlic and Madeira. Cover the dish and leave to marinate in a cool place for at least 4–6 hours, or preferably overnight for a more intense flavour.

3 Remove the steaks from the dish, reserving the marinade. Brush a little oil over a large heavy-based frying pan and heat until it is hot.

4 Add the steaks and cook over a high heat, according to taste. Allow about 3 minutes' cooking time per side for a medium steak or 2 minutes per side for rare. Remove the steaks from the frying pan and keep them warm.

5 Add the reserved marinade and the fresh beef stock to the pan and bring to the boil, then leave the sauce to bubble until it is well reduced.

6 Add the double cream to the pan, with salt to taste, and stir until it has slightly thickened. Serve the peppered steaks on warmed plates with the sauce.

Pork with Mozzarella and Sage

Here is a variation of the famous dish *saltimbocca alla romana* – the mozzarella adds a delicious creamy flavour.

Serves 2–3

225g/8oz pork tenderloin
1 garlic clove, crushed
75g/3oz mozzarella, cut
   into 6 slices
6 slices Parma ham
6 large sage leaves
25g/1oz/2 tbsp butter
salt and ground black
   pepper
potato wedges roasted in
   olive oil and green
   beans, to serve

1 Trim any excess fat from the pork, then cut the pork crossways into six pieces about 2.5cm/1in thick.

2 Stand each piece of tenderloin on its end and bat down with a rolling pin to flatten. Rub with garlic and set aside for 30 minutes in a cool place.

3 Place a slice of mozzarella on top of each pork steak and season with salt and pepper. Lay a slice of Parma ham on top of each, crinkling it a little to fit.

4 Press a sage leaf on to each and secure with a cocktail stick. Melt the butter in a large heavy-based frying pan and cook the pork for about 2 minutes on each side until you see the mozzarella melting. Remove the cocktail sticks and serve immediately with roasted potatoes and green beans.

Five-spice Lamb

This aromatic lamb casserole is a perfect dish to serve at an informal supper party.

Serves 4

30–45ml/2–3 tbsp oil
1.5kg/3–3½lb leg of
   lamb, boned and diced
1 onion, chopped
10ml/2 tsp grated fresh
   root ginger
1 garlic clove, crushed
5ml/1 tsp five-spice
   powder
30ml/2 tbsp hoi-sin sauce
15ml/1 tbsp soy sauce
300ml/½ pint/1¼ cups
   passata
250ml/8fl oz/1 cup lamb
   stock
1 red pepper, seeded and
   diced
1 yellow pepper, seeded
   and diced
30ml/2 tbsp chopped
   fresh coriander
15ml/1 tbsp sesame
   seeds, toasted
salt and ground black
   pepper

1 Preheat the oven to 160°C/325°F/Gas 3. In a large, flameproof casserole, heat 30ml/2 tbsp of the oil and then brown the diced lamb in batches over a high heat. Remove to a plate and set aside.

2 Add the onion, ginger and garlic to the casserole with a little more of the oil, if necessary, and cook for 5 minutes, or until softened.

3 Return the lamb to the casserole. Stir in the five-spice powder, hoi-sin sauce, soy sauce, passata and stock, and season to taste with salt and pepper. Bring to the boil, then cover with a tight-fitting lid and cook in the oven for about 1¼ hours.

4 Remove the casserole from the oven, stir in the peppers, then cover and return to the oven for a further 15 minutes, or until the lamb is very tender.

5 Sprinkle with the chopped fresh coriander and toasted sesame seeds. Serve hot accompanied by rice, if you wish.

Rich Beef Casserole

Use a full-bodied red wine such as a Burgundy to create the flavoursome sauce in this casserole.

Serves 4–6

900g/2lb chuck steak, cut
  into dice
2 onions, roughly chopped
1 bouquet garni
6 black peppercorns
15ml/1 tbsp red wine
  vinegar
1 bottle red wine
45–60ml/3–4 tbsp
  olive oil
3 celery sticks, thickly
  sliced

50g/2oz/½ cup plain flour
300ml/½ pint/1¼ cups
  beef stock
30ml/2 tbsp tomato purée
2 garlic cloves, crushed
175g/6oz chestnut
  mushrooms, halved
400g/14oz can artichoke
  hearts, drained
  and halved
chopped fresh parsley and
  thyme, to garnish

1 Combine the meat, onions, bouquet garni, peppercorns, vinegar and wine. Cover and leave to marinate overnight.

2 The next day, preheat the oven to 160°C/325°F/Gas 3. Strain the meat, reserving the marinade, and pat dry. Heat the oil in a large flameproof casserole and fry the meat and onions in batches, adding a little more oil if necessary. Remove and set aside. Add the celery and fry until browned, then remove this also and set it aside with the meat.

3 Sprinkle the flour into the casserole and cook for 1 minute. Gradually add the reserved marinade and the stock, and bring to the boil, stirring continuously. Return the meat, onions and celery to the casserole, then stir in the tomato purée and crushed garlic.

4 Cover the casserole with a tight-fitting lid and cook in the oven for about 2¼ hours. Stir in the mushrooms and artichokes, cover again and cook for a further 15 minutes, until the meat is tender. Garnish with parsley and thyme, and serve hot with creamy mashed potatoes, if you wish.

Pork Steaks with Gremolata

Gremolata is a popular Italian dressing of garlic, lemon and parsley – it adds a hint of sharpness to the pork.

Serves 4

30ml/2 tbsp olive oil
4 pork shoulder steaks
1 onion, chopped
2 garlic cloves, crushed
400g/14oz can tomatoes
30ml/2 tbsp tomato purée
150ml/¼ pint/⅔ cup dry
  white wine
bouquet garni
3 anchovy fillets, drained
  and chopped

salt and ground black
  pepper
salad leaves, to serve

For the gremolata
45ml/3 tbsp chopped
  fresh parsley
grated rind of ½ lemon
grated rind of 1 lime
1 garlic clove, chopped

1 Heat the oil in a large flameproof casserole and brown the pork steaks on both sides. Remove and set aside.

2 Add the onions to the casserole and cook until soft. Add the garlic and cook for 1–2 minutes. Chop the tomatoes and add with the tomato purée and wine. Add the bouquet garni, then boil rapidly for 3–4 minutes to reduce and thicken the sauce slightly. Return the pork to the casserole, then cover with a tight-fitting lid and cook for about 30 minutes. Stir in the chopped anchovies. Cover the casserole and cook for a further 15 minutes, or until the pork is tender.

3 Meanwhile, to make the gremolata, mix together the parsley, lemon and lime rinds and garlic.

4 Remove the pork steaks and discard the bouquet garni. Reduce the sauce over a high heat, if it is not already thick. Taste and adjust the seasoning if necessary.

5 Return the pork to the casserole, then sprinkle with the gremolata. Cover and cook for a further 5 minutes, then serve hot with salad leaves.

Beef Casserole and Dumplings

A traditional English recipe, this delicious casserole is topped with light herby dumplings for a filling meal.

Serves 4

15ml/1 tbsp oil
450g/1lb minced beef
16 button onions
2 carrots, thickly
   sliced
2 celery sticks, thickly
   sliced
25g/1oz/2 tbsp plain
   flour
600ml/1 pint/2½ cups
   beef stock

salt and ground black
   pepper

For the dumplings
115g/4oz/1 cup shredded
   vegetable suet
50g/2oz/4 tbsp plain
   flour
15ml/1 tbsp chopped
   fresh parsley

1 Preheat the oven to 180°C/350°F/Gas 4. Heat the oil in a flameproof casserole and fry the minced beef for 5 minutes until brown and sealed.

2 Add the onions; fry over a moderate heat for 5 minutes, stirring all the time.

3 Stir in the sliced carrots, the celery and the flour, then cook for a further 1 minute.

4 Add the beef stock and season to taste with salt and ground black pepper. Bring to the boil. Cover and cook in the oven for 1¼ hours.

5 For the dumplings, mix together the suet, flour and fresh parsley. Add sufficient cold water to form a smooth dough.

6 Roll the dumpling mixture into eight equal-size balls and place them around the top of the casserole. Return the casserole, uncovered, to the oven for another 20 minutes. Serve with broccoli florets, if liked.

Stilton Burgers

This tasty recipe contains a delicious surprise. The lightly melted Stilton cheese is encased in the crunchy burger.

Serves 4

450g/1lb minced beef
1 onion, finely chopped
1 celery stick, chopped
5ml/1 tsp mixed
   dried herbs
5ml/1 tsp mustard

50g/2oz/½ cup crumbled
   Stilton cheese
4 burger buns
salt and ground black
   pepper

1 Place the minced beef in a bowl with the chopped onion and celery. Mix together, then season with salt and pepper.

2 Stir in the herbs and mustard, bringing them together to form a firm mixture.

3 Divide the mixture into eight equal portions. Place four on a chopping board and flatten each one slightly.

4 Place the crumbled cheese in the centre of each.

5 Flatten the remaining mixture and place on top. Mould the mixture together, encasing the crumbled cheese, and shape into four burgers.

6 Grill under a moderate heat for 10 minutes, turning once, or until cooked through. Split the burger buns and place a burger inside each. Serve with a freshly made salad and some mustard pickle.

Cook's Tip
These burgers could be made with minced lamb or pork for a variation, but make sure they are thoroughly cooked and not pink inside.

Indian Curried Lamb Samosas

Authentic samosa pastry is rather difficult to make but these samosas work equally well using puff pastry.

Serves 4

15ml/1 tbsp oil	15ml/1 tbsp chopped fresh
1 garlic clove, crushed	coriander
175g/6oz minced lamb	225g/8oz ready-made
4 spring onions, finely	puff pastry
chopped	beaten egg, to glaze
10ml/2 tsp medium-hot	5ml/1 tsp cumin seeds
curry paste	salt and ground black
4 ready-to-eat dried	pepper
apricots, chopped	45ml/3 tbsp natural
1 small potato, diced	yogurt with chopped
10ml/2 tsp apricot chutney	fresh mint, to serve
30ml/2 tbsp frozen peas	fresh mint sprigs, to
squeeze of lemon juice	garnish

1 Preheat the oven to 220°C/425°F/Gas 7 and dampen a large non-stick baking sheet. Fry the garlic in the oil for 30 seconds, then add the lamb. Fry for about 5 minutes, stirring, until the meat is well browned.

2 Stir in the spring onion, curry paste, apricots and potato, and cook for 2–3 minutes. Then add the chutney, peas and 60ml/4 tbsp water. Cover and simmer for 10 minutes, stirring occasionally. Stir in the lemon juice and coriander, season to taste, remove and leave to cool.

3 Roll out the pastry and cut into four 15cm/6in squares. Place a quarter of the curry mixture in the centre of each square and brush the edges with beaten egg. Fold over to make a triangle and seal the edges. Knock up the edges with the back of a knife and make a small slit in the top of each.

4 Brush each samosa with beaten egg and sprinkle over the cumin seeds. Place on the damp baking sheet and bake for about 20 minutes. Serve garnished with mint sprigs and with the minty yogurt handed round separately.

Breton Pork and Bean Casserole

This is a traditional French dish, called *cassoulet*. There are many variations in the different regions of France.

Serves 4

30ml/2 tbsp olive oil	30ml/2 tbsp red wine
1 onion, chopped	15ml/1 tbsp tomato purée
2 garlic cloves, chopped	bouquet garni
450g/1lb lean shoulder of	400g/14oz can cannellini
pork, diced	beans, drained and
350g/12oz lean lamb	rinsed
(preferably leg), diced	50g/2oz/1 cup brown
225g/8oz coarse pork and	breadcrumbs
garlic sausage, cut	salt and ground black
into chunks	pepper
400g/14oz can chopped	green salad and French
tomatoes	bread, to serve

1 Preheat the oven to 160°C/325°F/Gas 3. Heat the oil in a large flameproof casserole and fry the onions and garlic until softened. Remove with a slotted spoon and reserve.

2 Add the pork, lamb and sausage chunks to the casserole and fry over a high heat until browned on all sides. Add the onions and garlic to the meat.

3 Stir in the chopped tomatoes, wine and tomato purée and add 300ml/½ pint/1¼ cups water. Season to taste with salt and pepper and add the bouquet garni. Cover and bring to the boil, then transfer the casserole to the preheated oven and cook for 1½ hours.

4 Remove the bouquet garni, stir in the beans and sprinkle the breadcrumbs over the top. Return to the oven, uncovered, for a further 30 minutes, until the top is golden brown. Serve hot with a green salad and French bread to mop up the juices.

Cook's Tip
Replace the lamb with duck breast, but be sure to drain off any fat before adding the breadcrumbs.

Pan-fried Mediterranean Lamb

The warm, summery flavours of the Mediterranean are combined for a simple weekday meal.

Serves 4

8 lean lamb cutlets
1 onion, thinly sliced
2 red peppers, seeded and
  sliced
400g/14oz can plum
  tomatoes
1 garlic clove, crushed

45ml/3 tbsp chopped
  fresh basil leaves
30ml/2 tbsp chopped
  black olives
salt and ground black
  pepper

1 Trim any excess fat from the lamb, then fry without fat in a non-stick frying pan until golden brown.

2 Add the onion and red peppers to the pan. Cook, stirring, for a few minutes to soften, then add the plum tomatoes, garlic and fresh basil leaves.

3 Cover and simmer for 20 minutes or until the lamb is tender. Stir in the olives, season to taste with salt and pepper and serve hot, with pasta if you wish.

Cook's Tip
The red peppers give this dish a slightly sweet taste. If you prefer, use green peppers for a more savoury stew.

Greek Lamb Pie

Ready-made filo pastry is so easy to use and gives a most professional look to this lamb and spinach pie.

Serves 4

sunflower oil, for
  brushing
450g/1lb minced lamb
1 onion, sliced
1 garlic clove, crushed
400g/14oz can plum
  tomatoes
30ml/2 tbsp chopped
  fresh mint

5ml/1 tsp grated nutmeg
350g/12oz young spinach
  leaves
275g/10oz packet
  ready-made filo pastry
5ml/1 tsp sesame seeds
salt and ground black
  pepper

1 Preheat the oven to 200°C/400°F/Gas 6. Lightly oil a 22cm/8½in round springform tin.

2 Fry the mince and onion without fat in a non-stick pan until golden. Add the garlic, tomatoes, mint and nutmeg and season with salt and pepper. Bring to the boil, stirring from time to time. Simmer, stirring occasionally, until most of the liquid has evaporated.

3 Wash the spinach and remove any tough stalks, then cook in only the water clinging to the leaves for about 2 minutes, until just wilted.

4 Lightly brush each sheet of filo pastry with oil and lay in overlapping layers in the tin, leaving enough overhanging to wrap over the top.

5 Spoon in the meat and spinach, then wrap the pastry over to enclose, scrunching it slightly. Sprinkle with sesame seeds and bake for about 25–30 minutes, or until golden and crisp. Serve hot, with salad or vegetables, as you wish.

Cheesy Pasta Bolognese

If you like lasagne, you will love this dish. It is especially popular with children too.

Serves 4

30ml/2 tbsp olive oil	sprig of fresh thyme
1 onion, chopped	225g/8oz/2 cups dried
1 garlic clove, crushed	penne pasta
1 carrot, diced	300ml/½ pint/1¼ cups
2 celery sticks, chopped	milk
2 rashers streaky bacon,	25g/1oz/2 tbsp butter
finely chopped	25g/1oz/2 tbsp plain flour
5 button mushrooms,	150g/5oz/1 cup diced
chopped	mozzarella cheese
450g/1lb lean minced beef	60ml/4 tbsp grated
120ml/4fl oz/½ cup red	Parmesan cheese
wine	salt and ground black
15ml/1 tbsp tomato purée	pepper
200g/7oz can chopped	fresh basil sprigs, to
tomatoes	garnish

1 Fry the onion, garlic, carrot and celery in the olive oil until softened. Add the bacon and fry for 3–4 minutes. Add the mushrooms, fry for 2 minutes, then fry the beef until brown.

2 Add the wine, tomato purée, 45ml/3 tbsp water, tomatoes and the sprig of fresh thyme. Bring to the boil, cover, and simmer for 30 minutes.

3 Preheat the oven to 200°C/400°F/Gas 6. Cook the pasta. Meanwhile, place the milk, butter and flour in a saucepan, heat gently, whisking until thickened. Stir in the mozzarella and half of the Parmesan cheeses, and season.

4 Drain the pasta and stir into the cheese sauce. Uncover the Bolognese sauce and boil rapidly for 2 minutes. Spoon the sauce into an ovenproof dish, top with the pasta mixture and sprinkle with the remaining Parmesan. Bake for 25 minutes, or until golden. Garnish with basil and serve hot.

Corned Beef and Egg Hash

This classic American hash is a popular brunch dish and should be served with chilli sauce for an authentic touch.

Serves 4

30ml/2 tbsp vegetable oil	1.5ml/¼ tsp grated
25g/1oz/2 tbsp butter	nutmeg
1 onion, finely chopped	1.5ml/¼ tsp paprika
1 small green pepper,	4 eggs
seeded and diced	salt and ground black
2 large boiled potatoes,	pepper
diced	chopped fresh parsley, to
350g/12oz can corned	garnish
beef, diced	chilli sauce, to serve

1 Heat the oil and butter together in a large frying pan and fry the onion for 5–6 minutes until softened. In a bowl, mix together the pepper, potatoes, corned beef, nutmeg and paprika; season to taste with salt and pepper. Add to the pan and toss gently to distribute the cooked onion. Press down lightly; fry over a moderate heat for 3–4 minutes, until a golden brown crust has formed on the bottom.

2 Stir the mixture through to distribute the crust, then repeat the frying twice, until the mixture is well browned.

3 Make four wells in the hash and crack an egg into each one. Cover and cook gently for about 4–5 minutes, until the egg whites are just set.

4 Sprinkle with chopped parsley and cut the hash into quarters. Serve hot with chilli sauce.

Cook's Tip
Put the can of corned beef in the fridge for about 30 minutes before using. It will firm up and you will be able to cut it into cubes more easily than if it is used at room temperature.

Best-ever American Burgers

These meaty quarter-pounders are far superior in taste and texture to anything you can buy ready-made.

Makes 4 burgers
15ml/1 tbsp vegetable oil
1 small onion, chopped
450g/1lb minced beef
1 large garlic clove, crushed
5ml/1 tsp ground cumin
10ml/2 tsp ground coriander
30ml/2 tbsp tomato purée or ketchup
5ml/1 tsp wholegrain mustard
dash of Worcestershire sauce
30ml/2 tbsp mixed chopped fresh herbs such as parsley, thyme and oregano or marjoram
15ml/1 tbsp lightly beaten egg
salt and ground black pepper
flour, for shaping
oil, for frying (optional)
mixed salad, chips and relish, to serve

1 Heat the oil in a frying pan, add the onion and cook for 5 minutes, until softened. Remove from the pan, drain on kitchen paper and leave to cool.

2 Mix together the beef, garlic, spices, tomato purée or ketchup, mustard, Worcestershire sauce, herbs, beaten egg and seasoning in a bowl. Stir in the cooled onions.

3 Sprinkle a board with flour and shape the mixture into four burgers with floured hands and a palette knife. Cover and chill in the fridge for 15 minutes.

4 Heat a little oil in a pan and fry the burgers over a moderate heat for about 5 minutes each side, depending on how rare you like them. Alternatively, cook under a moderate grill for the same time. Serve with salad, chips and relish.

Cook's Tip
If you prefer, make eight smaller burgers to serve in buns, with melted cheese and tomato slices.

Bacon and Sausage Sauerkraut

Juniper berries and crushed coriander seeds flavour this traditional dish from Alsace.

Serves 4
30ml/2 tbsp oil
1 large onion, thinly sliced
1 garlic clove, crushed
450g/1lb bottled sauerkraut, rinsed and drained
1 eating apple, cored and chopped
5 juniper berries
5 coriander seeds, crushed
450g/1lb piece of lightly smoked bacon loin roast
225g/8oz whole smoked pork sausage, pricked
175ml/6fl oz/¾ cup unsweetened apple juice
150ml/¼ pint/⅔ cup chicken stock
1 bay leaf
8 small salad potatoes

1 Preheat the oven to 180°C/350°F/Gas 4. Heat the oil in a flameproof casserole and fry the onion and garlic for about 3–4 minutes, until softened. Stir in the sauerkraut, apple, juniper berries and coriander seeds.

2 Lay the piece of bacon loin and the sausage on top of the sauerkraut, pour on the apple juice and stock, and add the bay leaf. Cover and bake in the oven for about 1 hour.

3 Remove from the oven and pop the potatoes into the casserole. Add a little more stock if necessary, cover and bake for a further 30 minutes, or until the potatoes are tender.

4 Just before serving, lift out the bacon and sausages on to a board and slice. Spoon the sauerkraut on to a warmed platter, top with the meat and surround with the potatoes.

Ginger Pork with Black Bean Sauce

Preserved black beans provide a unique flavour in this dish. Look for them in specialist Chinese food stores.

Serves 4

350g/12oz pork fillet
1 garlic clove, crushed
15ml/1 tbsp grated fresh
  root ginger
90ml/6 tbsp chicken stock
30ml/2 tbsp dry sherry
15ml/1 tbsp light soy
  sauce
5ml/1 tsp sugar
10ml/2 tsp cornflour
45ml/3 tbsp groundnut
  oil

2 yellow peppers, seeded
  and cut into strips
2 red peppers, seeded and
  cut into strips
1 bunch spring onions,
  sliced diagonally
45ml/3 tbsp preserved
  black beans, coarsely
  chopped
fresh coriander sprigs, to
  garnish

1   Cut the pork into thin slices across the grain of the meat. Put the slices into a dish and mix them with the garlic and ginger. Leave to marinate at room temperature for 15 minutes.

2   Blend together the stock, sherry, soy sauce, sugar and cornflour in a small bowl, then set the sauce mixture aside.

3   Heat the oil in a wok or large frying pan and stir-fry the marinated pork for 2–3 minutes. Add the peppers and spring onions and continue to stir-fry for a further 2 minutes.

4   Add the beans and sauce mixture and cook, stirring, until thick. Serve hot, garnished with the fresh coriander sprigs.

Cook's Tip
If you cannot find preserved black beans, use the same amount of black bean sauce instead.

Golden Pork and Apricot Casserole

The rich golden colour and warm spicy flavour of this simple casserole make it ideal for a chilly winter's day.

Serves 4

4 lean pork loin chops
1 onion, thinly sliced
2 yellow peppers, seeded
  and sliced
10ml/2 tsp medium
  curry powder
15g/½oz/1 tbsp plain
  flour

250ml/8fl oz/1 cup
  chicken stock
115g/4oz ready-to-eat
  dried apricots
30ml/2 tbsp wholegrain
  mustard
salt and ground black
  pepper

1   Trim the excess fat from the pork and fry without fat in a large heavy or non-stick saucepan until lightly browned.

2   Add the onion and yellow peppers to the pan and stir over a moderate heat for 5 minutes. Then stir in the curry powder and the flour.

3   Add the stock, stirring, then add the apricots and mustard. Cover with a tight-fitting lid and simmer for 25–30 minutes, until tender. Adjust the seasoning to taste and serve hot, with rice or new potatoes, if you wish.

Sukiyaki-style Beef

This dish incorporates all the traditional Japanese elements – meat, vegetables, noodles and beancurd.

Serves 4

450g/1lb thick rump steak
200g/7oz/3½ cups Japanese rice noodles
15ml/1 tbsp shredded suet
200g/7oz hard beancurd, cut into dice
8 shiitake mushrooms, trimmed
2 leeks, sliced into 2.5cm/1in lengths
90g/3½oz/scant 1 cup baby spinach, to serve

For the stock
15g/½oz/1 tbsp caster sugar
90ml/6 tbsp rice wine
45ml/3 tbsp dark soy sauce
120ml/4fl oz/½ cup water

1 Cut the beef into thin even-size slices.

2 Blanch the rice noodles in boiling water for 2 minutes, then strain well.

3 Mix together all the stock ingredients in a bowl.

4 Heat a wok, then add the suet. When the suet is melted, stir-fry the beef for 2–3 minutes until it is cooked, but still pink in colour.

5 Pour the stock over the beef.

6 Add the remaining ingredients and cook for 4 minutes, until the leeks are tender. Serve a selection of the different ingredients, with a few baby spinach leaves, to each person.

Cook's Tip
Add a touch of authenticity and serve this complete meal with chopsticks and a porcelain spoon to collect the stock juices.

Stir-fried Pork with Mustard

Fry the apples for this dish very carefully, because they will disintegrate if they are overcooked.

Serves 4

500g/1¼lb pork fillet
1 tart apple, such as Granny Smith
40g/1½oz/3 tbsp unsalted butter
15g/½oz/1 tbsp caster sugar
1 small onion, finely chopped
30ml/2 tbsp Calvados or brandy
15ml/1 tbsp Meaux or coarse grain mustard
15ml/¼ pint/⅔ cup double cream
30ml/2 tbsp chopped fresh parsley
salt and ground black pepper
fresh flat leaf parsley sprigs, to garnish

1 Cut the pork fillet into thin even size slices.

2 Peel and core the apple. Cut into thick slices.

3 Heat a wok, then add half the butter. When the butter is hot, add the apple slices, sprinkle over the sugar, and stir-fry for 2–3 minutes. Remove the apple and set aside. Wipe out the wok with kitchen paper.

4 Reheat the wok, then add the remaining butter and stir-fry the pork fillet and onion together for 2–3 minutes, until the pork is golden and the onion has begun to soften.

5 Stir in the Calvados or brandy and boil until it is reduced by half. Stir in the mustard.

6 Add the cream and simmer for about 1 minute, then stir in the parsley. Serve garnished with sprigs of flat leaf parsley.

Cook's Tip
If you haven't got a wok, use a large frying pan, preferably with deep, sloping sides.

Hungarian Beef Goulash

Spicy beef stew served with caraway flavoured dumplings
will satisfy even the largest appetites.

Serves 4

30ml/2 tbsp vegetable oil
1 kg/2lb braising steak,
   diced
2 onions, chopped
1 garlic clove, crushed
15g/½oz/1 tbsp plain
   flour
10ml/2 tsp paprika
5ml/1 tsp caraway seeds
400g/14oz can chopped
   tomatoes
300ml/½ pint/1¼ cups
   beef stock
1 large carrot, chopped
1 red pepper, seeded and
   chopped

soured cream, to serve
pinch of paprika, to
   garnish

For the dumplings

115g/4oz/1 cup
   self-raising flour
40g/2oz/½ cup shredded
   suet
15ml/1 tbsp chopped
   fresh parsley
2.5ml/½ tsp caraway
   seeds
salt and ground black
   pepper

1 Heat the oil in a flameproof casserole and fry the meat for
5 minutes over a high heat, stirring, until browned. Remove
with a slotted spoon. Add the onions and garlic and fry
gently for 5 minutes, until softened. Add the flour, paprika
and caraway seeds, stir and cook for 2 minutes.

2 Return the meat to the casserole; stir in the tomatoes and
stock. Bring to the boil, cover, simmer for 2 hours.

3 To make the dumplings, sift the flour and seasoning into a
bowl, add the suet, parsley, caraway seeds and about
45–60ml/3–4 tbsp water and mix to a soft dough. Divide
into eight pieces and roll into balls. Cover and reserve.

4 After 2 hours, stir the carrot and red pepper into the
goulash, and season. Drop the dumplings into the goulash,
cover and simmer for 25 minutes. Serve in bowls topped with
a spoonful of soured cream sprinkled with paprika.

Pork Satay with Peanut Sauce

These delightful little satay sticks from Thailand make a
good light meal or a drinks party snack.

Makes 8

½ small onion, chopped
2 garlic cloves, crushed
30ml/2 tbsp lemon juice
15ml/1 tbsp soy sauce
5ml/1 tsp ground
   coriander
2.5ml/½ tsp ground
   cumin
5ml/1 tsp ground turmeric
30ml/2 tbsp vegetable oil
450g/1lb pork tenderloin
fresh coriander sprigs, to
   garnish
boiled rice, to serve

For the sauce

50g/2oz creamed coconut,
   chopped
60ml/4 tbsp crunchy
   peanut butter
15ml/1 tbsp lemon juice

2.5ml/½ tsp ground
   cumin
2.5ml/½ tsp ground
   coriander
5ml/1 tsp soft brown
   sugar
15ml/1 tbsp soy sauce
1–2 dried red chillies,
   seeded and chopped
15ml/1 tbsp chopped fresh
   coriander

For the salad

½ small cucumber, peeled
   and diced
15ml/1 tbsp white wine
   vinegar
15ml/1 tbsp chopped fresh
   coriander
salt and ground black
   pepper

1 Process the first eight ingredients until smooth. Cut the
pork into strips, mix with the marinade, and chill. Preheat the
grill to hot. Thread two or three pork pieces on to each of
eight soaked skewers and grill for 2–3 minutes each side,
basting with the marinade.

2 To make the sauce, dissolve the creamed coconut in
150ml/¼ pint/⅔ cup boiling water. Put the remaining
ingredients into a saucepan, stir in the coconut, bring to the
boil, stirring, and simmer for 5 minutes.

3 Mix together all the salad ingredients. Arrange the satay
sticks on a platter, garnish with coriander sprigs and season.

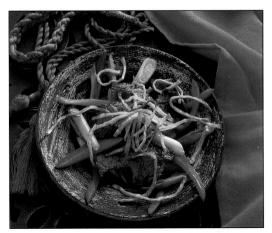

Stir-fried Pork with Lychees

No extra oil or fat is needed to cook this dish, as the pork produces enough on its own.

Serves 4

450g/1lb fatty pork,   175g/6oz lychees, peeled,
   such as belly pork,   stoned and cut into
   with the skin on or off   slivers
30ml/2 tbsp hoi-sin sauce   salt and ground black
4 spring onions, sliced   pepper
   diagonally   fresh lychees and parsley
              sprigs, to garnish

1   Cut the pork into bite-size pieces.

2   Pour the hoi-sin sauce over the pork and leave to marinate for at least 30 minutes.

3   Heat a wok, then add the pork and stir-fry for 5 minutes until crisp and golden. Add the spring onions and stir-fry for a further 2 minutes.

4   Scatter the lychee slivers over the pork, and season well with salt and pepper. Garnish with fresh lychees and fresh parsley sprigs, to serve.

Cook's Tip
Lychees have a very pretty pink skin which, when peeled, reveals a soft fleshy berry with a hard shiny stone. If you cannot buy fresh lychees, this dish can be made with drained canned lychees.

Sizzling Beef with Celeriac Straw

The crisp celeriac matchsticks look like fine pieces of straw when cooked and have a mild celery-like flavour.

Serves 4

450g/1lb celeriac   30ml/2 tbsp sherry
150ml/¼ pint/⅔ cup   vinegar
   vegetable oil   10ml/2 tsp
1 red pepper   Worcestershire sauce
6 spring onions   10ml/2 tsp tomato purée
450g/1lb rump steak   salt and ground black
60ml/4 tbsp beef stock   pepper

1   Peel the celeriac and then cut it into fine matchsticks, using a cleaver if you have one, or a large sharp knife.

2   Heat the wok, then add two-thirds of the oil. When the oil is hot, fry the celeriac matchsticks in batches until golden brown and crispy. Drain well on kitchen paper.

3   Chop the red pepper and the spring onions into 2.5cm/1in lengths, using diagonal cuts.

4   Chop the beef into strips, across the grain of the meat.

5   Heat a wok, then add the remaining oil. When the oil is hot, stir-fry the chopped spring onions and red pepper for about 2–3 minutes.

6   Add the beef strips and stir-fry for a further 3–4 minutes until well browned. Add the stock, vinegar, Worcestershire sauce and tomato purée. Season well with salt and pepper and serve with the celeriac "straw".

Cook's Tip
The Chinese use a large cleaver for preparing most vegetables. With a little practice, you will discover that it is the ideal kitchen utensil for cutting fine vegetable matchsticks and chopping thin strips of meat.

Turkish Lamb and Apricot Stew

Almond and parsley–flavoured couscous accompanies this rich stew of lamb, apricots and chick-peas.

Serves 4

1 large aubergine, diced	115g/4oz/1 cup canned
30ml/2 tbsp sunflower oil	chick-peas, drained
1 onion, chopped	5ml/1 tsp clear honey
1 garlic clove, crushed	salt and ground black
5ml/1 tsp ground	pepper
cinnamon	couscous, to serve
3 whole cloves	30ml/2 tbsp olive oil
450g/1lb boned leg of	30ml/2 tbsp chopped
lamb, diced	almonds, fried in a
400g/14oz can chopped	little oil
tomatoes	chopped fresh parsley, to
115g/4oz ready-to-eat	garnish
dried apricots	

1 Place the diced aubergine in a colander, sprinkle with salt and leave for about 30 minutes. Heat the oil in a large flameproof casserole and fry the onion and garlic for about 5 minutes, until softened but not browned.

2 Stir in the ground cinnamon and whole cloves and fry for a further 1 minute. Add the lamb and cook for 5–6 minutes more, stirring occasionally to brown the pieces evenly.

3 Rinse, drain and pat dry the aubergine with kitchen paper, add to the casserole and cook for 3 minutes, stirring well. Add the chopped tomatoes, 300ml/½ pint/1¼ cups water and the apricots, and season to taste with salt and pepper. Bring to the boil, then cover and simmer gently for about 45 minutes.

4 Stir the chick-peas and honey into the stew, then cook for a final 15–20 minutes, or until the lamb is tender. Serve the dish accompanied by couscous with the olive oil, fried almonds and chopped parsley stirred into it.

Curried Lamb and Lentils

This colourful curry is packed with protein and low in fat, and makes a flavoursome yet healthy meal.

Serves 4

8 lean boned lamb leg	475ml/16fl oz/2 cups
steaks (about 500g/	stock
1¼ lb total weight)	175g/6oz/1 cup green
1 onion, chopped	lentils
2 carrots, diced	salt and ground black
1 celery stick, chopped	pepper
15ml/1 tbsp hot curry	fresh coriander leaves, to
paste	garnish
30ml/2 tbsp tomato purée	boiled rice, to serve

1 In a large non-stick saucepan, fry the lamb steaks without fat until browned, turning once.

2 Add the vegetables and cook for 2 minutes, then stir in the curry paste, tomato purée, stock and lentils.

3 Bring to the boil, cover with a tight-fitting lid and simmer gently for 30 minutes until tender. Add some extra stock, if necessary. Season to taste and serve garnished with coriander and accompanied by rice.

Cook's Tip
Pick over the lentils carefully before adding them to the saucepan. They sometimes contain small stones which are unpleasant to find while eating a meal.

Middle-Eastern Lamb Kebabs

Skewered, grilled meats are a staple of Middle Eastern cooking. Here, marinated lamb is grilled with vegetables.

Makes 4

450g/1lb boned leg of
   lamb, diced
75ml/5 tbsp olive oil
15ml/1 tbsp chopped
   fresh oregano or
   thyme, or 10ml/2 tsp
   dried oregano
15ml/1 tbsp chopped
   fresh parsley
juice of ½ lemon

½ small aubergine,
   thickly sliced and
   quartered
4 baby onions, halved
2 tomatoes, quartered
4 fresh bay leaves
salt and ground black
   pepper
pitta bread and natural
   yogurt, to serve

1 Place the lamb in a bowl. Mix together the olive oil, oregano or thyme, parsley, lemon juice, salt and pepper. Pour over the lamb; mix well. Cover and marinate for about 1 hour.

2 Preheat the grill. Thread the marinated lamb, aubergine, onions, tomatoes and bay leaves alternately on to four large skewers. (If using wooden skewers, soak them first.)

3 Place the kebabs on a grill rack and brush the vegetables liberally with the leftover marinade. Cook the kebabs under a medium heat for about 8–10 minutes on each side, basting once or twice with the juices that have collected in the bottom of the grill pan. Serve the kebabs hot, accompanied by hot pitta bread and natural yogurt.

Cook's Tip

For a more piquant marinade, add one or two cloves of garlic, peeled and crushed.

Mexican Spiced Roast Leg of Lamb

Make sure you push the garlic slices deeply into the meat or they will burn and develop a bitter flavour.

Serves 4

1 small leg or half leg of
   lamb (about
   1.25kg/2½ lb)
15ml/1 tbsp dried
   oregano
5ml/1 tsp ground cumin
5ml/1 tsp hot chilli
   powder

2 garlic cloves
45ml/3 tbsp olive oil
30ml/2 tbsp red wine
   vinegar
salt and ground black
   pepper
fresh oregano sprigs, to
   garnish

1 Preheat the oven to 220°C/425°F/Gas 7. Place the leg of lamb on a large chopping board.

2 Place the oregano, cumin, chilli powder and one of the garlic cloves, crushed, into a bowl. Pour on half of the olive oil and mix well to form a paste. Set the paste aside.

3 Using a sharp knife, make a criss-cross pattern of fairly deep slits going through the skin and just into the meat of the leg of lamb. Press the spice paste into the meat slits with the back of a round-bladed knife. Peel and slice the remaining garlic clove thinly and cut each slice in half again. Push the pieces of garlic deeply into the slits made in the meat.

4 Mix the vinegar and remaining oil, pour over the joint and season with salt and pepper.

5 Bake for about 15 minutes at the higher temperature, then reduce the heat to 180°C/350°F/Gas 4 and cook for a further 1¼ hours (or a little longer if you like your meat well done). Serve the lamb with a delicious gravy made with the spicy pan juices and garnish with fresh oregano sprigs.

Boeuf Bourguignon

This French classic is named after the region it comes from, Burgundy, where the local red wine is used to flavour it.

Serves 4

30ml/2 tbsp olive oil
225g/8oz piece streaky bacon, diced
12 whole baby onions
900g/2lb braising steak, cut into 5cm/2in squares
1 large onion, thickly sliced
15g/½ oz/1 tbsp plain flour

about 450ml/¾ pint/1¾ cups red Burgundy wine
bouquet garni
1 garlic clove
225g/8oz button mushrooms, halved
salt and ground black pepper
chopped fresh parsley, to garnish

1 Heat the oil in a flameproof casserole and fry the bacon and baby onions for 7–8 minutes, until the onions have browned and the bacon fat is transparent. Remove with a slotted spoon and reserve.

2 Add the beef to the casserole and fry quickly on all sides until evenly browned. Add the sliced onion and continue cooking for 4–5 minutes.

3 Sprinkle over the flour and stir well. Pour over the wine and add the bouquet garni and garlic. Cover with a tightly fitting lid and simmer gently for about 2 hours. Stir in the reserved sautéed onions and bacon and add a little extra wine, if necessary.

4 Add the mushrooms. Cover again and cook for a further 30 minutes. Remove the bouquet garni and garlic and garnish with chopped fresh parsley.

Spiced Lamb Bake

A quite delicious South African shepherd's pie. The recipe was originally poached from the Afrikaners' Malay slaves.

Serves 4

15ml/1 tbsp vegetable oil
1 onion, chopped
675g/1½lb minced lamb
30ml/2 tbsp medium curry paste
30ml/2 tbsp mango chutney
30ml/2 tbsp freshly squeezed lemon juice

60ml/4 tbsp chopped, blanched almonds
30ml/2 tbsp sultanas
75g/3oz creamed coconut, crumbled
2 eggs
2 bay leaves
salt and ground black pepper

1 Preheat the oven to 180°C/350°F/Gas 4. Heat the oil in a frying pan and cook the chopped onion for 5–6 minutes, until softened but not browned.

2 Add the lamb and cook over a moderate heat, turning frequently, until browned all over. Stir in the curry paste, chutney, lemon juice, almonds and sultanas, season well with salt and pepper and cook for about 5 minutes.

3 Transfer the mixture to an ovenproof dish and cook in the oven, uncovered, for 10 minutes.

4 Meanwhile, dissolve the crumbled creamed coconut in 200ml/7fl oz/scant 1 cup boiling water and cool slightly. Beat in the eggs and a little seasoning.

5 Remove the dish from the oven and pour the coconut custard over the meat mixture. Lay the bay leaves on the top and return the dish to the oven for 30–35 minutes, or until the top is set and golden. Serve hot.

Greek Pasta Bake

Another excellent main meal (called *pastitsio* in Greece), this recipe is both economical and filling.

Serves 4
15ml/1 tbsp oil	2 large tomatoes
450g/1lb minced lamb	115g/4oz cup pasta
1 onion, chopped	shapes
2 garlic cloves, crushed	450g/1lb tub Greek-style
30ml/2 tbsp tomato purée	yogurt
25g/1oz/2 tbsp plain	2 eggs
flour	salt and ground black
300ml/½ pint/1¼ cups	pepper
lamb stock	green salad, to serve

1 Preheat the oven to 190°C/375°F/Gas 5. Heat the oil in a large saucepan and fry the lamb for 5 minutes. Add the onion and garlic and continue to fry for a further 5 minutes.

2 Stir in the tomato purée and flour. Cook for 1 minute.

3 Stir in the lamb stock and season to taste with salt and pepper. Bring to the boil and cook for 20 minutes.

4 Slice the tomatoes, place the meat in an ovenproof dish and arrange the tomatoes on top.

5 Bring a pan of salted water to the boil and cook the pasta shapes for 8–10 minutes until *al dente*. Drain well.

6 Mix together the pasta, yogurt and eggs. Spoon on top of the tomatoes and cook in the preheated oven for 1 hour. Serve hot with a crisp green salad.

Cook's Tip
Choose open pasta shapes for this dish rather than tubes so the sauce coats the pasta all over. Try shells, spirals or farfalle.

Bacon Koftas

These easy koftas are good for barbecues and summer grills, served with lots of salad.

Serves 4
225g/8oz lean smoked	finely grated rind of
back bacon, roughly	1 lemon
chopped	1 egg white
75g/3oz/1½ cups fresh	ground black pepper
wholemeal	pinch of paprika
breadcrumbs	lemon rind and fresh
2 spring onions, chopped	parsley leaves, to
15ml/1 tbsp chopped	garnish
fresh parsley	

1 Place the bacon in a food processor with the breadcrumbs, spring onions, parsley, lemon rind, egg white and pepper. Process the mixture until it is finely chopped and begins to bind together. Alternatively, use a mincer.

2 Divide the bacon mixture into eight even-size pieces and shape into long ovals around eight previously soaked wooden or bamboo skewers.

3 Sprinkle the koftas with paprika and cook under a hot grill or on a barbecue for about 8–10 minutes, turning them occasionally, until browned and cooked through. Garnish with lemon rind and parsley leaves, then serve hot with lemon rice and salad.

Cook's Tip
This is a good way to spread a little meat a long way as each portion requires only 50g/2oz bacon. Use good quality bacon, preferably dry cured, for this recipe.

Peking Beef and Pepper Stir-fry

Once the steak has marinated, this colourful dish can be prepared in just a few minutes.

Serves 4

350g/12oz rump or
  sirloin steak, sliced
  into strips
30ml/2 tbsp soy sauce
30ml/2 tbsp medium
  sherry
15ml/1 tbsp cornflour
5ml/1 tsp brown sugar
15ml/1 tbsp sunflower oil
15ml/1 tbsp sesame oil
1 garlic clove, finely
  chopped

15ml/1 tbsp grated fresh
  root ginger
1 red pepper, seeded and
  sliced
1 yellow pepper, seeded
  and sliced
115g/4oz/1 cup sugar
  snap peas
4 spring onions, cut into
  5cm/2in pieces
30ml/2 tbsp Chinese
  oyster sauce
hot noodles, to serve

1 In a bowl, mix together the steak strips, soy sauce, sherry, cornflour and brown sugar. Cover and leave to marinate for 30 minutes.

2 Heat the oils in a wok or large frying pan and stir-fry the garlic and ginger quickly for about 30 seconds. Add the peppers, sugar snap peas and spring onions and stir-fry over a high heat for 3 minutes.

3 Add the beef with the marinade juices to the wok or frying pan and stir-fry for a further 3–4 minutes.

4 Finally, pour in the oyster sauce and 60ml/4 tbsp water and stir until the sauce has thickened slightly. Serve immediately with hot noodles.

Texan Barbecued Ribs

This barbecue or oven-roast dish of pork spare ribs cooked in a sweet and sour sauce is a favourite in the United States.

Serves 4

1.5kg/3lb (about 16) lean
  pork spare ribs
1 onion, finely chopped
1 large garlic clove,
  crushed
120ml/4fl oz/½ cup
  tomato purée
30ml/2 tbsp orange juice
30ml/2 tbsp red wine
  vinegar
5ml/1 tsp mustard

10ml/2 tsp clear honey
25g/1oz/2 tbsp soft light
  brown sugar
dash of Worcestershire
  sauce
30ml/2 tbsp vegetable oil
salt and ground black
  pepper
chopped fresh parsley, to
  garnish

1 Preheat the oven to 200°C/400°F/Gas 6. Place the pork spare ribs in a large shallow roasting tin; bake for 20 minutes.

2 Meanwhile, in a saucepan mix together the onion, garlic, tomato purée, orange juice, wine vinegar, mustard, clear honey, brown sugar, Worcestershire sauce, oil and seasoning. Bring to the boil and simmer for about 5 minutes.

3 Remove the ribs from the oven and then reduce the oven temperature to 180°C/350°F/Gas 4. Spoon over half the sauce, covering the ribs well and bake for 20 minutes. Turn them over, baste with the remaining sauce and cook for about a further 25 minutes.

4 Sprinkle the spare ribs with parsley before serving and allow three or four ribs per person. Provide finger bowls for washing sticky fingers.

Skewers of Lamb with Mint

For a more substantial meal, serve these skewers on a bed of flavoured rice or couscous.

Serves 4

300ml/½ pint/1¼ cups
  Greek-style yogurt
½ garlic clove, crushed
generous pinch of saffron
  powder
30ml/2 tbsp chopped
  fresh mint
30ml/2 tbsp clear honey
45ml/3 tbsp olive oil
3 lamb neck fillets (about
  675g/1½lb total)

1 aubergine, cut into
  2.5cm/1in dice
2 small red onions,
  quartered
salt and ground black
  pepper
small fresh mint leaves,
  to garnish
mixed salad and hot pitta
  bread, to serve

1 Mix the yogurt, garlic, saffron, mint, honey, oil and pepper together in a shallow dish.

2 Trim the lamb and cut into 2.5cm/1in cubes. Add to the marinade and stir until well coated. Cover and leave to marinate for at least 4 hours, or preferably overnight.

3 Blanch the diced aubergine in a saucepan of boiling salted water for about 1–2 minutes. Drain well and then pat dry on kitchen paper.

4 Remove the diced lamb from the marinade. Thread the lamb, aubergine and onion pieces alternately on to skewers. If you are using wooden skewers, soak them in water first. This will prevent them from charring during grilling. Grill for 10–12 minutes, turning and basting occasionally with the marinade, until the lamb is tender.

5 Serve the skewers garnished with mint leaves and accompanied by a mixed salad and hot pitta bread.

Beef Stew with Red Wine

A slow-cooked casserole of tender beef in a red wine and tomato sauce, with black olives and red pepper.

Serves 6

75ml/5 tbsp olive oil
1.1kg/2½lb boned beef
  chuck, cut into
  3cm/1½in dice
1 onion, very finely
  sliced
2 carrots, chopped
45ml/3 tbsp finely
  chopped fresh parsley
1 garlic clove, chopped
1 bay leaf
a few fresh thyme sprigs
pinch of freshly ground
  nutmeg

250ml/8fl oz/1 cup red
  wine
400g/14oz can plum
  tomatoes, chopped,
  with their juice
120ml/4fl oz/½ cup beef
  or chicken stock
about 15 black olives,
  stoned and halved
salt and ground black
  pepper
1 large red pepper, cut
  into strips

1 Preheat the oven to 180°C/350°F/Gas 4. Brown the meat, in batches, in 45ml/3 tbsp of the oil in a large heavy-based flameproof casserole. Remove to a side plate as the meat is browned, and set aside until needed.

2 Add the remaining oil, the onion and carrots to the casserole. Cook over a low heat until the onion softens. Add the parsley and garlic, and cook for a further 3–4 minutes.

3 Return the meat to the casserole, raise the heat, and stir well to mix the vegetables with the meat. Stir in the bay leaf, thyme and nutmeg. Add the wine, bring to the boil and cook, stirring, for 4–5 minutes. Stir in the tomatoes, stock and olives, and mix well. Season to taste with salt and pepper. Cover the casserole with a tight-fitting lid and place in the centre of the preheated oven. Bake for 1½ hours.

4 Remove the casserole from the oven. Stir in the strips of pepper. Return the casserole to the oven and cook, uncovered, for 30 minutes more, or until the beef is tender.

Grilled Mixed Peppers

Soft smoky grilled peppers make a lovely combination with the slightly tart salsa.

Serves 4

4 medium peppers in
    different colours
45ml/3 tbsp chopped
    fresh flat-leaf parsley
45ml/3 tbsp chopped
    fresh dill
45ml/3 tbsp chopped
    fresh mint
1 small red onion, finely
    chopped
15ml/1 tbsp capers,
    coarsely chopped
50g/2oz/¼ cup Greek
    olives, pitted and
    sliced

1 fresh green chilli,
    seeded and finely
    chopped
60g/4 tbsp pistachios,
    chopped
75ml/5 tbsp extra-virgin
    olive oil
45ml/3 tbsp fresh lime
    juice
115g/4oz/½ cup
    medium-fat feta
    cheese, crumbled
25g/1oz gherkins, finely
    chopped

1 Preheat the grill. Place the whole peppers on a tray and grill until charred and blistered.

2 Place the peppers in a plastic bag and leave to cool.

3 Peel, seed and cut the peppers into even strips.

4 To make the salsa, mix all the remaining ingredients together, and stir in the pepper strips.

Vegetable and Tofu Kebabs

A colourful mixture of vegetables and tofu, skewered, glazed and grilled until tender.

Serves 4

1 yellow pepper
2 small courgettes
225g/8oz piece of
    firm tofu
8 cherry tomatoes
6 button mushrooms
15ml/1 tbsp wholegrain
    mustard

15ml/1 tbsp clear honey
30ml/2 tbsp olive oil
salt and ground black
    pepper
cooked mixed rice and
    wild rice, to serve
lime wedges and flat-leaf
    parsley, to garnish

1 Cut the pepper in half and remove the seeds. Cut each half into quarters and cut each quarter in half.

2 Top and tail the courgettes. Cut each courgette into seven or eight chunks.

3 Cut the tofu into 4cm/1½in pieces.

4 Thread the pepper pieces, courgette chunks, tofu, cherry tomatoes and mushrooms alternately on to four metal or bamboo skewers. If you are using bamboo skewers, soak them in a bowl of cold water first. This will prevent them from charring during grilling.

5 Whisk the mustard, honey and olive oil in a small bowl. Season to taste with salt and pepper.

6 Put the kebabs on to a baking sheet. Brush them with the mustard and honey glaze. Cook under the grill for 8 minutes, turning once or twice during cooking. Serve with a mixture of long grain and wild rice, and garnish with lime wedges and flat leaf parsley.

Soufflé Omelette

This delectable soufflé omelette is light and delicate enough to melt in the mouth.

Serves 1

2 eggs, separated
30ml/2 tbsp cold water
15ml/1 tbsp chopped
fresh coriander
7.5ml/½ tbsp olive oil

30ml/2 tbsp mango
chutney
25g/1oz/¼ cup grated
Jarlsberg cheese
salt and ground black
pepper

1 Beat the egg yolks together with the cold water, coriander and salt and pepper.

2 Whisk the egg whites until stiff peaks form and gently fold into the egg yolk mixture.

3 Heat the oil in a frying pan, pour in the egg mixture and reduce the heat. Do not stir. Cook until the omelette becomes puffy and golden brown on the underside (carefully lift one edge with a palette knife to check).

4 Spoon on the chutney and sprinkle on the Jarlsberg. Fold over and slide on to a warm plate. Eat immediately. (If preferred, before adding the chutney and cheese, place the pan under a hot grill to set the top.)

Cook's Tip
A light hand is essential to the success of this dish. Do not overmix the egg whites into the egg yolks or the mixture will be heavy.

Cheesy Bubble and Squeak

This London breakfast dish was originally made on Mondays with leftover vegetables from the Sunday lunch.

Serves 4

about 450g/1lb/3 cups
mashed potato
about 225g/8oz/4 cups
shredded cooked
cabbage or kale
1 egg, beaten
115g/4oz/1 cup grated
Cheddar cheese

pinch of freshly grated
nutmeg
salt and ground black
pepper
plain flour, for coating
oil, for frying

1 Mix the potatoes with the cabbage or kale, egg, cheese, nutmeg and seasoning. Divide and shape into eight patties.

2 Chill in the fridge for an hour or so, if possible, as this enables the mixture to become firm and makes it easier to fry. Toss the patties in the flour. Heat about 1cm/½in oil in a frying pan until it is quite hot.

3 Carefully slide the patties into the oil and fry on each side for about 3 minutes until golden and crisp. Drain on kitchen paper and serve hot and crisp.

Aubergine and Red Pepper Pâté

This simple pâté of baked aubergine, pink peppercorns and red peppers has more than a hint of garlic.

Serves 4

3 aubergines
2 fresh large red
   peppers
5 garlic cloves,
   unpeeled

7.5ml/1½ tsp pink
   peppercorns in brine,
   drained and crushed
30ml/2 tbsp chopped
   fresh coriander

1 Preheat the oven to 200°C/400°F/Gas 6. Arrange the whole aubergines, peppers and garlic cloves on a baking sheet and place in the oven. After 10 minutes remove the garlic cloves and turn over the aubergines and peppers.

2 Peel the garlic cloves and place in the bowl of a blender or food processor.

3 After a further 20 minutes remove the blistered and charred peppers from the oven and place in a plastic bag. Leave to cool.

4 After a further 10 minutes take out the aubergines. Split in half and scoop the flesh into a sieve placed over a bowl. Press the flesh with a spoon to remove the bitter juices.

5 Add the mixture to the garlic and process until smooth. Place in a large mixing bowl.

6 Peel and chop the red peppers and stir into the aubergine mixture. Mix in the pink peppercorns and chopped fresh coriander and serve at once.

Cook's Tip
Serve the pâté with Melba toast, if you like. Simply grill some slices of crustless white bread on both sides, being careful to remove any loose crumbs, then slice the crispy golden toasts horizontally.

Red Pepper Watercress Parcels

The peppery watercress flavour combines well with sweet red pepper in these crisp little filo pastry parcels.

Makes 8

3 red peppers
175g/6oz watercress
225g/8oz 1 cup ricotta
   cheese
50g/2oz/¼ cup toasted,
   chopped almonds

8 sheets filo pastry,
   thawed if frozen
30ml/2 tbsp olive oil
salt and ground black
   pepper

1 Preheat the oven to 190°C/375°F/Gas 5. Place the peppers under a hot grill until blistered and charred. Place in a plastic bag. When cool enough to handle, peel, seed and pat dry on kitchen paper.

2 Place the peppers and watercress in a food processor and pulse until coarsely chopped. Spoon into a bowl.

3 Mix in the ricotta and almonds, and season to taste with salt and pepper.

4 Working with one sheet of filo pastry at a time, cut out two 18cm/7in and two 5cm/2in squares from each sheet. Brush one large square with a little olive oil and place a second large square at an angle of 45 degrees to form a star shape.

5 Place one of the small squares in the centre of the star shape, brush lightly with olive oil and top with a second small square.

6 Top with one-eighth of the red pepper mixture. Bring the edges together to form a purse shape and twist to seal. Place on a lightly greased baking sheet and cook for 25–30 minutes until golden. Serve immediately.

Nutty Cheese Balls

An extremely quick and simple recipe. Try making a small version to serve as canapés at a drinks party.

Serves 4

225g/8oz/1 cup low-fat
  soft cheese such as
  Quark
50g/2oz/¹⁄₂ cup dolcelatte
  cheese
15ml/1 tbsp finely
  chopped onion
15ml/1 tbsp finely
  chopped celery stick
15ml/1 tbsp finely
  chopped fresh parsley

15ml/1 tbsp finely
  chopped gherkin
5ml/1 tsp brandy or port
  (optional)
pinch of paprika
50g/2oz/¹⁄₂ cup walnuts,
  roughly chopped
90ml/6 tbsp snipped
  fresh chives
salt and ground black
  pepper

1 Beat the soft cheese and dolcelatte together using a spoon, until quite smooth.

2 Mix in all the remaining ingredients, except the snipped chives, stirring well to combine.

3 Divide the mixture into 12 pieces and roll into balls.

4 Roll each ball gently in the snipped chives. Leave to chill in the fridge for about an hour before serving.

Cook's Tip
For an alternative look, mix the chives with the rest of the ingredients but omit the walnuts. Instead, chop the walnuts finely and use to roll on to the cheese balls.

Fried Tomatoes with Polenta Crust

This recipe works well with green tomatoes freshy picked from the garden or greenhouse.

Serves 4

4 large firm under-ripe
  tomatoes
115g/4oz/1 cup polenta
  or coarse cornmeal
5ml/1 tsp dried oregano
  or marjoram

2.5ml/¹⁄₂ tsp garlic
  powder
plain flour, for dredging
1 egg, beaten with
  seasoning
oil, for deep-frying

1 Cut the tomatoes into thick slices. Mix the polenta or cornmeal with the oregano or marjoram and garlic powder.

2 Put the flour, egg and polenta into different bowls. Dip the tomato slices into the flour, then into the egg and finally into the polenta or cornmeal.

3 Fill a shallow frying pan one-third full of oil and heat steadily until quite hot.

4 Slip the tomato slices into the oil carefully, a few at a time, and fry on each side until crisp. Remove and drain. Repeat with the remaining tomatoes, reheating the oil in between each batch. Serve with salad.

Cannellini Bean Purée

The slightly bitter radicchio and chicory make a wonderful marriage with the creamy citrus bean purée.

Serves 4

400g/14oz can cannellini beans
45ml/3 tbsp low-fat fromage blanc
finely grated rind and juice of 1 large orange
15ml/1 tbsp finely chopped fresh rosemary
4 heads of chicory
2 radicchio
15ml/1 tbsp walnut oil

1 Drain the beans, rinse, and drain again. Purée the beans in a food processor or blender with the fromage blanc, half the orange rind, orange juice and rosemary. Set aside.

2 Cut the heads of chicory in half lengthways.

3 Cut each radicchio into eight wedges.

4 Lay out the chicory and radicchio on a baking sheet and brush with walnut oil. Grill for 2–3 minutes. Serve with the purée and scatter over the remaining orange rind.

Cook's Tip
Substitute different beans for the cannellini beans, if you like. Try haricot, mung or broad beans instead.

Broccoli and Chestnut Terrine

Served hot or cold, this versatile terrine is just as suitable for a dinner party as for a picnic.

Serves 4–6

450g/1lb/4 cups broccoli florets
225g/8oz/2 cups cooked chestnuts, roughly chopped
50g/2oz/1 cup fresh wholemeal breadcrumbs
60ml/4 tbsp low-fat natural yogurt
30ml/2 tbsp finely grated Parmesan cheese
2 eggs, beaten
salt, freshly grated nutmeg and ground black pepper

1 Preheat the oven to 180°C/350°F/Gas 4. Base-line a 900g/2lb loaf tin with non-stick baking paper.

2 Blanch or steam the broccoli for 3–4 minutes until just tender. Drain well. Reserve a quarter of the smallest florets and chop the rest finely.

3 Mix together the chestnuts, breadcrumbs, yogurt and Parmesan, and season to taste with salt and pepper.

4 Fold in the chopped broccoli, reserved florets and the beaten eggs.

5 Spoon the broccoli mixture into the prepared tin.

6 Place in a roasting tin and pour in boiling water to come halfway up the sides of the loaf tin. Bake for 20–25 minutes. Remove from the oven and tip out on to a plate or tray. Serve cut into even slices.

Cook's Tip
If you do not have a non-stick loaf tin, grease it lightly with olive or sunflower oil after base-lining.

Baked Squash with Parmesan

Spaghetti squash is an unusual vegetable – when baked, the flesh separates into long strands.

Serves 2

1 spaghetti squash	1 shallot, chopped
115g/4oz/½ cup butter	5ml/1 tsp lemon juice
45ml/3 tbsp mixed	50g/2oz/scant ¾ cup
chopped fresh herbs	freshly grated
such as parsley, chives	Parmesan cheese
and oregano	salt and ground black
1 garlic clove, crushed	pepper

1 Preheat the oven to 180°C/350°F/Gas 4. Cut the squash in half lengthways. Place the halves, cut-side down, in a roasting tin. Pour a little water around them, then bake for about 40 minutes, until tender.

2 Meanwhile, put the butter, herbs, garlic, shallot and lemon juice in a food processor or blender and process until thoroughly blended and creamy in consistency. Season to taste with salt and pepper.

3 When the squash is tender, scrape out any seeds and cut a thin slice from the base of each half, so that they will sit level. Place the squash halves on warmed serving plates.

4 Using a fork, pull out a few of the spaghetti-like strands in the centre of each. Add a dollop of herb butter, then sprinkle with a little of the grated Parmesan. Serve the remaining herb butter and Parmesan separately, adding them as you pull out more strands.

Asparagus Rolls with Herb Sauce

For a taste sensation, try tender asparagus spears wrapped in crisp filo pastry served with a buttery herb sauce.

Serves 2

50g/2oz/4 tbsp butter	175g/6oz/¾ cup butter,
5 sheets filo pastry	softened
10 asparagus spears	15ml/1 tbsp chopped
	fresh herbs
For the sauce	salt and ground black
2 shallots, finely chopped	pepper
1 bay leaf	snipped fresh chives, to
150ml/¼ pint/⅔ cup dry	garnish
white wine	

1 Preheat the oven to 200°C/400°F/Gas 6. Melt the butter. Cut the filo pastry sheets in half. Brush a half sheet with melted butter. Fold one corner of the sheet down to the bottom edge to give a wedge shape.

2 Trim the asparagus, then lay a spear on top at the longest pastry edge and roll up towards the shortest edge. Make nine more rolls in the same way.

3 Lay the rolls on a greased baking sheet. Brush with the remaining melted butter. Bake in the preheated oven for about 8 minutes until golden.

4 Meanwhile, put the shallots, bay leaf and wine into a saucepan. Cover with a tight-fitting lid and cook over a high heat until the wine is reduced to 45–60ml/3–4 tbsp.

5 Strain the wine mixture into a bowl. Whisk in the butter, a little at a time, until the sauce is smooth and glossy.

6 Stir in the herbs and season to taste with salt and pepper. Return to the pan and keep the sauce warm. Serve the rolls on individual plates with a salad garnish, if liked. Serve the butter sauce separately, sprinkled with a few snipped chives.

Multi-mushroom Stroganoff

A pan-fry of sliced mushrooms swirled with soured cream makes a delicious accompaniment to pasta or rice.

Serves 3–4

45ml/3 tbsp olive oil
450g/1lb fresh mixed
  wild and cultivated
  mushrooms such as
  ceps, shiitakes or
  oysters, sliced
3 spring onions, sliced
2 garlic cloves, crushed
30ml/2 tbsp dry sherry or
  vermouth

300ml/½ pint/1¼ cups
  soured cream or crème
  fraîche
15ml/1 tbsp chopped
  fresh marjoram or
  thyme leaves
chopped fresh parsley, to
  garnish

1 Heat the oil in a large frying pan and fry the mushrooms gently, stirring them from time to time until they are softened and just cooked.

2 Add the spring onions, garlic and sherry or vermouth and cook for 1 minute more. Season well with salt and pepper.

3 Stir in the soured cream or crème fraîche and heat to just below boiling. Stir in the marjoram or thyme, then scatter over the parsley. Serve with rice, pasta or boiled new potatoes.

Cook's Tip
To create the most interesting flavour in this dish, use at least three different varieties of mushroom, preferably incorporating some woodland or wild mushrooms.

Ratatouille with Cheese Croûtons

Crunchy croûtons and creamy Camembert provide a tasty topping on hot, bought or home-made ratatouille.

Serves 2

3 thick slices white bread
225g/8oz firm
  Camembert cheese
60ml/4 tbsp olive oil

1 garlic clove, chopped
400g/14oz can ratatouille
fresh parsley sprigs, to
  garnish

1 Trim the crusts from the bread slices and discard. Cut the bread into 2.5cm/1in squares. Cut the Camembert cheese into 2.5cm/1in cubes.

2 Heat 45ml/3 tbsp of the oil in a frying pan and cook the bread over a high heat for 5 minutes, stirring constantly, until golden all over. Reduce the heat, add the garlic and cook for 1 minute more. Remove the croûtons with a slotted spoon.

3 Tip the ratatouille into a saucepan and place over a moderate heat, stirring occasionally, until hot.

4 Heat the remaining oil in the frying pan. Add the cheese cubes and sear over a high heat for 1 minute. Divide the hot ratatouille between two serving bowls, spoon the croûtons and cheese on top, garnish with parsley and serve at once.

Tofu and Crunchy Vegetables

High protein tofu is nicest if marinated lightly before it is cooked. If you use the smoked tofu, it's even tastier.

Serves 4

2 x 225g/8oz packets
   smoked tofu, diced
45ml/3 tbsp soy sauce
30ml/2 tbsp dry sherry or
   vermouth
15ml/1 tbsp sesame oil
45ml/3 tbsp groundnut
   or sunflower oil
2 leeks, thinly sliced
2 carrots, cut into sticks

1 large courgette, thinly
   sliced
115g/4oz baby corn,
   halved
115g/4oz button or
   shiitake mushrooms,
   sliced
15ml/1 tbsp sesame seeds
1 packet egg noodles,
   cooked

1 Marinate the tofu in the soy sauce, sherry or vermouth and sesame oil for at least 30 minutes. Drain and reserve the marinade for later.

2 Heat the groundnut or sunflower oil in a wok and stir-fry the tofu cubes until browned all over. Remove and reserve.

3 Stir-fry the leeks, carrots, courgette and baby corn, stirring and tossing for about 2 minutes. Add the mushrooms and cook for a further 1 minute.

4 Return the tofu to the wok and pour in the marinade. Heat until bubbling, then scatter over the sesame seeds.

5 Serve as soon as possible with the hot cooked noodles, dressed in a little sesame oil, if you wish.

Cook's Tip
The actual cooking of this dish takes just a few minutes, so have all the ingredients prepared before you start.

Sprouting Beans and Pak Choi

Supermarkets are becoming more cosmopolitan and many stock fresh ethnic vegetables.

Serves 4

45ml/3 tbsp groundnut
   oil
3 spring onions, sliced
2 garlic cloves, cut into
   slivers
2.5cm/1in piece fresh root
   ginger, cut into slivers
1 carrot, cut into thick
   sticks
150g/5oz/scant 1 cup
   sprouting beans
   (lentils, mung beans,
   chick-peas)
200g/7oz pak choi
   cabbage, shredded

50g/2oz/½ cup unsalted
   cashew nuts or halved
   almonds

For the sauce
45ml/3 tbsp light soy
   sauce
30ml/2 tbsp dry sherry
15ml/1 tbsp sesame oil
150ml/¼ pint/⅔ cup cold
   water
5ml/1 tsp cornflour
5ml/1 tsp clear honey
salt and ground black
   pepper

1 Heat the groundnut oil in a large wok and stir-fry the onions, garlic, ginger and carrot for 2 minutes. Add the sprouting beans and fry for another 2 minutes, stirring and tossing all the ingredients together.

2 Add the pak choi and cashew nuts or almonds and stir-fry until the cabbage leaves are just wilting. Quickly mix all the sauce ingredients together in a jug and pour them, stirring all the time, into the wok.

3 The vegetables will be coated in a thin glossy sauce. Season with salt and pepper and serve as soon as possible.

Cook's Tip
If you cannot find pak choi, use Chinese cabbage instead and prepare and cook in the same way.

Tomato Omelette Envelopes

These delicious chive omelettes are folded and filled with tomato and melting Camembert cheese.

Serves 2
1 small onion
4 tomatoes
30ml/2 tbsp vegetable oil
4 eggs
30ml/2 tbsp snipped
    fresh chives

115g/4oz Camembert
    cheese, rinded and
    diced
salt and ground black
    pepper

1 Cut the onion in half. Cut each half into thin wedges. Cut the tomatoes into wedges of similar size.

2 Heat 15ml/1 tbsp of the oil in a frying pan and cook the onion for 2 minutes over a moderate heat, then raise the heat and add the tomatoes. Cook for a further 2 minutes, then remove the pan from the heat.

3 Beat the eggs with the chives in a bowl. Season to taste with salt and pepper. Heat the remaining oil in an omelette pan. Add half the egg mixture and tilt the pan to spread thinly. Cook for 1 minute.

4 Flip the omelette over and cook for 1 minute more. Remove from the pan and keep hot. Make a second omelette with the remaining egg mixture.

5 Return the tomato mixture to a high heat. Add the cheese and toss the mixture over the heat for 1 minute.

6 Divide the mixture between the omelettes and fold them over. Serve at once. Add crisp lettuce leaves and chunks of granary bread, if you wish.

Cook's Tip
Add a few sliced mushrooms to the filling, if you wish, or use them in place of the tomatoes for a change.

Curried Eggs

Hard-boiled eggs are served on a mild creamy sauce base with just a hint of curry.

Serves 2
4 eggs
15ml/1 tbsp sunflower oil
1 small onion, chopped
2.5cm/1in piece of fresh
    root ginger, peeled and
    grated
2.5ml/½ tsp ground
    cumin
2.5ml/½ tsp garam
    masala
22.5ml/1½ tbsp tomato
    purée

10ml/2 tsp tandoori paste
10ml/2 tsp freshly
    squeezed lemon juice
50ml/2fl oz/¼ cup single
    cream
15ml/1 tbsp finely
    chopped fresh
    coriander
salt and ground black
    pepper
fresh coriander sprigs, to
    garnish

1 Put the eggs in a saucepan of water. Bring to the boil, lower the heat and simmer for 10 minutes.

2 Meanwhile, heat the oil in a frying pan and cook the onion for 2–3 minutes. Add the fresh root ginger and cook for a further 1 minute.

3 Stir in the ground cumin, garam masala, tomato purée, tandoori paste, lemon juice and cream. Cook for 1–2 minutes more, then stir in the coriander. Season with salt and pepper.

4 Drain the eggs, remove the shells and cut each egg in half. Spoon the sauce into a serving bowl, top with the eggs and garnish with fresh coriander. Serve at once.

Cook's Tip
If you store your eggs in the fridge, make sure you allow them to come to room temperature before you boil them. This way, they are less likely to crack.

Potatoes with Blue Cheese

We are so used to eating potatoes as a side dish, we tend to forget they can make a good main meal too, as here.

Serves 4

450g/1lb small new
  potatoes
small head of celery,
  sliced
small red onion, thinly
  sliced
115g/4oz blue cheese,
  mashed

150ml/¼ pint/⅔ cup
  single cream
salt and ground black
  pepper
90g/3½oz/scant 1 cup
  walnut pieces
30ml/2 tbsp chopped
  fresh parsley

1 Cover the potatoes with water and then boil for about 15 minutes, adding the sliced celery and onion to the pan for the last 5 minutes or so.

2 Drain the vegetables and put them into a shallow serving dish, making sure they are evenly distributed.

3 In a small saucepan slowly melt the cheese in the cream, stirring occasionally. Do not allow the mixture to boil but heat it until it scalds.

4 Season the sauce to taste. Pour it over the vegetables and scatter the walnuts and parsley over the top. Serve hot.

Cook's Tip
Choose any blue cheese you like, such as Stilton, Danish blue, blue vinney or blue brie.

Greek Spinach and Cheese Pies

These individual spinach, feta and Parmesan cheese pies are easy to make using ready-made filo pastry.

Makes 4

15ml/1 tbsp olive oil
1 small onion, finely
  chopped
275g/10oz/2½ cups fresh
  spinach, stalks
  removed
50g/2oz/4 tbsp butter,
  melted
4 sheets filo pastry

1 egg
large pinch of freshly
  grated nutmeg
75g/3oz/¾ cup crumbled
  feta cheese
15ml/1 tbsp grated
  Parmesan cheese
salt and ground black
  pepper

1 Preheat the oven to 190°C/375°F/Gas 5. Fry the onion in the oil for 5–6 minutes, until softened. Add the spinach leaves and cook, stirring, until the spinach has wilted and some of the liquid evaporated. Leave to cool.

2 Brush four 10cm/4in diameter loose-based tartlet tins with melted butter. Cut two sheets of filo into eight 14cm/4½in squares each. Cover the remaining sheets with a dish towel.

3 Brush four squares at a time with melted butter. Line the first tartlet tin with one square, gently easing it into the base and up the sides. Leave the edges overhanging. Lay the remaining squares on top of the first, turning them so the corners form a star shape. Repeat for the remaining tins.

4 Beat the egg with the nutmeg and seasoning, then stir in the cheeses and spinach. Divide the mixture between the tins and smooth level. Fold the overhanging over the filling.

5 Cut the third pastry sheet into eight 10cm/4in rounds. Brush with butter and place two on top of each tartlet. Press around the edges to seal. Brush the last pastry sheet with butter and cut into strips. Gently twist each strip and lay them on top of the tartlets. Bake for about 30–35 minutes, until golden. Serve hot or cold.

Chilli Beans with Basmati Rice

Red kidney beans, chopped tomatoes and hot chilli make a
great combination in this colourful, flavoursome dish.

Serves 4

350g/12oz/2 cups
  basmati rice
30ml/2 tbsp olive oil
1 large onion, chopped
1 garlic clove, crushed
15ml/12 tbsp hot chilli
  powder
15g/½oz/1 tbsp plain
  flour
15ml/1 tbsp tomato purée

400g/14oz can chopped
  tomatoes
400g/14oz can red kidney
  beans, drained
150ml/¼ pint/⅔ cup hot
  vegetable stock
chopped fresh parsley, to
  garnish
salt and ground black
  pepper

1 Wash the rice several times under cold running water.
Drain well. Bring a large saucepan of water to the boil. Add
the rice and cook for 10–12 minutes, until tender. Meanwhile,
heat the oil in a frying pan and cook the chopped onion and
garlic for about 2 minutes.

2 Stir the chilli powder and flour into the onion and garlic
mixture. Cook for 2 minutes more, stirring frequently.

3 Stir in the tomato purée and chopped tomatoes. Rinse and
drain the kidney beans well and add to the pan with the hot
vegetable stock. Cover and cook for a final 12 minutes,
stirring from time to time.

4 Season the chilli sauce to taste with salt and pepper. Drain
the rice and serve at once with the chilli beans, garnished with
a little chopped fresh parsley.

Cook's Tip
*Serve the chilli beans with a pasta of your choice or hot
pitta bread, if you prefer.*

Lentil Stir-fry

Mushrooms, artichoke hearts, sugar snap peas and green
lentils make a satisfying stir-fry supper.

Serves 2–3

115g/4oz/1 cup
  sugar snap peas
25g/1oz/2 tbsp butter
1 small onion, chopped
115g/4oz cup brown cap
  mushrooms, sliced
400g/14oz can artichoke
  hearts, drained and
  halved

400g/14oz can green
  lentils, drained
60ml/4 tbsp single cream
25g/1oz/¼ cup flaked
  almonds, toasted
salt and ground black
  pepper
French bread, to serve

1 Bring a saucepan of salted water to the boil, add the sugar
snap peas and cook for about 4 minutes until just tender.
Drain, refresh under cold running water, then drain again. Pat
the peas dry with kitchen paper and set aside.

2 Melt the butter in a frying pan and cook the chopped
onion for 2–3 minutes, stirring occasionally.

3 Add the sliced mushrooms to the onions. Stir until well
combined, then cook for 2–3 minutes until just tender. Add
the artichoke hearts, sugar snap peas and lentils to the pan.
Stir-fry for 2 minutes.

4 Stir in the cream and almonds and cook for 1 minute.
Season to taste with salt and pepper. Serve at once, with
chunks of French bread.

Cook's Tip
*Use dried green lentils if you prefer. Cook them
according to the manufacturer's instructions first and
then add them to the stir-fry with the artichokes and
sugar snap peas.*

Arabian Spinach

Stir-fry spinach with onions and spices, then mix in a can of chick-peas and you have a quick, delicious main meal.

Serves 4

30ml/2 tbsp olive or
   sunflower oil
1 onion, sliced
2 garlic cloves, crushed
400g/14oz/3½ cups
   spinach, washed and
   shredded

5ml/1 tsp cumin seeds
425g/15oz can
   chick-peas, drained
knob of butter
salt and ground black
   pepper

1 Heat the oil in a large frying pan or wok and fry the onion for about 5 minutes until softened. Add the garlic and cumin seeds, then fry for another minute.

2 Add the spinach, in stages, stirring until the leaves begin to wilt. Fresh spinach leaves condense down dramatically on cooking and they will all fit into the pan.

3 Stir in the chick-peas, butter and season with salt and pepper. Reheat until just bubbling, then serve hot. Drain off any pan juices, if you wish, but this dish is rather good served with a little sauce.

Courgettes en Papillote

An impressive dinner party accompaniment, these puffed paper parcels should be broken open at the table.

Serves 4

2 courgettes
1 leek
225g/8oz young
   asparagus, trimmed
4 tarragon sprigs

4 garlic cloves, unpeeled
1 egg, beaten
salt and ground black
   pepper

1 Preheat the oven to 200°C/400°F/Gas 6. Using a potato peeler, slice the courgettes lengthways into thin strips.

2 Cut the leek into very fine julienne strips and cut the asparagus evenly into 5cm/2in lengths.

3 Cut out four sheets of greaseproof paper measuring about 30 x 38cm/12 x 15in and fold in half. Draw a large curve to make a heart shape when unfolded. Cut along the inside of the line and open out.

4 Divide the courgettes, asparagus and leek evenly between each paper heart, positioning the filling on one side of the fold line, and topping each with a sprig of fresh tarragon and an unpeeled garlic clove. Season to taste with salt and pepper.

5 Brush the edges lightly with the beaten egg and fold over.

6 Pleat the edges together so that each parcel is completely sealed. Lay the parcels on a baking sheet and cook for about 10 minutes. Serve immediately.

Cook's Tip
Experiment with other vegetables and herbs such as sugar snap peas and mint, or baby carrots and rosemary. The possibilities are endless.

Green Lentil and Cabbage Salad

This warm crunchy salad makes a satisfying meal if served with crusty French bread or wholemeal rolls.

Serves 4–6

225g/8oz/1 cup Puy
  lentils
1.3 litres/2¼ pints/6 cups
  cold water
1 garlic clove
1 bay leaf
1 small onion, peeled and
  studded with 2 cloves
15ml/1 tbsp olive oil
1 red onion, finely sliced

2 garlic cloves, crushed
15ml/1 tbsp thyme leaves
350g/12oz/6 cups finely
  shredded cabbage
finely grated rind and
  juice of 1 lemon
15ml/1 tbsp raspberry
  vinegar
salt and ground black
  pepper

1 Rinse the lentils in cold water and place in a large saucepan with the water, peeled garlic clove, bay leaf and clove-studded onion. Bring to the boil and cook for about 10 minutes. Reduce the heat, cover the pan with a tight-fitting lid and simmer gently for 15–20 minutes. Drain and remove the onion, garlic and bay leaf.

2 Heat the oil in a large pan and cook the red onion, garlic and thyme for 5 minutes until softened.

3 Add the shredded cabbage and cook for 3–5 minutes until just cooked but still crunchy.

4 Stir in the cooked lentils, grated lemon rind and juice and the raspberry vinegar. Season with salt and pepper and serve.

Cook's Tip
Vary the type of cabbage you use in this recipe, if you like. Choose a white cabbage or a Savoy, or try fresh spring greens instead.

Tomato and Basil Tart

You could make individual tartlets instead of one large tart if you prefer, but reduce the baking time slightly.

Serves 6–8

175g/6oz/1½ cups flour
2.5ml/½ tsp salt
115g/4oz/½ cup butter or
  margarine, chilled
45–75ml/3–5 tbsp water
30ml/2 tbsp extra virgin
  olive oil

For the filling
175g/6oz mozzarella
  cheese, thinly sliced

12 fresh basil leaves,
  6 roughly torn
4–5 tomatoes, cut into
  5mm/¼ in slices
salt and ground black
  pepper
60ml/4 tbsp freshly
  grated Parmesan
  cheese

1 Place the flour and salt in a bowl, then rub in the butter until the mixture resembles breadcrumbs. Add 45ml/3 tbsp water and combine with a fork until the dough holds together. Mix in more water if needed. Gather the dough into a ball, wrap in greaseproof paper and chill for 40 minutes. Preheat the oven to 190°C/375°F/Gas 5.

2 Roll out the pastry to a thickness of 5mm/¼in and use to line a 28cm/11in fluted loose-bottomed flan tin. Prick the base and chill for 20 minutes in the fridge.

3 Line the pastry with a sheet of baking parchment. Fill with dried beans. Place the flan tin on a baking sheet; bake blind for 15 minutes. Remove from the oven. Leave the oven on.

4 Remove the beans and paper. Brush the pastry with oil. Line with the mozzarella. Sprinkle the torn basil over the top.

5 Arrange the tomato slices over the cheese. Dot with the whole basil leaves. Season with salt and pepper, Parmesan and oil. Bake for 35 minutes. If the cheese exudes a lot of liquid during baking, tilt the tin and spoon it off to keep the pastry crisp. Serve hot or at room temperature.

Spinach and Potato Galette

**Creamy layers of potato, spinach and fresh herbs make a
warming and filling supper dish.**

Serves 6
*900g/2lb large potatoes
450g/1lb/4 cups fresh
    spinach
400g/14oz/1¾ cups low-
    fat cream cheese
15ml/1 tbsp grainy
    mustard*

*2 eggs
50g/2oz mixed chopped
    fresh herbs such as
    chives, parsley, chervil
    or sorrel
salt and ground black
    pepper*

1 Preheat the oven to 180°C/350°F/Gas 4. Base-line a deep
23cm/9in round cake tin with non-stick baking paper. Place
the potatoes in a large saucepan and cover with cold water.
Bring to the boil and cook for 10 minutes. Drain well and
allow to cool slightly before slicing thinly.

2 Wash the spinach and place in a large pan with only the
water that is clinging to the leaves. Cover and cook, stirring
once, until the spinach has just wilted. Drain well in a sieve
and squeeze out the excess moisture with the back of a spoon.
Chop the spinach finely.

3 Beat together the cream cheese, mustard and eggs, then
stir in the chopped spinach and fresh herbs.

4 Place a layer of the sliced potatoes in the lined tin,
arranging them in concentric circles. Top with a spoonful of
the cream cheese mixture and spread out. Continue layering,
seasoning with salt and pepper as you go, until all the
potatoes and the cream cheese mixture are used up.

5 Cover the tin with a piece of foil, scrunched around the
edge, and place in a roasting tin.

6 Half-fill the roasting tin with boiling water and cook the
galette in the oven for 45–50 minutes. Turn out on to a plate
and serve hot or cold.

Cowboy Hot-pot

**A great dish to serve as a children's main meal, which
adults will enjoy too – if they are allowed to join the posse.**

Serves 4–6
*45ml/3 tbsp sunflower oil
1 onion, sliced
1 fresh red pepper, sliced
1 sweet potato or
    2 carrots, chopped
115g/4oz/scant ½ cup
    chopped green beans
400g/14oz can baked
    beans
200g/7oz can sweetcorn
15ml/1 tbsp tomato purée*

*5ml/1 tsp barbecue spice
    seasoning
115g/4oz cheese
    (preferably smoked),
    diced
450g/1lb potatoes, thinly
    sliced
25g/1oz/2 tbsp butter,
    melted
salt and ground black
    pepper*

1 Preheat the oven to 190°C/375°F/Gas 5. Heat the oil in a
frying pan and gently fry the onion, pepper and sweet potato
or carrots until softened but not browned.

2 Add the green beans, baked beans, sweetcorn (and liquid),
tomato purée and barbecue spice seasoning. Bring to the boil,
then simmer for 5 minutes.

3 Cover the vegetable and cheese mixture with the sliced
potato, brush with butter, season with salt and pepper and
bake for 30–40 minutes until golden brown on top and the
potato is cooked.

Cook's Tip
*Use any vegetable mixture you like in this versatile
hot-pot, according to what you have to hand.*

Quorn with Ginger, Chilli and Leeks

Quorn easily absorbs different flavours and retains a good firm texture, making it ideal for stir-frying.

Serves 4

225g/8oz packet Quorn, diced
45ml/3 tbsp dark soy sauce
30ml/2 tbsp dry sherry or vermouth
10ml/2 tsp honey
150ml/¼ pint/⅔ cup vegetable stock
10ml/2 tsp cornflour
45ml/3 tbsp sunflower or groundnut oil
3 leeks, thinly sliced
1 red chilli, seeded and sliced
2.5cm/1in piece fresh root ginger, peeled and shredded
salt and ground black pepper

1 Toss the Quorn in the soy sauce and sherry or vermouth until well coated and leave to marinate for about 30 minutes.

2 Strain the Quorn from the marinade and reserve the juices in a jug. Mix the marinade with the honey, vegetable stock and cornflour to make a paste.

3 Heat the oil in a wok or large frying pan and, when hot, stir-fry the Quorn until it is crisp on the outside. Remove the Quorn and set aside.

4 Reheat the oil and stir-fry the leeks, chilli and ginger for about 2 minutes until they are just soft. Season to taste with salt and pepper.

5 Return the Quorn to the pan, together with the marinade, and stir well until the liquid is thick and glossy. Serve hot with rice or egg noodles.

Cook's Tip
Quorn is a versatile, microprotein food, now available in most supermarkets. If you cannot find it, you could use tofu instead.

Chinese Potatoes with Chilli Beans

This oriental-inspired dish gains particular appeal by way of its tasty sauce.

Serves 4

4 potatoes, cut into thick chunks
3 spring onions, sliced
1 large fresh chilli, seeded and sliced
30ml/2 tbsp sunflower or groundnut oil
2 garlic cloves, crushed
400g/14oz can red kidney beans
30ml/2 tbsp dark soy sauce
15ml/1 tbsp sesame oil
salt and ground black pepper
15ml/1 tbsp sesame seeds, to sprinkle
chopped fresh coriander or parsley, to garnish

1 Boil the potatoes until they are just tender. Take care not to overcook them. Drain and reserve.

2 In a large frying pan or wok, stir-fry the spring onions and chilli in the oil for about 1 minute, then add the garlic and fry for a few seconds longer.

3 Rinse and drain the kidney beans, then add them to the pan with the potatoes, stirring well. Finally add the soy sauce and sesame oil.

4 Season to taste with salt and pepper and cook the vegetables until they are well heated through. Sprinkle with the sesame seeds and the chopped fresh coriander or parsley.

Sweetcorn and Bean Tamale Pie

This is a hearty dish with a cheesy polenta topping which covers sweetcorn and kidney beans in a rich hot sauce.

Serves 4

2 corn on the cob
30ml/2 tbsp vegetable oil
1 onion, chopped
2 garlic cloves, crushed
1 red pepper, seeded and
  chopped
2 green chillies, seeded
  and chopped
10ml/2 tsp ground
  cumin
450g/1lb ripe tomatoes,
  peeled, seeded and
  chopped
15ml/1 tbsp tomato purée
425g/15oz can red kidney
  beans, drained and
  rinsed

15ml/1 tbsp chopped fresh
  oregano
oregano leaves, to garnish

For the topping
115g/4oz/1 cup polenta
15g/½oz/1 tbsp plain
  flour
2.5ml/½ tsp salt
10ml/2 tsp baking powder
1 egg, lightly beaten
120ml/4fl oz/½ cup milk
15g/½oz/1 tbsp butter,
  melted
50g/2oz/½ cup grated
  smoked Cheddar cheese

1 Preheat the oven to 220°C/425°F/Gas 7. Husk the corn on the cob, then par-boil for 8 minutes. Drain, leave to cool slightly, then remove the kernels with a sharp knife.

2 Fry the onion, garlic and pepper in the oil for 5 minutes, until softened. Add the chillies and cumin; fry for 1 minute. Stir in the tomatoes, tomato purée, beans, corn kernels and oregano. Season to taste. Simmer, uncovered, for 10 minutes.

3 To make the topping, mix the polenta, flour, salt, baking powder, egg, milk and butter to form a thick batter.

4 Transfer the bean mixture to an ovenproof dish, spoon the polenta mixture over and spread evenly. Bake for 30 minutes. Remove from the oven, sprinkle the cheese over the top, then bake for a further 5–10 minutes, until golden.

Pepper and Potato Tortilla

Traditionally a Spanish dish, tortilla is best eaten cold in chunky wedges and makes an ideal picnic food.

Serves 4

2 potatoes
45ml/3 tbsp olive oil
1 large onion, thinly
  sliced
2 garlic cloves, crushed
1 green pepper, thinly
  sliced

1 red pepper, thinly sliced
6 eggs, beaten
115g/4oz/1 cup grated
  mature Cheddar or
  Mahón cheese
salt and ground black
  pepper

1 Do not peel the potatoes, but wash them well. Par-boil them for about 10 minutes, then drain and, when they are cool enough to handle, slice them thickly. Switch on the grill so that it warms up while you prepare the rest of the dish.

2 In a large non-stick or well seasoned frying pan, heat the oil and fry the onion, garlic and pepper over a moderate heat for 5 minutes until softened.

3 Add the potatoes and continue frying, stirring from time to time until the potatoes are completely cooked and the vegetables are soft. Add a little extra oil if the pan seems rather too dry.

4 Pour in half the beaten eggs, then sprinkle over half the grated Cheddar or Mahón cheese, then the rest of the egg. Season with salt and pepper and finish with a layer of cheese.

5 Continue to cook over a low heat, without stirring, half covering the pan with a lid to help set the eggs.

6 When the mixture is firm, flash the pan under the hot grill to seal the top just lightly. Leave the tortilla in the pan to cool. This helps it firm up further and makes it easier to turn out. Cut into generous wedges to serve.

Chick-pea Stew

This hearty chick-pea and vegetable stew is delicious served with garlic-flavoured mashed potato.

Serves 4

30ml/2 tbsp olive oil
1 small onion, finely
*   chopped*
225g/8oz carrots, halved
*   lengthways and thinly*
*   sliced*
2.5ml/½ tsp ground
*   cumin*
5ml/1 tsp ground
*   coriander*
25g/1oz/2 tbsp plain
*   flour*

225g/8oz courgettes,
*   sliced*
200g/7oz can sweetcorn,
*   drained*
400g/14oz can
*   chick-peas, drained*
30ml/2 tbsp tomato purée
200ml/7fl oz/scant 1 cup
*   hot vegetable stock*
salt and ground black
*   pepper*
mashed potato, to serve

1 Heat the oil in a frying pan. Add the onion and carrots. Toss the vegetables to coat them in the oil, then cook over a moderate heat for 4 minutes.

2 Add the ground cumin, coriander and flour. Stir and cook for 1 minute more.

3 Cut the courgette slices in half. Add them to the pan with the sweetcorn, chick-peas, tomato purée and vegetable stock. Stir well. Cook for 10 minutes, stirring frequently.

4 Taste the stew and season to taste with salt and pepper. Serve at once with mashed potato.

Cook's Tip
To make garlic-flavoured mashed potato, peel and crush a garlic clove, fry it lightly in butter, then stir into the mashed potato until well combined.

Potato and Broccoli Stir-fry

This wonderful stir-fry combines potato, broccoli and red pepper with just a hint of fresh ginger.

Serves 2

450g/1lb potatoes
45ml/3 tbsp groundnut
*   oil*
50g/2oz/4 tbsp butter
1 small onion, chopped
1 red pepper, seeded and
*   chopped*

225g/8oz broccoli, broken
*   into florets*
2.5cm/1in piece of fresh
*   root ginger, peeled and*
*   grated*
salt and ground black
*   pepper*

1 Peel the potatoes and cut them into 1cm/½in dice.

2 Heat the oil in a large frying pan and cook the potatoes for 8 minutes over a high heat, stirring and tossing occasionally, until browned and just tender.

3 Drain off the oil. Add the butter to the potatoes in the pan. As soon as it melts, add the chopped onion and red pepper. Stir-fry for 2 minutes.

4 Add the broccoli florets and ginger to the pan. Stir-fry for 2–3 minutes more, taking care not to break up the potatoes. Season to taste with salt and pepper and serve at once.

Vegetables with Lentil Bolognese

Instead of a cheese sauce, it makes a pleasant change to top lightly steamed vegetables with a delicious lentil sauce.

Serves 6

1 small cauliflower
  broken into florets
225g/8oz/2 cups broccoli
  florets
2 leeks, thickly sliced
225g/8oz Brussels
  sprouts, halved if large

**For the lentil
Bolognese sauce**
1 onion, chopped
2 garlic cloves, crushed
2 carrots, coarsely grated
2 celery sticks, chopped

45ml/3 tbsp olive oil
115g/4oz/½ cup red
  lentils
400g/14oz can chopped
  tomatoes
30ml/2 tbsp tomato purée
450ml/¾ pint/2 cups
  stock
15ml/1 tbsp fresh
  marjoram, chopped,
  or 5ml/1 tsp dried
  marjoram
salt and ground black
  pepper

1 In a large saucepan, gently fry the onion, garlic, carrots and celery in the oil for about 5 minutes, until they are soft. Add the lentils, tomatoes, tomato purée, stock, marjoram and seasoning. Bring the mixture to the boil, then partially cover with a lid and simmer for 20 minutes until thick and soft.

2 Place all the vegetables in a steamer over a pan of boiling water and cook for 8–10 minutes until just tender.

3 Drain and place in a shallow serving dish. Spoon the sauce on top, stirring slightly to mix. Serve hot.

Black Bean and Vegetable Stir-fry

This colourful and very flavoursome vegetable mixture is coated in a classic Chinese sauce.

Serves 4

8 spring onions
225g/8oz button
  mushrooms
1 red pepper
1 green pepper
2 large carrots
60ml/4 tbsp sesame oil
2 garlic cloves, crushed

60ml/4 tbsp black bean
  sauce
90ml/6 tbsp warm water
225g/8oz/scant 3 cups
  beansprouts
salt and ground black
  pepper

1 Thinly slice the spring onions and button mushrooms. Set aside in separate bowls.

2 Cut both the peppers in half, remove the seeds and slice the flesh into thin strips.

3 Cut the carrots in half. Cut each half into thin strips lengthways. Stack the slices and cut through them to make very fine strips.

4 Heat the oil in a large wok or frying pan until very hot and stir-fry the spring onions and garlic for 30 seconds.

5 Add the mushrooms, peppers and carrots. Stir-fry for a further 5–6 minutes over a high heat until the vegetables are just beginning to soften.

6 Mix the black bean sauce with the water. Add to the wok or pan and cook for another 3–4 minutes. Stir in the beansprouts and stir-fry for a final 1 minute until all the vegetables are coated in the sauce. Season to taste with salt and pepper. Serve at once.

Tomato and Okra Stew

Okra is an unusual and delicious vegetable. It releases a sticky sap when cooked, which helps to thicken the stew.

Serves 4

15ml/1 tbsp olive oil
1 onion, chopped
400g/14oz can pimientos, drained
2 x 400g/14oz cans chopped tomatoes
275g/10oz okra
30ml/2 tbsp chopped fresh parsley
salt and ground black pepper

1 Heat the oil in a saucepan and cook the chopped onion for about 2–3 minutes.

2 Roughly chop the pimientos and add to the onion. Add the chopped tomatoes and mix well.

3 Cut the tops off the okra and cut into halves or quarters if large. Add to the tomato sauce in the pan. Season to taste with plenty of salt and pepper.

4 Bring the vegetable stew to the boil, then lower the heat, cover the pan with a tight-fitting lid and simmer for 12 minutes until the vegetables are tender and the sauce has thickened. Stir in the chopped parsley and serve at once.

Cook's Tip
Okra is now available all year round. Do not buy them any longer than 7.5–10cm/3–4in and look for clean, dark green pods – a brown tinge indicates staleness. When preparing, if the ridges look tough or damaged, scrape them with a sharp knife.

Chunky Vegetable Paella

This Spanish rice dish is now enjoyed the world over. This version includes aubergine and chick-peas.

Serves 6

large pinch of saffron strands
1 aubergine, cut into thick chunks
90ml/6 tbsp olive oil
1 large onion, thickly sliced
3 garlic cloves, crushed
1 yellow pepper, sliced
1 red pepper, sliced
10ml/2 tsp paprika
225g/8oz/1¼ cups risotto rice
600ml/1 pint/2½ cups stock
450g/1lb fresh tomatoes, skinned and chopped
115g/4oz sliced mushrooms
115g/4oz/scant ½ cup cut green beans
400g/14oz can chick-peas

1 Steep the saffron in 45ml/3 tbsp hot water. Sprinkle the aubergine with salt, leave to drain in a colander for 30 minutes, then rinse and dry.

2 In a large paella or frying pan, heat the oil and fry the onion, garlic, peppers and aubergine for about 5 minutes, stirring occasionally. Sprinkle in the paprika and stir again.

3 Mix in the rice, then pour in the stock, tomatoes, saffron and seasoning. Bring to the boil, then simmer the mixture for about 15 minutes, uncovered, shaking the pan frequently and stirring from time to time.

4 Stir in the mushrooms, green beans and chick-peas (with their liquid). Continue cooking for a further 10 minutes, then serve hot, direct from the pan.

Onion and Gruyère Tart

The secret of this tart is to cook the onions very slowly until they almost caramelize.

Serves 4

175g/6oz/1½ cups plain flour	15 – 30ml/1 – 2 tbsp wholegrain mustard
pinch of salt	2 eggs, plus 1 egg yolk
75g/3oz/6 tbsp butter, diced	300ml/½ pint/1 cup double cream
1 egg yolk	75g/3oz/generous ½ cup grated Gruyère cheese
For the filling	pinch of freshly grated nutmeg
50g/2oz/4 tbsp butter	salt and ground black pepper
450g/1lb onions, thinly sliced	

1 To make the pastry, sift the flour and salt into a bowl. Add the butter and rub into the flour with your fingertips until the mixture resembles fine breadcrumbs. Add the egg yolk and 15ml/1 tbsp cold water and mix to a firm dough. Chill in the fridge for 30 minutes.

2 Preheat the oven to 200°C/400°F/Gas 6. Knead the pastry, then roll it out on a lightly floured work surface and use to line a 23cm/9in loose-based flan tin. Prick the base all over with a fork, line the pastry case with greaseproof paper and fill with baking beans.

3 Bake the pastry case blind for 15 minutes. Remove the paper and beans and bake for a further 10 – 15 minutes, until the pastry case is crisp. Meanwhile, melt the butter in a saucepan, add the onions, cover with a tight-fitting lid and cook for 20 minutes, stirring occasionally, until golden.

4 Reduce the oven temperature to 180°C/350°F/Gas 4. Spread the pastry case with mustard and top with the onions. Mix together the eggs, egg yolk, cream, cheese, nutmeg and seasoning. Pour over the onions. Bake for 30 – 35 minutes, until golden. Serve warm.

Potato and Spinach Gratin

Pine nuts add a satisfying crunch to this gratin of wafer-thin potato slices and spinach in a creamy cheese sauce.

Serves 2

450g/1lb potatoes	115g/4oz/1 cup grated mature Cheddar cheese
1 garlic clove, crushed	
3 spring onions, thinly sliced	25g/1oz/¼ cup pine nuts
150ml/¼ pint/⅔ cup single cream	salt and ground black pepper
250ml/8fl oz/1 cup milk	lettuce and tomato salad, to serve
225g/8oz frozen chopped spinach, thawed	

1 Peel the potatoes and cut them carefully into wafer-thin slices. Spread them out in a large, heavy-based, non-stick frying pan.

2 Scatter the crushed garlic and sliced spring onions evenly over the potatoes.

3 Pour the cream and milk over the potatoes. Place the pan over a gentle heat, cover and cook for 8 minutes or until the potatoes are tender.

4 Using both hands, squeeze the spinach dry. Add the spinach to the potatoes, mixing lightly. Cover the pan with a tight-fitting lid and cook for 2 minutes more.

5 Season to taste with salt and pepper, then spoon the mixture into a gratin dish. Preheat the grill.

6 Sprinkle the grated cheese and pine nuts over the spinach mixture. Lightly toast under the grill for 2 – 3 minutes until the topping is golden. A simple lettuce and tomato salad makes an excellent accompaniment to this dish.

Stuffed Peppers

Sweet peppers can be stuffed and baked with a variety of fillings, from cooked vegetables to rice or pasta.

Serves 6

6 peppers, any colour
200g/7oz/generous 1 cup rice
60ml/4 tbsp olive oil
1 large onion, chopped
3 anchovy fillets, chopped
2 garlic cloves, finely chopped
3 tomatoes, peeled and cut into small dice

60ml/4 tbsp white wine
45ml/3 tbsp finely chopped fresh parsley
114g/4oz/scant ½ cup mozzarella
90ml/6 tbsp freshly grated Parmesan cheese
salt and ground black pepper

1 Cut the tops off the peppers. Scoop out the seeds and the fibrous insides. Blanch the peppers and their tops in a large saucepan of boiling water for 3–4 minutes. Remove, and stand upside down on wire racks to drain.

2 Boil the rice according to the packet instructions, but drain and rinse it in cold water 3 minutes before the recommended cooking time has elapsed. Drain again.

3 Sauté the onion in the oil until soft. Mash in the anchovies and garlic. Add the tomatoes and wine; cook for 5 minutes.

4 Preheat the oven to 190°C/375°F/Gas 5. Remove the tomato mixture from the heat. Stir in the rice, parsley, the mozzarella and 60ml/4 tbsp of the Parmesan cheese. Season to taste with salt and pepper.

5 Pat the insides of the peppers dry with kitchen paper. Sprinkle with salt and pepper. Stuff the peppers. Sprinkle the tops with the remaining Parmesan and a little oil. Arrange the peppers in a shallow baking dish. Pour in enough water to come 1cm/½in up the sides of the peppers. Bake for 25 minutes. Serve at once.

Broccoli and Ricotta Cannelloni

When piping the filling into the cannelloni tubes, hold them upright on the work surface.

Serves 4

12 dried cannelloni tubes, 7.5cm/3in long
450g/1lb/4 cups broccoli florets
75g/3oz/1½ cups fresh breadcrumbs
150ml/¼ pint/⅔ cup milk
60ml/4 tbsp olive oil, plus extra for brushing
225g/8oz/1 cup ricotta cheese
pinch of grated nutmeg
90ml/6 tbsp freshly grated Parmesan or Pecorino cheese

salt and ground black pepper
30ml/2 tbsp pine nuts, for sprinkling

For the tomato sauce
30ml/2 tbsp olive oil
1 onion, finely chopped
1 garlic clove, crushed
2 x 400g/14oz cans chopped tomatoes
15ml/1 tbsp tomato purée
4 black olives, stoned and chopped
5ml/1 tsp dried thyme

1 Preheat the oven to 190°C/375°F/Gas 5 and grease an ovenproof dish. Bring a saucepan of water to the boil, add a little olive oil and simmer the pasta, uncovered, until nearly cooked. Boil the broccoli until tender. Drain the pasta and rinse under cold water. Drain the broccoli, then process in a food processor or blender until smooth.

2 Mix together the breadcrumbs, milk and oil. Add the ricotta, broccoli purée, nutmeg, 60ml/4 tbsp Parmesan cheese and seasoning.

3 For the sauce, fry the onions and garlic in the oil for 5 minutes. Stir in the tomatoes, tomato purée, olives and thyme, and season. Boil for 2 minutes; pour in the dish.

4 Open the pasta tubes. Pipe in the filling using a 1cm/½in nozzle pipe. Arrange in the dish. Brush with olive oil, then sprinkle over the remaining cheese and pine nuts. Bake for 30 minutes, or until golden on top.

Pasta with Spring Vegetables

If you are not fond of fennel, use a small onion instead. Prepare in the same way.

Serves 4

115g/4oz/1 cup broccoli
  florets
115g/4oz baby leeks
225g/8oz asparagus
1 small fennel bulb
115g/4oz/1 cup fresh or
  frozen peas
40g/1½oz/3 tbsp butter
1 shallot, chopped
300ml/½ pint/1¼ cups
  double cream

45ml/3 tbsp mixed
  chopped fresh herbs,
  such as parsley, thyme
  and sage
350g/12oz/3 cups dried
  penne pasta
salt and ground black
  pepper
freshly grated Parmesan
  cheese, to serve

1 Divide the broccoli florets into tiny sprigs. Cut the leeks and asparagus diagonally into 5cm/2in lengths. Trim the fennel bulb and remove any tough outer leaves. Cut into wedges, leaving the layers attached at the root ends so the pieces stay intact.

2 Cook each vegetable separately in boiling salted water until just tender – use the same water for each vegetable. Drain well and keep warm.

3 Melt the butter in a separate saucepan, and cook the chopped shallot, stirring occasionally, until softened but not browned. Stir in the herbs and cream and cook for a few minutes, until slightly thickened.

4 Meanwhile, cook the pasta in boiling salted water for 10 minutes or according to the instructions on the packet. Drain well and add to the sauce with all the vegetables. Toss gently to combine and season to taste with plenty of pepper.

5 Serve the pasta hot, with plenty of freshly grated Parmesan cheese.

Pasta Carbonara

A classic Roman dish traditionally made with spaghetti, which is equally delicious with fresh egg tagliatelle.

Serves 4

350–450g/12oz–1lb
  fresh tagliatelle
15ml/1 tbsp olive oil
225g/8oz piece of ham,
  bacon or pancetta, cut
  into 2.5cm/1in sticks
115g/4oz button
  mushrooms, sliced

4 eggs, lightly beaten
75ml/5 tbsp single cream
salt and ground black
  pepper
30ml/2 tbsp finely grated
  Parmesan cheese
fresh basil sprigs, to
  garnish

1 Cook the pasta in a pan of boiling salted water, with a little oil added, for 6–8 minutes or until al dente.

2 Meanwhile, heat the oil in a frying pan and fry the ham for 3–4 minutes, then add the mushrooms and fry for a further 3–4 minutes. Turn off the heat and reserve. Lightly beat the eggs and cream together in a bowl and season well with salt and pepper.

3 When the pasta is cooked, drain it well and return to the pan. Add the ham, mushrooms and any pan juices and stir into the pasta.

4 Pour in the eggs, cream and half the Parmesan cheese. Stir well and as you do this the eggs will cook in the heat of the pasta. Pile on to warmed serving plates, sprinkle with the remaining Parmesan and garnish with basil.

Spinach and Hazelnut Lasagne

Use frozen spinach in this hearty and satisfying dish if you are short of time.

Serves 4

900g/2lb/8 cups fresh
 spinach
300ml/½ pint/1¼ cups
 vegetable stock
1 onion, finely chopped
1 garlic clove, crushed
75g/3oz/¾ cup hazelnuts
30ml/2 tbsp chopped
 fresh basil

6 sheets lasagne
400g/14oz can chopped
 tomatoes
250ml/8fl oz/1 cup
 low-fat fromage frais
salt and ground black
 pepper
flaked hazelnuts and
 chopped fresh parsley

1 Preheat the oven to 200°C/400°F/Gas 6. Wash the spinach; cook with no extra water over a high heat for 2 minutes until wilted. Drain well. Simmer the onion and garlic in 30ml/ 2 tbsp stock until soft. Stir in the spinach, hazelnuts and basil.

2 In a large ovenproof dish, layer the spinach, lasagne and tomatoes; season as you go. Pour in the remaining stock. Spread the fromage frais over the top. Bake for 45 minutes. Serve hot, sprinkled with hazelnuts and chopped parsley.

Tagliatelle with Hazelnut Pesto

Hazelnuts are used instead of pine nuts in the pesto sauce, providing a healthier, lower-fat option.

Serves 4

2 garlic cloves, crushed
25g/1oz fresh basil leaves
25g/1oz/¼ cup chopped
 hazelnuts

200g/7oz/scant 1 cup soft
 cheese
225g/8oz tagliatelle
ground black pepper

1 Place the garlic, basil, hazelnuts and cheese in a food processor or blender and process to a thick paste.

2 Cook the tagliatelle in lightly salted boiling water until just tender, then drain well.

3 Spoon the sauce into the hot pasta, tossing until melted. Sprinkle with pepper and serve hot.

Cook's Tip
If fresh tuna is available, use 450g/1lb, cut into small chunks and add after step 2. Simmer for 6–8 minutes, then add the chilli, olives and pasta.

Spaghetti with Tuna Sauce

Use 450g/1lb fresh spaghetti in place of the dried pasta in this piquant dish, if you prefer.

Serves 4
Cook 225g/8oz spaghetti, drain and keep hot. Boil 1 garlic clove and 400g/14oz can chopped tomatoes and simmer for 2–3 minutes. Add 425g/15oz canned tuna and 2.5ml/½ tsp chilli sauce (optional), 4 black olives and the spaghetti. Heat well and season to taste.

Penne with Broccoli and Chilli

For a milder sauce you could omit the chilli, but it does give
this dish a great kick.

Serves 4

450g/1lb/4 cups small
  broccoli florets
30ml/2 tbsp stock
1 garlic clove, crushed
1 small red chilli, finely
  sliced, or 2.5ml/½ tsp
  chilli sauce

60ml/4 tbsp natural
  low-fat yogurt
30ml/2 tbsp toasted pine
  nuts or cashew nuts
350g/12oz/3¾ cups
  penne
salt and ground black
  pepper

1 Add the pasta to a large pan of lightly salted boiling water
and return to the boil. Place the broccoli in a steamer basket
over the top. Cover and cook for 8–10 minutes until both are
just tender. Drain.

2 Heat the stock and add the crushed garlic and chilli or
chilli sauce. Stir over a low heat for 2–3 minutes.

3 Stir in the broccoli, pasta and yogurt. Adjust the seasoning,
sprinkle with nuts and serve hot.

Linguine with Pesto Sauce

Pesto originates in Liguria, where the sea breezes are said
to give the local basil a particularly fine flavour.

Serves 5–6

65g/2½oz fresh basil
  leaves
3–4 garlic cloves, peeled
45ml/3 tbsp pine nuts
2.5ml/½ tsp salt
75ml/5 tbsp extra virgin
  olive oil

50g/2oz/scant ¾ cup
  freshly grated
  Parmesan cheese
60ml/4 tbsp freshly
  grated Pecorino cheese
salt and ground black
  pepper
500g/1¼lb linguine

1 Place the basil, garlic, pine nuts, salt and olive oil in a food
processor or blender and process until smooth. Remove to a
bowl. (If desired, the sauce may be frozen at this point, before
the cheeses are added.)

2 Add the cheeses and stir to combine thoroughly. Season to
taste with salt and pepper.

3 Cook the pasta in a large saucepan of rapidly boiling
salted water until it is *al dente*. Just before draining it, take
about 60ml/4 tbsp of the cooking water and stir it into the
pesto sauce.

4 Drain the pasta and toss with the sauce. Serve at once,
with extra cheese if wished.

Cook's Tip
*Pecorino cheese is not as widely available as Parmesan.
If you cannot find it, use all Parmesan instead.*

Spaghetti with Herb Sauce

Fresh herbs make a wonderful aromatic sauce – the heat from the pasta releases their flavour to delicious effect.

Serves 4

50g/2oz chopped mixed
  fresh herbs such as
  parsley, basil and
  thyme
2 garlic cloves, crushed
60ml/4 tbsp pine nuts,
  toasted
150ml/¼ pint/⅔ cup
  olive oil

350g/12oz dried
  spaghetti
60ml/4 tbsp freshly
  grated Parmesan
  cheese
salt and ground black
  pepper
fresh basil leaves, to
  garnish

1 Put the herbs, garlic and half the pine nuts into a food processor or blender. With the machine running slowly, add the oil and process to form a thick purée.

2 Cook the spaghetti in plenty of boiling salted water for about 8 minutes, until *al dente*. Drain thoroughly.

3 Transfer the herb purée to a large warm bowl, then add the spaghetti and Parmesan. Toss well to coat the pasta with the sauce. Season with salt and peppper, sprinkle the remaining pine nuts and the basil leaves on top and serve hot.

Tagliatelle with Saffron Mussels

Tagliatelle is served with mussels in a saffron and cream sauce in this recipe, but use other pasta if you prefer.

Serves 4

1.75kg/4 – 4½lb live
  mussels in the shell
150ml/¼ pint/⅔ cup dry
  white wine
2 shallots, finely
  chopped
350g/12oz dried
  tagliatelle
25g/1oz/2 tbsp butter
2 garlic cloves, crushed

250ml/8fl oz/1 cup
  double cream
large pinch of saffron
  strands
1 egg yolk
salt and ground black
  pepper
30ml/2 tbsp chopped
  fresh parsley, to
  garnish

1 Scrub the mussels well under cold running water. Remove the beards and discard any mussels that are open. Place the mussels in a large saucepan with the wine and shallots. Cover with a tight-fitting lid and cook over a high heat, shaking the pan occasionally, for 5–8 minutes until the mussels have opened. Drain the mussels, reserving the liquid. Discard any that remain closed. Shell all but a few of the mussels and keep warm. Bring the reserved cooking liquid to the boil, then reduce by half. Strain into a jug.

2 Cook the pasta in a large pan of boiling salted water for 10 minutes or according to the instructions on the packet.

3 Meanwhile, melt the butter in a frying pan and fry the garlic for 1 minute. Pour in the mussel liquid, cream and saffron strands. Heat gently until the sauce thickens slightly. Remove the pan from the heat and stir in the egg yolk and shelled mussels, and season to taste with salt and pepper.

4 Drain the tagliatelle and transfer to warmed serving bowls. Spoon the sauce over and sprinkle with chopped parsley. Garnish with the mussels in shells and serve at once.

Pasta Rapido with Parsley Pesto

Here's a fresh, lively sauce that will stir the appetite and pep up any pasta supper.

Serves 4

450g/1lb/4 cups dried
  pasta
75g/3oz/¾ cup whole
  almonds
50g/2oz/½ cup flaked
  almonds toasted
25g/1oz/generous ¼ cup
  freshly grated
  Parmesan cheese
pinch of salt

For the sauce
40g/1½oz fresh flat leaf
  parsley
2 garlic cloves, crushed
45ml/3 tbsp olive oil
45ml/3 tbsp lemon juice
5ml/1 tsp sugar
250ml/8fl oz/1 cup
  boiling water

1 Bring a large saucepan of salted water to the boil and cook the pasta according to the instructions on the packet. Toast the whole and flaked almonds separately under a moderate grill until golden brown. Set the flaked almonds aside.

2 To make the sauce, chop the parsley finely in a food processor. Add the whole almonds and reduce to a fine consistency. Add the garlic, olive oil, lemon juice, sugar and water. Combine to make a sauce.

3 Drain the pasta and combine with half of the sauce. (The remainder of the sauce will keep in a screw-top jar in the fridge for up to ten days.) Top with freshly grated Parmesan cheese and the flaked almonds.

Macaroni Cheese with Mushrooms

This macaroni cheese is served in a light creamy sauce with mushrooms and topped with pine nuts.

Serves 4

450g/1lb quick-cooking
  elbow macaroni
45ml/3 tbsp olive oil
225g/8oz button
  mushrooms, sliced
2 fresh thyme sprigs
50g/2oz/4 tbsp plain
  flour
1 vegetable stock cube
600ml/1 pint/2½ cups
  milk

2.5ml/½ tsp celery salt
5ml/1 tsp Dijon mustard
175g/6oz/1½ cups grated
  Cheddar
25g/1oz/generous ¼ cup
  freshly grated
  Parmesan cheese
25g/1oz/¼ cup pine nuts
salt and ground black
  pepper

1 Bring a saucepan of salted water to the boil and cook the macaroni according to the instructions on the packet.

2 Heat the oil in a heavy saucepan and cover and cook the mushrooms and thyme over a gentle heat for 2–3 minutes. Stir in the flour and draw from the heat, add the stock cube and stir continuously until evenly blended. Add the milk a little at a time, stirring after each addition. Add the celery salt, mustard and Cheddar cheese and season to taste with salt and pepper. Stir and simmer for about 1–2 minutes, until the sauce has thickened.

3 Preheat a moderate grill. Drain the macaroni well, toss into the sauce and turn out into four individual dishes or one large flameproof gratin dish. Scatter with grated Parmesan cheese and pine nuts, then grill until brown and bubbly.

Pasta with Roasted Pepper Sauce

Add other vegetables such as French beans or courgettes or even chick-peas to make this sauce more substantial.

Serves 4

2 fresh red peppers
2 yellow peppers
45ml/3 tbsp olive oil
1 onion, sliced
2 garlic cloves, crushed
400g/14oz can chopped
plum tomatoes

2.5ml/½ tsp mild chilli
powder
450g/1lb/4 cups dried
pasta shells or spirals
salt and ground black
pepper
freshly grated Parmesan
cheese, to serve

1 Preheat the oven to 200°C/400°F/Gas 6. Place the peppers on a baking sheet and bake for about 20 minutes or until they are beginning to char. Alternatively, grill the peppers, turning them from time to time.

2 Rub the skins off the peppers under cold water. Halve, remove the seeds and roughly chop the flesh.

3 Heat the oil in a saucepan and cook the onion and garlic gently for 5 minutes until soft and golden.

4 Stir in the chilli powder, cook for 2 minutes, then add the tomatoes and peppers. Bring to the boil and simmer for about 10–15 minutes until slightly thickened and reduced. Season with salt and pepper to taste.

5 Bring a pan of salted water to the boil and cook the pasta according to the instructions on the packet. Drain well and toss with the sauce. Serve piping hot with lots of freshly grated Parmesan cheese.

Stir-fried Vegetables with Pasta

This is a colourful oriental-style dish, easily prepared using pasta instead of Chinese noodles.

Serves 4

1 carrot
175g/6oz small
courgettes
175g/6oz runner or other
green beans
175g/6oz baby corn cobs
450g/1lb ribbon pasta
such as tagliatelle
pinch of salt
30ml/2 tbsp corn oil, plus
extra for tossing the
pasta

1cm/½in piece fresh root
ginger, peeled and
finely chopped
2 garlic cloves, finely
chopped
90ml/6 tbsp yellow bean
sauce
6 spring onions, sliced
into 2.5cm/1in lengths
30ml/2 tbsp dry sherry
5ml/1 tsp sesame seeds

1 Slice the carrot and courgettes diagonally into chunks. Slice the beans diagonally, then cut the baby corn cobs diagonally in half.

2 Cook the pasta in plenty of boiling salted water according to the instructions on the packet. Drain, then rinse under hot water. Toss in a little oil.

3 Heat 30ml/2 tbsp oil until smoking in a wok or frying pan and add the ginger and garlic. Stir-fry for 30 seconds, then add the carrots, beans and courgettes.

4 Stir-fry for 3–4 minutes then stir in the yellow bean sauce. Stir-fry for 2 minutes, add the spring onions, sherry and pasta and stir-fry for a further 1 minute until piping hot. Sprinkle with sesame seeds and serve immediately.

Tagliatelle with Gorgonzola Sauce

Gorgonzola is a creamy Italian blue cheese. You could use Danish Blue or Pipo Crème instead.

Serves 4

25g/1oz/2 tbsp butter, plus extra for tossing the pasta
225g/8oz Gorgonzola cheese
150ml/¼ pint/⅔ cup double or whipping cream
30ml/2 tbsp dry vermouth
5ml/1 tsp cornflour
30ml/1 tbsp chopped fresh sage
450g/1lb tagliatelle
salt and ground black pepper

1 Melt 25g/1oz/2 tbsp butter in a heavy saucepan (it needs to be thick-based to prevent the cheese from burning). Stir in 175g/6oz/1½ cups crumbled Gorgonzola cheese and stir over a very gentle heat for 2–3 minutes until the cheese is melted.

2 Pour in the cream, vermouth and cornflour, whisking well to amalgamate. Stir in the chopped sage, then season to taste with salt and pepper. Cook, whisking all the time, until the sauce boils and thickens. Set aside.

3 Boil the pasta in plenty of salted water according to the instructions on the packet. Drain well and toss with a little butter to coat evenly.

4 Reheat the sauce gently, whisking well. Divide the pasta among four serving bowls, top with the sauce and sprinkle over the remaining cheese. Serve immediately.

Cook's Tip
If you do not have vermouth, use a good quality dry sherry in its place.

Rigatoni with Garlic Crumbs

A hot and spicy dish – halve the quantity of chilli if you would prefer a milder flavour.

Serves 4–6

45ml/3 tbsp olive oil
2 shallots, chopped
8 rashers streaky bacon, chopped
10ml/2 tsp crushed dried chillies
400g/14oz can chopped tomatoes with herbs
6 slices white bread, crusts removed
115g/4oz/½ cup butter
2 garlic cloves, chopped
450g/1lb/4 cups rigatoni
salt and ground black pepper

1 Heat the oil in a saucepan and fry the shallots and bacon gently for 6–8 minutes until golden. Add the dried chillies and chopped tomatoes, half-cover with a lid and simmer for about 20 minutes.

2 Meanwhile, place the bread in a blender or food processor and process to fine crumbs.

3 Heat the butter in a frying pan and stir-fry the garlic and breadcrumbs until golden and crisp. (Be careful not to let the crumbs catch and burn.)

4 Bring a pan of lightly salted water to the boil and cook the pasta according to the instructions on the packet. Drain well.

5 Toss the pasta with the tomato sauce and divide among four serving bowls.

6 Sprinkle with the crumbs and serve immediately.

Cook's Tip
If you are preparing this dish for vegetarians leave out the bacon, or replace it with sliced mushrooms.

Pasta with Tomatoes and Rocket

This pretty-coloured pasta dish relies for its success on the slightly peppery taste of the rocket.

Serves 4

450g/1lb/4 cups pasta
    shells
450g/1lb ripe cherry
    tomatoes
45ml/3 tbsp olive oil

75g/3oz fresh rocket
salt and ground black
    pepper
Parmesan cheese
    shavings, to serve

1 Bring a saucepan of water to the boil and cook the pasta according to the instructions on the packet. Drain well.

2 Halve the tomatoes. Trim, wash and dry the rocket.

3 Heat the oil in a large saucepan and gently cook the tomatoes for barely 1 minute. The tomatoes should only just be heated through and not be allowed to disintegrate.

4 Add the pasta to the pan, then the rocket. (Roughly tear any rocket leaves that are over-large.) Carefully stir to mix and heat through. Season to taste with salt and pepper. Serve hot, with plenty of shaved Parmesan cheese.

Cook's Tip
Rocket is increasingly available in supermarkets. However, if you cannot find it, it is easy to grow in the garden or in a window-box.

Pasta Spirals with Pepperoni

A warming supper dish, this pepperoni and tomato sauce could be served on any type of pasta.

Serves 4

1 onion
1 red pepper
1 green pepper
30ml/2 tbsp olive oil,
    plus extra for tossing
    the pasta
800g/1¾lb canned
    chopped tomatoes
30ml/2 tbsp tomato purée

10ml/2 tsp paprika
175g/6oz pepperoni or
    chorizo
45ml/3 tbsp chopped
    fresh parsley
450g/1lb/4 cups green
    pasta spirals
salt and ground black
    pepper

1 Chop the onion. Halve and seed the peppers, removing the cores, then cut the flesh into dice.

2 Heat the oil in a saucepan and cook the onion for about 2 minutes, until beginning to colour. Stir in the peppers, tomatoes, tomato purée and paprika, bring to the boil and simmer uncovered for 15–20 minutes until the sauce is reduced and thickened.

3 Slice the sausage and stir into the sauce with about half the chopped parsley. Season to taste with salt and pepper.

4 While the sauce is simmering, cook the pasta in plenty of boiling salted water according to the instructions on the packet. Drain well. Toss the pasta with the remaining parsley in a little extra olive oil. Divide among warmed bowls and top with the sauce.

Cook's Tip
All types of sausages are suitable to include in this dish. If using raw sausages, add them with the onion and cook thoroughly.

Pasta with Tuna and Capers

Pasta shapes are tossed in a flavoursome sauce made with tuna, capers, anchovies and fresh basil.

Serves 4

400g/14oz can tuna fish
  in oil
30ml/2 tbsp olive oil
2 garlic cloves, crushed
800g/1¾ lb canned
  chopped tomatoes
6 canned anchovy fillets,
  drained
30ml/2 tbsp capers in
  vinegar, drained

30ml/2 tbsp chopped
  fresh basil
salt and ground black
  pepper
450g/1lb/4 cups
  garganelle, penne or
  rigatoni
fresh basil sprigs, to
  garnish

1 Drain the oil from the tuna into a saucepan, add the olive oil and heat gently until it stops spitting.

2 Add the garlic and fry until golden. Stir in the tomatoes and simmer for 25 minutes until thickened.

3 Flake the tuna and cut the anchovies in half. Stir into the sauce with the capers and chopped basil. Season to taste with salt and pepper.

4 Cook the pasta in plenty of boiling salted water according to the instructions on the packet. Drain well and toss with the sauce. Garnish with fresh basil sprigs.

Cook's Tip
This piquant sauce could be made without the addition of tomatoes – just heat the oil, add the other ingredients and heat through gently before tossing with the pasta.

Pasta Bows with Smoked Salmon

In Italy, pasta cooked with smoked salmon is becoming very fashionable. This is a quick and luxurious sauce.

Serves 4

6 spring onions, sliced
50g/2oz/4 tbsp butter
90ml/6 tbsp dry white
  wine or vermouth
450ml/¾ pint/1¾ cups
  double cream
pinch of freshly grated
  nutmeg
225g/8oz smoked salmon

30ml/2 tbsp chopped
  fresh dill or 15ml/
  1 tbsp dried dill
freshly squeezed lemon
  juice
450g/1lb/4 cups pasta
  bows
salt and ground black
  pepper

1 Slice the spring onions finely. Melt the butter in a saucepan and fry the spring onions for about 1 minute until they begin to soften.

2 Add the wine or vermouth and boil hard to reduce to about 30ml/2 tbsp. Stir in the cream and add salt, pepper and nutmeg to taste. Bring to the boil and simmer for about 2–3 minutes until slightly thickened.

3 Cut the smoked salmon into 2.5cm/1in squares and stir into the sauce with the dill. Taste and add a little lemon juice. Keep the sauce warm.

4 Cook the pasta in plenty of boiling salted water according to the instructions on the packet. Drain well. Toss the pasta with the sauce and serve immediately.

Cook's Tip
This dish could also be prepared with canned salmon, broken into bite-size pieces, if you prefer.

Pasta with Prawns and Feta Cheese

This dish contains a delicious combination of fresh prawns and sharp-tasting feta cheese.

Serves 4

450g/1lb/4 cups medium
  raw prawns
6 spring onions
50g/2oz/4 tbsp butter
225g/8oz feta cheese

small bunch fresh chives
450g/1lb/4 cups penne,
  garganelle or rigatoni
salt and ground black
  pepper

1 Remove the heads from the prawns by twisting and pulling off. Peel the prawns and discard the shells. Chop the spring onions.

2 Melt the butter in a frying pan and cook the prawns. When they turn pink, add the spring onions and cook gently for 1 minute more.

3 Cut the feta cheese into 1cm/½in dice. Stir the dice into the prawn mixture and season to taste with pepper.

4 Cut the chives into 2.5cm/1in lengths and stir half into the prawn mixture.

5 Bring a saucepan of salted water to the boil and cook the pasta according to the instructions on the packet. Drain well, pile into a warmed serving dish and top with the sauce. Scatter with the remaining chives and serve.

Cook's Tip
Substitute goat's cheese for the feta cheese if you like; prepare the dish in the same way.

Tagliatelle with Prosciutto

This is a simple dish, prepared in minutes from the best ingredients, with a thick covering of Parmesan cheese.

Serves 4

115g/4oz prosciutto
450g/1lb tagliatelle
75g/3oz/6 tbsp butter
50g/2oz/½ cup grated
  Parmesan cheese

salt and ground black
  pepper
a few fresh sage leaves, to
  garnish

1 Cut the prosciutto into strips of the same width as the tagliatelle. Cook the pasta in plenty of boiling salted water according to the instructions on the packet.

2 Meanwhile, melt the butter gently in a saucepan and heat the prosciutto strips through, but do not fry.

3 Drain the tagliatelle well and pile into a warm serving dish. Sprinkle all the Parmesan cheese over the top.

4 Pour the buttery prosciutto over the top of the tagliatelle and Parmesan. Season well with pepper and garnish with the sage leaves.

Cook's Tip
Buy Parmesan cheese in a block and grate it yourself. The flavour is far superior to that of ready-grated Parmesan cheese.

Cannelloni al Forno

This recipe provides a lighter, healthier alternative to the usual beef-filled, béchamel-coated version.

Serves 4–6

450g/1lb boned chicken breast, skinned and cooked	squeeze of lemon juice
	12–18 cannelloni tubes
	1 jar of passata
225g/8oz mushrooms	50g/2oz/scant ¾ cup
2 garlic cloves, crushed	freshly grated
30ml/2 tbsp chopped	Parmesan cheese
fresh parsley	salt and ground black
15ml/1 tbsp chopped	pepper
fresh tarragon	fresh parsley sprig, to
1 egg, beaten	garnish

1 Preheat the oven to 200°C/400°F/Gas 6. Place the chicken in a food processor and blend until finely minced. Transfer to a bowl and set aside.

2 Place the mushrooms, garlic, parsley and tarragon in the food processor and blend until finely minced. Beat the mushroom mixture into the chicken with the egg, salt and pepper and lemon juice to taste.

3 Bring a saucepan of salted water to the boil and cook the cannelloni according to the instructions on the packet. Drain well on a clean dish towel.

4 Place the filling in a piping bag fitted with a large plain nozzle. Use this to fill each tube of cannelloni.

5 Lay the filled cannelloni tightly together in a single layer in a buttered shallow ovenproof dish. Spoon over the passata and sprinkle with Parmesan cheese. Bake in the oven for 30 minutes or until brown and bubbling. Serve garnished with a sprig of parsley.

Fettuccine all'Alfredo

A classic from Rome, this dish is simply pasta tossed with double cream, butter and freshly grated Parmesan cheese.

Serves 4

25g/1oz/2 tbsp butter	salt and ground black
150ml/¼ pint/⅔ cup	pepper
double cream, plus	50g/2oz/scant ¾ cup
60ml/4 tbsp extra	freshly grated
450g/1lb fettuccine	Parmesan cheese, plus
pinch of freshly grated	extra to serve
nutmeg	

1 Place the butter and 150ml/¼ pint/⅔ cup cream in a heavy saucepan, bring to the boil and simmer for 1 minute until slightly thickened.

2 Bring a saucepan of salted water to the boil and cook the fettuccine according to the instructions on the packet, but for about 2 minutes' less time. The pasta should still be a little firm or *al dente*.

3 Drain the pasta very thoroughly and turn into the pan with the cream sauce.

4 Place the pan on the heat and turn the pasta in the sauce to coat it evenly.

5 Add the remaining cream, the cheese, salt and pepper to taste and a little grated nutmeg. Toss until well coated and heated through. Serve immediately with some extra grated Parmesan cheese.

Cook's Tip
Popular additions to this recipe are fresh or frozen peas, and thin strips of ham if you are not catering for vegetarians.

Onion and Gorgonzola Pizzettes

Serves 4

1 quantity Basic Pizza
   Dough (see below)
30ml/2 tbsp garlic oil
2 small red onions
150g/5oz Gorgonzola

2 garlic cloves
10ml/2 tsp chopped fresh
   sage
pinch of black pepper

Preheat the oven to 220°C/425°F/Gas 7. Divide the dough into eight pieces and roll out each one on a lightly floured surface to a small oval about 5mm/¼in thick. Place well apart on two greased baking sheets and prick with a fork. Brush the bases well with 15ml/1 tbsp of the garlic oil. Halve, then slice the onions into thin wedges. Scatter over the pizza bases. Remove the rind from the Gorgonzola. Cut the cheese into small cubes, then scatter it over the onions. Cut the garlic lengthways into thin strips and sprinkle over, along with the sage. Drizzle the remaining oil on top and grind over plenty of pepper. Bake for 10–15 minutes until crisp and golden. Serve immediately.

Basic Pizza Dough

Makes one 25–30cm/10–12in round pizza base

175g/6oz/1½ cups strong
   white flour
1.25ml/¼ tsp salt
5ml/1 tsp easy-blend
   dried yeast

120–150ml/4–5fl oz/
   ½–¾ cup lukewarm
   water
15ml/1 tbsp olive oil

Sift the flour and salt into a large mixing bowl and stir in the yeast. Make a well in the centre; pour in the water and oil. Mix to a soft dough. Knead the dough on a lightly floured board for 10 minutes until smooth and elastic. Place in a greased bowl, cover with clear film and leave to double in size for about 1 hour. Turn out on to a lightly floured surface, knead gently for 2–3 minutes and use as required.

Feta and Roasted Garlic Pizza

This is a pizza for garlic lovers. Mash down the cloves as you eat – they should be soft and sweet-tasting.

Serves 4

1 garlic bulb, unpeeled
45ml/3 tbsp olive oil
1 red pepper, seeded and
   quartered
1 yellow pepper, seeded
   and quartered
2 plum tomatoes

1 quantity Basic Pizza
   Dough (see below left)
175g/6oz/1½ cups feta,
   crumbled
pinch of black pepper
15–30ml/1–2 tbsp
   chopped fresh oregano,
   to garnish

1 Preheat the oven to 220°C/425°F/Gas 7. Break the garlic into cloves, discarding the outer papery layers. Toss in 15ml/1 tbsp of the olive oil.

2 Place the peppers skin-side up on a baking sheet and grill, turning them until the skins are evenly charred. Place in a covered bowl for 10 minutes, then peel off the skins. Cut the flesh into strips.

3 Make a slash in the skin of each tomato, then put them in a bowl and pour over boiling water. Leave for 30 seconds, then plunge into cold water. Peel, seed and roughly chop the flesh. Divide the pizza dough into four pieces and roll out each one on a lightly floured surface to an equal-sized circle of about 13cm/5in diameter.

4 Place the dough circles well apart on two greased baking sheets, then push up the dough edges to form a thin rim around the edges of the sheets. Brush the dough circles with half the remaining oil and scatter over the chopped tomatoes. Top with the peppers, crumbled feta cheese and garlic cloves. Drizzle over the remaining oil and season to taste with pepper. Bake in the oven for 15–20 minutes until crisp and golden. Garnish with chopped oregano; serve immediately.

Mussel and Leek Pizzettes

Serve these subtly flavoured seafood pizzettes with a crisp green salad for a light lunch.

Serves 4
450g/1lb live mussels
120ml/4fl oz/½ cup dry white wine
1 quantity Basic Pizza Dough (see page 158)
15ml/1 tbsp olive oil
50g/2oz Gruyère cheese
50g/2oz mozzarella
2 small leeks
salt and ground black pepper

1 Preheat the oven to 220°C/425°F/Gas 7. Place the mussels in a bowl of cold water to soak, and scrub well. Remove the beards and discard any mussels that are open.

2 Place the mussels in a saucepan. Pour over the dry white wine, cover with a tight-fitting lid and cook over a high heat, shaking the pan occasionally, for 5–10 minutes until the mussels have opened.

3 Drain off the cooking liquid. Remove the mussels from their shells, discarding any that remain closed. Leave to cool.

4 Divide the dough into four pieces and roll out each one on a lightly floured surface to a 13cm/5in circle. Place well apart on two greased baking sheets, then push up the dough edges to form a thin trim. Brush the pizza bases with the oil. Grate the cheeses and sprinkle half evenly over the bases.

5 Thinly slice the leeks, then scatter over the cheese. Bake for 10 minutes, then remove from the oven.

6 Arrange the mussels on top. Season with salt and pepper and sprinkle over the remaining cheese. Bake for a further 5–10 minutes until crisp and golden. Serve immediately.

Cook's Tip
Frozen or canned mussels can also be used but will give a different flavour and texture to these pizzettes.

Wild Mushroom Pizzettes

Fresh wild mushrooms add a distinctive flavour to these pizzettes, which make an ideal starter.

Serves 4
45ml/3 tbsp olive oil
350g/12oz fresh mixed wild mushrooms, washed and sliced
2 shallots, chopped
2 garlic cloves, finely chopped
30ml/2 tbsp chopped fresh mixed thyme and flat leaf parsley
1 quantity Basic Pizza Dough (see page 158)
40g/1½oz/generous ¼ cup grated Gruyère cheese
30ml/2 tbsp freshly grated Parmesan
salt and ground black pepper

1 Preheat the oven to 220°C/425°F/Gas 7. Heat 30ml/2 tbsp of the oil in a frying pan and fry the mushrooms, shallots and garlic over a moderate heat, stirring occasionally, until all the juices have evaporated.

2 Stir in half the herbs and seasoning, then set aside to cool.

3 Divide the dough into four pieces and roll out each one on a lightly floured surface to a 13cm/5in circle. Place well apart on two greased baking sheets, then push up the dough edges to form a thin rim. Brush the pizza bases with the remaining oil and top with the wild mushroom mixture.

4 Mix together the Gruyère and Parmesan, then sprinkle over. Bake for 15–20 minutes until crisp and golden. Remove from the oven and scatter over the remaining herbs to serve.

Cook's Tip
If you cannot find wild mushrooms, a mixture of cultivated mushrooms, such as shiitake, oyster and chestnut, would do just as well.

Ham, Pepper and Mozzarella Pizzas

Succulent roasted peppers, salty Parma ham and creamy
mozzarella make a delicious topping for these pizzas.

Serves 2

4 thick slices ciabatta
   bread
1 red pepper, roasted and
   peeled
1 yellow pepper, roasted
   and peeled

4 slices Parma ham, cut
   into thick strips
75g/3oz mozzarella
pinch of black pepper
tiny fresh basil leaves, to
   garnish

1 Lightly toast the slices of ciabatta bread on both sides until
they are golden.

2 Cut the roast peppers into thick strips and arrange on the
toasted bread with the Parma ham.

3 Thinly slice the mozzarella and arrange on top. Grind over
plenty of pepper. Place under a hot grill for 2–3 minutes until
the cheese is bubbling.

4 Arrange the basil leaves on top and serve immediately.

Fruity French Bread Pizza

This recipe uses French bread as a base instead of the more
usual pizza dough, for a change.

Serves 4

2 small baguettes
1 jar ready-made tomato
   sauce or pizza topping
75g/3oz sliced cooked
   ham
4 rings canned pineapple,
   drained and chopped

½ small green pepper,
   seeded and cut into
   thin strips
75g/3oz mature Cheddar
   cheese
salt and ground black
   pepper

1 Preheat the oven to 200°C/400°F/Gas 6. Cut the baguettes
in half lengthways and toast the outsides under a grill until
crisp and golden.

2 Spread the tomato sauce or pizza topping over the toasted
baguette halves.

3 Cut the ham into strips and arrange on the baguettes with
the pineapple and pepper. Season with salt and pepper.

4 Grate the Cheddar and sprinkle over the top. Bake or grill
for 15–20 minutes until crisp and golden. Serve immediately.

Cook's Tip
*These pizzas may be grilled instead of baked in the
oven. Cook them for the same length of time under a
moderate heat but check that they do not burn.*

Marinara Pizza

The combination of garlic, good quality olive oil and oregano gives this pizza an unmistakably Italian flavour.

Serves 2–3

60ml/4 tbsp olive oil
675g/1½ lb plum
    tomatoes, peeled,
    seeded and chopped
1 pizza base, 25–30cm/
    10–12in diameter
    (see page 158)

4 garlic cloves, cut into
    slivers
15ml/1 tbsp chopped
    fresh oregano
salt and ground black
    pepper

1 Preheat the oven to 220°C/425°F/Gas 7. In a saucepan, heat 30ml/2 tbsp of the oil. Add the tomatoes and cook, stirring frequently for about 5 minutes until soft.

2 Place the tomatoes in a metal sieve and leave them to drain for about 5 minutes.

3 Transfer the tomatoes to a food processor or blender and purée until smooth.

4 Brush the pizza base with half the remaining oil. Spoon over the tomatoes and sprinkle with garlic and oregano. Drizzle over the remaining oil and season to taste. Bake for 15–20 minutes until crisp and golden. Serve at once.

Cook's Tip
Ready-made pizza bases are available from most supermarkets and come in a range of sizes. It is useful to keep a few in the freezer.

Quattro Formaggi

Rich and cheesy, these individual pizzas are quick to make, and the aroma of melting cheese is irresistible.

Serves 4

1 quantity Basic Pizza
    Dough (see page 158)
15ml/1 tbsp garlic oil
½ small red onion, very
    thinly sliced
50g/2oz dolcelatte
50g/2oz mozzarella

50g/2oz/½ cup grated
    Gruyère
30ml/2 tbsp freshly
    grated Parmesan
15ml/1 tbsp chopped
    fresh thyme
pinch of black pepper

1 Preheat the oven to 220°C/425°F/Gas 7. Divide the dough into four pieces and roll out each one on a lightly floured surface into a 13cm/5in circle. Place well apart on two greased baking sheets, then push up the dough edges to make a thin rim. Brush with garlic oil and top with the red onion.

2 Cut the dolcelatte and mozzarella into dice and scatter over the bases. Mix together the Gruyère, Parmesan and thyme and sprinkle over.

3 Grind over plenty of pepper. Bake for 15–20 minutes until crisp and golden and the cheeses are bubbling. Serve hot.

Pizza with Fresh Vegetables

This pizza can be made with any vegetable combination.
Blanch or sauté before baking in the oven.

Serves 4

400g/14oz peeled plum
    tomatoes, weighed
    whole (or canned
    without their juice)
2 broccoli spears
225g/8oz fresh asparagus
2 small courgettes
75ml/5 tbsp olive oil
50g/2oz/½ cup shelled
    peas, fresh or frozen
4 spring onions, sliced

1 quantity Basic Pizza
    Dough (see page 158)
75g/3oz/generous ½ cup
    diced mozzarella
    cheese
10 fresh basil leaves, torn
    into pieces
2 garlic cloves, finely
    chopped
salt and ground black
    pepper

1 Preheat the oven to 240°C/475°F/Gas 9 for at least
20 minutes before baking the pizza. Strain the tomatoes
through the medium holes of a food mill placed over a bowl,
scraping in all the pulp.

2 Peel the broccoli stems and asparagus, and blanch with the
courgettes in a large saucepan of boiling unsalted water for
4–5 minutes. Drain and cut into bite-size pieces.

3 Heat 30ml/2 tbsp of the olive oil in a small saucepan. Stir
in the peas and spring onions, and cook for 5–6 minutes,
stirring frequently. Remove from the heat.

4 Roll out the pizza dough to a 25cm/10in circle and place
on a greased baking sheet. Spread the puréed tomatoes on to
the dough, leaving the rim uncovered. Add all the other
vegetables, spreading them evenly over the tomatoes.

5 Sprinkle with the mozzarella, basil, garlic, salt and pepper
and remaining olive oil. Immediately place the pizza in the
oven. Bake for about 20 minutes, or until the crust is golden
brown and the cheese has melted.

Four Seasons Pizza

The topping on this pizza is divided into four quarters, one
for each "season", creating a colourful effect.

Serves 4

450g/1lb peeled plum
    tomatoes, weighed
    whole (or canned
    without their juice)
75ml/5 tbsp olive oil
115g/4oz mushrooms,
    thinly sliced
1 garlic clove, finely
    chopped
1 quantity Basic Pizza
    Dough (see page 158)
350g/12oz/scant 2½ cups
    diced mozzarella

4 thin slices of ham, cut
    into 5cm/2in squares
32 black olives, stoned
    and halved
8 artichoke hearts,
    preserved in oil,
    drained and cut in
    half
5ml/1 tsp oregano leaves,
    fresh or dried
salt and ground black
    pepper

1 Preheat the oven to 240°C/475°F/Gas 9 for at least
20 minutes before baking the pizza. Strain the tomatoes
through the medium holes of a food mill placed over a bowl,
scraping in all the pulp.

2 Heat 30ml/2 tbsp of the oil in a saucepan and lightly sauté
the mushrooms. Stir in the garlic and set aside.

3 Roll out the pizza dough to a 25cm/10in circle and place
on a greased baking sheet. Spread the puréed tomatoes on the
prepared pizza dough, leaving the rim uncovered. Sprinkle
evenly with the mozzarella. Spread the mushrooms over one
quarter of the pizza.

4 Arrange the ham on another quarter, and the olives and
artichoke hearts on the two remaining quarters. Sprinkle with
oregano, salt and pepper, and the remaining olive oil.
Immediately place the pizza in the oven. Bake for about
15–20 minutes, or until the crust is golden brown and the
topping is bubbling.

Fiorentina Pizza

Spinach is the star ingredient of this pizza. A grating of nutmeg heightens its flavour.

Serves 2–3

175g/6oz/1½ cups fresh
  spinach
45ml/3 tbsp olive oil
1 small red onion, thinly
  sliced
1 pizza base, 25–30cm/
  10–12in diameter
  (see page 158)

1 jar ready-made tomato
  sauce or pizza topping
pinch of freshly grated
  nutmeg
150g/5oz mozzarella
1 egg
25g/1oz/¼ cup grated
  Gruyère cheese

1 Preheat the oven to 220°C/425°F/Gas 7. Remove the stalks from the spinach and wash the leaves in plenty of cold water. Drain well and pat dry with kitchen paper.

2 Heat 15ml/1 tbsp of the oil in a large frying pan and fry the onion until softened. Add the spinach and continue to fry until just wilted. Drain off any excess liquid.

3 Brush the pizza base with half the remaining oil. Spread over the tomato sauce or pizza topping, then top with the spinach mixture. Grate over some nutmeg.

4 Thinly slice the mozzarella and arrange over the spinach. Drizzle over the remaining oil. Bake for 10 minutes, then remove from the oven.

5 Make a small well in the centre of the pizza and drop the egg into the hole.

6 Sprinkle over the Gruyère and return to the oven for a further 5–10 minutes until crisp and golden.

Chilli Beef Pizza

Minced beef and red kidney beans combined with oregano, cumin and chillies give this pizza a Mexican character.

Serves 4

30ml/2 tbsp olive oil
1 red onion, finely
  chopped
1 garlic clove, crushed
½ red pepper, seeded and
  finely chopped
175g/6oz lean minced
  beef
2.5ml/½ tsp ground
  cumin
2 fresh red chillies, seeded
  and chopped
115g/4oz/scant ½ cup
  (drained weight)
  canned red kidney
  beans, rinsed

1 jar ready-made tomato
  sauce or pizza topping
15ml/1 tbsp chopped
  fresh oregano
50g/2oz/½ cup grated
  mozzarella
75g/3oz/¾ cup grated
  oak-smoked Cheddar
1 pizza base, 25-30cm/
  10-12in diameter
  (see page 158)
salt and ground black
  pepper

1 Preheat the oven to 220°C/425°F/Gas 7. Heat 15ml/1 tbsp of the oil in a frying pan and gently fry the onion, garlic and pepper until soft. Increase the heat, add the beef, and brown well, stirring constantly.

2 Add the cumin and chillies and continue to cook, stirring, for about 5 minutes. Add the beans and seasoning.

3 Spread the tomato sauce over the pizza base.

4 Spoon over the beef mixture, then scatter over the oregano.

Tuna, Anchovy and Caper Pizza

This pizza makes a substantial supper dish for two to three people when accompanied by a simple salad.

Serves 2–3

For the pizza dough
115g/4oz/1 cup
  self-raising flour
115g/4oz/1 cup
  self-raising wholemeal
  flour
pinch of salt
50g/2oz/4 tbsp butter,
  diced
about 150ml/¼ pint/
  ⅔ cup milk

For the topping
30ml/2 tbsp olive oil

1 jar ready-made tomato
  sauce or pizza topping
1 small red onion
200g/7oz can tuna,
  drained
15ml/1 tbsp capers
12 black olives, stoned
45ml/3 tbsp freshly
  grated Parmesan
  cheese
50g/2oz can anchovy
  fillets, drained and
  halved lengthways
ground black pepper

1 Place the flour and salt in a bowl and rub in the butter until the mixture resembles fine breadcrumbs. Add the milk and mix to a soft dough with a wooden spoon. Knead on a lightly floured surface until smooth.

2 Preheat the oven to 220°C/425°F/Gas 7. Roll out the dough on a lightly floured surface to a 25cm/10in circle. Place on a greased baking sheet and brush with 15ml/4 tbsp of the oil. Spread the tomato sauce or pizza topping evenly over the dough, leaving the edge uncovered.

3 Cut the onion into thin wedges and arrange on top. Roughly flake the tuna with a fork and scatter over the onion. Sprinkle over the capers, black olives and Parmesan cheese. Place the anchovy fillets over the top of the pizza in a criss-cross pattern. Drizzle over the remaining oil, then grind over plenty of pepper. Bake for 15–20 minutes until crisp and golden. Serve immediately.

Salmon and Avocado Pizza

Smoked and fresh salmon make a delicious pizza topping when mixed with avocado.

Serves 3–4

150g/5oz salmon fillet
120ml/4fl oz/½ cup dry
  white wine
1 pizza base, 25–30cm/
  10–12in diameter (see
  page 158)
15ml/1 tbsp olive oil
400g/14oz can chopped
  tomatoes, drained well
115g/4oz/scant 1 cup
  grated mozzarella
1 small avocado

10ml/2 tsp lemon juice
30ml/2 tbsp crème
  fraîche
75g/3oz smoked salmon,
  cut into strips
15ml/1 tbsp capers
30ml/2 tbsp snipped
  fresh chives, to
  garnish
ground black pepper

1 Preheat the oven to 220°C/425°F/Gas 7. Place the salmon fillet in a frying pan, pour over the wine and season with pepper. Bring slowly to the boil over a gentle heat, remove from the heat, cover with a tight-fitting lid and cool. (The fish will cook in the cooling liquid.) Skin and flake the salmon into small pieces, removing any bones.

2 Brush the pizza base with the oil and spread the drained tomatoes over the top. Sprinkle over 50g/2oz/scant ½ cup of mozzarella. Bake for 10 minutes, then remove from the oven.

3 Meanwhile, halve, stone and peel the avocado. Cut the flesh into small dice and toss carefully in the lemon juice.

4 Dot teaspoonfuls of the crème fraîche over the pizza base.

5 Arrange the fresh and smoked salmon, avocado, capers and remaining mozzarella on top. Season to taste with pepper. Bake for 5–10 minutes until crisp and golden.

6 Sprinkle over the chives and serve immediately.

Mushroom and Pancetta Pizzas

Use any type and combination of mushrooms you like for these simple yet tasty individual pizzas.

Serves 4

1 quantity Basic Pizza
  Dough (see page 158)
60ml/4 tbsp olive oil
2 garlic cloves, crushed
225g/8oz fresh mixed
  ceps and chestnut
  mushrooms, roughly
  chopped

75g/3oz pancetta,
  roughly chopped
15ml/1 tbsp chopped
  fresh oregano
45ml/3 tbsp freshly
  grated Parmesan
  cheese
salt and ground black
  pepper

1 Preheat the oven to 220°C/425°F/Gas 7. Divide the dough into four pieces and roll out each one on a lightly floured surface to a 13cm/5in circle. Place well apart on two greased baking sheets.

2 Heat 30ml/2 tbsp of the olive oil in a frying pan and fry the garlic and mushrooms gently until the mushrooms are tender and the juices have evaporated. Season to taste with salt and pepper, then cool.

3 Brush the pizza bases with 15ml/1 tbsp oil, then spoon over the mushrooms. Scatter over the pancetta and oregano. Sprinkle with Parmesan and drizzle over the remaining oil. Bake for 10–15 minutes, until crisp. Serve immediately.

Cook's Tip
Pancetta is available in larger supermarkets and Italian delicatessens. If you cannot find it, use thickly sliced fried bacon instead.

Pepperoni Pizza

Mixed peppers, mozzarella cheese and pepperoni make a delicious topping for this luxurious pizza.

Serves 4

For the sauce
30ml/2 tbsp olive oil
1 onion, finely chopped
1 garlic clove, crushed
400g/14oz can chopped
  tomatoes with herbs
15ml/1 tbsp tomato purée

For the pizza base
275g/10oz/2½ cups plain
  flour
2.5ml/½ tsp salt
5ml/1 tsp easy-blend
  dried yeast
30ml/2 tbsp olive oil

For the topping
½ each red, yellow and
  green pepper, sliced
  into rings
150g/5oz mozzarella
  cheese, sliced
75g/3oz pepperoni
  sausage, thinly sliced
8 black olives, stoned
3 sun-dried tomatoes,
  chopped
2.5ml/½ tsp dried
  oregano
olive oil, for drizzling

1 For the sauce, fry the onions and garlic in the oil until softened. Add the tomatoes and tomato purée. Boil rapidly for 5 minutes until reduced slightly. Leave to cool.

2 To make the pizza base, sift the flour and salt into a bowl. Sprinkle over the yeast and make a well in the centre. Pour in 175ml/6fl oz/¾ cup warm water and the olive oil. Mix to a soft dough. Knead the dough on a lightly floured surface for about 5–10 minutes, until smooth. Roll out to a 25cm/10in round, press up the edges slightly and place on a greased baking sheet.

3 Spread over the tomato sauce and top with the peppers, mozzarella, pepperoni, olives and tomatoes. Sprinkle over the oregano and drizzle with olive oil. Cover loosely and leave in a warm place for 30 minutes. Meanwhile, preheat the oven to 220°C/425°F/ Gas 7. Bake for 25–30 minutes then serve.

Farmhouse Pizza

This is the ultimate party pizza. Served cut into fingers, it is ideal for a large and hungry gathering.

Serves 8

90ml/6 tbsp olive oil
225g/8oz button
  mushrooms, sliced
2 quantities Basic Pizza
  Dough (see page 158)
1 jar ready-made tomato
  sauce or pizza topping
300g/10oz mozzarella
  cheese, thinly sliced
115g/4oz wafer thin
  smoked ham slices

6 bottled artichoke hearts
  in oil, drained and
  sliced
50g/2oz can anchovy
  fillets, drained and
  halved lengthways
10 black olives, stoned
  and halved
30ml/2 tbsp chopped
  fresh oregano
15ml/3 tbsp grated
  Parmesan cheese
ground black pepper

1 Preheat the oven to 220°C/425°F/Gas 7. In a large frying pan, heat 30ml/2 tbsp of the oil. Gently fry the mushrooms for 5 minutes until all the juices have evaporated. Remove from the heat and leave to cool.

2 Roll out the dough on a lightly floured surface to make a 30 x 25cm/12 x 10in rectangle. Transfer to a greased baking sheet, then push up the dough edges to form a thin rim. Brush with 30ml/2 tbsp of the oil.

3 Spread the tomato sauce or pizza topping over the dough, then arrange the sliced mozzarella over the sauce.

4 Scrunch up the ham and arrange on top with the artichoke hearts, mushrooms and anchovies.

5 Dot with the olives, then sprinkle over the oregano and Parmesan. Drizzle over the remaining oil and season to taste with pepper. Bake for about 25 minutes until crisp and golden. Serve immediately.

Crab and Parmesan Calzonelli

These miniature calzone owe their popularity to their impressive presentation.

Makes 10–12

1 quantity Basic Pizza
  Dough (see page 158)
115g/4oz mixed prepared
  crab meat, defrosted if
  frozen
15ml/1 tbsp double cream
30ml/2 tbsp freshly
  grated Parmesan

30ml/2 tbsp chopped
  fresh parsley
1 garlic clove, crushed
salt and ground black
  pepper
fresh parsley sprigs, to
  garnish

1 Preheat the oven to 200°C/400°F/Gas 6. Roll out the pizza dough on a lightly floured surface to 3mm/⅛ in thick. Using a 7.5cm/3in plain round pastry cutter, stamp out ten to twelve circles of dough.

2 In a bowl, mix together the crab meat, cream, Parmesan, parsley and garlic, and season to taste with salt and pepper.

3 Spoon a little of the filling on to one half of each circle. Dampen the edges of the dough with water and fold over to enclose the filling.

4 Seal the edges by pressing with a fork. Place well apart on two greased baking sheets. Bake for 10–15 minutes until golden. Garnish with parsley sprigs.

Cook's Tip
If you prefer, use prawns instead of crab meat. If frozen, make sure they are fully thawed first.

Ham and Mozzarella Calzone

A calzone is a kind of "inside-out" pizza – the dough is on the outside and the filling on the inside.

Serves 2

1 quantity Basic Pizza
  Dough (see page 158)
115g/4oz/½ cup ricotta
  cheese
30ml/2 tbsp freshly
  grated Parmesan
1 egg yolk
30ml/2 tbsp chopped
  fresh basil

75g/3oz cooked ham,
  finely chopped
75g/3oz mozzarella, cut
  into small dice
olive oil, for brushing
salt and ground black
  pepper

1 Preheat the oven to 220°C/425°F/Gas 7. Divide the dough in half and roll out each piece on a lightly floured surface to an 18cm/7in circle.

2 In a bowl, mix together the ricotta and Parmesan cheeses, egg yolk, basil and seasoning.

3 Spread the mixture over half of each circle, leaving a 2.5cm/1in border, then scatter the ham and mozzarella on top. Dampen the edges with water, then fold over the other half of dough to enclose the filling.

4 Press the edges firmly together to seal. Place on two greased baking sheets. Brush with oil and make a small hole in the top of each to allow the steam to escape. Bake for 15–20 minutes until golden. Serve immediately.

Cook's Tip
For a vegetarian version, replace the ham with fried mushrooms or chopped cooked spinach.

Aubergine and Shallot Calzone

Aubergines, shallots and sun-dried tomatoes make an unusual filling for calzone.

Serves 2

45ml/3 tbsp olive oil
3 shallots, chopped
4 baby aubergines
1 garlic clove, chopped
50g/2oz (drained weight)
  sun-dried tomatoes in
  oil, chopped
1.5ml/¼ tsp dried red
  chilli flakes
10ml/2 tsp chopped fresh
  thyme

1 quantity Basic Pizza
  Dough (see page 158)
75g/3oz/generous ½ cup
  dried mozzarella
salt and ground black
  pepper
15–30ml/1–2 tbsp
  freshly grated
  Parmesan cheese, to
  serve

1 Preheat the oven to 220°C/425°F/Gas 7. Trim the baby aubergines, then cut into small dice.

2 Fry the shallots in some oil until soft. Add the aubergines, garlic, sun-dried tomatoes, red chilli flakes, thyme and season to taste. Cook for 4–5 minutes, stirring frequently, until the aubergine is beginning to soften.

3 Divide the dough in half and roll out each piece on a lightly floured surface to an 18cm/7in circle. Spread the aubergine mixture over half of each circle, leaving a 2.5cm/1in border, then scatter the mozzarella over.

4 Dampen the edges with water, then fold the other half of dough over to enclose the filling. Press the edges firmly together to seal. Place on two greased baking sheets.

5 Brush with half the remaining oil and make a small hole in the top of each to allow the steam to escape. Bake for about 15–20 minutes until golden. Remove from the oven and brush with the remaining oil. Sprinkle over the Parmesan and serve the calzone immediately.

Root Vegetable Couscous

Harissa is a very fiery Tunisian chilli sauce which can be bought ready-made from Middle-Eastern shops.

Serves 4

350g/12oz/2¼ cups
    couscous
45ml/3 tbsp olive oil
4 baby onions, halved
675g/1½lb fresh mixed
    root vegetables such as
    carrots, swede, turnip,
    celeriac and sweet
    potatoes, cubed
2 garlic cloves, crushed
pinch of saffron strands
2.5ml/½ tsp each ground
    cinnamon and ginger
2.5ml/½ tsp ground
    turmeric
5ml/1 tsp each ground
    cumin and coriander
15ml/1 tbsp tomato purée
450ml/¾ pint/1¾cups
    hot vegetable stock

1 small fennel bulb,
    quartered
115g/4oz/1 cup cooked or
    canned chick-peas
50g/2oz/½ cup seedless
    raisins
30ml/2 tbsp chopped
    fresh coriander
30ml/2 tbsp chopped
    fresh flat leaf parsley
salt and ground black
    pepper

For the spiced sauce
15ml/1 tbsp olive oil
15ml/1 tbsp lemon juice
15ml/1 tbsp chopped
    fresh coriander
2.5–5ml/½–1 tsp
    harissa

1 Put the couscous in a bowl, cover with hot water; drain. Gently fry the onions for 3 minutes, then add the root vegetables and fry for 5 minutes. Add the garlic and spices and cook for 1 minute, stirring. Transfer the vegetable mixture to a large deep saucepan. Stir in the tomato purée, stock, fennel, chick-peas, raisins, chopped coriander and flat leaf parsley. Bring to the boil. Put the couscous into a muslin-lined steamer and place this over the vegetable mixture. Cover and simmer for 20 minutes, or until the vegetables are tender.

2 To make the sauce, mix all the ingredients into 250ml/8fl oz/1 cup of the vegetable liquid. Spoon the couscous on to a plate and pile the vegetables on top. Serve at once, handing round the sauce separately.

Risotto with Mushrooms

The addition of wild mushrooms gives a lovely woodland flavour to this risotto.

Serves 3–4

25g/1oz dried wild
    mushrooms, preferably
    porcini
175g/6oz fresh cultivated
    mushrooms
juice of ½ lemon
75g/3oz/6 tbsp butter
30ml/2 tbsp finely
    chopped fresh parsley
900ml/1½ pints/3¾cups
    meat or chicken stock,
    preferably home-made
30ml/2 tbsp olive oil

1 small onion, finely
    chopped
275g/10oz/1½ cups
    medium grain risotto
    rice, such as arborio
120ml/4fl oz/½ cup dry
    white wine
salt and ground black
    pepper
45ml/3 tbsp freshly
    grated Parmesan
    cheese

1 Place the dried mushrooms in a small bowl with about 350ml/12fl oz/1½ cups warm water. Leave to soak for at least 40 minutes. Rinse the mushrooms. Filter the soaking water through a strainer lined with kitchen paper, and reserve. Place in a pan with the stock; simmer until needed.

2 Slice the mushrooms. Toss with the lemon juice. Melt a third of the butter in a large frying pan. Stir in the mushrooms and cook until they begin to brown. Stir in the parsley, cook for 30 seconds more, and remove to a side dish.

3 Heat another third of the butter with the olive oil in the mushroom pan. Cook the onion until golden. Add the rice and stir for 1–2 minutes. Add all the mushrooms. Pour in the wine, cook until it evaporates. Add the stock until it evaporates; cook the rice until *al dente*, about 20–35 minutes.

4 Remove the risotto pan from the heat. Stir in the remaining butter and the Parmesan. Grind in a little pepper, and taste again for salt; adjust if necessary. Allow the risotto to rest for 3–4 minutes before serving.

Tomato Risotto

Use plum tomatoes in this dish, if possible, for their fresh
vibrant flavour and meaty texture.

Serves 4

675g/1½lb firm ripe
    tomatoes
50g/2oz/4 tbsp butter
1 onion, finely chopped
1.2 litres/2 pints/5 cups
    vegetable stock
275g/10oz/1¼ cups
    arborio rice
400g/14oz can cannellini
    beans

50g/2oz/½ cup finely
    grated Parmesan
    cheese
salt and ground black
    pepper
10–12 fresh basil leaves,
    shredded, and freshly
    grated Parmesan
    cheese, to serve

1 Halve the tomatoes and scoop out the seeds into a sieve
placed over a bowl. Press the seeds with a spoon to extract all
the juice. Set aside.

2 Grill the tomatoes skin-side up until the skins are evenly
blackened and blistered. Rub off the skins and dice the flesh.

3 Melt the butter in a large frying pan and cook the onion
for 5 minutes until beginning to soften. Add the tomatoes, the
reserved juice and seasoning, then cook, stirring occasionally,
for about 10 minutes. Meanwhile, bring the vegetable stock to
the boil in another pan.

4 Add the rice to the tomatoes and stir to coat, then add a
ladleful of the stock and stir gently until absorbed. Repeat,
adding a ladleful of stock at a time, until all the stock is
absorbed and the rice is tender and creamy.

5 Stir in the cannellini beans and grated Parmesan and heat
through for a few minutes. Just before serving the risotto,
sprinkle each portion with shredded basil leaves and
shavings of Parmesan.

Grilled Polenta with Peppers

Grilled slices of herby polenta are topped with yellow and
red pepper strips for a delicious, colourful dish.

Serves 4

115g/4oz/scant 1 cup
    polenta
25g/1oz/2 tbsp butter
15–30ml/1–2 tbsp
    mixed chopped herbs
    such as parsley, thyme
    and sage
melted butter, for
    brushing
60ml/4 tbsp olive oil
1–2 garlic cloves, cut
    into slivers

2 roasted red peppers,
    peeled and cut into
    strips
2 roasted yellow peppers,
    peeled and cut into
    strips
15ml/1 tbsp balsamic
    vinegar
salt and ground black
    pepper
fresh herb sprigs, to
    garnish

1 Bring 600ml/1 pint/2½ cups salted water to the boil in a
heavy saucepan. Trickle in the polenta, beating continuously,
then cook gently for 15–20 minutes, stirring occasionally,
until the mixture is no longer grainy and comes away from
the sides of the pan.

2 Remove the pan from the heat and beat in the butter, herbs
and plenty of pepper.

3 Pour the polenta into a small pudding basin, smooth the
surface and leave until cold and firm.

4 Turn out the polenta on to a board and cut into thick slices.
Brush the polenta slices with melted butter and grill each side
for about 4–5 minutes, until golden brown.

5 Meanwhile, heat the olive oil in a frying pan, add the
garlic and peppers and stir-fry for 1–2 minutes. Stir in the
balsamic vinegar and seasoning.

6 Spoon the pepper mixture over the polenta slices and
garnish with fresh herb sprigs. Serve hot.

Okra Fried Rice

This spicy rich dish is given a creamy consistency by the natural juices of the sliced okra.

Serves 3–4

30ml/2 tbsp vegetable oil
15g/½oz/1 tbsp butter or margarine
1 garlic clove, crushed
½ red onion, finely chopped
115g/4oz okra, topped and tailed
30ml/2 tbsp diced green and red peppers
2.5ml/½ tsp dried thyme
2 green chillies, finely chopped

2.5ml/½ tsp five-spice powder
1 vegetable stock cube
30ml/2 tbsp soy sauce
15ml/1 tbsp chopped fresh coriander
225g/8oz/2½ cups cooked rice
salt and ground black pepper
fresh coriander sprigs, to garnish

1 Heat the oil and butter or margarine in a frying pan or wok and cook the garlic and onion over a moderate heat for 5 minutes until soft.

2 Thinly slice the okra, add to the pan or wok and sauté gently for 6–7 minutes.

3 Add the green and red peppers, thyme, chillies and five-spice powder and cook for 3 minutes, then crumble in the stock cube.

4 Add the soy sauce, coriander and rice and heat through, stirring well. Season to taste with salt and pepper. Serve hot, garnished with coriander sprigs.

Cook's Tip
Reduce the amount of chopped green chilli you include in this dish, if you wish.

Asparagus and Cheese Risotto

Arborio rice is *the* risotto rice and gives this authentic Italian dish a unique creamy texture.

Serves 4

1.5ml/¼ tsp saffron strands
750ml/1¼ pints/3⅓ cups hot chicken stock
25g/1oz/2 tbsp butter
30ml/2 tbsp olive oil
1 large onion, finely chopped
2 garlic cloves, finely chopped
225g/8oz/1¼ cups arborio rice
300ml/½ pint/1¼ cups dry white wine

225g/8oz asparagus tips (or asparagus cut into 5cm/2in lengths), cooked
75g/3oz/1 cup finely grated Parmesan cheese
salt and ground black pepper
fresh Parmesan cheese shavings and fresh basil sprigs, to garnish
ciabatta bread rolls and green salad, to serve

1 Sprinkle the saffron over the stock and leave to infuse for 5 minutes. Heat the butter and oil in a frying pan and fry the onion and garlic for about 6 minutes until softened.

2 Add the rice and stir-fry for 1–2 minutes to coat the grains with the butter and oil. Pour on 300ml/½ pint/1¼ cups of the stock and saffron. Cook gently, stirring frequently, until it is absorbed. Repeat with another 300ml/½ pint/1¼ cups stock. When that is absorbed, add the wine and carry on cooking and stirring until the rice has a creamy consistency.

3 Add the asparagus and remaining stock, and stir until the liquid is absorbed and the rice is tender. Stir in the Parmesan cheese and season to taste with salt and pepper.

4 Spoon the risotto on to warmed plates and garnish with the Parmesan cheese shavings and fresh basil. Serve with hot ciabatta rolls and a crisp green salad, if you wish.

Louisiana Rice

Minced pork and chicken livers with mixed vegetables make a tasty dish that is a meal in itself.

Serves 4

60ml/4 tbsp vegetable oil
1 small aubergine, diced
225g/8oz minced pork
1 green pepper, seeded
   and chopped
2 celery sticks, chopped
1 onion, chopped
1 garlic clove, crushed
5ml/1 tsp cayenne pepper
5ml/1 tsp paprika
5ml/1 tsp ground black
   pepper
2.5ml/½ tsp salt

5ml/1 tsp dried thyme
2.5ml/½ tsp dried
   oregano
475ml/16fl oz/2 cups
   chicken stock
225g/8oz chicken livers,
   minced
150g/5oz/¼ cup long
   grain rice
1 bay leaf
45ml/3 tbsp chopped
   fresh parsley
celery leaves, to garnish

1 Heat the oil in a frying pan until really hot, then stir-fry the aubergine for about 5 minutes. Add the pork and cook for about 6–8 minutes, until browned, using a wooden spoon to break up any lumps.

2 Add the pepper, celery, onion, garlic, cayenne pepper, paprika, pepper, salt, thyme and oregano. Cover and cook over a high heat for 5–6 minutes, stirring frequently from the bottom to scrape up and distribute the crispy bits of pork.

3 Pour on the chicken stock and stir to clean the bottom of the pan. Cover and cook for 6 minutes over a moderate heat. Stir in the chicken livers, cook for a further 2 minutes, then stir in the rice and add the bay leaf.

4 Reduce the heat, cover and simmer for about 6–7 minutes more. Turn off the heat and leave to stand for a further 10–15 minutes until the rice is tender. Remove the bay leaf and stir in the chopped parsley. Serve the rice hot, garnished with the celery leaves.

Indian Pilau Rice

Basmati rice is the most popular choice for Indian dishes, but you could use long grain rice instead.

Serves 4

225g/8oz/1¼ cups
   basmati rice, rinsed
   well
1 small onion, finely
   chopped
1 garlic clove, crushed
30ml/2 tbsp vegetable oil
5ml/1 tsp fennel seeds
15ml/1 tbsp sesame seeds
2.5ml/½ tsp ground
   turmeric
5ml/1 tsp ground cumin

1.5ml/¼ tsp salt
2 whole cloves
4 cardamom pods, lightly
   crushed
5 black peppercorns
450ml/¾ pint/1¼ cups
   chicken stock
15ml/1 tbsp ground
   almonds
fresh coriander sprigs,
   to garnish

1 Soak the rice in water for 30 minutes. Heat the oil in a saucepan, add the onions and garlic, then fry them gently for 5–6 minutes, until softened.

2 Stir in the fennel and sesame seeds, the turmeric, cumin, salt, cloves, cardamom pods and peppercorns and fry for about 1 minute. Drain the rice well, add to the pan and stir-fry for a further 3 minutes.

3 Pour on the chicken stock. Bring to the boil, then cover with a tight-fitting lid, reduce the heat to very low and then simmer gently for 20 minutes, without removing the lid, until all the liquid has been absorbed.

4 Remove from the heat and leave to stand for 2–3 minutes. Fluff up the rice with a fork and stir in the ground almonds. Garnish with coriander sprigs.

Cook's Tip
Soak the rice for 30 minutes in cold water before cooking, if you have time.

Chinese Special Fried Rice

This staple of Chinese cuisine consists of a mixture of chicken, shrimps and vegetables with fried rice.

Serves 4

175g/6oz/1 cup long
  grain white rice
45ml/3 tbsp groundnut
  oil
1 garlic clove, crushed
4 spring onions, finely
  chopped
115g/4oz/1 cup diced
  cooked chicken
115g/4oz/1 cup peeled,
  cooked shrimps
50g/2oz/½ cup frozen
  peas

1 egg, beaten with a
  pinch of salt
50g/2oz lettuce, finely
  shredded
30ml/2 tbsp light soy
  sauce
pinch of caster sugar
salt and ground black
  pepper
15ml/1 tbsp chopped,
  roasted cashew nuts,
  to garnish

1   Rinse the rice in two to three changes of warm water to wash away some of the starch. Drain well.

2   Put the rice in a saucepan and add 15ml/1 tbsp of the oil and 350ml/12fl oz/1½ cups water. Cover and bring to the boil, stir once, then cover and simmer for 12–15 minutes, until nearly all the water has been absorbed. Turn off the heat and leave, covered, to stand for 10 minutes. Fluff up with a fork and leave to cool.

3   Heat the remaining oil in a wok or frying pan and stir-fry the garlic and spring onions for 30 seconds.

4   Add the chicken, shrimps and peas and stir-fry for about 1–2 minutes, then add the cooked rice and stir-fry for a further 2 minutes. Pour in the egg and stir-fry until just set. Stir in the lettuce, soy sauce, sugar and seasoning.

5   Transfer to a warmed serving bowl, sprinkle with the chopped cashew nuts and serve immediately.

Lemony Bulgur Wheat Salad

This Middle-Eastern salad, called *tabbouleh*, is delicious as an accompaniment to grilled meats or fish, or on its own.

Serves 4

225g/8oz/1½ cups bulgur
  wheat
4 spring onions, finely
  chopped
75ml/5 tbsp each chopped
  fresh mint and parsley
15ml/1 tbsp chopped
  fresh coriander

2 tomatoes, skinned and
  chopped
juice of 1 lemon
75ml/5 tbsp olive oil
salt and ground black
  pepper
fresh mint sprigs, to
  garnish

1   Place the bulgur wheat in a bowl, pour on enough boiling water to cover and leave to soak for 20 minutes.

2   After soaking, place the bulgur wheat in a large sieve and drain thoroughly. Transfer to a bowl.

3   Stir in the spring onions, herbs, tomatoes, lemon juice, olive oil and seasoning. Mix well and chill in the fridge for about an hour. Garnish with mint.

Cook's Tip
Add some stoned, halved black olives to the salad just before serving, if you wish.

Tanzanian Vegetable Rice

Serve this tasty rice with baked chicken, or a fish dish and a delicious fresh relish – *kachumbali.*

Serves 4

350g/12oz/2 cups basmati rice
45ml/3 tbsp vegetable oil
1 onion, chopped
750ml/1¼ pints/3 cups vegetable stock or water
2 garlic cloves, crushed
115g/4oz/1 cup sweetcorn
½ fresh red or green pepper, chopped
1 large carrot, grated

1 Wash the rice in a sieve under cold water, then leave to drain for about 15 minutes.

2 Heat the oil in a large saucepan and fry the onion for a few minutes over a moderate heat until just soft.

3 Add the rice and stir-fry for about 10 minutes, taking care to keep stirring all the time so that the rice doesn't stick to the base of the pan.

4 Add the stock or water and the garlic and stir well. Bring to the boil and cook over a high heat for 5 minutes, then reduce the heat, cover with a tight-fitting lid and cook the rice for 20 minutes.

5 Scatter the corn over the rice, then spread the pepper on top and lastly sprinkle over the grated carrot.

6 Cover tightly and steam over a low heat until the rice is cooked, then mix together with a fork and serve immediately.

Rice with Seeds and Spices

A change from plain boiled rice, this spicy dish makes a colourful accompaniment for curries or grilled meats.

Serves 4

5ml/1 tsp sunflower oil
2.5ml/½ tsp ground turmeric
6 cardamom pods, lightly crushed
5ml/1 tsp coriander seeds, lightly crushed
1 garlic clove, crushed
200g/7oz/1 cup basmati rice
400ml/14fl oz/1⅔ cups stock
120ml/4fl oz/½ cup natural yogurt
15ml/1 tbsp each toasted sunflower seeds and toasted sesame seeds
salt and ground black pepper
fresh coriander leaves, to garnish

1 Heat the oil in a non-stick frying pan and fry the spices and garlic for about 1 minute, stirring all the time.

2 Add the rice and stock, bring to the boil, then cover and simmer for 15 minutes or until just tender.

3 Stir in the yogurt and the toasted sunflower and sesame seeds. Adjust the seasoning and serve hot, garnished with coriander leaves.

Cook's Tip
Although basmati rice gives the best texture and flavour, you could substitute ordinary long grain rice if you prefer.

Lemon and Herb Risotto Cake

This unusual rice dish can be served as a main course with salad, or as a satisfying side dish.

Serves 4

1 small leek, thinly sliced	30ml/2 tbsp chopped
600ml/1 pint/2½ cups	fresh parsley
chicken stock	75g/3oz/generous ½ cup
225g/8oz/1¼ cups	grated mozzarella
arborio rice	cheese
finely grated rind of	salt and ground black
1 lemon	pepper
30ml/2 tbsp chopped	fresh parsley and lemon
fresh chives	wedges, to garnish

1 Preheat the oven to 200°C/400°F/Gas 6. Lightly oil a 22cm/8½in round loose-bottomed cake tin.

2 Cook the leek in a large saucepan with 45ml/3 tbsp stock, stirring over a moderate heat, to soften. Add the rice and the remaining stock.

3 Bring to the boil. Cover the pan with a tight-fitting lid and simmer gently, stirring occasionally, for about 20 minutes, or until all the liquid is absorbed.

4 Stir in the lemon rind, herbs, cheese and seasoning. Spoon into the tin, cover with foil and bake for 30–35 minutes or until lightly browned. Turn out and serve in slices, garnished with parsley and lemon wedges.

Cook's Tip
This risotto cake is equally delicious served cold, so makes ideal picnic food.

Bulgur and Lentil Pilaff

Bulgur wheat is very easy to cook and can be used in almost any way you would normally use rice, hot or cold.

Serves 4

5ml/1 tsp olive oil	225g/8oz/1¼ cups bulgur
1 large onion, thinly	wheat
sliced	about 750ml/1¼ pints/
2 garlic cloves, crushed	3⅓ cups stock or water
5ml/1 tsp ground	115g/4oz button
coriander	mushrooms, sliced
5ml/1 tsp ground cumin	115g/4oz/⅔ cup green
5ml/1 tsp ground	lentils
turmeric	salt, ground black pepper
2.5ml/½ tsp ground	and cayenne pepper
allspice	

1 Heat the oil in a non-stick saucepan and fry the onion, garlic and spices for 1 minute, stirring.

2 Stir in the bulgur wheat and cook, stirring, for about 2 minutes, until lightly browned. Add the stock or water, mushrooms and lentils.

3 Simmer over a very gentle heat for about 25–30 minutes, until the bulgur wheat and lentils are tender and all the liquid is absorbed. Add more stock or water, if necessary.

4 Season well with salt, black pepper and cayenne pepper and serve hot.

Cook's Tip
Green lentils can be cooked without presoaking, as they cook quite quickly and keep their shape. However, if you have time, soaking them first will shorten the cooking time slightly.

Minted Couscous Castles

Couscous, flavoured with mint and then moulded, makes
an unusual accompaniment to a meal.

Serves 6

225g/8oz/1¼ cups
  couscous
475ml/16fl oz/2 cups
  boiling stock
15ml/1 tbsp freshly
  squeezed lemon juice
2 tomatoes, diced

30ml/2 tbsp chopped
  fresh mint
oil, for brushing
salt and ground black
  pepper
fresh mint sprigs, to
  garnish

1 Place the couscous in a bowl and pour over the boiling
stock. Cover the bowl and leave to stand for 30 minutes, until
all the stock is absorbed and the grains are tender.

2 Stir in the lemon juice with the tomatoes and chopped
mint. Adjust the seasoning with salt and pepper.

3 Brush the insides of four cups or individual moulds with
oil. Spoon in the couscous mixture and pack down firmly.
Chill in the fridge for several hours.

4 Turn out and serve cold, or alternatively, cover and heat
gently in a low oven or microwave, then turn out and serve
hot, garnished with mint.

Cook's Tip

*Most couscous is sold ready-cooked so can be prepared
as above. However, some types require steaming first,
so check the instructions on the packet.*

Creole Jambalaya

This version of jambalaya is made with chicken instead of
the more traditional ham.

Serves 6

4 chicken thighs, boned,
  skinned and diced
about 300ml/½ pint/
  1¼ cups chicken stock
1 large green pepper,
  seeded and sliced
3 celery sticks, sliced
4 spring onions, sliced
400g/14oz can tomatoes
5ml/1 tsp ground cumin

5ml/1 tsp ground allspice
2.5ml/½ tsp cayenne
  pepper
5ml/1 tsp dried thyme
300g/10oz/1½ cups long
  grain rice
200g/7oz/scant 2 cups
  peeled, cooked prawns
salt and ground black
  pepper

1 Fry the chicken in a non-stick saucepan without fat,
turning occasionally, until golden brown.

2 Add 15ml/1 tbsp stock with the pepper, celery and
onions. Cook for a few minutes to soften, then add the
tomatoes, spices and thyme.

3 Stir in the rice and remaining stock. Cover closely and
cook for about 20 minutes, stirring occasionally, until the rice
is tender. Add more stock if necessary.

4 Add the peeled prawns and heat well. Season to taste and
serve with a crisp salad, if you wish.

Red Fried Rice

This vibrant rice dish owes its appeal to the bright colours
of red onion, red pepper and cherry tomatoes.

Serves 2
115g/4oz/⅝ cup rice
30ml/2 tbsp groundnut
  oil
1 small red onion,
  chopped
1 red pepper, seeded and
  chopped

225g/8oz cherry
  tomatoes, halved
2 eggs, beaten
salt and ground black
  pepper

1 Wash the rice several times under cold running water.
Drain well. Bring a large saucepan of water to the boil, add
the rice and cook for 10–12 minutes.

2 Meanwhile, heat the oil in a wok until very hot and stir-fry
the onion and red pepper for 2–3 minutes. Add the cherry
tomatoes and stir-fry for a further 2 minutes.

3 Pour in the beaten eggs all at once. Cook for 30 seconds
without stirring, then stir to break up the eggs as they set.

4 Drain the cooked rice thoroughly, add to the wok and toss
it over the heat with the vegetable and egg mixture for
3 minutes. Season the fried rice with salt and pepper to taste.

Cook's Tip
*Use basmati rice for this dish, if possible. Its slightly
crunchy texture complements the softness of the egg.*

Kedgeree

Popular for breakfast in Victorian times, kedgeree has its
origins in *khichri*, an Indian rice and lentil dish.

Serves 4
500g/1¼lb smoked
  haddock
115g/4oz/scant ½ cup
  long grain rice
30ml/2 tbsp lemon juice
150ml/¼ pint/⅔ cup
  single or soured cream
pinch of freshly grated
  nutmeg
pinch of cayenne pepper

2 hard-boiled eggs, peeled
  and cut into wedges
50g/2oz/4 tbsp butter,
  diced
30ml/2 tbsp chopped
  fresh parsley
salt and ground black
  pepper
fresh parsley sprigs, to
  garnish

1 Poach the haddock, just covered by water, for about
10 minutes, until the flesh flakes easily. Lift the fish from the
cooking liquid with a draining spoon, then remove any skin
and bones. Flake the flesh.

2 Pour the rice into a measuring jug and note the volume,
then tip out, pour the fish cooking liquid into the jug and top
up with water, until it measures twice the volume of the rice.

3 Bring the fish cooking liquid to the boil, add the rice, stir,
then cover with a tight-fitting lid and simmer for about
15 minutes, until the rice is tender and the liquid absorbed.
While the rice is cooking, preheat the oven to 180°C/350°F/
Gas 4, and butter a baking dish.

4 Remove the rice from the heat and stir in the lemon juice,
cream, flaked fish, nutmeg and cayenne. Add the egg wedges
to the rice mixture and stir in gently.

5 Tip the rice mixture into the baking dish, dot with butter
and bake for about 25 minutes.

6 Stir the chopped parsley into the kedgeree, adjust the
seasoning to taste and garnish with fresh parsley sprigs.

Nut Pilaff with Omelette Rolls

This pilaff combines a wonderful mixture of textures – soft
fluffy rice with crunchy nuts and omelette rolls.

Serves 2

175g/6oz/1 cup basmati
   rice
15ml/1 tbsp sunflower oil
1 small onion, chopped
1 red pepper, finely diced
350ml/12fl oz/1½ cups
   hot vegetable stock
2 eggs

25g/1oz/¼ cup salted
   peanuts
15ml/1 tbsp soy sauce
salt and ground black
   pepper
fresh parsley sprigs, to
   garnish

1 Wash the rice several times under cold running water.
Drain thoroughly. Heat half the oil in a large frying pan and
fry the onion and red pepper for 2–3 minutes, then stir in the
rice and stock. Bring to the boil and cook for 10 minutes until
the rice is tender.

2 Meanwhile, beat the eggs lightly and season to taste with
salt and pepper. Heat the remaining oil in a second large
frying pan. Pour in the eggs and tilt the pan to cover the base
thinly. Cook the omelette for 1 minute, then flip it over and
cook the other side for 1 minute.

3 Slide the omelette on to a clean board and roll it up tightly.
Cut the omelette roll into eight slices.

4 Stir the peanuts and the soy sauce into the pilaff and add
pepper to taste. Turn the pilaff into a serving dish, then
arrange the omelette rolls on top and garnish with the parsley.
Serve at once.

Cook's Tip
*Try salted cashew nuts or toasted flaked almonds in
this dish for a change.*

Aubergine Pilaff

This hearty dish is made with bulgur wheat, aubergine and
pine nuts, subtly flavoured with fresh mint.

Serves 2

2 aubergines
60–90ml/4–6 tbsp
   sunflower oil
1 small onion, finely
   chopped
175g/6oz/1 cup bulgur
   wheat
450ml/¾ pint/1¼ cups
   vegetable stock

30ml/2 tbsp pine nuts,
   toasted
15ml/1 tbsp chopped
   fresh mint
salt and ground black
   pepper
lime and lemon wedges
   and fresh mint sprigs,
   to garnish

1 Top and tail the aubergines. Using a sharp knife, cut them
into neat sticks and then into 1cm/½in dice.

2 Heat 60ml/4 tbsp of the oil in a large frying pan and sauté
the onion for 1 minute.

3 Add the diced aubergine. Cook over a high heat, stirring
frequently, for about 4 minutes until just tender. Add the
remaining oil if needed.

4 Stir in the bulgur wheat, mixing well, then pour in the
vegetable stock. Bring to the boil, then lower the heat and
simmer for 10 minutes or until all the liquid has evaporated.
Season with salt and pepper to taste.

5 Add the pine nuts, stir gently with a wooden spoon, then
stir in the mint.

6 Spoon the pilaff on to individual plates and garnish each
portion with lime and lemon wedges. Sprinkle with torn mint
leaves for extra colour.

Cabbage with Bacon

In this dish, smoked bacon enhances the flavour of cabbage, making it a delicious vegetable accompaniment.

Serves 2–4

30ml/2 tbsp oil	500g/1¼ lb cabbage,
1 onion, finely chopped	shredded
115g/4oz smoked bacon,	salt and ground black
finely chopped	pepper

1 Heat the oil in a large saucepan and cook the onion and bacon for about 7 minutes, stirring occasionally.

2 Add the cabbage and season with salt and pepper. Stir for a few minutes over a moderately high heat until the cabbage begins to lose volume.

3 Continue to cook the cabbage, stirring it frequently for 8–10 minutes until tender, but still crisp. (For softer cabbage, cover the pan for part of the cooking.) Serve immediately.

Cook's Tip
This dish is equally delicious if prepared using spring greens instead of cabbage. To make a more substantial dish to serve for lunch or supper, add some chopped button mushrooms and some skinned, seeded and chopped tomatoes.

Braised Red Cabbage

Lightly spiced with a sharp, sweet flavour, this dish goes well with roast pork, duck and game dishes.

Serves 4–6

1kg/2lb red cabbage	15g/½oz/1 tbsp dark
2 onions, chopped	brown sugar
2 cooking apples, peeled,	45ml/3 tbsp red wine
cored and grated	vinegar
5ml/1 tsp freshly grated	25g/1oz/2 tbsp butter or
nutmeg	margarine, cut into
1.5ml/¼ tsp ground	dice
cloves	salt and ground black
1.5ml/¼ tsp ground	pepper
cinnamon	

1 Preheat the oven to 160°C/325°F/Gas 3. Cut away and discard the large white ribs from the outer cabbage leaves using a large sharp knife, then finely shred the cabbage.

2 Layer the shredded cabbage in a large ovenproof dish with the onions, apples, spices, sugar and seasoning. Pour over the vinegar and add the diced butter or margarine.

3 Cover the ovenproof dish and cook in the oven for about 1½ hours, stirring a couple of times, until the cabbage is very tender. Serve hot.

Cook's Tip
This recipe can be cooked in advance. Bake the cabbage for 1½ hours, then leave to cool. To complete the cooking, bake in the oven at the same temperature for about 30 minutes, stirring occasionally.

Lemony Carrots

The carrots are cooked until just tender in lemony stock which is then thickened to make a light tangy sauce.

Serves 4

600ml/1 pint/2½ cups water	pinch of freshly grated nutmeg
450g/1lb carrots, thinly sliced	20g/¾ oz/1½ tbsp butter
bouquet garni	15ml/½oz/1 tbsp plain flour
15ml/1 tbsp freshly squeezed lemon juice	salt and ground black pepper

1 Bring the water to the boil in a large saucepan, then add the carrots, bouquet garni, lemon juice, nutmeg and seasoning and simmer until the carrots are tender. Remove the carrots using a slotted spoon, then keep warm.

2 Boil the cooking liquid hard until it has reduced to about 300ml/½ pint/1¼ cups. Discard the bouquet garni.

3 Mash 15g/½ oz/1 tbsp of the butter and all of the flour together, then gradually whisk into the simmering reduced cooking liquid, whisking well after each addition, then simmer for about 3 minutes, until the sauce has thickened.

4 Return the carrots to the pan, heat through in the sauce, then remove from the heat. Stir in the remaining butter and serve immediately.

Ratatouille

Ratatouille may be served hot or cold, as a starter, side dish or vegetarian main course.

Serves 4

2 large aubergines, roughly chopped	1 fresh rosemary sprig
4 courgettes, roughly chopped	1 fresh thyme sprig
150ml/¼ pint/⅔ cup olive oil	5ml/1 tsp coriander seeds, crushed
2 onions, sliced	3 plum tomatoes, skinned, seeded and chopped
2 garlic cloves, chopped	8 basil leaves, roughly torn
1 large red pepper, seeded and roughly chopped	salt and ground black pepper
2 large yellow peppers, seeded and roughly chopped	fresh parsley or basil sprigs, to garnish

1 Place the aubergines in a colander, sprinkle with salt and place a plate with a weight on top to extract the bitter juices. Leave for 30 minutes.

2 Heat the olive oil in a large saucepan and gently fry the onions for about 6–7 minutes until just softened. Add the garlic and cook for a further 2 minutes.

3 Rinse, drain and pat dry the aubergines with kitchen paper. Add to the pan with the peppers, increase the heat and sauté until the peppers are just turning brown.

4 Add the herbs and coriander seeds, then cover the pan and cook gently for about 40 minutes.

5 Add the tomatoes and season to taste with salt and pepper. Cook gently for a further 10 minutes, until the vegetables are soft but not too mushy. Remove the sprigs of herbs. Stir in the torn basil leaves and check the seasoning. Leave to cool slightly and serve warm or cold, garnished with sprigs of parsley or basil.

Parsnips with Almonds

Parsnips have an affinity with most nuts, so you could use walnuts or hazelnuts instead of the almonds.

Serves 4

450g/1lb small parsnips
35g/1¼oz/scant 3 tbsp
  butter
25g/1oz/¼ cup flaked
  almonds
15g/½oz/1 tbsp soft light
  brown sugar

pinch of ground mixed
  spice
15ml/1 tbsp lemon juice
salt and ground black
  pepper
chopped fresh chervil or
  parsley, to garnish

1 Cook the parsnips in boiling salted water until almost tender. Drain well. When the parsnips are cool enough to handle, cut each in half across its width, then quarter these halves lengthways.

2 Heat the butter in a frying pan and cook the parsnips and almonds gently, stirring and turning carefully until they are lightly flecked with brown.

3 Mix together the sugar and mixed spice, sprinkle over the parsnips and stir to mix, then trickle over the lemon juice. Season to taste with salt and pepper and heat for 1 minute. Serve sprinkled with chopped fresh chervil or parsley.

Turnips with Orange

Sprinkle toasted nuts such as flaked almonds or chopped walnuts over the turnips to add contrast.

Serves 4

50g/2oz/4 tbsp butter
15ml/1 tbsp oil
1 small shallot, finely
  chopped
450g/1lb small turnips,
  quartered

300ml/½ pint/1¼ cups
  freshly squeezed
  orange juice
salt and ground black
  pepper

1 Heat the butter and oil in a saucepan and cook the shallot gently, stirring occasionally, until soft but not coloured.

2 Add the turnips to the shallot and heat. Shake the pan frequently until the turnips start to absorb the butter and oil.

3 Pour the orange juice on to the turnips, then simmer gently for about 30 minutes, until the turnips are tender and the orange juice is reduced to a buttery sauce. Season with salt and pepper, if required, and serve hot.

Red Cabbage with Pears and Nuts

A sweet and sour, spicy red cabbage dish, with the added crunch of pears and walnuts.

Serves 6

15ml/1 tbsp walnut oil
1 onion, sliced
2 whole star anise
5ml/1 tsp ground
    cinnamon
pinch of ground cloves
450g/1lb red cabbage,
    finely shredded
25g/1oz/2 tbsp dark
    brown sugar
45ml/3 tbsp red wine
    vinegar
300ml/½ pint/1¼ cup
    red wine
150ml/¼ pint/scant
    ¾ cup port
2 pears, cut into
    1cm/½in cubes
115g/4oz/½ cup raisins
salt and ground black
    pepper
115g/4oz/½ cup walnut
    halves

1 Heat the oil in a large pan. Add the onion and cook gently for about 5 minutes until softened.

2 Add the star anise, cinnamon, cloves and cabbage and cook for about 3 minutes more.

3 Stir in the sugar, vinegar, red wine and port. Cover the pan and simmer gently for 10 minutes, stirring occasionally.

4 Stir in the cubed pears and raisins and cook for a further 10 minutes or until the cabbage is tender. Season to taste. Mix in the walnut halves and serve.

Swiss Soufflé Potatoes

Baked potatoes are great for cold weather eating, and are both economical and satisfying.

Serves 4

4 baking potatoes
115g/4oz/scant 1 cup
    grated Gruyère cheese
115g/4oz/½ cup herb-
    flavoured butter
60ml/4 tbsp double cream
2 eggs, separated
salt and ground black
    pepper

1 Preheat the oven to 220°C/425°F/Gas 7. Scrub the potatoes, then prick them all over with a fork. Bake for about 1–1½ hours until tender. Remove them from the oven and reduce the temperature to 180°C/350°F/Gas 4.

2 Cut each potato in half and scoop out the flesh into a bowl. Return the potato shells to the oven to crisp them up while making the filling.

3 Mash the potato flesh using a fork then add the Gruyère, herb-flavoured butter, cream and egg yolks, and season to taste with salt and pepper. Beat well until smooth.

4 Whisk the egg whites in a separate bowl until stiff peaks form, then fold into the potato mixture.

5 Pile the mixture back into the potato shells and bake for 20–25 minutes, until risen and golden brown.

Cook's Tip
Choose a floury variety of potato for this dish for the best results.

Thai Vegetables with Noodles

This dish makes a delicious vegetarian supper on its own, or it could be served as an accompaniment.

Serves 4

225g/8oz/4 cups egg
  noodles
15ml/1 tbsp sesame oil
45ml/3 tbsp groundnut
  oil
2 garlic cloves, thinly
  sliced
2.5cm/1in piece fresh root
  ginger, finely chopped
2 fresh red chillies, seeded
  and sliced
115g/4oz/1 cup broccoli
  florets
115g/4oz baby sweetcorn

175g/6oz shiitake or
  oyster mushrooms,
  sliced
1 bunch spring onions,
  sliced
115g/4oz pak choi or
  Chinese leaves,
  shredded
115g/4oz/generous 1 cup
  beansprouts
15–30ml/1–2 tbsp dark
  soy sauce
salt and ground black
  pepper

1 Bring a saucepan of salted water to the boil and cook the egg noodles according to the instructions on the packet. Drain well and toss in the sesame oil. Set aside.

2 Heat the groundnut oil in a wok or large frying pan and stir-fry the garlic and ginger for 1 minute. Add the chillies, broccoli, baby sweetcorn and mushrooms and stir-fry for a further 2 minutes.

3 Add the spring onions, shredded pak choi or Chinese leaves and beansprouts and stir-fry for another 2 minutes.

4 Toss in the drained noodles with the soy sauce and pepper.

5 Continue to cook over a high heat, stirring, for a further 2–3 minutes, until the ingredients are well mixed and warmed through. Serve at once.

Cauliflower with Three Cheeses

The mingled flavours of three cheeses give a new twist to cauliflower cheese.

Serves 4

4 baby cauliflowers
250ml/8fl oz/1 cup single
  cream
75g/3oz dolcelatte cheese,
  diced
75g/3oz mozzarella
  cheese, diced

45ml/3 tbsp freshly
  grated Parmesan
  cheese
pinch of freshly grated
  nutmeg
ground black pepper
toasted breadcrumbs, to
  garnish

1 Cook the cauliflowers in a large saucepan of boiling salted water for 8–10 minutes, until just tender.

2 Meanwhile, put the cream into a small pan with the cheeses. Heat gently until the cheeses have melted, stirring occasionally. Season to taste with nutmeg and pepper.

3 When the cauliflowers are cooked, drain them thoroughly and place one on each of four warmed plates.

4 Spoon a little of the cheese sauce over each cauliflower and sprinkle each with a few of the toasted breadcrumbs. Serve at once.

Cook's Tip
For a more economical dish or if baby cauliflowers are not available, use one large cauliflower instead. Cut it into quarters with a large sharp knife and remove the central core.

Potato Gnocchi with Sauce

These delicate potato dumplings are dressed with a tasty creamy hazelnut sauce.

Serves 4
675g/1½ lb large potatoes
115g/4oz/1 cup plain
   flour

For the hazelnut sauce
115g/4oz/½ cup
   hazelnuts, roasted
1 garlic clove, roughly
   chopped

½ tsp grated lemon rind
½ tsp lemon juice
30ml/2 tbsp sunflower oil
150g/5oz/¾ cup low-fat
   fromage blanc
salt and ground black
   pepper

1 Place 65g/2½ oz of the hazelnuts in a blender with the garlic, grated lemon rind and juice. Blend until coarsely chopped. Gradually add the oil and blend until smooth. Spoon into a bowl and mix in the fromage blanc. Season.

2 Place the potatoes in a pan of cold water. Bring to the boil and cook for 20–25 minutes. Drain well in a colander. While still warm, peel and purée the potatoes by passing them through a food mill into a bowl.

3 Add the flour a little at a time (you may not need all of the flour, as potatoes vary in texture). Stop adding flour when the mixture is smooth and slightly sticky. Add salt to taste.

4 Roll the mixture out on to a floured board to form a sausage 1cm/½in in diameter. Cut into 2cm/¾in lengths.

5 Take one piece at a time and press it on to a floured fork. Roll each piece slightly while pressing it along the prongs and off the fork. Flip on to a floured plate or tray. Continue with the rest of the mixture. Cook the gnocchi in a large pan of boiling water for about 3–4 minutes. When cooked, they will rise to the surface. Drain and serve with the hazelnut sauce.

Winter Vegetable Hot-pot

Use whatever vegetables you have to hand in this richly flavoured and substantial one-pot meal.

Serves 4
2 onions, sliced
4 carrots, sliced
1 small swede, sliced
2 parsnips, sliced
3 small turnips, sliced
½ celeriac, cut into
   matchsticks
2 leeks, thinly sliced
30ml/2 tbsp mixed
   chopped fresh herbs
   such as parsley and
   thyme

1 garlic clove, chopped
1 bay leaf, crumbled
300ml/½ pint/1¼ cups
   vegetable stock
15g/½oz/1 tbsp plain
   flour
675g/1½lb red-skinned
   potatoes, scrubbed and
   thinly sliced
50g/2oz/4 tbsp butter
salt and ground black
   pepper

1 Preheat the oven to 190°C/375°F/Gas 5. Arrange all the vegetables, except the potatoes, in layers in a large casserole with a tight-fitting lid, seasoning them lightly with salt and pepper and sprinkling them with chopped herbs, garlic and crumbled bay leaf as you go.

2 Blend the vegetable stock into the flour and pour over the vegetables. Arrange the potatoes in overlapping layers on top. Dot with butter and cover tightly.

3 Cook in the oven for 1¼ hours, or until the vegetables are tender. Remove the lid from the casserole and cook for a further 15–20 minutes until the top layer of potatoes is golden and crisp at the edges. Serve hot.

Cook's Tip
Make sure the root vegetables are cut into even-size slices so they cook uniformly.

Beans with Tomatoes

Young runner beans should not have "strings" down the sides, but older ones will. Remove them before cooking.

Serves 4

675g/1½lb/2 cups sliced
  runner beans
40g/1½oz/3 tbsp butter
4 ripe tomatoes, peeled
  and chopped

salt and ground black
  pepper
chopped fresh tarragon,
  to garnish

1 Bring a saucepan of water to the boil, add the beans, return to the boil and cook for 3 minutes. Drain well.

2 Heat the butter in a pan, add the tomatoes and beans and season with salt and pepper. Cover the pan with a tight-fitting lid and simmer gently for about 10–15 minutes, until the beans are tender.

3 Tip the beans and tomatoes into a warm serving dish and sprinkle over the chopped tarragon to garnish. Serve hot as an accompaniment to grilled meats, poultry or fish.

Rosemary Roasties

The potatoes are roasted with their skins on, giving them far more flavour than traditional roast potatoes.

Serves 4

1kg/2lb small red
  potatoes
10ml/2 tsp walnut or
  sunflower oil

30ml/2 tbsp fresh
  rosemary leaves
salt and paprika

1 Preheat the oven to 240°C/475°F/Gas 9. Leave the potatoes whole with the skins on, or if large, cut in half. Place the potatoes in a large saucepan of cold water and bring to the boil, then drain immediately.

2 Return the potatoes to the saucepan and drizzle the walnut or sunflower oil over them. Shake the pan to coat the potatoes evenly in the oil.

3 Tip the potatoes into a shallow roasting tin. Sprinkle with rosemary, salt and paprika. Roast for 30 minutes or until crisp. Served hot, these potatoes are good with roast lamb.

Vegetable Ribbons

This mixed vegetable side dish looks impressive and will delight dinner party guests.

Serves 4

Using a vegetable peeler or sharp knife, cut 3 medium carrots and 3 medium courgettes into thin ribbons. Bring 120ml/4 fl oz/½ cup chicken stock to the boil, add the carrots. Return the stock to the boil; add the courgettes. Boil rapidly for 2–3 minutes, or until the vegetable ribbons are just tender. Stir in 30ml/2 tbsp chopped fresh parsley, season lightly with salt and ground black pepper, and serve hot.

Courgette and Tomato Bake

A *tian* is a heavy earthenware dish in which many French vegetable dishes are cooked. This is one example.

Serves 4

45ml/3 tbsp olive oil
1 onion, chopped
1 garlic clove, crushed
3 rashers lean bacon, chopped
4 courgettes, grated
2 tomatoes, skinned, seeded and chopped
115g/4oz/scant ¼ cup cooked long grain rice
10ml/2 tsp chopped fresh thyme
15ml/1 tbsp chopped fresh parsley
60ml/4 tbsp grated Parmesan cheese
2 eggs, lightly beaten
15ml/1 tbsp fromage frais
salt and ground black pepper

1 Preheat the oven to 180°C/350°F/Gas 4. Grease a shallow ovenproof dish with a little olive oil.

2 Heat the oil in a frying pan and fry the onion and garlic for 5 minutes until softened.

3 Add the bacon and fry for 2 minutes, then stir in the courgettes and fry for a further 8 minutes, stirring from time to time and letting some of the liquid evaporate. Remove the pan from the heat.

4 Add the tomatoes, cooked rice, herbs, 30ml/2 tbsp of the Parmesan cheese, the eggs and fromage frais, and season to taste with salt and pepper. Mix together well.

5 Spoon the courgette mixture into the dish and sprinkle over the remaining Parmesan cheese. Bake for 45 minutes, until set and golden. Serve hot.

Cook's Tip
For a dinner party, divide the mixture among four lightly greased individual gratin dishes and bake for about 25 minutes until set and golden.

Spanish Green Beans with Ham

Judias verdes con jamón are green beans cooked with the Spanish raw-cured Serrano ham.

Serves 4

450g/1lb French beans
45ml/3 tbsp olive oil
1 onion, thinly sliced
2 garlic cloves, finely chopped
75g/3oz Serrano ham, chopped
salt and ground black pepper

1 Cook the beans, left whole, in boiling salted water for about 5–6 minutes, until they are just tender but still with a little bit of bite.

2 Meanwhile, heat the oil in a saucepan and fry the onions for 5 minutes, until softened and translucent. Add the garlic and ham and cook for a further 1–2 minutes.

3 Drain the beans, then add them to the pan and cook, stirring occasionally, for 2–3 minutes. Season well with salt and pepper and serve hot.

Cook's Tip
Serrano ham is increasingly available in large supermarkets and has the advantage of being cheaper than Parma ham. However, if you cannot find it, use Parma ham or bacon instead.

Sweet Potatoes with Bacon

This sweet potato dish is often served for Thanksgiving in North America to celebrate the settlers' first harvest.

Serves 4

2 large sweet potatoes
  (450g/1lb each),
  washed
50g/2oz/½ cup soft light
  brown sugar
30ml/2 tbsp lemon juice
40g/1½ oz/3 tbsp butter

4 rashers smoked streaky
  bacon, cut into thin
  strips
salt and ground black
  pepper
sprig of flat leaf parsley,
  to garnish

1 Preheat the oven to 190°C/375°F/Gas 5 and lightly butter a shallow ovenproof dish. Cut the unpeeled sweet potatoes crossways into four and place the pieces in a pan of boiling water. Cover with a tight-fitting lid and cook until just tender, about 25 minutes.

2 Drain the potatoes and, when cool enough to handle, peel and slice quite thickly. Arrange in a single layer, overlapping, in the prepared dish.

3 Sprinkle over the sugar and lemon juice and dot with butter. Top with the bacon and season with salt and pepper.

4 Bake uncovered for 35–40 minutes, basting once or twice, until the potatoes are tender.

5 Preheat the grill to a high heat. Grill the potatoes for about 2–3 minutes, until they are browned and the bacon crispy. Serve hot, garnished with parsley.

Potatoes Baked with Tomatoes

This simple hearty dish from the south of Italy is best made with fresh tomatoes but canned plum tomatoes will do.

Serves 6

2 large red or yellow
  onions, thinly sliced
900g/2¼ lb potatoes,
  peeled and thinly
  sliced
450g/1lb fresh tomatoes
  (or canned, with their
  juice), sliced
90ml/6 tbsp olive oil

115g/4oz/1 cup freshly
  grated Parmesan or
  mature Cheddar
  cheese
salt and ground black
  pepper
50ml/2fl oz/¼ cup water
a few fresh basil leaves, to
  garnish (optional)

1 Preheat the oven to 180°C/350°F/Gas 4. Brush a large baking dish generously with oil.

2 Arrange a layer of onions in the dish, followed by layers of potatoes and tomatoes. Pour on a little of the oil, and sprinkle with the cheese. Season with salt and pepper.

3 Repeat until the vegetables are used up, ending with an overlapping layer of potatoes and tomatoes. Tear the basil leaves into pieces, and add them here and there among the vegetables. Sprinkle the top with cheese and a little oil.

4 Pour on the water. Bake for 1 hour, or until tender.

5 If the top begins to brown too much, place a sheet of foil or a flat baking sheet on top of the dish. Serve hot, garnished with basil leaves, if you wish.

Aubergine Baked with Cheeses

This famous dish, with its rich tomato sauce, is a speciality of Italy's southern regions.

Serves 4–6

900g/2lb aubergines
flour, for coating
oil, for frying
40g/1½oz/½ cup freshly
   grated Parmesan
   cheese
400g/14oz mozzarella
   cheese, sliced very
   thinly
salt and ground black
   pepper

For the tomato sauce
60ml/4 tbsp olive oil
1 onion, very finely
   chopped
1 garlic clove, chopped
450g/1lb fresh tomatoes,
   or canned, chopped,
   with their juice
a few fresh basil leaves or
   parsley sprigs

1 Cut the aubergines into 1cm/½in rounds, sprinkle with salt, and leave to drain for about 1 hour.

2 For the tomato sauce, cook the onion in the oil until translucent. Stir in the garlic and the tomatoes (if using fresh tomatoes, add 45ml/3 tbsp water). Season to taste; add the basil or parsley. Cook for 30 minutes. Purée in a food mill.

3 Pat the aubergine slices dry, coat them lightly in flour. Heat a little oil in a large non-stick frying pan. Add one layer of aubergines, and cook over low to moderate heat with the pan covered until they soften. Turn, and cook on the other side. Remove from the pan, repeat with the remaining slices.

4 Preheat the oven to 180°C/350°F/Gas 4. Grease a wide shallow baking dish or tin. Spread a little tomato sauce in the base. Cover with a layer of aubergine. Sprinkle with a few teaspoons of Parmesan, season to taste with salt and pepper, and cover with a layer of mozzarella. Spoon on some tomato sauce. Repeat until all the ingredients are used up, ending with a covering of the tomato sauce and a sprinkling of Parmesan. Sprinkle with a little olive oil, and bake for about 45 minutes, until golden and bubbling.

Stuffed Onions

These savoury onions make a good light lunch or supper. Small onions could be stuffed and served as a side dish.

Serves 6

6 large onions
75g/3oz/scant ½ cup
   ham, cut into small
   dice
1 egg
50g/2oz/½ cup dried
   breadcrumbs
45ml/3 tbsp finely
   chopped fresh parsley
1 garlic clove, chopped

pinch of freshly grated
   nutmeg
75g/3oz/¾ cup freshly
   grated cheese such as
   Parmesan or mature
   Cheddar
90ml/6 tbsp olive oil
salt and ground black
   pepper

1 Peel the onions without cutting through the bases. Cook them in a large pan of boiling water for about 20 minutes. Drain, and refresh in plenty of cold water.

2 Using a small sharp knife, cut around and scoop out each central section. Remove about half the inside (save it for soup). Lightly salt the empty cavities, and leave the onions to drain upside down.

3 Preheat the oven to 200°C/400°F/Gas 6. Beat the ham into the egg in a small bowl. Stir in the breadcrumbs, parsley, garlic, nutmeg and all but 45ml/3 tbsp of the grated cheese. Add 45ml/3 tbsp of the oil, and season with salt and pepper.

4 Pat the insides of the onions dry with kitchen paper. Stuff them using a small spoon. Arrange the onions in one layer in an oiled baking dish.

5 Sprinkle the tops with the remaining cheese and then with oil. Bake for 45 minutes, or until the onions are tender and golden on top.

Baked Fennel with Parmesan Cheese

Fennel is widely eaten in Italy, both raw and cooked. It is delicious married with the sharpness of Parmesan.

Serves 4–6
200g/2lb fennel bulbs, washed and cut in half
50g/2oz/4 tbsp butter

40g/1½oz/½ cup freshly grated Parmesan cheese

1 Cook the fennel bulbs in a large saucepan of boiling water until softened but not mushy. Drain well. Preheat the oven to 200°C/400°F/Gas 6.

2 Cut the fennel bulbs lengthways into four or six pieces. Place them in a buttered baking dish.

3 Dot with butter. Sprinkle with the grated Parmesan. Bake in the hot oven until the cheese is golden brown, about 20 minutes. Serve at once.

Cook's Tip
For a more substantial version of this dish, finely chop 75g/3oz ham and scatter it over the fennel before topping with the Parmesan cheese.

Courgettes with Sun-dried Tomatoes

Sun-dried tomatoes have a concentrated sweet flavour that goes well with courgettes.

Serves 6
10 sun-dried tomatoes, dry or preserved in oil and drained
175ml/6fl oz/¾ cup warm water
75ml/5 tbsp olive oil
1 large onion, finely sliced

2 garlic cloves, finely chopped
900g/2lb courgettes, cut into thin strips
salt and ground black pepper

1 Slice the tomatoes into thin strips. Place in a bowl with the warm water. Allow to stand for 20 minutes.

2 Heat the oil in a large frying pan or saucepan and then cook the onion over low to moderate heat until it softens but does not brown.

3 Stir in the garlic and the courgettes. Cook for about 5 minutes, continuing to stir the mixture.

4 Stir in the tomatoes and their soaking liquid. Season to taste with salt and pepper. Raise the heat slightly and cook until the courgettes are just tender. Serve hot or cold.

Broccoli Cauliflower Gratin

Broccoli and cauliflower combine well, and this dish is much lighter than a classic cauliflower cheese.

Serves 4

1 small cauliflower
(about 250g/9oz)
1 head broccoli (about
250g/9oz)
120ml/4fl oz/½ cup
natural low-fat yogurt
75g/3oz/¼ cup grated
reduced-fat Cheddar
cheese

5ml/1 tsp wholegrain
mustard
30ml/2 tbsp wholemeal
breadcrumbs
salt and ground black
pepper

1 Break the cauliflower and broccoli into florets and cook in lightly salted boiling water for 8–10 minutes, until just tender. Drain well and transfer to a flameproof dish.

2 Mix together the yogurt, grated cheese and mustard, then season the mixture with pepper and spoon over the cauliflower and broccoli.

3 Sprinkle the breadcrumbs over the top and place under a moderately hot grill until golden brown. Serve hot.

Cook's Tip
When preparing the cauliflower and broccoli, discard the tougher parts of the stalks, then break the florets into even-size pieces so they will cook evenly.

Tex-Mex Baked Potatoes with Chilli

A spicy chilli bean sauce tops baked potatoes and is served with a dollop of soured cream.

Serves 4

2 large potatoes
15ml/1 tbsp oil
1 garlic clove, crushed
1 small onion, chopped
½ small red pepper,
seeded and chopped
225g/8oz lean minced
beef
½ small fresh red chilli,
seeded and chopped
5ml/1 tsp ground cumin
pinch of cayenne pepper
200g/7oz can chopped
tomatoes
30ml/2 tbsp tomato purée

2.5ml/½ tsp dried
oregano
2.5ml/½ tsp dried
marjoram
200g/7oz can red kidney
beans, drained and
rinsed
15ml/1 tbsp chopped
fresh coriander
salt and ground black
pepper
60ml/4 tbsp soured
cream
chopped fresh parsley, to
garnish

1 Preheat the oven to 220°C/425°F/Gas 7. Rub the potatoes with a little oil and pierce with skewers. Bake them on the top shelf for 30 minutes before beginning to cook the chilli.

2 Heat the oil in a pan and fry the garlic, onion and pepper gently for 4–5 minutes, until softened.

3 Add the beef and fry until browned all over, then stir in the chilli, cumin, cayenne pepper, tomatoes, tomato purée, 60ml/4 tbsp water and the herbs. Cover with a tight-fitting lid and simmer for about 25 minutes, stirring occasionally.

4 Remove the lid, stir in the kidney beans and cook for 5 minutes. Turn off the heat and stir in the chopped fresh coriander. Season to taste and set aside.

5 Cut the baked potatoes in half and place them in serving bowls. Top with the chilli mixture and a dollop of soured cream, then garnish with chopped fresh parsley.

Bombay Spiced Potatoes

This Indian potato dish uses a delicately aromatic mixture of whole and ground spices.

Serves 4

4 large potatoes (Maris Piper or King Edward), diced
60ml/4 tbsp sunflower oil
1 garlic clove, finely chopped
10ml/2 tsp brown mustard seeds
5ml/1 tsp black onion seeds (optional)
5ml/1 tsp ground turmeric
5ml/1 tsp ground cumin
5ml/1 tsp ground coriander
5ml/1 tsp fennel seeds
salt and ground black pepper
generous squeeze of lemon juice
chopped fresh coriander and lemon wedges, to garnish

1 Bring a saucepan of salted water to the boil, add the potatoes and simmer for about 4 minutes, until just tender. Drain well.

2 Heat the oil in a large frying pan and add the garlic along with all the whole and ground spices. Stir-fry gently for 1–2 minutes, until the mustard seeds start to pop.

3 Add the potatoes and stir-fry over a moderate heat for about 5 minutes, until heated through and well coated with the spicy oil.

4 Season well and sprinkle over the lemon juice. Garnish with chopped fresh coriander and lemon wedges. Serve as an accompaniment to curries or strongly flavoured meat dishes.

Cook's Tip
Look out for black onion seeds – kalonji – in Indian or Pakistani food stores.

Spanish Chilli Potatoes

The Spanish name for this dish, *patatas bravas*, means fierce, hot potatoes. Reduce the amount of chilli if you wish.

Serves 4

900g/2lb new or salad potatoes
60ml/4 tbsp olive oil
1 onion, finely chopped
2 garlic cloves, crushed
15ml/1 tbsp tomato purée
200g/7oz can chopped tomatoes
15ml/1 tbsp red wine vinegar
2–3 small dried red chillies, seeded and chopped finely, or 5–10ml/1–2 tsp hot chilli powder
5ml/1 tsp paprika
salt and ground black pepper
fresh flat leaf parsley sprig, to garnish

1 Boil the potatoes in their skins for 10–12 minutes or until just tender. Drain them well and leave to cool, then cut in half and set aside.

2 Heat the oil in a large saucepan and fry the onions and garlic for 5–6 minutes, until just softened. Stir in the tomato purée, tomatoes, vinegar, chilli and paprika and simmer for about 5 minutes.

3 Add the potatoes and mix into the sauce mixture until well coated. Cover with a tight-fitting lid and simmer gently for about 8–10 minutes, or until the potatoes are tender. Season well and transfer to a warmed serving dish. Serve garnished with a sprig of flat leaf parsley.

Spicy Jacket Potatoes

These lightly spiced potatoes make a glorious snack, light lunch or accompaniment to a meal.

Serves 2–4

2 large baking potatoes
5ml/1 tsp sunflower oil
1 small onion, chopped
2.5cm/1in piece fresh
*   ginger root, grated*
5ml/1 tsp ground cumin
5ml/1 tsp ground
*   coriander*

2.5ml/½ tsp ground
*   turmeric*
generous pinch of garlic
*   salt*
natural yogurt and fresh
*   coriander sprigs, to*
*   serve*

1 Preheat the oven to 190°C/375°F/Gas 5. Prick the potatoes with a fork. Bake for 40 minutes, or until soft.

2 Cut the potatoes in half and scoop out the flesh. Heat the oil in a non-stick frying pan; fry the onion for a few minutes to soften. Stir in the ginger, cumin, coriander and turmeric.

3 Stir over a gentle heat for about 2 minutes, then add the potato flesh, and garlic salt to taste.

4 Cook the potato mixture for a further 2 minutes, stirring occasionally. Spoon the mixture back into the potato shells and top each with a spoonful of natural yogurt and a sprig or two of fresh coriander. Serve hot.

Two Beans Provençal

A tasty side dish, these beans would complement a simple main course of grilled meat, poultry or fish.

Serves 4

5ml/1 tsp olive oil
1 small onion, finely
*   chopped*
1 garlic clove, crushed
225g/8oz/scant 1 cup
*   French beans*

225g/8oz/scant 1 cup
*   runner beans*
2 tomatoes, skinned and
*   chopped*
salt and ground black
*   pepper*

1 Heat the oil in a heavy-based or non-stick frying pan and sauté the chopped onion over a moderate heat until softened but not browned.

2 Add the garlic, the French and runner beans and the tomatoes, then season well and cover tightly.

3 Cook over a fairly gentle heat, shaking the pan from time to time, for about 30 minutes, or until the beans are tender. Serve hot.

Cook's Tip

For a dry version of this dish, omit the tomatoes. Simply fry the onion and garlic until softened, boil the beans in lightly salted water until tender, then stir into the rich mixture and combine well.

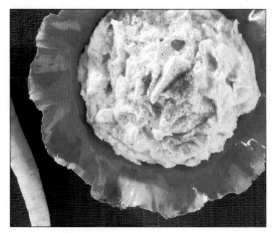

Chinese Crispy Seaweed

In northern China they use a special kind of seaweed for this dish, but spring greens make a good alternative.

Serves 4

225g/8oz spring greens
groundnut or sunflower
  oil, for deep-frying
1.5ml/¼ tsp salt

10ml/2 tsp soft light
  brown sugar
30 – 45ml/2 – 3 tbsp
  toasted, flaked
  almonds

1 Cut out and discard any tough stalks from the spring greens. Place about six leaves on top of each other and roll up into a tight roll.

2 Using a sharp knife, slice across into thin shreds. Lay on a tray and leave to dry for about 2 hours.

3 Heat about 5–7.5cm/2–3in of oil in a wok or pan to 190°C/375°F. Carefully place a handful of the leaves into the oil – it will bubble and spit for the first 10 seconds and then die down. Deep fry for about 45 seconds, or until a slightly darker green – do not let the leaves burn.

4 Remove with a slotted spoon, drain on kitchen paper and transfer to a serving dish. Keep warm in the oven while frying the remainder.

5 When you have fried all the shredded leaves, sprinkle with the salt and sugar and toss lightly. Garnish with the toasted almonds.

Cook's Tip
Make sure that your deep frying pan is deep enough to allow the oil to bubble up during cooking. The pan should be less than half full.

Leek and Parsnip Purée

Vegetable purées are popular in Britain and France served with meat, chicken or fish dishes.

Serves 4

2 large leeks, sliced
3 parsnips, sliced
knob of butter
45ml/3 tbsp top of the
  milk or single
  cream
30ml/2 tbsp fromage frais

generous squeeze of
  lemon juice
salt and ground black
  pepper
large pinch of freshly
  grated nutmeg, to
  garnish

1 Steam or boil the leeks and parsnips together for about 15 minutes, until tender. Drain well, then place in a food processor or blender.

2 Add the remaining ingredients to the processor or blender. Combine them all until really smooth, then check the seasoning. Transfer to a warmed bowl and garnish with a sprinkling of nutmeg.

Middle-Eastern Vegetable Stew

This spiced dish of mixed vegetables can be served as a side dish or as a vegetarian main course.

Serves 4–6

45ml/3 tbsp vegetable or
  chicken stock
1 green pepper, seeded
  and sliced
2 courgettes, sliced
2 carrots, sliced
2 celery sticks, sliced
2 potatoes, diced
400g/14oz can chopped
  tomatoes
5ml/1 tsp chilli powder

30ml/2 tbsp chopped
  fresh mint
15ml/1 tbsp ground
  cumin
400g/14oz can
  chick-peas, drained
salt and ground black
  pepper
fresh mint sprigs,
  to garnish

1 Heat the vegetable or chicken stock in a large flameproof casserole until boiling, then add the sliced pepper, courgettes, carrot and celery. Stir over a high heat for 2–3 minutes, until the vegetables are just beginning to soften.

2 Add the potatoes, tomatoes, chilli powder, mint and cumin. Add the chick-peas and bring to the boil.

3 Reduce the heat, cover the casserole with a tight-fitting lid and simmer for 30 minutes, or until all the vegetables are tender. Season to taste with salt and pepper and serve hot, garnished with mint leaves.

Summer Vegetable Braise

Tender young vegetables are ideal for quick cooking in a minimum of liquid. Use any vegetable mixture you like.

Serves 4

175g/6oz baby carrots
175g/6oz/1½ cups sugar
  snap peas or
  mange-touts
115g/4oz baby corn cobs
90ml/6 tbsp vegetable
  stock

10ml/2 tsp lime juice
salt and ground black
  pepper
chopped fresh parsley and
  snipped fresh chives,
  to garnish

1 Place the carrots, peas and baby corn cobs in a large heavy-based saucepan with the vegetable stock and lime juice. Bring to the boil.

2 Cover the pan and reduce the heat, then simmer for about 6–8 minutes, shaking the pan occasionally, until the vegetables are just tender.

3 Season the vegetables to taste with salt and pepper, then stir in the chopped fresh parsley and snipped chives. Cook the vegetables for a few seconds more, stirring them once or twice until the herbs are well mixed, then serve at once with grilled lamb chops or roast chicken.

Cook's Tip
You can cook a winter version of this dish using seasonal root vegetables. Cut them into even slice chunks and cook for slightly longer.

Straw Potato Cake

These potatoes are so–named in France because of their resemblance to a woven straw doormat.

Serves 4
450g/1lb baking potatoes
22.5ml/1½ tbsp melted
  butter

15ml/1 tbsp vegetable oil
salt and ground black
  pepper

1 Peel the potatoes and grate them coarsely, then immediately toss them with the melted butter and season with salt and pepper.

2 Heat the oil in a large frying pan. Add the potato mixture and press down to form an even layer that covers the pan. Cook over a moderate heat for 7–10 minutes until the base is well browned.

3 Loosen the potato cake by shaking the pan or running a thin palette knife under it.

4 To turn it over, invert a large baking sheet over the frying pan and, holding it tightly against the pan, turn them both over together. Lift off the frying pan, return it to the heat and add a little more oil if it looks dry. Slide the potato cake into the frying pan and continue cooking until it is crisp and browned on the second side. Serve hot.

Cook's Tip
Make several small potato cakes instead of one large one, if you prefer. Simply adjust the cooking time.

Sautéed Wild Mushrooms

This is a quick dish to prepare and makes an ideal side dish for all kinds of grilled and roast meats.

Serves 6
900g/2lb fresh mixed
  wild and cultivated
  mushrooms such as
  morels, porcini,
  chanterelles, oyster or
  shiitake
30ml/2 tbsp olive oil
25g/1oz/2 tbsp unsalted
  butter
2 garlic cloves, chopped

3 or 4 shallots, finely
  chopped
45–60ml/3–4 tbsp
  chopped fresh parsley,
  or a mixture of
  different chopped fresh
  herbs
salt and ground black
  pepper

1 Wash and carefully dry the mushrooms. Trim the stems and cut the mushrooms into quarters, or slice if they are very large.

2 Heat the oil in a large frying pan over a moderately high heat. Add the butter and swirl to melt, then stir in the prepared mushrooms and cook for 4–5 minutes until beginning to brown.

3 Add the garlic and shallots to the pan and cook for a further 4–5 minutes until the mushrooms are tender and any liquid given off has evaporated. Season to taste with salt and pepper and stir in the parsley or mixed herbs and serve hot.

Cook's Tip
Use as many different varieties of cultivated and wild mushrooms as you can find to create a tasty and attractive dish.

Celeriac Purée

Many chefs add potato to celeriac purée, but this recipe highlights the pure flavour of the vegetable.

Serves 4

1 large celeriac (about
   750g/1¾ lb), peeled
15g/½oz/1 tbsp butter

pinch of grated nutmeg
salt and ground black
   pepper

1 Cut the celeriac into large dice, put in a saucepan with enough cold water to cover and add a little salt. Bring to the boil over a moderately high heat and cook gently for about 10–15 minutes until tender.

2 Drain the celeriac, reserving a little of the cooking liquid, and place in a food processor fitted with a metal blade or a blender. Process until smooth, adding a little of the cooking liquid if it needs thinning.

3 Stir in the butter and season to taste with salt, pepper and nutmeg. Reheat, if necessary, before serving.

Creamy Spinach Purée

Crème fraîche or béchamel sauce usually gives this dish its creamy richness. Here is a quick light alternative.

Serves 4

675g/1½lb/4½ cups leaf
   spinach, stems
   removed
115g/4oz/½ cup full or
   medium-fat soft cheese

milk (if required)
pinch of freshly grated
   nutmeg
salt and ground black
   pepper

1 Rinse the spinach, shake lightly and place in a deep frying pan or wok. Cook over a moderate heat for about 3–4 minutes until wilted. Drain in a colander, pressing with the back of a spoon. The spinach does not need to be completely dry.

2 Purée the spinach and soft cheese in a food processor fitted with a metal blade or a blender until well blended, then transfer to a bowl. If the purée is too thick to fall easily from a spoon, add a little milk, spoonful by spoonful. Season to taste with salt, pepper and nutmeg. Transfer to a heavy-based saucepan and reheat gently before serving.

Cannellini Bean Purée

This inexpensive dip is a healthy multi-purpose option; use low-fat fromage frais to lower its calorie content.

Serves 4

Drain 400g/14 oz can cannellini beans, rinse, drain again. Purée in a blender or food processor with 45ml/3 tbsp fromage blanc, grated zest, rind and juice of 1 large orange and 15ml/1 tbsp finely chopped fresh rosemary. Set aside. Cut 4 heads of chicory in half lengthwise and cut 2 medium radicchio into 8 wedges. Lay them on a baking tray and brush with 15ml/1 tbsp walnut oil. Grill for 2–3 minutes. Serve with the purée; scatter over the orange rind.

New Potato and Chive Salad

The secret of a good potato salad is to mix the potatoes with the dressing while they are still hot so that they absorb it.

Serves 4– 6

*675g/1½lb new potatoes
4 spring onions
45ml/3 tbsp olive oil
15ml/1 tbsp white wine
    vinegar
4ml/¾ tsp Dijon mustard*

*175ml/6fl oz/¾ cup good
    quality mayonnaise
45ml/3 tbsp snipped
    fresh chives
salt and ground black
    pepper*

1 Cook the potatoes, unpeeled, in boiling salted water until tender. Meanwhile, finely chop the white parts of the spring onions along with a little of the green parts.

2 Whisk together the oil, vinegar and mustard. Drain the potatoes well, then immediately toss lightly with the vinegar mixture and spring onions and leave to cool. Stir the mayonnaise and chives into the potatoes and chill in the fridge until ready to serve with grilled pork, lamb chops or roast chicken.

Watercress Potato Salad Bowl

New potatoes are good hot or cold, and this colourful and nutritious salad makes the most of them.

Serves 4

*450g/1lb small new
    potatoes, unpeeled
1 bunch watercress
200g/7oz cherry
    tomatoes, halved
30ml/2 tbsp pumpkin
    seeds*

*45ml/3 tbsp low-fat
    fromage frais
15ml/1 tbsp cider vinegar
5ml/1 tsp soft light
    brown sugar
salt and paprika*

1 Cook the potatoes in lightly salted boiling water until just tender, then drain and leave to cool.

2 Toss together the potatoes, watercress, tomatoes and pumpkin seeds. Place the fromage frais, vinegar, sugar, salt and paprika in a screw-top jar and shake well to mix. Pour over the salad just before serving.

Frankfurter Salad

A last minute salad you can throw together using store-cupboard ingredients.

Serves 4

Boil 700g/1½lb new potatoes in salted water for 20 minutes. Drain, cover and keep warm. Hard-boil 2 eggs for 12 minutes, shell and quarter. Score the skins of 350g/12oz frankfurters cork-screw fashion, cover with boiling water and simmer for 5 minutes. Drain, cover and keep warm. Distribute the leaves of 1 butterhead lettuce and 225g/8 oz young spinach among 4 plates, moisten the potatoes and frankfurters with dressing and scatter over the salad. Finish with the eggs, season and serve.

Salad Niçoise

Serve this rich and filling salad as a main course, simply with crusty bread.

Serves 4

90ml/6 tbsp olive oil
30ml/2 tbsp tarragon
    vinegar
5ml/1 tsp tarragon or
    Dijon mustard
1 small garlic clove,
    crushed
115g/4oz/1 cup French
    beans
12 small new potatoes
3–4 Little Gem lettuces,
    roughly chopped
200g/7oz can tuna in oil,
    drained

6 anchovy fillets, halved
    lengthways
12 black olives, stoned
4 tomatoes, chopped
4 spring onions, finely
    chopped
10ml/2 tsp capers
30ml/2 tbsp pine nuts
2 hard-boiled eggs,
    chopped
salt and ground black
    pepper
crusty bread, to serve

1 Mix the oil, vinegar, mustard, garlic and seasoning with a wooden spoon in the base of a large salad bowl.

2 Cook the French beans and potatoes in separate saucepans of boiling salted water until just tender. Drain and add to the bowl with the lettuce, tuna, anchovies, olives, tomatoes, spring onions and capers.

3 Just before serving, toast the pine nuts in a small frying pan until lightly browned.

4 Sprinkle over the salad while still hot, add the eggs and toss all the ingredients together well. Serve with chunks of hot crusty bread.

Cook's Tip
Look out for salad potatoes, such as Charlotte, Belle de Fontenay or Pink Fir Apple, to use in this recipe.

Caesar Salad

Any crisp lettuce will do in this delicious salad, which was created by Caesar Cardini in the 1920s.

Serves 4

1 large cos lettuce
4 thick slices white or
    granary bread,
    without crusts
45ml/3 tbsp olive oil
1 garlic clove, crushed

For the dressing
1 egg
1 garlic clove, chopped

30ml/2 tbsp lemon juice
dash of Worcestershire
    sauce
3 anchovy fillets, chopped
120ml/4fl oz/½ cup olive
    oil
75ml/5 tbsp grated
    Parmesan cheese
salt and ground black
    pepper

1 Preheat the oven to 220°C/425°F/Gas 7. Separate, rinse and dry the lettuce leaves. Tear the outer leaves roughly and chop the heart. Arrange the lettuce in a large salad bowl.

2 Dice the bread and mix with the olive oil and garlic in a separate bowl until the bread has soaked up the oil. Lay the bread dices on a baking sheet and place in the oven for about 6–8 minutes (keeping an eye on them) until golden. Remove and leave to cool.

3 To make the dressing, break the egg into the bowl of a food processor or blender and add the garlic, lemon juice, Worcestershire sauce and one of the anchovy fillets. Process until smooth.

4 With the motor running, pour in the olive oil in a thin stream until the dressing has the consistency of single cream. Season to taste with salt and pepper, if needed.

5 Pour the dressing over the salad leaves and toss well, then toss in the garlic croûtons, Parmesan cheese and finally the remaining anchovies and serve immediately.

Tuna and Bean Salad

This substantial salad makes a good light meal, and can be very quickly assembled from canned ingredients.

Serves 4–6

2 x 400g/14oz cans
  cannellini or borlotti
  beans
2 x 200g/7oz cans tuna
  fish, drained
60ml/4 tbsp extra virgin
  olive oil

30ml/2 tbsp lemon juice
salt and ground black
  pepper
15ml/1 tbsp chopped
  fresh parsley
3 spring onions, thinly
  sliced

1 Pour the beans into a large strainer and rinse under cold water. Drain well. Place in a serving dish.

2 Break the tuna into fairly large flakes with a fork and arrange over the beans.

3 Make the dressing by combining the oil with the lemon juice in a small bowl. Season with salt and pepper, and stir in the parsley. Mix well. Pour over the beans and tuna.

4 Sprinkle the spring onions over the salad and toss well before serving.

Cook's Tip
If you prefer a milder onion flavour, gently sauté the spring onions in a little oil until softened, but not browned, before adding them to the salad.

Grilled Pepper Salad

This colourful salad is a southern Italian creation; all the ingredients thrive in the Mediterranean sun.

Serves 6

4 large peppers, red or
  yellow or a
  combination of both
30ml/2 tbsp capers in
  salt, vinegar or brine,
  rinsed
18–20 black or green
  olives

For the dressing
90ml/6 tbsp extra virgin
  olive oil
2 garlic cloves, chopped
30ml/2 tbsp balsamic or
  wine vinegar
salt and ground black
  pepper

1 Place the peppers under a hot grill and turn occasionally until they are black and blistered on all sides. Remove from the heat and place in a paper bag. Leave for 5 minutes.

2 Peel the peppers, then cut them into quarters. Remove the stems and seeds.

3 Cut the peppers into strips, and arrange them in a serving dish. Distribute the capers and olives evenly over them.

4 To make the dressing, mix the oil and garlic together in a small bowl, crushing the garlic with a spoon to release as much flavour as possible. Mix in the vinegar, and season to taste with salt and pepper. Pour over the salad, mix well, and allow to stand for at least 30 minutes before serving.

Cook's Tip
Skinning the peppers brings out their delicious sweet flavour and is well worth the extra effort.

Chicken Liver and Tomato Salad

Warm salads are especially welcome during the autumn months when the evenings are growing shorter and cooler.

Serves 4

*225g/½lb young
    spinach, stems
    removed
1 frisée lettuce
105ml/7 tbsp groundnut
    or sunflower oil
175g/6oz rindless bacon,
    cut into strips*

*3 slices day-old bread,
    without crusts, cut
    into short fingers
450g/1lb chicken livers
115g/4oz cherry tomatoes
salt and ground black
    pepper*

1 Wash and spin the salad leaves. Place in a salad bowl. Heat 60ml/4 tbsp of the oil in a large frying pan and cook the bacon for 3–4 minutes until crisp and brown. Remove the bacon with a slotted spoon and leave to drain on a piece of kitchen paper.

2 To make the croûtons, fry the bread in the bacon-flavoured oil, tossing until crisp and golden. Drain on kitchen paper.

3 Heat the remaining 45ml/3 tbsp of oil in the frying pan and fry the chicken livers briskly for 2–3 minutes. Transfer the livers to the salad leaves, add the bacon, croûtons and tomatoes. Season with salt and pepper, toss and serve.

Cook's Tip
Although fresh chicken livers are preferable, frozen ones could be used in this salad. It is important to make sure they are completely thawed before cooking.

Maryland Salad

Chicken, sweetcorn, bacon, banana and watercress are combined here in a sensational main-course salad.

Serves 4

*4 free-range chicken
    breasts, boned
225g/8oz rindless
    unsmoked bacon
4 baby sweetcorn
40g/1½oz/3 tbsp soft
    butter, softened
4 ripe bananas, peeled
    and halved
4 firm tomatoes, halved
4 escarole or butterhead
    lettuces*

*1 bunch watercress
    (about 115g/4oz)
salt and ground black
    pepper*

For the dressing
*75ml/5 tbsp groundnut
    oil
15ml/1 tbsp white wine
    vinegar
10ml/1 tsp maple syrup
10ml/2 tsp mild mustard*

1 Season the chicken breasts, brush with oil and barbecue or grill for 15 minutes, turning once. Barbecue or grill the bacon for 8–10 minutes or until crisp.

2 Bring a large saucepan of salted water to the boil. Trim the baby sweetcorn or leave the husks on if you prefer. Boil for 20 minutes. For extra flavour, brush with butter and brown over the barbecue or under the grill. Barbecue or grill the bananas and tomatoes for 6–8 minutes. You can brush these with butter too if you wish.

3 To make the dressing, combine the oil, vinegar, maple syrup and mustard with 15ml/1 tbsp water in a screw-top jar and shake well.

4 Wash, spin thoroughly and dress the escarole or butterhead lettuce and the watercress.

5 Distribute the salad leaves among four large plates. Slice the chicken and arrange over the leaves with the bacon, banana, sweetcorn and tomatoes.

Leeks with Mustard Dressing

Pour the dressing over the leeks while they are still warm so that they absorb the mustardy flavours.

Serves 4

8 slim leeks (each about 13cm/5in long)
5–10ml/1–2 tsp Dijon mustard
10ml/2 tsp white wine vinegar
1 hard-boiled egg, halved lengthways
75ml/5 tbsp light olive oil
10ml/2 tsp chopped fresh parsley
salt and ground black pepper

1 Steam the leeks over a saucepan of boiling water until they are just tender.

2 Meanwhile, stir together the mustard and vinegar in a bowl. Scoop the egg yolk into the bowl and mash thoroughly into the vinegar mixture using a fork.

3 Gradually work in the oil to make a smooth sauce, then season to taste with salt and pepper.

4 Lift the leeks out of the steamer and place on several layers of kitchen paper, then cover the leeks with several more layers of kitchen paper and pat dry.

5 Transfer the leeks to a serving dish while still warm, spoon the dressing over them and leave to cool. Finely chop the egg white using a large sharp knife, then mix with the chopped fresh parsley and scatter over the leeks. Chill in the fridge until ready to serve.

Cook's Tip
Pencil-slim baby leeks are increasingly available nowadays, and are beautifully tender. Use three or four of these smaller leeks per serving.

Lettuce and Herb Salad

For a really quick salad, look out for pre-packed bags of mixed baby lettuce leaves in the supermarket.

Serves 4

½ cucumber
mixed lettuce leaves
1 bunch watercress (about 115g/4oz)
1 chicory head, sliced
45ml/3 tbsp mixed chopped fresh herbs such as parsley, thyme, tarragon, chives and chervil

For the dressing
15ml/1 tbsp white wine vinegar
5ml/1 tsp prepared mustard
75ml/5 tbsp olive oil
salt and ground black pepper

1 Peel the cucumber, if you wish, then cut it in half lengthways and scoop out the seeds. Thinly slice the flesh. Tear the lettuce leaves into bite-size pieces.

2 Toss the cucumber, lettuce, watercress, chicory and herbs together in a bowl, or arrange them in the bowl in layers, if you prefer.

3 To make the dressing, mix the vinegar and mustard together, then whisk in the oil and seasoning.

4 Stir the dressing, then pour over the salad, toss lightly to coat the salad vegetables and leaves. Serve at once.

Cook's Tip
Do not dress the salad until just before serving, otherwise the lettuce leaves will wilt.

Goat's Cheese Salad

The robust flavours of the goat's cheese and buckwheat combine especially well with figs and walnuts in this salad.

Serves 4

175g/6oz/1 cup couscous
30ml/2 tbsp toasted
   buckwheat
1 hard-boiled egg
30ml/2 tbsp chopped
   fresh parsley
60ml/4 tbsp olive oil,
   preferably Sicilian
45ml/3 tbsp walnut oil
115g/4oz rocket

½ frisée lettuce
175g/6oz crumbly white
   goat's cheese
50g/2oz/½ cup broken
   walnuts, toasted
4 ripe figs, trimmed and
   almost cut into four
   (leaving the pieces
   joined at the base)

1 Place the couscous and buckwheat in a bowl, cover with boiling water and leave to soak for 15 minutes. Place in a sieve if necessary to drain off any remaining water, then spread out on a metal tray and allow to cool.

2 Shell the hard-boiled egg and pass it through a fine grater.

3 Toss the egg, parsley and couscous in a bowl. Combine the two oils and use half to moisten the couscous mixture.

4 Wash and spin the salad leaves, dress with the remaining oil and distribute among four large plates.

5 Pile the couscous in the centre of the leaves, crumble on the goat's cheese, scatter with toasted walnuts, and add the trimmed figs.

Cook's Tip
Serve this strongly flavoured salad with a gutsy red wine from the Rhône or South of France.

Waldorf Ham Salad

Waldorf salad originally consisted of apples, celery and mayonnaise. This ham version is a meal in itself.

Serves 4

3 apples, peeled
15ml/1 tbsp lemon juice
2 slices cooked ham
   (about 175g/6oz each)
3 celery sticks
150ml/¼ pint/⅔ cup
   mayonnaise
1 escarole or Batavia
   lettuce

1 small radicchio, finely
   shredded
½ bunch watercress
45ml/3 tbsp walnut oil or
   olive oil
2oz/50g/½ cup walnut
   pieces, toasted
salt and ground black
   pepper

1 Core, slice and shred the apples finely. Moisten with lemon juice to keep them white. Cut the cooked ham into 5cm/2in strips, then cut the celery into similar-size pieces, and combine in a bowl.

2 Add the mayonnaise to the apples, ham and celery and stir to combine well.

3 Wash and spin the salad leaves. Shred the leaves finely, then toss with the walnut or olive oil. Distribute the leaves among four plates. Pile the mayonnaise mixture in the centre, scatter with toasted walnuts, season to taste with salt and pepper, and serve at once.

Baby Leaf Salad with Croûtons

Cripsy ciabatta croûtons give a lovely crunch to this mixed leaf and avocado salad.

Serves 4
15ml/1 tbsp olive oil
1 garlic clove, crushed
15ml/1 tbsp freshly
    grated Parmesan
    cheese
15ml/1 tbsp chopped
    fresh parsley
4 slices ciabatta bread,
    crusts removed, cut
    into small dice
1 large bunch watercress
large handful of rocket

1 bag mixed baby salad
    leaves, including oak
    leaf and cos lettuce
1 ripe avocado

For the dressing
45ml/3 tbsp olive oil
15ml/1 tbsp walnut oil
juice of ½ lemon
2.5ml/½ tsp Dijon
    mustard
salt and ground black
    pepper

1 Preheat the oven to 190°C/375°F/Gas 5. Put the oil, garlic, Parmesan, parsley and bread in a bowl and toss to coat well. Spread out the diced bread on a baking sheet and bake for about 8 minutes until crisp. Leave to cool.

2 Remove any coarse or discoloured stalks or leaves from the watercress and place in a serving bowl with the rocket and baby salad leaves.

3 Halve the avocado and remove the stone. Peel and cut into chunks, then add it to the salad bowl.

4 To make the dressing, mix together the oils, lemon juice, mustard and seasoning in a small bowl or screw-top jar until evenly blended. Pour over the salad and toss well. Sprinkle over the croûtons and serve at once.

Wild Rice with Grilled Vegetables

Grilling brings out the delicious and varied flavour of these summer vegetables.

Serves 4
225g/8oz/1¼ cups wild
    and long grain rice
    mixture
1 large aubergine, thickly
    sliced
1 red, 1 yellow and 1
    green pepper, seeded
    and cut into quarters
2 red onions, sliced
225g/8oz brown cap or
    shiitake mushrooms
2 small courgettes, cut in
    half lengthways

olive oil, for brushing
30ml/2 tbsp chopped
    fresh thyme

For the dressing
90ml/6 tbsp extra virgin
    olive oil
30ml/2 tbsp balsamic
    vinegar
2 garlic cloves, crushed
salt and ground black
    pepper

1 Put the rice mixture in a saucepan of cold salted water. Bring to the boil, reduce the heat, cover with a tight-fitting lid and cook gently for 30–40 minutes or according to the packet instructions, until all the grains are tender.

2 To make the dressing, mix together the olive oil, vinegar, garlic and seasoning in a small bowl or screw-topped jar until well blended. Set aside while you grill the vegetables.

3 Arrange the vegetables on a grill rack. Brush with olive oil and grill for 8–10 minutes, until tender and well browned, turning them occasionally and brushing again with oil.

4 Drain the rice and toss in half the dressing. Tip into a serving dish and arrange the grilled vegetables on top. Pour over the remaining dressing and scatter over the chopped fresh thyme.

Russian Salad

Russian salad became fashionable in the hotel dining rooms of Europe in the 1920s and 1930s.

Serves 4

115g/4oz large button mushrooms
120ml/4fl oz/½ cup mayonnaise
15ml/1 tbsp freshly squeezed lemon juice
350g/12oz peeled, cooked prawns
1 large dill pickle, finely chopped, or 30ml/2 tbsp capers
115g/4oz broad beans
115g/4oz small new potatoes, scrubbed or scraped

115g/4oz young carrots, trimmed and peeled
115g/4oz baby sweetcorn
115g/4oz baby turnips, trimmed
15ml/1 tbsp olive oil, preferably French or Italian
4 eggs, hard-boiled and shelled
pinch of salt, pepper and paprika
25g/1oz canned anchovies, cut into fine strips, to garnish

1 Slice the mushrooms thinly, then cut into matchsticks. Combine the mayonnaise and lemon juice. Fold the mayonnaise into the mushrooms and prawns, add the dill pickle or capers, then season to taste with salt and pepper.

2 Bring a large saucepan of salted water to the boil, add the broad beans, and cook for 3 minutes. Drain and cool under running water, then pinch the beans between thumb and forefinger to release them from their tough skins. Boil the potatoes for 20 minutes and the remaining vegetables for 6 minutes. Drain and cool under running water.

3 Toss the vegetables with oil and divide among four shallow bowls. Spoon on the dressed prawns and place a hard-boiled egg in the centre. Garnish the egg with strips of anchovy and sprinkle with paprika.

Crunchy Coleslaw

Home-made coleslaw is quite quick and easy to make – and it tastes fresh, crunchy and wonderful.

Serves 4–6

¼ firm white cabbage
1 small onion, finely chopped
2 celery sticks, thinly sliced
2 carrots, coarsely grated
5–10ml/1–2 tsp caraway seeds (optional)
1 eating apple, cored and chopped (optional)

50g/2oz/½ cup walnuts, chopped (optional)
salt and ground black pepper

For the dressing

45ml/3 tbsp mayonnaise
30ml/2 tbsp single cream or natural yogurt
5ml/1 tsp grated lemon rind

1 Cut and discard the core from the cabbage quarter, then shred the leaves finely. Place them in a large bowl.

2 Toss the onion, celery and carrot into the cabbage, plus the caraway seeds, apple and walnuts, if using. Season well with salt and pepper.

3 Mix the dressing ingredients together in a small bowl, then stir into the vegetables. Cover the salad with clear film and allow to stand for 2 hours, stirring occasionally, then chill lightly in the fridge before serving.

Pear and Roquefort Salad

Choose ripe but firm Comice or Williams' pears for this attractive and deeply flavoursome salad.

Serves 4

3 ripe pears
lemon juice
about 175g/6oz mixed
   fresh salad leaves
175g/6oz Roquefort
   cheese
50g/2oz/½ cup hazelnuts,
   toasted and chopped

For the dressing
30ml/2 tbsp hazelnut oil
45ml/3 tbsp olive oil
15ml/1 tbsp cider vinegar
5ml/1 tsp Dijon mustard
salt and ground black
   pepper

1 To make the dressing, mix together the oils, vinegar and mustard in a bowl or screw-top jar. Season to taste with salt and pepper.

2 Peel, core and slice the pears and toss them in lemon juice.

3 Divide the salad leaves among four serving plates, then place the pears on top. Crumble the cheese and scatter over the salad along with the toasted hazelnuts. Spoon over the dressing and serve at once.

Mediterranean Mixed Pepper Salad

Serve this colourful salad either as a tasty starter or as an accompaniment to cold meats for lunch or supper.

Serves 4

2 red peppers, halved and
   seeded
2 yellow peppers, halved
   and seeded
150ml/¼ pint/⅔ cup
   olive oil

1 onion, thinly sliced
2 garlic cloves, crushed
generous squeeze of
   lemon juice
chopped fresh parsley, to
   garnish

1 Grill the pepper halves for about 5 minutes, until the skin has blistered and blackened. Pop them into a polythene bag, seal and leave for 5 minutes.

2 Meanwhile, heat 30ml/2 tbsp of the olive oil in a frying pan and fry the onion for about 5–6 minutes, until softened and translucent. Remove from the heat and reserve.

3 Take the peppers out of the bag and peel off the skins. Discard the pepper skins and slice each pepper half into fairly thin strips.

4 Place the peppers, cooked onions and any oil from the pan into a bowl. Add the crushed garlic, pour in the remaining olive oil, add a generous squeeze of lemon juice and season to taste. Mix well, cover and marinate for 2–3 hours, stirring the mixture once or twice.

5 Just before serving, garnish the pepper salad with chopped fresh parsley.

Californian Salad

Full of vitality and vitamins, this is a lovely light and healthy salad for sunny summer days.

Serves 4

1 small crisp lettuce, torn
   into pieces
225g/8oz/2 cups young
   spinach leaves
2 carrots, coarsely grated
115g/4oz cherry
   tomatoes, halved
2 celery sticks, thinly
   sliced
75g/3oz/1/2 cup raisins
50g/2oz/1/2 cup blanched
   almonds or unsalted
   cashew nuts, halved

30ml/2 tbsp sunflower
   seeds
30ml/2 tbsp sesame
   seeds, lightly toasted

For the dressing
45ml/3 tbsp extra virgin
   olive oil
30ml/2 tbsp cider vinegar
10ml/2 tsp clear honey
juice of 1 small orange
salt and ground black
   pepper

1 Put the salad vegetables, raisins, almonds or cashew nuts and seeds into a large bowl.

2 Put all the dressing ingredients into a screw-top jar, shake them up well and pour over the salad.

3 Toss the salad thoroughly and divide it among four small salad bowls. Serve chilled, sprinkled with salt and pepper.

Scandinavian Cucumber and Dill

This unusual salad is particularly complementary to hot and spicy food.

Serves 4

2 cucumbers
30ml/2 tbsp snipped
   fresh chives
30ml/2 tbsp chopped
   fresh dill

150ml/1/4 pint/2/3 cup
   soured cream or
   fromage frais
salt and ground black
   pepper

1 Slice the cucumbers as thinly as possible, preferably in a food processor or with a slicer.

2 Place the slices in layers in a colander set over a plate to catch the juices. Sprinkle each layer evenly, but not too heavily, with salt.

3 Leave the cucumber to drain for up to 2 hours, then lay out the slices on a clean dish towel and pat them dry.

4 Mix the cucumber with the herbs, cream or fromage frais and plenty of pepper. Serve as soon as possible.

Cook's Tip
The juices in this salad continue forming after salting,
so only dress it when you are ready to serve.

Chicory, Fruit and Nut Salad

Mildly bitter chicory is wonderful with sweet fruit, and is delicious when complemented by a creamy curry sauce.

Serves 4

45ml/3 tbsp mayonnaise
15ml/1 tbsp Greek-style yogurt
15ml/1 tbsp mild curry paste
90ml/6 tbsp single cream
½ iceberg lettuce
2 heads of chicory
50g/2oz/1 cup flaked coconut
50g/2oz/½ cup cashew nuts
2 red eating apples
75g/3oz/½ cup currants

1 Mix together the mayonnaise, Greek-style yogurt, curry paste and single cream in a small bowl. Cover and chill in the fridge until required.

2 Tear the iceberg lettuce into even-size pieces and put into a salad bowl.

3 Cut the root end off each head of chicory and discard. Slice the chicory and add it to the salad bowl. Preheat the grill.

4 Spread out the coconut flakes on a baking sheet. Grill for 1 minute until golden. Tip into a bowl and set aside. Toast the cashew nuts for 2 minutes until golden.

5 Quarter the apples and cut out the cores. Slice the apple quarters and add to the lettuce with the toasted coconut, cashew nuts and currants.

6 Spoon the dressing over the salad, toss lightly and serve.

Cook's Tip
Choose a sweet, well-flavoured variety of red apple for this salad, such as Braeburn or Royal Gala.

Tzatziki

This Greek salad is typically served with grilled lamb and chicken, but is also good with salmon and trout.

Serves 4

1 cucumber
5ml/1 tsp salt
45ml/3 tbsp finely chopped fresh mint, plus a few springs to garnish
1 clove garlic, crushed
5ml/1 tsp caster sugar
200ml/7 fl oz strained Greek-style yogurt
paprika, to garnish (optional)

1 Peel the cucumber. Reserve a little to use as a garnish if you wish and cut the rest in half lengthways. Remove the seeds with a teaspoon and discard. Slice the cucumber thinly and combine with salt. Leave for about 15-20 minutes. Salt will soften the cucumber and draw out any bitter juices.

2 Combine the mint, garlic, sugar and yogurt in a bowl, reserving a few sprigs of mint as decoration.

3 Rinse the cucumber in a sieve under cold running water to flush away the salt. Drain well and combine with the yogurt. Decorate with cucumber and mint. Serve cold, garnished with paprika if you wish.

Cook's Tip
If preparing tzatziki in a hurry, leave out the method for salting the cucumber at the end of step 1. The cucumber will have a more crunchy texture, and will be slightly less sweet.

Tomato and Bread Salad

This salad is a traditional peasant dish from Tuscany which was created to use up bread that was several days old.

Serves 4

400g/14oz stale white or
  brown bread or rolls
4 large tomatoes
1 large red onion, or
  6 spring onions
a few fresh basil leaves,
  to garnish

For the dressing
60ml/4 tbsp extra virgin
  olive oil
30ml/2 tbsp white wine
  vinegar
salt and ground black
  pepper

1 Cut the bread or rolls into thick slices. Place in a shallow bowl and soak with cold water. Leave for at least 30 minutes.

2 Cut the tomatoes into chunks. Place in a serving bowl. Finely slice the onion or spring onions, and add them to the tomatoes. Squeeze as much water out of the bread as possible, and add it to the vegetables.

3 Mix together the dressing ingredients. Season to taste with salt and pepper. Pour it over the salad and mix well. Decorate with the basil leaves. Allow to stand in a cool place for at least 2 hours before serving.

Fennel and Orange Salad

This salad originated in Sicily, following the seventeenth-century custom of serving fennel at a meal's end.

Serves 4

2 large fennel bulbs
  (about 675g/1½ lb
  total)
2 sweet oranges
2 spring onions,
  to garnish

For the dressing
60ml/4 tbsp extra virgin
  olive oil
30ml/2 tbsp fresh lemon
  juice
salt and ground black
  pepper

1 Wash the fennel bulbs and remove any brown or stringy outer leaves. Slice the bulbs and stems into thin pieces. Place in a shallow serving bowl.

2 Peel the oranges with a sharp knife, cutting away the white pith. Slice thinly. Cut each slice into thirds. Arrange over the fennel, adding any juice from the oranges.

3 To make the dressing, mix the oil and lemon juice together. Season with salt and pepper. Pour the dressing over the salad and mix well.

4 Slice the white and green sections of the spring onions thinly. Sprinkle over the salad.

Parmesan and Poached Egg Salad

Soft poached eggs, hot garlic croûtons and cool crisp salad leaves make an unforgettable combination.

Serves 2

½ small loaf white bread
75ml/5 tbsp extra virgin
  olive oil
2 eggs
115g/4oz mixed salad
  leaves

2 garlic cloves, crushed
2.5ml/½ tbsp white wine
  vinegar
30ml/2 tbsp freshly
  shaved Parmesan
  cheese
black pepper

1 Remove the crust from the bread. Cut the bread into 2.5cm/1in cubes.

2 Heat 30ml/2 tbsp of the oil in a frying pan and cook the bread for about 5 minutes, tossing the cubes occasionally, until they are golden brown.

3 Meanwhile, bring a saucepan of water to the boil. Slide in the eggs carefully, one at a time. Gently poach the eggs for 4 minutes until lightly cooked.

4 Divide the salad leaves between two plates. Remove the croûtons from the pan and arrange them over the leaves. Wipe the pan clean with kitchen paper.

5 Heat the remaining oil in the pan and cook the garlic and vinegar over a high heat for about 1 minute. Pour the warm dressing over the salad leaves and croûtons.

6 Place a poached egg on each salad. Scatter with shavings of Parmesan cheese and a little freshly ground black pepper.

Cook's Tip
Add a dash of vinegar to the water before poaching the eggs. This helps to keep the whites together. To ensure that a poached egg has a good shape, swirl the water with a spoon before sliding in the egg.

Classic Greek Salad

If you have ever visited Greece you'll know that a Greek salad with a chunk of bread makes a delicious filling meal.

Serves 4

1 cos lettuce
½ cucumber, halved
  lengthways
4 tomatoes
8 spring onions
75g/3oz Greek black
  olives

115g/4oz feta cheese
90ml/6 tbsp white wine
  vinegar
150ml/¼ pint/⅔ cup
  extra virgin olive oil
salt and ground black
  pepper

1 Tear the lettuce leaves into pieces and place them in a large serving bowl. Slice the cucumber and add to the bowl.

2 Cut the tomatoes into wedges and put them into the bowl.

3 Slice the spring onions. Add them to the bowl along with the olives and toss well.

4 Cut the feta cheese into dice and add to the salad.

5 Put the vinegar and olive oil into a small bowl and season to taste with salt and pepper. Whisk well. Pour the dressing over the salad and toss to combine. Serve at once with extra olives and chunks of bread, if you wish.

Cook's Tip
This salad can be assembled in advance, but should only be dressed just before serving. Keep the dressing at room temperature as chilling deadens its flavours.

Potato Salad with Egg and Lemon

Potato salads are a popular addition to any salad spread and are enjoyed with an assortment of cold meats and fish.

Serves 4

900g/2lb new potatoes,
    scrubbed or scraped
1 onion, finely chopped
1 hard-boiled egg
300ml/½ pint/1¼ cups
    mayonnaise
1 garlic clove, crushed

finely grated juice and
    zest of 1 lemon
60ml/4 tbsp chopped
    fresh parsley
salt and ground black
    pepper

1 Bring the potatoes to the boil in a saucepan of salted water. Simmer for 20 minutes. Drain and allow to cool. Cut the potatoes into large dice, season with salt and pepper to taste, and combine with the onion.

2 Shell the hard-boiled egg and grate into a mixing bowl, then add the mayonnaise. Combine the garlic and lemon rind and juice in a small bowl and stir into the mayonnaise.

Cook's Tip
Use an early season variety of potato for this salad or look out for baby salad potatoes. They will not disintegrate when boiled and have a sweet flavour.

Sweet Turnip Salad

The robust flavoured turnip partners well with the taste of horseradish and caraway seeds in this delicious salad.

Serves 4

350g/12oz turnips
2 spring onions, white
    part only, chopped
15g/½oz/1 tbsp caster
    sugar

pinch of salt
30ml/2 tbsp creamed
    horseradish
10ml/2 tsp caraway seeds

1 Peel, slice and shred the turnips – or you could grate them if you wish.

2 Add the spring onions, sugar and salt, then rub together with your hands to soften the turnip.

3 Fold in the creamed horseradish and caraway seeds and serve the salad immediately.

Queen of Puddings

This pudding was developed from a seventeenth-century recipe by Queen Victoria's chefs at Buckingham Palace.

Serves 4

75g/3oz/1½ cups fresh
  breadcrumbs
50g/2oz/4 tbsp caster
  sugar, plus
  5ml/1 tsp grated rind
  of 1 lemon

600ml/1 pint/2½ cups
  milk
4 eggs
45ml/3 tbsp raspberry
  jam, warmed

1 Stir the breadcrumbs, 25g/1oz/2 tbsp of the sugar and the lemon rind together in a heatproof bowl. Bring the milk to the boil in a saucepan, then stir into the breadcrumbs.

2 Separate three of the eggs and beat the yolks with the whole egg. Stir into the breadcrumb mixture, pour into a buttered baking dish and leave to stand for 30 minutes. Meanwhile, preheat the oven to 160°C/325°F/Gas 3. Bake the pudding for 50–60 minutes, until set.

3 Whisk the egg whites in a large clean bowl until stiff but not dry, then gradually whisk in just under 25g/1oz/2tbsp caster sugar until the mixture is thick and glossy, taking care not to overwhip.

4 Spread the jam over the pudding, then spoon over the meringue to cover the top completely. Evenly sprinkle about 5ml/1tsp sugar over the meringue, then bake for a further 15 minutes, until the meringue is beginning to turn a light golden colour.

Pear and Blackberry Brown Betty

All this delicious fruity pudding needs to go with it is some hot home-made custard, pouring cream or ice cream.

Serves 4–6

75g/3oz/6 tbsp butter,
  diced
175g/6oz/3 cups
  breadcrumbs
450g/1lb ripe pears
450g/1lb/4 cups
  blackberries

grated rind and juice of 1
  small orange
115g/4oz/½ cup
  demerara sugar
extra demerara sugar, for
  sprinkling

1 Preheat the oven to 180°C/350°F/Gas 4. Heat the butter in a heavy-based frying pan over a moderate heat and add the breadcrumbs. Stir until golden.

2 Peel and core the pears, then cut them into thick slices and mix with the blackberries, orange rind and juice.

3 Mix the demerara sugar with the breadcrumbs, then layer with the fruit in a 900ml/1½ pint/3 cup buttered baking dish, beginning and ending with a layer of sugared breadcrumbs.

4 Sprinkle the extra demerara sugar over the top. Cover the baking dish, then bake the pudding for 20 minutes. Uncover the pudding, then bake for a further 30–35 minutes, until the fruit is cooked and the top is brown and crisp.

Baked Stuffed Apples

When apples are plentiful, this traditional pudding is a popular and easy choice.

Serves 4

75g/3oz/scant 1 cup
  ground almonds
25g/1oz/2 tbsp butter,
  softened
5ml/1 tsp clear honey

1 egg yolk
50g/2oz dried apricots,
  chopped
4 cooking apples,
  preferably Bramleys

1 Preheat the oven to 200°C/400°F/Gas 6. Beat together the almonds, butter, honey, egg yolk and apricots.

2 Stamp out the cores from the cooking apples using a large apple corer, then score a line with the point of a sharp knife around the circumference of each apple.

3 Lightly grease a shallow baking dish, then arrange the cooking apples in the dish.

4 Divide the apricot mixture among the cavities in the apples, then bake in the oven for 45–60 minutes, until the apples are fluffy.

Kentish Cherry Batter Pudding

Kent, known as the "Garden of England", is particularly well known for cherries and the dishes made from them.

Serves 4

45ml/3 tbsp Kirsch
  (optional)
450g/1lb dark cherries,
  stoned
50g/2oz/½ cup plain
  flour
50g/2oz/4 tbsp caster
  sugar

2 eggs, separated
300ml/½ pint/¼ cup
  milk
75g/3oz/6 tbsp butter,
  melted
caster sugar, for
  sprinkling

1 Sprinkle the Kirsch, if using, over the cherries in a small bowl and leave them to soak for about 30 minutes.

2 Mix the flour and sugar together, then slowly stir in the egg yolks and milk to make a smooth batter. Stir in half the butter and leave for 30 minutes.

3 Preheat the oven to 220°C/425°F/Gas 7, then pour the remaining butter into a 600ml/1 pint/2½ cup baking dish and put in the oven to heat.

4 Whisk the egg whites until stiff peaks form, then fold into the batter with the cherries and Kirsch, if using. Pour into the dish and bake for 15 minutes.

5 Reduce the oven temperature to 180°C/350°F/Gas 4 and bake for 20 minutes, or until golden and set in the centre. Serve sprinkled with sugar.

Sticky Toffee Pudding

If you prefer, use pecan nuts instead of walnuts in this delightfully gooey pudding.

Serves 6

115g/4oz/1 cup toasted
  walnuts, chopped
175g/6oz/¾ cup butter
175g/6oz/1½ cups soft
  brown sugar

60ml/4 tbsp double cream
30ml/2 tbsp lemon juice
2 eggs, beaten
115g/4oz/1 cup
  self-raising flour

1   Grease a 900ml/1½ pint/3¾ cup pudding basin and add half the nuts.

2   Heat 50g/2oz/4 tbsp of the butter with 50g/2oz/4 tbsp of the sugar, the cream and 15ml/1 tbsp of the lemon juice in a small saucepan, stirring until smooth. Pour half into the pudding basin, then swirl to coat it a little way up the sides.

3   Beat the remaining butter and sugar until light and fluffy, then gradually beat in the eggs. Fold in the flour and the remaining nuts and lemon juice and spoon into the basin.

4   Cover the basin with greaseproof paper with a pleat folded in the centre, then tie securely with string.

5   Steam the pudding for 1¼ hours, or until it is completely set in the centre.

6   Just before serving, gently warm the remaining sauce. Unmould the pudding on to a warm plate and pour over the warm sauce.

Easy Chocolate and Orange Soufflé

The base in this soufflé is a simple semolina mixture, rather than the thick white sauce of most soufflés.

Serve 4

50g/2oz/scant ½ cup
  semolina
50g/2oz/scant ½ cup soft
  brown sugar
600ml/1 pint/2½ cups
  milk
grated rind of 1 orange

90ml/6 tbsp fresh orange
  juice
3 eggs, separated
65g/2½oz plain
  chocolate, grated
icing sugar, for
  sprinkling

1   Preheat the oven to 200°C/400°F/Gas 6. Butter a shallow 1.75 litre/3 pint/7½ cup ovenproof dish.

2   Pour the milk into a heavy-based saucepan, sprinkle over the semolina and brown sugar, then heat, stirring the mixture all the time, until boiling and thickened.

3   Remove the pan from the heat; beat in the orange rind and juice, egg yolks and all but 15ml/1 tbsp of the chocolate.

4   Whisk the egg whites until stiff but not dry, then lightly fold into the semolina mixture in three batches. Spoon the mixture into the dish and bake for about 30 minutes until just set in the centre and risen. Sprinkle the top with the reserved chocolate and the icing sugar, then serve immediately.

Plum and Walnut Crumble

Walnuts add a lovely crunch to the fruit layer in this rich crumble – almonds would be equally good.

Serves 4 – 6

75g/3oz/¾ cup walnut
   pieces
900g/2lb plums
75g/6oz/1½ cups
   demerara sugar

75g/3oz/6 tbsp butter or
   ·hard margarine, cut
   into dice
75g/6oz/1½ cups plain
   flour

1 Preheat the oven to 180°C/350°F/Gas 4. Spread the nuts on a baking sheet and place in the oven for 8 – 10 minutes, until evenly coloured.

2 Butter a 1.2 litre/2 pint/5 cup baking dish. Halve and stone the plums, then put them into the dish and stir in the nuts and half of the demerara sugar.

3 Rub the butter or margarine into the flour until the mixture resembles coarse crumbs. (Alternatively, use a food processor.) Stir in the remaining sugar and continue to rub in until fine crumbs are formed.

4 Cover the fruit with the crumb mixture and press it down lightly. Bake the pudding for about 45 minutes, until the top is golden brown and the fruit tender.

Cook's Tip
To make an oat and cinnamon crumble, substitute rolled oats for half the flour in the crumble mixture and add 2.5–5ml/½ –1 tsp ground cinnamon, to taste.

Baked Rice Pudding

Canned rice pudding simply cannot compare with this creamy home-made version, especially if you like the skin.

Serves 4

50g/2oz/¼ cup pudding
   rice
25g/1oz/2 tbsp soft light
   brown sugar ·
50g/2oz/4 tbsp butter
900ml/1½ pints/3¾ cups
   milk

small strip of lemon rind
pinch of freshly grated
   nutmeg
fresh mint sprigs, to
   decorate
raspberries, to serve

1 Preheat the oven to 150°C/300°F/Gas 2, then butter a 1.2 litre/2 pint/5 cup shallow baking dish.

2 Put the rice, sugar and butter into the dish, stir in the milk and lemon rind and sprinkle a little nutmeg over the surface.

3 Bake the rice pudding in the oven for about 2½ hours, stirring after 30 minutes and another couple of times during the next 2 hours until the rice is tender and the pudding has a thick and creamy consistency.

4 If you like skin on top, leave the rice pudding undisturbed for the final 30 minutes of cooking (otherwise, stir it again). Serve hot, decorated with fresh mint sprigs and raspberries.

Cook's Tip
Baked rice pudding is even more delicious with fruit. Add some sultanas, raisins or chopped ready-to-eat dried apricots to the pudding, or serve it alongside sliced fresh peaches or nectarines, fresh raspberries or fresh strawberries.

Floating Islands in Plum Sauce

This unusual, low-fat pudding is simpler to make than it looks, and is quite delicious.

Serves 4

450g/1lb red plums
300ml/½ pint/1¼ cups
    apple juice
2 egg whites

30ml/2 tbsp concentrated
    apple juice syrup
pinch of freshly grated
    nutmeg

1 Halve the plums and remove the stones. Place them in a wide saucepan with the apple juice.

2 Bring to the boil, then cover with a tight-fitting lid and leave to simmer gently until the plums are tender.

3 Meanwhile, place the egg whites in a clean, dry bowl and whisk until stiff peaks form.

4 Gradually whisk in the apple juice syrup, whisking until the meringue holds fairly firm peaks.

5 Using a tablespoon, scoop the meringue mixture into the gently simmering plum sauce. (You may need to cook the "islands" in two batches.)

6 Cover again and allow to simmer gently for 2–3 minutes, until the meringues are just set. Serve straight away, sprinkled with a little freshly grated nutmeg.

Cook's Tip
For ease of preparation when you are entertaining, the plum sauce can be made in advance and reheated just before you cook the meringues.

Souffléed Rice Pudding

The inclusion of fluffy egg whites in this rice pudding makes it unusually light.

Serves 4

65g/2½oz/¼ cup short
    grain pudding rice
45ml/3 tbsp clear honey
750ml/1¼ pints/3⅓ cups
    semi-skimmed milk

1 vanilla pod or 2.5ml/
    ½ tsp vanilla essence
2 egg whites
5ml/1 tsp finely grated
    nutmeg

1 Place the pudding rice, clear honey and the milk in a heavy-based or non-stick saucepan and bring to the boil. Add the vanilla pod, if using.

2 Reduce the heat and cover with a tight-fitting lid. Leave to simmer gently for about 1–1¼ hours, stirring occasionally to prevent sticking, until most of the liquid has been absorbed.

3 Remove the vanilla pod from the saucepan, or if using vanilla essence, add this to the rice mixture now. Preheat the oven to 220°C/425°F/Gas 7.

4 Place the egg whites in a clean dry bowl and whisk until stiff peaks form.

5 Using a metal spoon or spatula, fold the egg whites evenly into the rice mixture and tip into a 1 litre/1¾ pint/4 cup ovenproof dish.

6 Sprinkle with grated nutmeg and bake for 15–20 minutes, until the pudding is well risen and golden brown. Serve hot.

Cabinet Pudding

Dried and glacé fruit, sponge cake and ratafias, spiked with brandy if you wish, make a rich pudding.

Serves 4

25g/1oz/2½ tbsp raisins, chopped
30ml/2 tbsp brandy (optional)
25g/1oz glacé cherries, halved
25g/1oz angelica, chopped
2 trifle sponge cakes

50g/2oz ratafias
2 eggs
2 egg yolks
25g/1oz/2 tbsp sugar
450ml/¾ pint/1¼ cups single cream or milk
few drops of vanilla essence

1 Soak the raisins in the brandy, if using, for several hours.

2 Butter a 750ml/1¼ pint/3⅓ cup charlotte mould and arrange some of the cherries and angelica in the base.

3 Dice the sponge cakes and crush the ratafias. Mix with the remaining cherries and angelica, raisins and brandy, if using, and spoon into the mould.

4 Lightly whisk together the eggs, egg yolks and sugar. Bring the cream or milk just to the boil, then stir into the egg mixture with the vanilla essence.

5 Strain the egg mixture into the mould, then set aside for 15–30 minutes.

6 Preheat the oven to 160°C/325°F/Gas 3. Place the mould in a roasting tin, cover with baking paper and pour in boiling water. Bake for 1 hour, or until set. Leave for 2–3 minutes, then turn out on to a warm plate.

Eve's Pudding

The tempting apples beneath the sponge topping are the reason for this pudding's name.

Serves 4–6

115g/4oz/½ cup butter, softened
115g/4oz/½ cup caster sugar
2 eggs, beaten
grated rind and juice of 1 lemon
90g/3½oz/scant 1 cup self-raising flour

40g/1½oz/generous ¼ cup ground almonds
115g/4oz/½ cup soft brown sugar
500–675g/1½lb cooking apples, cored and thinly sliced
25g/1oz/¼ cup flaked almonds

1 Beat together the butter and caster sugar in a large mixing bowl until the mixture is very light and fluffy.

2 Gradually beat the eggs into the butter mixture, beating well after each addition, then fold in the lemon rind, flour and ground almonds.

3 Mix the brown sugar, apples and lemon juice, tip into the dish, add the sponge mixture, then the almonds. Bake for 40–45 minutes, until golden.

Surprise Lemon Pudding

The surprise is a delicious tangy lemon sauce that forms beneath the light topping in this pudding.

Serves 4

75g/3oz/6 tbsp butter, softened	grated rind and juice of 4 lemons
175g/6oz/1½ cups soft brown sugar	50g/2oz/½ cup self-raising flour
4 eggs, separated	120ml/4fl oz/½ cup milk

1 Preheat the oven to 180°C/350°F/Gas 4, then butter an 18cm/7in soufflé dish or cake tin and stand it in a roasting tin.

2 Beat the butter and sugar together in a large bowl until pale and very fluffy. Beat in one egg yolk at a time, beating well after each addition and gradually beating in the lemon rind and juice until well mixed; do not worry if the mixture curdles a little at this stage.

3 Sift the flour and stir into the lemon mixture until well mixed, then gradually stir in the milk.

4 Whisk the egg whites in a separate bowl until stiff peaks form but the whites are not dry, then lightly, but thoroughly, fold into the lemon mixture in three batches. Carefully pour the mixture into the soufflé dish or cake tin, then pour boiling water into the roasting tin to come halfway up the sides.

5 Bake the pudding in the centre of the oven for about 45 minutes, or until risen, just firm to the touch and golden brown on top. Serve at once.

Castle Puddings with Custard

These attractive puddings may be baked in ramekin dishes if you do not have dariole moulds.

Serves 4

about 45ml/3 tbsp blackcurrant, strawberry or raspberry jam	130g/4½oz/generous 1 cup self-raising flour
115g/4oz/½ cup butter, softened	**For the custard**
115g/4oz/½ cup caster sugar	450ml/¾ pint/1 scant cup milk
2 eggs, beaten	4 eggs
few drops of vanilla essence	15–25g/½–1oz/1–2 tbsp sugar
	few drops of vanilla essence

1 Preheat the oven to 180°C/350°F/Gas 4. Butter eight dariole moulds. Put about 10ml/2 tsp of your chosen jam in the base of each mould.

2 Beat the butter and sugar together until light and fluffy, then gradually beat in the eggs, beating well after each addition, and add the vanilla essence towards the end. Lightly fold in the flour, then divide the mixture among the moulds. Bake the puddings for about 20 minutes until well risen and a light golden colour.

3 To make the sauce, whisk the eggs and sugar together. Bring the milk to the boil in a heavy, preferably non-stick, saucepan, then slowly pour on to the sweetened egg mixture, stirring constantly.

4 Return the milk to the pan and heat very gently, stirring, until the mixture thickens enough to coat the back of a spoon; do not allow to boil. Cover the pan and remove from the heat.

5 Remove the moulds from the oven, leave to stand for a few minutes, then turn the puddings on to warmed plates and serve with the custard.

Bread and Butter Pudding

An unusual version of a classic recipe, this pudding is made with French bread and mixed dried fruit.

Serves 4–6

4 ready-to-eat dried apricots, finely chopped
15ml/1 tbsp raisins
30ml/2 tbsp sultanas
15ml/1 tbsp chopped mixed peel
1 French loaf (about 200g/7oz), thinly sliced
50g/2oz/4 tbsp butter, melted
450ml/¼ pint/1¾ cups milk
150ml/¼ pint/⅔ cup double cream

115g/4oz/½ cup caster sugar
3 eggs
2.5ml/½ tsp vanilla essence
30ml/2 tbsp whisky

For the cream
150ml/¼ pint/⅔ cup double cream
30ml/2 tbsp Greek-style yogurt
15–30ml/1–2 tbsp whisky
15g/½ oz/1 tbsp caster sugar

1 Preheat the oven to 180°C/350°F/Gas 4. Butter a deep 1.5 litre/2½ pint/6¼ cup ovenproof dish. Mix together the dried fruits. Brush the bread on both sides with butter. Fill the dish with alternate layers of bread and dried fruit starting with fruit and finishing with bread. Heat the milk and cream in a saucepan until just boiling. Whisk together the sugar, eggs and vanilla essence.

2 Whisk the milk mixture into the eggs, then strain into the dish. Sprinkle the whisky over the top. Press the bread down, cover with foil and leave to stand for 20 minutes.

3 Place the dish in a roasting tin half filled with water and bake for 1 hour, or until the custard is just set. Remove the foil and cook for 10 minutes more, until golden. Just before serving, heat all the cream ingredients in a small pan, stirring. Serve with the hot pudding.

Chocolate Amaretti Peaches

This dessert is quick and easy to prepare, yet sophisticated enough to serve at the most elegant dinner party.

Serves 4

115g/4oz amaretti biscuits, crushed
50g/2oz plain chocolate, chopped
grated rind of ½ orange
15ml/1 tbsp clear honey
1.5ml/¼ tsp ground cinnamon

1 egg white, lightly beaten
4 firm ripe peaches
150ml/¼ pint/⅔ cup white wine
15g/½oz/1 tbsp caster sugar
whipped cream, to serve

1 Preheat the oven to 190°C/375°F/Gas 5. Mix together the crushed amaretti biscuits, chocolate, orange rind, honey and cinnamon in a bowl. Add the beaten egg white and mix to bind the mixture together.

2 Halve and stone the peaches and fill the cavities with the chocolate mixture, mounding it up slightly.

3 Arrange the stuffed peaches in a lightly buttered shallow ovenproof dish which will just hold the fruit comfortably. Pour the wine into a measuring jug and stir in the sugar.

4 Pour the wine mixture around the peaches. Bake for 30–40 minutes, until the peaches are tender. Serve at once with a little of the cooking juices spooned over and the whipped cream.

Cook's Tip
Prepare this dessert using fresh nectarines or apricots instead of peaches, if you wish.

Warm Autumn Compôte

This is a simple yet quite sophisticated dessert featuring succulent ripe autumnal fruits.

Serves 4

75g/3oz/generous ¼ cup
   caster sugar
1 bottle red wine
1 vanilla pod, split
1 strip pared lemon rind

4 pears
2 purple figs, quartered
225g/8oz/2 cups
   raspberries
lemon juice, to taste

1 Put the caster sugar and red wine in a large saucepan and heat gently until the sugar has completely dissolved. Add the vanilla pod and lemon rind and bring to the boil. Reduce the heat and simmer for 5 minutes.

2 Peel and halve the pears, then scoop out the cores, using a melon baller or teaspoon. Add the pears to the syrup and poach for about 15 minutes, turning them several times so they colour evenly.

3 Add the quartered figs and poach for a further 5 minutes, until the fruits are tender.

4 Transfer the poached pears and figs to a serving bowl using a slotted spoon, then scatter over the raspberries.

5 Return the syrup to the heat and boil rapidly to reduce slightly and concentrate the flavour. Add a little lemon juice to taste. Strain the syrup over the fruits and serve warm.

Apple Soufflé Omelette

Apples sautéed until they are slightly caramelized make a delicious autumn filling for this sweet omelette.

Serves 2

4 eggs, separated
30ml/2 tbsp single cream
15g/½oz/1 tbsp caster
   sugar
15g/½oz/1 tbsp butter
sifted icing sugar, for
   dredging

For the filling
1 eating apple, peeled,
   cored and sliced
25g/1oz/2 tbsp butter
25g/1oz/2 tbsp soft light
   brown sugar
45ml/3 tbsp single cream

1 To make the filling, sauté the apple slices in the butter and sugar until just tender. Stir in the cream and keep warm, while making the omelette.

2 Place the egg yolks in a bowl with the cream and sugar and beat well. Whisk the egg whites until stiff peaks form, then fold into the yolk mixture.

3 Melt the butter in a large heavy-based frying pan, pour in the soufflé mixture and spread evenly. Cook for 1 minute until golden underneath, then place under a hot grill to brown the top.

4 Slide the omelette on to a plate, spoon the apple mixture on to one side, then fold over. Dredge the icing sugar over thickly, then quickly mark in a criss-cross pattern with a hot metal skewer. Serve the omelette immediately.

Cook's Tip
In the summer months, make the filling for the omelette using fresh raspberries or strawberries.

Warm Lemon and Syrup Cake

This simple cake is made special by the lemony syrup which is poured over it when baked.

Serves 8

3 eggs
175g/6oz/¾ cup butter, softened
175g/6oz/¾ cup caster sugar
175g/6oz/1½ cups self-raising flour
50g/2oz/½ cup ground almonds
1.5ml/¼ tsp freshly grated nutmeg

50g/2oz candied lemon peel, finely chopped
grated rind of 1 lemon
30ml/2 tbsp freshly squeezed lemon juice
poached pears, to serve

For the syrup
175g/6oz/¾ cup caster sugar
juice of 3 lemons

1 Preheat the oven to 180°C/350°F/Gas 4. Lightly grease and base-line a deep round 20cm/8in cake tin.

2 Place all the cake ingredients in a large bowl and beat well for 2–3 minutes, until light and fluffy.

3 Tip the mixture into the prepared tin, spread level and bake for 1 hour, or until golden and firm to the touch.

4 To make the syrup, put the caster sugar, lemon juice and 75ml/5 tbsp water in a saucepan. Heat gently, stirring until the sugar has completely dissolved, then boil, without stirring, for 1–2 minutes.

5 Turn out the cake on to a plate with a rim. Prick the surface of the cake all over with a fork, then pour over the hot syrup. Leave to soak for about 30 minutes. Serve the cake warm with thin wedges of poached pears.

Papaya and Pineapple Crumble

Crumbles are always popular with children and adults, but you can ring the changes with this exotic variation.

Serves 4–6
For the topping
175g/6oz/1½ cups plain flour
75g/3oz/6 tbsp butter, diced
75g/3oz/generous ¼ cup caster sugar
75g/3oz/½ cup mixed chopped nuts

For the filling
1 medium-ripe pineapple
1 large ripe papaya
15g/½oz/1 tbsp caster sugar
5ml/1 tsp mixed spice
grated rind of 1 lime
natural yogurt, to serve

1 Preheat the oven to 180°C/350°F/Gas 4. To make the topping, sift the flour into a bowl and rub in the butter until the mixture resembles breadcrumbs. Stir in the caster sugar and mixed chopped nuts.

2 Peel the pineapple, remove the eyes, then cut in half. Cut away the core and cut the flesh into bite-size chunks. Halve the papaya and scoop out the seeds using a spoon. Peel, then cut the flesh into similar size pieces.

3 Put the pineapple and papaya chunks into a large pie dish. Sprinkle over the sugar, mixed spice and lime rind and toss gently to mix.

4 Spoon the crumble topping over the fruit and spread out evenly with a fork, but don't press it down. Bake in the oven for 45–50 minutes, until golden brown. Serve the crumble hot or warm with natural yogurt.

Zabaglione

A much-loved simple Italian pudding traditionally made with Marsala, an Italian fortified wine.

Serves 4

4 egg yolks
50g/2oz/4 tbsp caster
  sugar

60ml/4 tbsp Marsala
amaretti biscuits, to serve

1 Place the egg yolks and caster sugar in a large heatproof bowl and whisk with an electric whisk until the mixture is pale and thick.

2 Gradually add the Marsala, about 15ml/1 tbsp at a time, whisking well after each addition (at this stage the mixture will be quite runny).

3 Place the bowl over a saucepan of gently simmering water and continue to whisk for at least 5–7 minutes, until the mixture becomes thick and mousse-like; when the beaters are lifted they should leave a thick trail on the surface of the mixture. (If you don't beat the mixture for long enough, the zabaglione will be too runny and will probably separate.)

4 Pour into four warmed stemmed glasses and serve immediately with the amaretti biscuits for dipping.

Cook's Tip
If you don't have any Marsala, substitute Madeira, a medium-sweet sherry or a dessert wine.

Thai-fried Bananas

This is a very simple and quick Thai pudding – bananas are simply fried in butter, brown sugar and lime juice.

Serves 4

40g/1½oz/3 tbsp
  unsalted butter
4 large slightly under-
  ripe bananas
15ml/1 tbsp desiccated
  coconut

50g/2oz/4 tbsp soft light
  brown sugar
60ml/4 tbsp lime juice
2 lime slices, to decorate
thick and creamy natural
  yogurt, to serve

1 Heat the butter in a large frying pan or wok and fry the bananas for 1–2 minutes on each side, or until they are lightly golden in colour.

2 Meanwhile, dry fry the coconut in a small frying pan until lightly browned and reserve.

3 Sprinkle the sugar into the pan with the bananas, add the lime juice and cook, stirring, until dissolved. Sprinkle the coconut over the bananas, decorate with lime slices and serve with the thick and creamy yogurt.

Crêpes Suzette

This dish is a classic of French cuisine and still enjoys worldwide popularity as a dessert or a daytime treat.

Makes 8

115g/4oz/1 cup plain flour
pinch of salt
1 egg
1 egg yolk
300ml/½ pint/1¼ cups
   semi-skimmed milk
15g/½oz/1 tbsp butter,
   melted, plus extra, for
   shallow frying

For the sauce
2 large oranges
50g/2oz/4 tbsp butter
50g/2oz/½ cup soft light
   brown sugar
15ml/1 tbsp Grand
   Marnier
15ml/1 tbsp brandy

1 Sift the flour and salt into a bowl and make a well in the centre. Crack the egg and extra yolk into the well. Stir the eggs to incorporate all the flour. When the mixture thickens, gradually pour in the milk, beating well after each addition, until a smooth batter is formed. Stir in the butter, transfer to a jug, cover and chill for 30 minutes. Heat a shallow frying pan, add a little butter and heat until sizzling. Pour in a little batter, tilting the pan to cover the base. Cook over a moderate heat for 1–2 minutes until lightly browned underneath, then flip and cook for a further minute. Make eight crêpes and stack them on a plate.

2 Pare the rind from one of the oranges and reserve about 5ml/1 tsp. Squeeze the juice from both oranges.

3 To make the sauce, melt the butter in a large frying pan and heat the sugar with the rind and juice until dissolved and gently bubbling. Fold each crêpe in quarters. Add to the pan one at a time, coat in the sauce and fold in half again. Move to the side of the pan to make room for the others.

4 Pour on the Grand Marnier and brandy and cook gently for 2–3 minutes, until the sauce has slightly caramelized. Sprinkle with the reserved orange rind and serve at once.

Bananas with Rum and Raisins

Choose almost-ripe bananas with evenly coloured skins, all yellow or just green at the tips for this dessert.

Serves 4

40g/1½oz/scant ¼ cup
   seedless raisins
75ml/5 tbsp dark rum
50g/2oz/4 tbsp unsalted
   butter
50g/2oz/½ cup soft light
   brown sugar
4 bananas, peeled and
   halved lengthways

1.5ml/¼ tsp grated
   nutmeg
1.5ml/¼ tsp ground
   cinnamon
30ml/2 tbsp slivered
   almonds, toasted
chilled cream or vanilla
   ice cream, to serve
   (optional)

1 Put the raisins in a bowl with the rum. Leave them to soak for about 30 minutes to plump up.

2 Melt the butter in a frying pan, add the sugar and stir until completely dissolved. Add the bananas and cook for a few minutes until tender.

3 Sprinkle the spices over the bananas, then pour over the rum and raisins. Carefully set alight using a long taper and stir gently to mix.

4 Scatter over the slivered almonds and serve immediately with chilled cream or vanilla ice cream, if you wish.

Cook's Tip
Stand well back when you set the rum alight and shake the pan gently until the flames subside.

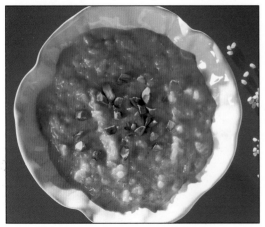

Orange Rice Pudding

In Spain, Greece, Italy and Morocco rice puddings are a favourite dish, especially when sweetened with honey.

Serves 4

50g/2oz/¼ cup short grain pudding rice
600ml/1 pint/2½ cups milk
30–45ml/2–3 tbsp clear honey, to taste

finely grated rind of ½ small orange
150ml/¼ pint/⅔ cup double cream
15ml/1 tbsp chopped pistachios, toasted

1 Mix the rice with the milk, honey and orange rind in a saucepan and bring to the boil, then reduce the heat, cover with a tight-fitting lid and simmer very gently for about 1¼ hours, stirring regularly.

2 Remove the lid and continue cooking and stirring for about 15–20 minutes, until the rice is creamy.

3 Pour in the cream and simmer for 5–8 minutes longer. Serve the rice sprinkled with the chopped toasted pistachios in individual warmed bowls.

Apple and Blackberry Nut Crumble

This much-loved dish of Bramley apples and blackberries is topped with a golden, sweet crumble.

Serves 4

900g/2lb (about 4 medium) Bramley apples, peeled, cored and sliced
115g/4oz/½ cup butter, cubed
115g/4oz/½ cup soft light brown sugar
175g/6oz/1½ cups blackberries

75g/3oz/¾ cup wholemeal flour
75g/3oz/¾ cup plain flour
2.5ml/½ tsp ground cinnamon
45ml/3 tbsp chopped mixed nuts, toasted
custard, cream or ice cream, to serve

1 Preheat the oven to 180°C/350°F/Gas 4. Lightly butter a 1.2 litre/2 pint/5 cup ovenproof dish.

2 Place the apples in a saucepan with 25g/1oz/2 tbsp of the butter, 25g/1oz/2 tbsp of the sugar and 15ml/1 tbsp water. Cover with a tight-fitting lid and cook gently for about 10 minutes, until just tender but still holding their shape.

3 Remove from the heat and gently stir in the blackberries. Spoon the mixture into the ovenproof dish and set aside while you make the topping.

4 To make the crumble topping, sift the flours and cinnamon into a bowl (tip in any of the bran left in the sieve). Add the remaining 75g/3oz/6 tbsp butter and rub into the flour with your fingertips until the mixture resembles fine breadcrumbs (or you can use a food processor).

5 Stir in the remaining 75g/3oz/generous ¼ cup sugar and the nuts and mix well. Sprinkle the crumble topping over the fruit. Bake for 35–40 minutes, until the top is golden brown. Serve hot with custard, cream or ice cream.

Apple Strudel

This Austrian pudding, traditionally made with strudel pastry, is just as good prepared with filo pastry.

Serves 4–6

75g/3oz/¾ cup
   hazelnuts, chopped
   and roasted
30ml/2 tbsp nibbed
   almonds, roasted
50g/2oz/4 tbsp demerara
   sugar
2.5ml/½ tsp ground
   cinnamon
grated rind and juice of
   ½ lemon

2 large Bramley cooking
   apples, peeled, cored
   and chopped
50g/2oz/⅓ cup sultanas
4 large sheets filo pastry
50g/2oz/4 tbsp unsalted
   butter, melted
sifted icing sugar, for
   dusting
cream, custard or yogurt,
   to serve

1 Preheat the oven to 190°C/375°F/Gas 5. In a bowl mix together the hazelnuts, almonds, sugar, cinnamon, lemon rind and juice, apples and sultanas. Set aside.

2 Lay one sheet of filo pastry on a clean dish towel and brush with melted butter. Lay a second sheet on top and brush again with melted butter. Repeat with the remaining two sheets.

3 Spread the fruit and nut mixture over the pastry, leaving a 7.5cm/3in border at each of the shorter ends. Fold the pastry ends in over the filling. Roll up from one long edge to the other, using the dish towel to help.

4 Carefully transfer the strudel to a greased baking sheet, placing it seam-side down. Brush all over with butter and bake for 30–35 minutes, until golden and crisp. Dust the strudel generously with icing sugar and serve while still hot with cream, custard or yogurt.

Banana, Maple and Lime Crêpes

Crêpes are a treat any day of the week, and they can be made in advance and stored in the freezer for convenience.

Serves 4

115g/4oz/1 cup plain
   flour
1 egg white
250ml/8fl oz/1 cup
   skimmed milk
50ml/2 fl oz/¼ cup cold
   water
sunflower oil, for frying

For the filling
4 bananas, sliced
45ml/3 tbsp maple or
   golden syrup
30ml/2 tbsp freshly
   squeezed lime juice
strips of lime rind, to
   decorate

1 Beat together the flour, egg white, milk and water until smooth and bubbly. Chill in the fridge until needed.

2 Heat a small amount of oil in a non-stick frying pan and pour in enough batter just to coat the base. Swirl it around the pan to coat evenly.

3 Cook until golden, then toss or turn and cook the other side. Place on a plate, cover with foil and keep hot while making the remaining pancakes.

4 To make the filling, place the bananas, syrup and lime juice in a saucepan and simmer gently for 1 minute. Spoon into the pancakes and fold into quarters. Sprinkle with shreds of lime rind to decorate. Serve hot, with yogurt or fromage frais, if you wish.

Cook's Tip
To freeze the crêpes, interleaf them with non-stick baking paper and seal in a plastic bag. They should be used within 3 months.

Spiced Pears in Cider

Any variety of pear can be used for cooking, but choose a firm variety such as Conference for this recipe.

Serves 4
4 medium-firm pears	25g/1oz/2 tbsp light
250ml/8fl oz/1 cup dry	muscovado sugar
cider	5ml/1 tsp arrowroot
thinly pared strip of	ground cinnamon, to
lemon rind	sprinkle
1 cinnamon stick	

1 Peel the pears thinly, leaving them whole with the stalks on. Place in a saucepan with the cider, lemon rind and cinnamon. Cover and simmer gently, turning the pears occasionally for 15–20 minutes, or until tender.

2 Lift out the pears. Boil the syrup, uncovered, to reduce by about half. Remove the lemon rind and cinnamon stick, then stir in the sugar.

3 Mix the arrowroot with 15ml/1 tbsp cold water in a small bowl until smooth, then stir into the syrup. Bring to the boil and stir over the heat until thickened and clear.

4 Pour the sauce over the pears and sprinkle with ground cinnamon. Leave to cool slightly, then serve warm with fromage frais, if you wish.

Cook's Tip
Whole pears look impressive but if you prefer they can be halved and cored before cooking. This will shorten the cooking time slightly.

Fruity Bread Pudding

A delicious old-fashioned family favourite is given a lighter, healthier touch in this version.

Serves 4
75g/3oz/⅓ cup mixed	1 large banana, sliced
dried fruit	150ml/¼ pint/⅔ cup
150ml/¼ pint/⅔ cup	skimmed milk
apple juice	15g/½oz/1 tbsp
115g/4oz stale brown or	demerara sugar
white bread, diced	natural yogurt, to serve
5ml/1 tsp mixed spice	

1 Preheat the oven to 200°C/400°F/Gas 6. Place the mixed dried fruit in a small saucepan with the apple juice and bring to the boil.

2 Remove the pan from the heat and stir in the diced bread, mixed spice and banana. Spoon the mixture into a shallow 1.2 litre/2 pint/5 cup ovenproof dish; pour over the milk.

3 Sprinkle with demerara sugar and bake for about 25–30 minutes, until firm and golden brown. Serve hot or cold with natural yogurt.

Cook's Tip
Different types of bread will absorb varying amounts of liquid, so you may need to adjust the amount of milk used to allow for this.

Crunchy Gooseberry Crumble

Gooseberries are perfect for traditional family puddings such as this extra special crumble.

Serves 4

500g/1¼lb/4¼ cups gooseberries	60ml/4 tbsp sunflower oil
50g/2oz/4 tbsp caster sugar	50g/2oz/4 tbsp demerara sugar
75g/3oz/1 cup rolled oats	30ml/2 tbsp chopped walnuts
75g/3oz/¼ cup wholemeal flour	natural yogurt or custard, to serve

1 Preheat the oven to 200°C/400°F/Gas 6. Place the gooseberries in a saucepan with the caster sugar. Cover the pan and cook over a low heat for 10 minutes, until the gooseberries are just tender. Tip into an ovenproof dish.

2 To make the crumble, place the oats, flour and oil in a bowl and stir with a fork until evenly mixed.

3 Stir in the demerara sugar and walnuts, then spread evenly over the gooseberries. Bake for 25–30 minutes, or until golden and bubbling. Serve hot with yogurt or custard.

Cook's Tip
When gooseberries are out of season substitute other fruits, such as apples, plums or rhubarb.

Gingerbread Upside-down Pudding

A proper pudding goes down well on a cold winter's day. This one is quite quick to make and looks very impressive.

Serves 4–6

sunflower oil, for brushing	2.5ml/½ tsp bicarbonate of soda
15g/½oz/1 tbsp soft brown sugar	7.5ml/1½ tsp ground ginger
4 peaches, halved and stoned, or canned peach halves, drained	5ml/1 tsp ground cinnamon
8 walnut halves	115g/4oz/½ cup molasses sugar
For the base	1 egg
130g/4½oz/½ cup wholemeal flour	120ml/4fl oz/½ cup skimmed milk
	50ml/2fl oz/¼ cup sunflower oil

1 Preheat the oven to 180°C/350°F/Gas 4. Brush the base and sides of a 23cm/9in round springform cake tin with oil. Sprinkle the soft brown sugar evenly over the base.

2 Arrange the peaches, cut-side down, in the tin with a walnut half in each.

3 To make the base, sift together the flour, bicarbonate of soda, ginger and cinnamon, then stir in the sugar. Beat together the egg, milk and oil, then mix into the dry ingredients until smooth.

4 Pour the mixture evenly over the peaches and bake for 35–40 minutes, until firm to the touch. Turn out on to a serving plate. Serve hot with yogurt or custard, if liked.

Cook's Tip
The soft brown sugar caramelizes during baking, creating a delightfully sticky topping.

Lemon Meringue Pie

In this popular dish, light meringue topping crowns the delicious citrus-filled pie.

Makes an 18.5cm/7½in pie

115g/4oz/1 cup plain
    flour
50g/2oz/4 tbsp butter,
    cubed
25g/1oz/3 tbsp ground
    almonds
25g/1oz/2 tbsp caster
    sugar
1 egg yolk

For the filling
juice of 3 lemons

finely grated rind of 2
    lemons
45ml/3 tbsp cornflour
75g/3oz/generous ¼ cup
    caster sugar
2 egg yolks
15g/½ oz/1 tbsp butter

For the meringue
2 egg whites
115g/4oz/½ cup caster
    sugar

1   Rub the butter into the flour until the mixture resembles breadcrumbs. Stir in the almonds and sugar, add the egg yolk and 30ml/2 tbsp cold water. Mix until the pastry comes together. Knead on a lightly floured surface, then wrap and chill in the fridge for about 30 minutes.

2   Preheat a baking sheet at 200°C/400°F/Gas 6. Roll out the pastry and use to line a 18.5cm/7½in fluted loose-based flan tin. Prick the base. Line with greaseproof paper and fill with baking beans. Place the tin on the baking sheet and bake blind for 12 minutes. Remove the paper and beans and bake for a further 5 minutes. Allow to cool. Reduce the temperature to 150°C/300°F/Gas 2.

3   For the filling, blend the lemon juice, rind and cornflour. Pour into a saucepan and add 150ml/¼ pint/⅔ cup water. Bring to the boil, stirring until smooth and thickened. Remove and beat in the sugar and egg yolks, then add the butter. Spoon into the pastry case. For the meringue, whisk the egg whites until stiff, then gradually whisk in the sugar until thick and glossy. Pile on top of the filling. Bake for 30–35 minutes, or until golden.

Apple and Orange Pie

A simple but tasty two-fruit pie: make sure you choose really juicy oranges or even blood oranges.

Serves 4

400g/14oz ready-made
    shortcrust pastry
3 oranges, peeled
900g/2lb cooking apples,
    cored and thickly
    sliced

25g/1oz/2 tbsp demerara
    sugar
beaten egg, to glaze
caster sugar, for
    sprinkling

1   Roll out the pastry on a lightly floured surface to about 2cm/¾in larger than the top of a 1.2 litre/2 pint/5 cup pie dish. Cut off a narrow strip around the edge of the pastry and fit on the rim of the pie dish.

2   Preheat the oven to 190°C/375°F/Gas 5. Hold one orange at a time over a bowl to catch the juice; cut down between the membranes to remove the segments.

3   Mix the segments and juice, the apples and sugar in the pie dish. Place a pie funnel in the centre of the dish.

4   Dampen the pastry strip. Cover the dish with the rolled out pastry and press the edges to the pastry strip. Brush the top with beaten egg, then bake for 35–40 minutes, until lightly browned. Sprinkle with caster sugar before serving.

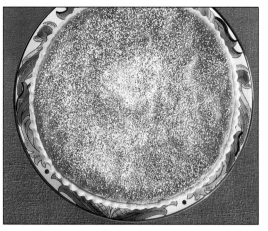

Bakewell Tart

Although the pastry base technically makes this a tart, the original recipe calls it a pudding.

Serves 4

225g/8oz ready-made
   puff pastry
30ml/2 tbsp raspberry or
   apricot jam
2 eggs
2 egg yolks
115g/4oz/½ cup caster
   sugar

115g/4oz/½ cup butter,
   melted
50g/2oz/⅔ cup ground
   almonds
few drops of almond
   essence
sifted icing sugar, for
   dredging

1 Preheat the oven to 200°C/400°F/Gas 6. Roll out the pastry on a lightly floured surface and use it to line an 18cm/7in pie plate or fluted loose-based flan tin. Spread the jam over the base of the pastry case.

2 Whisk the eggs, egg yolks and sugar together in a large bowl until thick and pale.

3 Gently stir the butter, ground almonds and almond essence into the mixture.

4 Pour the mixture into the pastry case and bake for about 30 minutes, until the filling is just set and browned. Dredge with icing sugar before eating hot, warm or cold.

Cook's Tip

Since the pastry case isn't baked blind first, place a baking sheet in the oven while it preheats, then place the pie dish or flan tin on the hot sheet. This will ensure that the base of the pastry case cooks through.

Yorkshire Curd Tart

The distinguishing characteristic of this tart is the allspice, or "clove pepper" as it was once known locally.

Serves 8

225g/8oz/2 cups plain
   flour
115g/4oz/½ cup butter,
   cubed
1 egg yolk

For the filling
large pinch of allspice
90g/3½oz/1 scant cup
   soft light brown sugar

3 eggs, beaten
grated rind and juice of
   1 lemon
40g/1½oz/3 tbsp butter,
   melted
450g/1lb/2 cups curd
   cheese
75g/3oz/½ cup raisins or
   sultanas

1 Place the flour in a bowl. Add the butter and rub it into the flour with your fingertips until the mixture resembles breadcrumbs. (Alternatively, you can use a food processor.) Stir the egg yolk into the flour mixture with a little water to bind the dough together.

2 Turn the dough on to a lightly floured surface, knead lightly and briefly, then form into a ball. Roll out the pastry thinly and use to line a 20cm/8in fluted loose-based flan tin. Chill for 15 minutes in the fridge.

3 Preheat the oven to 190°C/375°F/Gas 5. To make the filling, mix the allspice with the sugar, then stir in the eggs, lemon rind and juice, melted butter, curd cheese and the raisins or sultanas.

4 Pour the filling into the pastry case, then bake for about 40 minutes until the pastry is cooked and the filling is lightly set and golden brown. Serve still slightly warm, cut into wedges, with cream, if you wish.

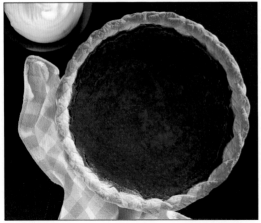

American Spiced Pumpkin Pie

This traditional pie is served in the United States and Canada at Thanksgiving, when pumpkins are plentiful.

Serves 4–6

175g/6oz/1½ cups plain
    flour
pinch of salt
75g/3oz/6 tbsp unsalted
    butter
15g/½oz/1 tbsp caster
    sugar
450g/1lb peeled fresh
    pumpkin, diced, or
    400g/14oz canned
    pumpkin, drained

115g/4oz/1 cup soft light
    brown sugar
1.5ml/¼ tsp salt
1.5ml/¼ tsp ground
    allspice
2.5ml/½ tsp ground
    cinnamon
2.5ml/½ tsp ground
    ginger
2 eggs, lightly beaten
120ml/4fl oz/½ cup
    double cream
whipped cream, to serve

1 Place the flour in a bowl with a pinch of salt. Rub in the butter until the mixture resembles breadcrumbs. Add the sugar and 30–45ml/2–3 tbsp water. Mix to a soft dough. Knead briefly, flatten into a round, wrap and chill for 1 hour.

2 Preheat the oven to 200°C/400°F/Gas 6 with a baking sheet inside. If using fresh pumpkin, steam for 15 minutes, then cool. Purée in a food processor or blender until smooth.

3 Line a 23.5cm/9½in x 2.5cm/1in deep pie tin with the pastry. Prick the base. Cut out leaf shapes from the excess pastry and mark veins with the back of a knife. Brush the edges with water and stick on the leaves. Chill.

4 Mix together the pumpkin purée, sugar, salt, spices, eggs and cream and pour into the pastry case. Place on the preheated baking sheet and bake for 15 minutes. Then reduce the temperature to 180°C/350°F/Gas 4 and cook for a further 30 minutes, or until the filling is set and the pastry golden. Serve warm with whipped cream.

Pear and Blueberry Pie

A variation on plain blueberry pie, this pudding is just as delicious served cold as it is warm.

Serves 4

225g/8oz/2 cups plain
    flour
pinch of salt
50g/2oz/4 tbsp lard, diced
50g/2oz/4 tbsp butter,
    diced
675g/1½ lb/4½ cups
    blueberries
25g/1oz/2 tbsp caster
    sugar

15ml/1 tbsp arrowroot
2 ripe but firm pears,
    peeled, cored and
    sliced
2.5ml/½ tsp ground
    cinnamon
grated rind of ½ lemon
beaten egg, to glaze
caster sugar, for
    sprinkling

1 Sift the flour and salt into a bowl. Rub in the fats until the mixture resembles fine breadcrumbs. Mix to a dough with 45ml/3 tbsp cold water. Chill for 30 minutes.

2 Place 225g/8oz/2 cups of the blueberries in a saucepan with the sugar. Cover with a lid and cook gently until the blueberries have softened. Press through a nylon sieve. Blend the arrowroot with 30ml/2 tbsp cold water and add to the blueberries. Bring to the boil, stirring until thickened. Allow to cool slightly.

3 Preheat the oven to 190°C/375°F/Gas 5 with a baking sheet inside. Roll out just over half the pastry on a lightly floured surface and use to line a 20cm/8in shallow pie dish.

4 Mix together the remaining blueberries, the pears, ground cinnamon and lemon rind and spoon into the dish. Pour over the blueberry purée.

5 Use the remaining pastry to cover the pie. Make a slit in the centre. Brush with egg and sprinkle with caster sugar. Bake on the baking sheet for 40–45 minutes, until golden. Serve warm, with crème fraîche, if you wish.

Mississippi Pecan Pie

For a truly authentic touch of the Deep South, use maple syrup instead of golden syrup in this rich dessert.

Serves 4–6

For the pastry
115g/4oz/1 cup plain flour
50g/2oz/4 tbsp butter
25g/1oz/2 tbsp caster sugar
1 egg yolk

For the filling
175g/6oz/5 tbsp golden syrup

50g/2oz/⅓ cup dark muscovado sugar
50g/2oz/4 tbsp butter
3 eggs, lightly beaten
2.5ml/½ tsp vanilla essence
150g/5oz/1¼ cups pecan nuts
fresh cream or ice cream, to serve

1 Place the flour in a bowl. Dice the butter, then rub it into the flour with your fingertips until the mixture resembles breadcrumbs. (Alternatively use a food processor.) Stir in the sugar, egg yolk and about 30ml/2 tbsp cold water. Mix to a dough and knead on a lightly floured surface until smooth.

2 Roll out the pastry and use it to line a 20cm/8in fluted loose-based flan tin. Prick the base, then line with greaseproof paper and fill with baking beans. Chill for 30 minutes in the fridge. Preheat the oven to 200°C/400°F/Gas 6.

3 Bake the pastry case blind for 10 minutes. Remove the paper and beans and continue to bake for 5 more minutes. Reduce the oven temperature to 180°C/350°F/Gas 4.

4 To make the filling, heat the syrup, sugar and butter in a saucepan until the sugar dissolves. Remove from the heat and cool slightly. Whisk in the eggs and vanilla essence and stir in the pecan nuts.

5 Pour into the pastry case and bake for 35–40 minutes, until the filling is set. Serve with cream or ice cream.

Upside-down Apple Tart

Cox's Pippin apples are perfect to use in this tart because they hold their shape so well.

Serves 4

For the pastry
50g/2oz/4 tbsp butter, softened
40g/1½oz/3 tbsp caster sugar
1 egg
115g/4oz/1 cup plain flour
pinch of salt

For the apple layer
75g/3oz/generous ¼ cup butter, softened
75g/3oz/scant ½ cup soft light brown sugar
10 Cox's Pippin apples, peeled, cored and thickly sliced
whipped cream, to serve

1 For the pastry, cream the butter and sugar until pale and creamy. Beat in the egg, sift in the flour and salt and mix to a soft dough. Knead, wrap and chill for 1 hour.

2 For the apple layer, grease a 23cm/9in cake tin, then add 50g/2oz/4 tbsp of the butter. Place on the hob and melt the butter. Remove from the heat and sprinkle over 50g/2oz/4 tbsp of the sugar. Arrange the apple slices on top, sprinkle with the remaining sugar and dot with the remaining butter.

3 Preheat the oven to 230°C/450°F/Gas 8. Place the cake tin on the hob again over a low to moderate heat for about 15 minutes, until a light golden caramel forms on the base.

4 Roll out the pastry on a lightly floured surface to around the same size as the tin and lay it on top of the apples. Tuck the pastry edges down around the sides of the apples.

5 Bake for about 20–25 minutes, until the pastry is golden. Remove from the oven and leave to stand for 5 minutes.

6 Place an upturned plate on top of the tin and, holding the two together with a dish towel, turn the apple tart out on to the plate. Serve while still warm with whipped cream.

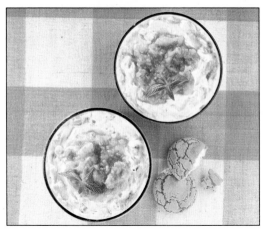

Gooseberry and Elderflower Cream

When elderflowers are in season, instead of using the cordial, cook two to three elderflower heads with the gooseberries.

Serves 4

*500g/1¼ lb/4¼ cups
  gooseberries
300ml/½ pint/1¼ cups
  double cream
about 115g/4oz/1 cup
  sifted icing sugar, to
  taste*

*30ml/2 tbsp elderflower
  cordial or orange
  flower water
  (optional)
fresh mint sprigs, to
  decorate
almond biscuits, to serve*

1 Place the gooseberries in a heavy saucepan, cover and cook over a low heat, shaking the pan occasionally, until the gooseberries are tender. Tip the gooseberries into a bowl, crush them, then leave to cool completely.

2 Beat the cream until soft peaks form, then fold in half of the crushed gooseberries. Sweeten with icing sugar and add the elderflower cordial, or orange flower water to taste, if using. Sweeten the remaining gooseberries.

3 Layer the cream mixture and the crushed gooseberries in four dessert dishes or tall glasses, then cover and chill. Decorate the dessert with the fresh mint sprigs and serve with almond biscuits.

Cook's Tip
If preferred, the cooked gooseberries can be puréed and sieved instead of crushed.

Eton Mess

This dish forms part of the picnic meals enjoyed by parents and pupils at Eton school.

Serves 4

*500g/1¼ lb/4¼ cups
  strawberries, roughly
  chopped
45–50ml/3–4 tbsp
  Kirsch*

*300ml/½ pint/1¼ cups
  double cream
6 small white meringues
fresh mint sprigs, to
  decorate*

1 Put the strawberries in a bowl, sprinkle over the Kirsch, then cover and chill in the fridge for 2–3 hours.

2 Whip the cream until soft peaks form, then gently fold in the strawberries with their juices.

3 Crush the meringues into rough chunks, then scatter over the strawberry mixture and fold in gently.

4 Spoon the strawberry mixture into a glass serving bowl, decorate with the fresh mint sprigs and serve immediately.

Cook's Tip
If you would prefer to make a less rich version of this dessert, use Greek-style or thick and creamy natural yogurt instead of part or all of the cream. Simply beat the yogurt gently before adding the strawberries.

Cranachan

Crunchy toasted oatmeal and soft raspberries combine to give this dessert a lovely texture.

Serves 4

60ml/4 tbsp clear honey
45ml/3 tbsp whisky
50g/2oz/¾ cup medium
 oatmeal
300ml/½ pint/1¼ cups
 double cream

350g/12oz/3 cups
 raspberries
fresh mint sprigs, to
 decorate

1 Gently warm the honey in the whisky, then leave to cool.

2 Preheat the grill. Spread the oatmeal in a very shallow layer in the grill pan and toast, stirring occasionally, until browned. Leave to cool.

3 Whip the cream in a large bowl until soft peaks form, then gently stir in the oats, honey and whisky until well combined.

4 Reserve a few raspberries for decoration, then layer the remainder with the oat mixture in four tall glasses. Cover and chill in the fridge for 2 hours.

5 About 30 minutes before serving, transfer the glasses to room temperature. Decorate with the reserved raspberries and mint sprigs.

Old English Trifle

If you are making this pudding for children, replace the sherry and brandy with orange juice.

Serves 6

75g/3oz day-old sponge
 cake, broken into
 bite-size pieces
8 ratafias, broken into
 halves
100ml/3½fl oz/⅓ cup
 medium sherry
30ml/2 tbsp brandy
350g/12oz/3 cups
 prepared fruit such as
 raspberries, peaches or
 strawberries
300ml/½ pint/1¼ cups
 double cream

40g/1½oz/scant ½ cup
 toasted flaked
 almonds, to decorate
strawberries, to decorate

For the custard
4 egg yolks
25g/1oz/2 tbsp caster
 sugar
450ml/¾ pint/1¼ cups
 single or whipping
 cream
few drops of vanilla
 essence

1 Put the sponge cake and ratafias in a glass serving dish, then sprinkle over the sherry and brandy and leave until they have been absorbed.

2 To make the custard, whisk the egg yolks and caster sugar together. Bring the cream to the boil in a heavy saucepan, then pour on to the egg yolk mixture, stirring constantly.

3 Return the mixture to the pan and heat very gently, stirring all the time with a wooden spoon, until the custard thickens enough to coat the back of the spoon; do not allow to boil. Leave to cool, stirring occasionally.

4 Put the fruit in an even layer over the sponge cake and ratafias in the serving dish, then strain the custard over the fruit and leave to set. Lightly whip the cream, spread it over the custard, then chill the trifle well. Decorate with flaked almonds and strawberries just before serving.

Cherry Syllabub

This recipe follows the style of the earliest syllabubs and produces a frothy creamy layer over a liquid one.

Serves 4

225g/8oz/2 cups ripe
    dark cherries, stoned
    and chopped
30ml/2 tbsp Kirsch
2 egg whites
30ml/2 tbsp lemon juice

150ml/¼ pint/⅔ cup
    sweet white wine
75g/3oz/generous ¼ cup
    caster sugar
300ml/½ pint/1¼ cups
    double cream

1 Divide the chopped cherries among six tall dessert glasses and sprinkle over the Kirsch.

2 In a clean bowl, whisk the egg whites until stiff peaks form. Gently fold in the lemon juice, wine and sugar.

3 In a separate bowl (but using the same whisk), lightly beat the cream, then fold into the egg white mixture. Spoon the cream mixture over the cherries, then chill overnight in the fridge.

Damask Cream

It is important not to move this simple, light, yet elegant dessert while it is setting, otherwise it will separate.

Serves 4

600ml/1 pint/2½ cups
    milk
40g/1½oz/3 tbsp caster
    sugar
several drops of triple-
    strength rose water

10ml/2 tsp rennet
60ml/4 tbsp double cream
sugared rose petals, to
    decorate (optional)

1 Gently heat the milk and 25g/1oz/2 tbsp of the sugar, stirring, until the sugar has melted and the temperature of the mixture feels neither hot nor cold. Stir rose water to taste into the milk, then remove the saucepan from the heat and stir in the rennet.

2 Pour the milk into a serving dish and leave undisturbed for 2–3 hours, until set. Stir the remaining sugar into the cream, then carefully spoon over the junket. Decorate with sugared rose petals, if you wish.

Mandarins in Orange-flower Syrup

Mandarins, tangerines, clementines, mineolas: any of these lovely citrus fruits are suitable to use in this recipe.

Serves 4

Pare some rind from one mandarin and cut it into fine shreds for decoration. Squeeze the juice from two mandarins and reserve it. Peel eight further mandarins, removing the white pith. Arrange the whole fruit in a wide dish. Mix the reserved juice, 1 tbsp confectioner's sugar and 2 tsp orange-flower water and pour it over the fruit. Cover and chill. Blanch the rind in boiling water for 30 seconds. Drain, cool and sprinkle over the mandarins, with pistachio nuts, to serve.

Chocolate Blancmange

For a special dinner party, flavour the blancmange with peppermint essence, crème de menthe or orange liqueur.

Serves 4

60ml/4 tbsp cornflour
600ml/1 pint/2½ cups
  milk
40g/1½ oz/3 tbsp caster
  sugar

50–115g/2–4oz plain
  chocolate, chopped
vanilla essence, to taste
chocolate curls, to
  decorate

1 Rinse a 750ml/1¼ pint/3⅔ cup fluted mould with cold water and leave it upside down to drain. Blend the cornflour to a smooth paste with a little of the milk.

2 Bring the remaining milk to the boil, preferably in a non-stick saucepan, then pour on to the blended mixture, stirring all the time.

3 Pour all the milk back into the saucepan and bring slowly to the boil over a low heat, stirring all the time until the mixture boils and thickens. Remove the pan from the heat, then add the sugar, chopped chocolate and a few drops of vanilla essence. Stir until the chocolate has melted.

4 Pour the chocolate mixture into the mould and leave in a cool place for several hours to set.

5 To unmould the blancmange, place on a large serving plate, then holding the plate and mould firmly together, invert them. Give both plate and mould a gentle but firm shake to loosen the blancmange, then lift off the mould. Scatter white and plain chocolate curls over the top of the blancmange to decorate and serve at once.

Cook's Tip
If you prefer, set the blancmange in four or six individual moulds.

Honeycomb Mould

These honeycomb moulds have a fresh lemon flavour. The layered mixture looks most attractive.

Serves 4

30ml/2 tbsp cold water
15g/½ oz gelatine
2 eggs, separated
75g/3oz/generous ¼ cup
  caster sugar

475ml/16fl oz/2 cups
  milk
grated rind of 1 small
  lemon
60ml/4 tbsp lemon juice

1 Chill four individual moulds or, if you prefer, use a 1.2 litre/2 pint/5 cup jelly mould. Mix together the water and the gelatine and leave to soften for 5 minutes. Place the bowl over a small saucepan of hot water and stir from time to time until dissolved.

2 Meanwhile, whisk the egg yolks and sugar together until pale, thick and fluffy.

3 Bring the milk to the boil in a heavy, preferably non-stick, saucepan, then slowly pour on to the egg yolk mixture, stirring all the time.

4 Return the milk mixture to the pan, then heat gently, stirring continuously until thickened. Do not allow to boil or it will curdle. Remove from the heat and stir in the grated lemon rind and juice.

5 Stir 2 or 3 spoonfuls of the lemon mixture into the gelatine, and then stir this back into the saucepan. In a clean dry bowl, whisk the egg whites until they are stiff but not too dry, then gently fold into the mixture in the saucepan in three batches, being careful to retain the oil.

6 Rinse the moulds or mould with cold water and drain well, then pour in the lemon mixture. Leave to cool, then cover and chill in the fridge until set. To serve, invert on to four individual or one serving plate.

Peach Melba

The original dish created for the opera singer Dame Nelli Melba had peaches and ice cream served upon an ice swan.

Serves 4

300g/11oz/scant 2 cups raspberries	*2 large ripe peaches or 425g/15oz can sliced peaches*
squeeze of lemon juice	
icing sugar, to taste	*8 scoops vanilla ice cream*

1 Press the raspberries through a non-metallic sieve.

2 Add a little lemon juice to the raspberry purée and sweeten to taste with icing sugar.

3 Dip fresh peaches in boiling water for 4–5 seconds, then slip off the skins, halve along the indented line, then slice; or tip canned peaches into a sieve and drain them.

4 Place two scoops of ice cream in each individual glass dish, top with peach slices, then pour over the raspberry purée. Serve immediately.

Summer Pudding

You may use any seasonal berries you wish in this unique and ever-popular dessert.

Serves 4

about 8 thin slices day-old white bread, crusts removed	*800g/1¼lb/4½ cups mixed summer fruits*
	about 25g/1oz/2 tbsp sugar

1 Cut a round from one slice of bread to fit in the base of a 1.2 litre/2 pint/5 cup pudding basin, then cut strips of bread about 5cm/2in wide to line the basin, overlapping the strips.

2 Gently heat the fruit, sugar and 30ml/2 tbsp water in a large heavy-based saucepan, shaking the pan occasionally, until the juices begin to run.

3 Reserve about 45ml/3 tbsp fruit juice, then spoon the fruit and remaining juice into the basin, taking care not to dislodge the bread.

4 Cut the remaining bread to fit entirely over the fruit. Stand the basin on a plate and cover with a saucer or small plate that will just fit inside the top of the basin. Place a heavy weight on top. Chill the pudding and the reserved fruit juice overnight in the fridge.

5 Run a knife carefully around the inside of the basin rim, then invert the pudding on to a cold serving plate. Pour over the reserved juice and serve.

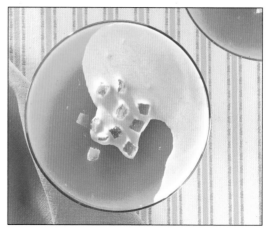

Boodles Orange Fool

This fruit fool has become the speciality of Boodles Club, a gentlemen's club in London's St James's area.

Serves 4

4 trifle sponge cakes, cubed	grated rind and juice of 2 oranges
300ml/½ pint/1¼ cups double cream	grated rind and juice of 1 lemon
25–50g/1–2oz/2–4 tbsp caster sugar	orange and lemon slices and rind, to decorate

1 Line the bottom and halfway up the sides of a large glass serving bowl or china dish with the cubed trifle sponge cakes.

2 Whip the cream with the sugar until it starts to thicken, then gradually whip in the fruit juices, adding the fruit rinds towards the end.

3 Carefully pour the cream mixture into the bowl or dish, taking care not to dislodge the sponge. Cover and chill for about 3–4 hours. Serve the fool decorated with orange and lemon slices and rind.

Apricot and Orange Jelly

You could also make this light dessert using nectarines or peaches instead of apricots.

Serves 4

350g/12oz well-flavoured fresh ripe apricots, stoned	15ml/1 tbsp gelatine single cream, to serve finely chopped candied orange peel, to decorate
50–75g/2–3oz/about ⅓ cup sugar	
about 300ml/½ pint/ 1¼ cups freshly squeezed orange juice	

1 Heat the apricots, sugar and 120ml/4fl oz/½ cup of the orange juice, stirring until the sugar has dissolved. Simmer gently until the apricots are tender.

2 Press the apricot mixture through a nylon sieve into a small measuring jug.

3 Pour 45ml/3 tbsp orange juice into a small heatproof bowl, sprinkle over the gelatine and leave for about 5 minutes, until softened.

4 Place the bowl over a saucepan of hot water and heat until the gelatine has dissolved. Pour into the apricot mixture slowly, stirring all the time. Make up to 600ml/1 pint/ 2½ cups with the orange juice.

5 Pour the apricot mixture into four individual dishes and chill in the fridge until set. Pour a thin layer of cream over the surface of the jellies before serving, decorated with candied orange peel.

Summer Berry Medley

Make the most of seasonal fruits in this refreshing dessert.
The sauce is also good swirled into plain fromage frais.

Serves 4–6

175g/6oz/1½ cups
   redcurrants, stripped
   from their stalks
175g/6oz/1½ cups
   raspberries
50g/2oz/¼ cup caster
   sugar
30–45ml/2–3 tbsp
   crème de framboise

450–675g/1–1½lb/
   4½ cups fresh mixed
   soft summer fruits
   such as strawberries,
   raspberries,
   blueberries,
   redcurrants and
   blackcurrants
vanilla ice cream, to
   serve

1 Place the redcurrants in a bowl with the raspberries, caster
sugar and crème de framboise. Cover and leave to macerate
for 1–2 hours.

2 Put the macerated fruit with its juices in a saucepan and
cook gently for 5–6 minutes, stirring occasionally, until the
fruit is just tender.

3 Pour the fruit into a blender or food processor and process
until smooth. Press through a nylon sieve to remove any pips.
Leave to cool, then chill in the fridge.

4 Divide the mixed soft fruit among four individual glass
serving dishes and pour over the sauce. Serve with scoops of
vanilla ice cream.

Brown Bread Ice Cream

This delicious textured ice cream is best served with a
blackcurrant sauce spiked with crème de cassis.

Serves 6

50g/2oz/½ cup roasted
   and chopped
   hazelnuts, ground
75g/3oz/1½ cups
   wholemeal
   breadcrumbs
50g/2oz/½ cup demerara
   sugar
3 egg whites
115g/4oz/½ cup caster
   sugar
300ml/½ pint/1¼ cups
   double cream

few drops of vanilla
   essence

For the sauce
225g/8oz/2 cups
   blackcurrants
75g/3oz/generous ¼ cup
   caster sugar
15ml/1 tbsp crème de
   cassis
fresh mint sprigs, to
   decorate

1 Combine the hazelnuts and breadcrumbs on a baking
sheet, then sprinkle over the demerara sugar. Place under a
moderate grill and cook until crisp and browned.

2 Whisk the egg whites in a bowl until stiff, then gradually
whisk in the caster sugar until thick and glossy. Whip the
cream until soft peaks form and fold into the meringue with
the breadcrumb mixture and vanilla essence.

3 Spoon the mixture into a 1.2 litre/2 pint/5 cup loaf tin.
Smooth the top level, then cover and freeze until firm.

4 To make the sauce, put the blackcurrants in a small bowl
with the sugar. Toss gently to mix and leave for about
30 minutes. Purée the blackcurrants in a food processor or
blender, then press through a nylon sieve until smooth. Add
the crème de cassis and chill in the fridge.

5 To serve, arrange a slice of ice cream on a plate, spoon over
a little sauce and decorate with fresh mint sprigs.

Raspberry Meringue Gâteau

This rich hazelnut meringue is filled with raspberries and cream and served with a raspberry sauce.

Serves 6

4 egg whites
225g/8oz/1 cup caster sugar
few drops of vanilla essence
5ml/1 tsp distilled malt vinegar
115g/4oz/1 cup roasted and chopped hazelnuts, ground
300ml/½ pint/1¼ cups double cream
350g/12oz/3 cups raspberries

sifted icing sugar, for dusting
raspberries and fresh mint sprigs, to decorate

For the sauce
225g/8oz/2 cups raspberries
45–60ml/3–4 tbsp icing sugar, sifted
15ml/1 tbsp orange liqueur

1 Preheat the oven to 180°C/350°F/Gas 4. Grease and base-line two 20cm/8in sandwich tins.

2 Whisk the egg whites until stiff peaks form, then gradually whisk in the caster sugar a tablespoon at a time. Continue whisking for a minute or two until very stiff, then fold in the vanilla essence, vinegar and hazelnuts. Transfer the mixture to the sandwich tins. Bake for 50–60 minutes, until crisp. Remove from the tins and cool.

3 Meanwhile, make the sauce. Purée the raspberries with the icing sugar and orange liqueur in a food processor or blender, then press through a fine nylon sieve to remove any pips. Chill the sauce in the fridge until ready to serve.

4 Whip the cream until soft peaks form, then fold in the raspberries. Use to sandwich the meringue rounds together.

5 Dust the top of the gâteau with icing sugar. Decorate with raspberries and mint sprigs and serve with the sauce.

Iced Chocolate and Nut Gâteau

Autumn hazelnuts add crunchiness to this popular iced dinner-party dessert.

Serves 6–8

75g/3oz/¾ cup shelled hazelnuts
about 32 sponge fingers
150ml/¼ pint/⅔ cup cold strong black coffee
30ml/2 tbsp Cognac or other brandy

450ml/¾ pint/1¾ cups double cream
75g/3oz/scant 1 cup icing sugar, sifted
150g/5oz plain chocolate
icing sugar and cocoa powder, for dusting

1 Preheat the oven to 200°C/400°F/Gas 6. Spread out the hazelnuts on a baking sheet and toast them in the oven for 5 minutes until golden. Transfer the nuts to a clean dish towel and rub off the skins. Cool, then chop finely.

2 Line a 1.2 litre/2 pint/5 cup loaf tin with clear film and cut the sponge fingers to fit the base and sides. Reserve the remaining biscuits.

3 Mix the coffee with the Cognac or other brandy in a shallow dish. Dip the sponge fingers briefly into the coffee mixture and return to the tin, sugary-side down.

4 Whip the cream with the icing sugar until it holds soft peaks. Roughly chop 75g/3oz of the chocolate, and fold into the cream with the hazelnuts.

5 Melt the remaining chocolate in a heatproof bowl set over a saucepan of barely simmering water. Cool, then fold into the cream mixture. Spoon into the tin.

6 Moisten the remaining biscuits in the coffee mixture and lay over the filling. Wrap and freeze until firm.

7 Remove the gâteau from the freezer 30 minutes before serving. Turn out on to a serving plate and dust with icing sugar and cocoa powder.

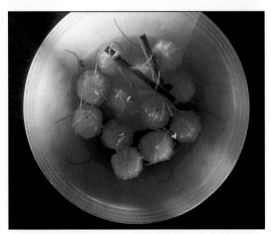

Blackberry Brown Sugar Meringue

A rich pudding which is elegant enough in presentation to be served at an autumnal dinner party.

Serves 6

For the meringue
175g/6oz/1½ cups soft
    light brown sugar
3 egg whites
5ml/1 tsp distilled malt
    vinegar
2.5ml/½ tsp vanilla
    essence

For the filling
350–450g/12oz–1lb/
    3–4 cups blackberries
30ml/2 tbsp crème de
    cassis
300ml/½ pint/1¼ cups
    double cream
15ml/1 tbsp icing sugar,
    sifted
small blackberry leaves,
    to decorate (optional)

1 Preheat the oven to 160°C/325°F/Gas 3. Draw a 20cm/8in circle on a sheet of non-stick baking paper, turn over and place on a baking sheet. Spread the brown sugar out on a baking sheet, dry in the oven for 8–10 minutes, then sieve.

2 Whisk the egg whites in a bowl until stiff. Add half the dried brown sugar, 15g/½oz/1 tbsp at a time, whisking well after each addition. Add the vinegar and vanilla essence, then fold in the remaining sugar.

3 Spoon the meringue on to the drawn circle on the paper, making a hollow in the centre. Bake for 45 minutes, then turn off the oven and leave the meringue in the oven with the door slightly open, until cold. Meanwhile, place the blackberries in a bowl, sprinkle over the crème de cassis and leave to macerate for 30 minutes.

4 When the meringue is cold, carefully peel off the non-stick baking paper and transfer the meringue to a serving plate. Lightly whip the cream with the icing sugar and spoon into the centre. Top with the blackberries and decorate with small blackberry leaves, if liked. Serve at once.

Clementines in Cinnamon Caramel

The combination of sweet, yet sharp clementines and caramel sauce with a hint of spice is divine.

Serves 4–6

8–12 clementines
225g/8oz/1 cup
    granulated sugar
300ml/½ pint/1¼ cups
    hand-hot water

2 cinnamon sticks
30ml/2 tbsp orange-
    flavoured liqueur
25g/1oz/¼ cup shelled
    pistachio nuts

1 Pare the rind from two clementines using a vegetable peeler and cut it into fine strips. Set aside.

2 Peel the clementines, removing all the pith but keeping them intact. Put the fruits in a serving bowl.

3 Gently heat the sugar in a pan until it dissolves and turns a rich golden brown. Immediately turn off the heat.

4 Pour the water into the pan, protecting your hand with a dish towel (the mixture will bubble and splutter). Bring slowly to the boil, stirring until the caramel dissolves. Add the shredded peel and cinnamon sticks, then simmer for 5 minutes. Stir in the liqueur.

5 Leave the syrup to cool for about 10 minutes, then pour over the clementines. Cover the bowl and chill for several hours or overnight.

6 Blanch the pistachio nuts in boiling water. Drain, cool and remove the dark outer skins. Scatter over the clementines and serve at once.

Chocolate Chestnut Roulade

Don't worry if this moist sponge cracks as you roll it – this is the sign of a good roulade.

Serves 8

175g/6oz plain chocolate
30ml/2 tbsp strong black coffee
5 eggs, separated
175g/6oz/1 cup caster sugar
250ml/18fl oz/1 cup double cream
225g/8oz unsweetened chestnut purée
45 – 60ml/3 – 4 tbsp icing sugar, plus extra for dusting
single cream, to serve

1 Preheat the oven to 180°C/350°F/Gas 4, then line and oil a 33 x 23cm/13 x 9in Swiss roll tin; use non-stick baking paper. Melt the chocolate in a bowl, then stir in the coffee. Leave to cool slightly.

2 Whisk the egg yolks and sugar together until thick and light, then stir in the cooled chocolate mixture. Whisk the egg whites in another bowl until stiff. Stir a spoonful into the chocolate mixture to lighten it, then gently fold in the rest.

3 Pour the mixture into the prepared tin, and spread level. Bake for 20 minutes. Remove from the oven, cover with a dish towel and leave to cool in the tin for several hours.

4 Whip the cream until soft peaks form. Mix together the chestnut purée and icing sugar; fold into the whipped cream.

5 Dust a sheet of greaseproof paper with icing sugar. Turn out the roulade on to this paper and peel off the lining paper. Trim the sides. Gently spread the chestnut cream evenly over the roulade to within 2.5cm/1in of the edges. Using the greaseproof paper to help you, carefully roll up the roulade as tightly and evenly as possible. Chill the roulade for about 2 hours, then dust liberally with icing sugar. Cut into thick slices. Serve with a little single cream poured over each slice.

Pasta Timbales with Apricot Sauce

If orzo cannot be found, other small soup pastas can be used for this dessert, which is made like a rice pudding.

Serves 4

100g/4oz/1 cup orzo
75g/3oz/⅓ cup caster sugar
pinch of salt
25g/1oz/2 tbsp butter
1 vanilla pod, split
750ml/1¼ pints/3⅔ cups milk
300ml/10fl oz/1¼ cups ready-made custard
45ml/3 tbsp Kirsch
15ml/1 tbsp powdered gelatine
oil, for greasing
400g/14oz canned apricots in juice
lemon juice
fresh flowers, to decorate (optional)

1 Place the pasta, sugar, pinch of salt, butter, vanilla pod and milk into a heavy saucepan and bring to the boil. Turn down the heat and simmer for 25 minutes until the pasta is tender and most of the liquid is absorbed. Stir frequently to prevent it from sticking.

2 Remove the vanilla pod and transfer the pasta to a bowl to cool. Stir in the custard and add 30ml/2 tbsp of the Kirsch.

3 Sprinkle the gelatine over 45ml/2 tbsp water in a small bowl set in a pan of barely simmering water. Allow to become spongy and heat gently to dissolve. Stir into the pasta.

4 Lightly oil 4 timbale moulds and spoon in the pasta. Chill for 2 hours until set.

5 Meanwhile, liquidize the apricots, pass through a sieve and add lemon juice and Kirsch to taste. Dilute with a little water if too thick. Loosen the timbales from their moulds and turn out on to individual plates. Serve with apricot sauce, decorated with fresh flowers if you wish.

Coffee Jellies with Amaretti Cream

This impressive dessert is very easy to prepare. For the best results, use a high–roasted Arabica bean for the coffee.

Serves 4

75g/3oz/generous ¼ cup caster sugar
450ml/¾ pint/1¾ cups hot strong coffee
30–45ml/2–3 tbsp dark rum or coffee liqueur
20ml/4 tsp gelatine

For the amaretti cream
150ml/¼ pint/⅔ cup double cream

15ml/1 tbsp icing sugar, sifted
10–15ml/2–3 tsp instant coffee granules dissolved in 15ml/4 tbsp hot water
6 large amaretti biscuits, crushed

1 Put the sugar in a saucepan with 75ml/5 tbsp water and stir over a gentle heat until dissolved. Increase the heat and allow the syrup to boil steadily, without stirring, for about 3–4 minutes.

2 Stir the hot coffee and rum or coffee liqueur into the syrup, then sprinkle the gelatine over the top and stir the mixture until it is completely dissolved.

3 Carefully pour the coffee jelly mixture into four wetted 150ml/¼ pint/⅔ cup moulds, allow to cool and then leave in the fridge for several hours until set.

4 To make the amaretti cream, lightly whip the cream with the icing sugar until the mixture holds stiff peaks. Stir in the coffee, then gently fold in all but 30ml/2 tbsp of the crushed amaretti biscuits.

5 Unmould the jellies on to four individual serving plates and spoon a little of the amaretti cream to one side. Dust over the reserved amaretti crumbs and serve at once.

Chocolate Date Torte

A stunning cake that tastes wonderful. Rich and gooey – it's a chocoholic's delight!

Serves 8

4 egg whites
115g/4oz/½ cup caster sugar
200g/7oz plain chocolate
175g/6oz Medjool dates, stoned and chopped
175g/6oz/1½ cups walnuts or pecan nuts, chopped

5ml/2 tsp vanilla essence, plus a few extra drops

For the frosting
200g/7oz/scant 1 cup fromage frais
200g/7oz/scant 1 cup mascarpone
icing sugar, to taste

1 Preheat the oven to 180°C/350°F/Gas 4. Lightly grease and base-line a 20cm/8in springform cake tin.

2 To make the frosting, mix together the fromage frais and mascarpone, and a few drops of vanilla essence and icing sugar to taste, then set aside.

3 Whisk the egg whites in a bowl until stiff peaks form. Whisk in 30ml/2 tbsp of the caster sugar until the meringue is thick and glossy, then fold in the remainder.

4 Chop 175g/6oz of the chocolate. Carefully fold into the meringue with the dates, nuts and 5ml/1 tsp of the vanilla essence. Pour into the prepared tin, spread level and bake for about 45 minutes, until risen around the edges.

5 Allow to cool in the tin for about 10 minutes, then turn out on to a wire rack. Peel off the lining paper and leave until completely cold. When cool, swirl the frosting over the top of the torte.

6 Melt the remaining chocolate in a bowl over hot water. Spoon into a small paper piping bag, snip off the top and drizzle the chocolate over the torte. Chill in the fridge before serving, cut into wedges.

Crème Caramel

This creamy, caramel-flavoured custard from France enjoys worldwide popularity.

Serves 4–6

115g/4oz/½ cup granulated sugar	6 eggs
300ml/½ pint/1¼ cups milk	75g/3oz/generous ¼ cup caster sugar
300ml/½ pint/1¼ cups single cream	2.5ml/½ tsp vanilla essence

1 Preheat the oven to 150°C/300°F/Gas 2 and half-fill a large roasting tin with water. Place the granulated sugar in a saucepan with 60ml/4 tbsp water and heat gently, swirling the pan occasionally, until the sugar has dissolved. Increase the heat and boil for a good caramel colour. Immediately pour the caramel into an ovenproof soufflé dish. Place in the roasting tin and set aside.

2 To make the egg custard, heat the milk and cream together in a pan until almost boiling. Meanwhile, beat the eggs, caster sugar and vanilla essence together in a bowl using a large balloon whisk.

3 Whisk the hot milk into the eggs and sugar, then strain the liquid through a sieve into the soufflé dish, on top of the cooled caramel base.

4 Transfer the tin to the centre of the oven and bake for about 1½–2 hours (topping up the water level after 1 hour), or until the custard has set in the centre. Lift the dish carefully out of the water and leave to cool, then cover and chill overnight in the fridge.

5 Loosen the sides of the chilled custard with a knife and then place an inverted plate (large enough to hold the caramel sauce that will flow out as well) on top of the dish. Holding the dish and plate together, turn upside down and give the whole thing a quick shake to release the crème caramel.

Australian Hazelnut Pavlova

A hazelnut meringue base is topped with orange cream, nectarines and raspberries in this lovely dessert.

Serves 4–6

3 egg whites	15ml/1 tbsp orange juice
175g/6oz/1 cup caster sugar	30ml/2 tbsp natural thick and creamy yogurt
5ml/1 tsp cornflour	2 ripe nectarines, stoned and sliced
5ml/1 tsp white wine vinegar	225g/8oz/2 cups raspberries, halved
40g/1½oz/generous ¼ cup chopped roasted hazelnuts	15–30ml/1–2 tbsp redcurrant jelly, warmed
250ml/8fl oz/1 cup double cream	

1 Preheat the oven to 140°C/275°F/Gas 1. Lightly grease a baking sheet. Draw a 20cm/8in circle on a sheet of baking parchment. Place pencil-side down on the baking sheet.

2 Place the egg whites in a clean, dry, grease-free bowl and whisk with an electric mixer until stiff peaks form. Whisk in the caster sugar 15g/½oz/1 tbsp at a time, whisking well after each addition.

3 Add the cornflour, vinegar and hazelnuts and fold in carefully with a large metal spoon.

4 Spoon the meringue on to the marked circle and spread out to the edges, making a dip in the centre.

5 Bake for about 1¼–1½ hours, until crisp. Leave to cool completely and transfer to a serving platter.

6 Whip the double cream and orange juice until the mixture is just thick, stir in the yogurt and spoon on to the meringue. Top with the prepared fruit and drizzle over the warmed redcurrant jelly. Serve immediately.

Chinese Fruit Salad

For an unusual fruit salad with an oriental flavour, try this mixture of fruits in a tangy lime and lychee syrup.

Serves 4

115g/4oz/½ cup caster
  sugar
thinly pared rind and
  juice of 1 lime
400g/14oz can lychees in
  syrup
1 ripe mango, stoned and
  sliced

1 eating apple, cored and
  sliced
2 bananas, chopped
1 star fruit, sliced
  (optional)
5ml/1 tsp sesame seeds,
  toasted

1 Place the caster sugar in a small saucepan with the lime rind and 300ml/ ½ pint/1¼ cups water. Heat gently until the sugar dissolves completely, then increase the heat and boil gently for about 7–8 minutes. Remove the saucepan from the heat and leave on one side to cool the syrup.

2 Drain the lychees into a jug and pour the juice into the cooled lime syrup with the lime juice. Place all the prepared fruit in a bowl and pour over the lime and lychee syrup. Chill in the fridge for about 1 hour. Just before serving, sprinkle with toasted sesame seeds.

Cook's Tip
Try different combinations of fruit in this salad. You might like to include pawpaw, kiwi fruit or pineapple for a change.

Apricot and Almond Jalousie

Jalousie **means "shutter", and the slatted pastry topping of this pie looks exactly like French window shutters.**

Serves 4

225g/8oz ready-made
  puff pastry
a little beaten egg
90ml/6 tbsp apricot
  conserve

25g/1oz/2 tbsp caster
  sugar
30ml/2 tbsp flaked
  almonds
cream, to serve

1 Preheat the oven to 220°C/425°F/Gas 7. Roll out the pastry on a lightly floured surface and cut into a square measuring 30cm/12in. Cut in half to make two rectangles.

2 Place one piece of pastry on a wetted baking sheet and brush all round the edges with beaten egg. Spread over the apricot conserve.

3 Fold the remaining rectangle in half lengthways and cut about eight diagonal slits from the centre fold to within about 1cm/½in from the edge all the way along.

4 Unfold the cut pastry and lay it on top of the pastry on the baking sheet. Press the pastry edges together well to seal and knock them up with the back of a knife.

5 Brush the slashed pastry with water and sprinkle over the caster sugar and flaked almonds.

6 Bake in the oven for 25–30 minutes, until well risen and golden brown. Remove the jalousie from the oven and leave to cool. Serve sliced, with cream or natural yogurt.

Cook's Tip
Make smaller individual jalousies and serve them with morning coffee, if you like. Use other flavours of fruit conserve for a change.

Baked American Cheesecake

The lemon-flavoured cream cheese provides a subtle filling for this classic dessert.

Makes 9 squares
For the base
175g/6oz/1½ cups crushed digestive biscuits
40g/1½oz/3 tbsp butter, melted

For the topping
450g/1lb/2½ cups curd cheese or full-fat soft cheese
115g/4oz/½ cup caster sugar

3 eggs
finely grated rind of 1 lemon
15ml/1 tbsp lemon juice
2.5ml/½ tsp vanilla essence
15ml/1 tbsp cornflour
30ml/2 tbsp soured cream
150ml/¼ pint/⅔ cup soured cream and
1.5ml/¼ tsp ground cinnamon, to decorate

1 Preheat the oven to 170°C/325°F/Gas 3. Lightly grease and line an 18cm/7in square loose-based cake tin.

2 Place the crushed biscuits and butter in a bowl and mix well. Tip into the base of the prepared cake tin and press down firmly with a potato masher.

3 Place the cheese in a bowl, add the sugar and beat well until smooth. Add the eggs one at a time, beating well after each addition and then stir in the lemon rind and juice, the vanilla essence, cornflour and soured cream. Beat until the mixture is completely smooth.

4 Pour the mixture on to the biscuit base and smooth the top level. Bake for 1¼ hours, or until the cheesecake has set in the centre. Turn off the oven but leave the cheesecake inside until completely cold.

5 Remove the cheesecake from the tin, top with the soured cream and swirl with the back of a spoon. Sprinkle with cinnamon and cut into squares.

Mango Ice Cream

Canned mangoes are used to make this deliciously rich and creamy ice cream, which has an oriental flavour.

Serves 4–6
2 x 425g/15oz cans sliced mango, drained
50g/2oz/¼ cup caster sugar
30ml/2 tbsp lime juice
15ml/1 tbsp gelatine

350ml/12fl oz/1½ cups double cream, lightly whipped
fresh mint sprigs, to decorate

1 Reserve four slices of mango for decoration and chop the remainder. Place the mango pieces in a bowl with the caster sugar and lime juice.

2 Put 45ml/3 tbsp hot water in a small heatproof bowl and sprinkle over the gelatine. Place over a saucepan of gently simmering water and stir until dissolved. Pour on to the mango mixture and mix well.

3 Add the lightly whipped cream and fold into the mango mixture. Pour the mixture into a plastic freezer container and freeze until half frozen.

4 Place the half-frozen ice cream in a food processor or blender and process until smooth. Spoon back into the container and return to the freezer to freeze completely.

5 Remove from the freezer 10 minutes before serving and place in the fridge. Serve scoops of ice cream decorated with pieces of the reserved sliced mango and fresh mint sprigs.

Rippled Chocolate Ice Cream

Rich, smooth and packed with chocolate, this heavenly ice cream is an all-round-the-world chocoholics' favourite.

Serves 4

60ml/4 tbsp chocolate
 and hazelnut spread
450ml/¾ pint/1¾ cups
 double cream
15ml/1 tbsp icing sugar

50g/2oz plain chocolate,
 chopped
plain chocolate curls, to
 decorate

1 Mix together the chocolate and hazelnut spread and 75ml/5 tbsp of the double cream in a bowl.

2 Place the remaining cream in a second bowl, sift in the icing sugar and beat until softly whipped.

3 Lightly fold in the chocolate and hazelnut mixture with the chopped chocolate until the mixture is rippled. Transfer to a plastic freezer container and freeze for 3–4 hours, until firm.

4 Remove the ice cream from the freezer about 10 minutes before serving to allow it to soften slightly. Spoon or scoop into dessert dishes or glasses and top each serving with a few plain chocolate curls.

Fruited Rice Ring

This pudding ring looks beautiful but you could stir the fruit in and serve in individual dishes instead.

Serves 4

65g/2½oz/¼ cup short
 grain pudding rice
900ml/1½ pints/3¾ cups
 semi-skimmed milk
1 cinnamon stick
175g/6oz dried fruit
 salad

175ml/6fl oz/¾ cup
 orange juice
40g/1½oz/3 tbsp caster
 sugar
finely grated rind of
 1 small orange

1 Place the rice, milk and cinnamon stick in a large saucepan and bring to the boil. Cover and simmer, stirring occasionally, for about 1½ hours, until all the liquid is absorbed.

2 Meanwhile, place the fruit and orange juice in a pan and bring to the boil. Cover and simmer very gently for about 1 hour, until tender and all the liquid is absorbed.

3 Remove the cinnamon stick from the rice and discard. Stir in the caster sugar and orange rind.

4 Tip the cooked fruit salad into the base of a lightly oiled 1.5 litre/2½ pint/6 cup ring mould. Spoon the rice over, smoothing it down firmly. Chill in the fridge.

5 Run a knife around the edge of the mould and turn out the rice carefully on to a serving plate.

Apricot Mousse

This light fluffy dessert can be made with any dried fruits instead of apricots – try dried peaches, prunes or apples.

Serves 4

300g/10oz ready-to-eat dried apricots
300ml/½ pint/1¼ cups fresh orange juice
200g/7oz/¾ cup low-fat fromage frais
2 egg whites
fresh mint, to decorate

1 Place the apricots in a saucepan with the orange juice and heat gently until boiling. Cover the pan and simmer gently for 3 minutes.

2 Cool slightly, then place in a food processor or blender and process until smooth. Stir in the fromage frais.

3 Whisk the egg whites until stiff enough to hold soft peaks, then fold gently into the apricot mixture.

4 Spoon the mousse into four stemmed glasses or one large serving dish. Chill in the fridge before serving. Decorate with sprigs of fresh mint.

Cook's Tip
To make a speedier, fool-type dessert, omit the egg whites and simply swirl together the apricot mixture and the fromage frais.

Apple Foam with Blackberries

Any seasonal soft fruit can be used for this lovely dessert if blackberries are not available.

Serves 4

225g/8oz/2 cups blackberries
150ml/¼ pint/generous ½ cup apple juice
5ml/1 tsp powdered gelatine
15ml/1 tbsp clear honey
2 egg whites

1 Place the blackberries in a saucepan with 60ml/4 tbsp of the apple juice and heat gently until the fruit is soft. Remove from the heat, cool, then chill in the fridge.

2 Sprinkle the gelatine over the remaining apple juice in a small pan and stir over a gentle heat until dissolved. Stir in the honey.

3 Whisk the egg whites until stiff peaks form. Continue whisking hard and gradually pour in the hot gelatine mixture until well mixed.

4 Quickly spoon the foam into rough mounds on individual plates. Chill. To serve, spoon the blackberries and juice around the foam rounds.

Cook's Tip
Make sure you dissolve the gelatine over a very low heat. It must not boil, or it will lose its setting ability.

Raspberry Passion Fruit Swirls

If passion fruit is not available, this simple dessert can be made with raspberries alone.

Serves 4

300g/11oz/generous
2½ cups raspberries
2 passion fruit
350ml/12fl oz/1⅓ cups
low-fat fromage frais

25g/1oz/2 tbsp caster
sugar
raspberries and sprigs of
fresh mint, to decorate

1 Mash the raspberries in a small bowl with a fork until the juice runs. Scoop out the passion fruit pulp into a separate bowl with the fromage frais and sugar and mix well.

2 Spoon alternate spoonfuls of the raspberry pulp and the fromage frais mixture into stemmed glasses or one large serving dish, stirring lightly to create a swirled effect.

3 Decorate the desserts with whole raspberries and sprigs of fresh mint. Serve chilled.

Creamy Mango Cheesecake

This low-fat cheesecake is as creamy as any other, but makes a healthier dessert option.

Serves 4

115g/4oz/1¼ cups
rolled oats
40g/1½oz/3 tbsp
sunflower margarine
30ml/2 tbsp clear honey
1 large ripe mango
300g/10oz/1¼ cups low-
fat soft cheese

150ml/¼ pint/⅔ cup
low-fat natural yogurt
finely grated rind of
1 small lime
45ml/3 tbsp apple juice
20ml/4 tsp gelatine
fresh mango and lime
slices, to decorate

1 Preheat the oven to 200°C/400°F/Gas 6. Mix together the oats, margarine and honey; press into the base of a 20cm/8in loose-bottomed cake tin. Bake for 12–15 minutes. Cool.

2 Peel, stone and roughly chop the mango. Process with the cheese, yogurt and lime rind until smooth. Heat the apple juice until boiling, sprinkle the gelatine over it, stir to dissolve, then stir into the cheese mixture. Pour into the tin and chill until set. Turn out and decorate with mango and lime slices.

Frudités with Honey Dip

This dish is shared and would be ideal to serve at an informal lunch or supper party.

Serves 4

Place 225g/8oz/1 cup Greek-style yogurt in a dish, beat until smooth, then stir in 45ml/3 tbsp clear honey, leaving a marbled effect. Cut a selection of fruits into wedges or bite-size pieces or leave whole, depending on your choice. Arrange on a platter with the bowl of dip in the centre. Serve chilled.

Boston Banoffee Pie

This dessert's rich, creamy, toffee-style filling just can't be resisted – but who cares!

Serves 4–6

150g/5oz/1¼ cups plain
　flour
225g/8oz/1 cup butter
50g/2oz/¼ cup caster
　sugar
½ x 400g/14oz can
　skimmed, sweetened
　condensed milk

115g/4oz/⅔ cup soft
　light brown sugar
30ml/2 tbsp golden syrup
2 small bananas, sliced
a little lemon juice
whipped cream and
　grated plain chocolate

1 Preheat the oven to 160°C/325°F/Gas 3. Place the flour and 115g/4oz/ ½ cup of the butter in a bowl, then stir in the caster sugar. Squeeze the mixture together with your hands until it forms a dough. Press into the base of a 20cm/8in loose-based fluted flan tin. Bake blind for 25 – 30 minutes, until the pastry is lightly browned.

2 Place the remaining butter with the condensed milk, brown sugar and golden syrup into a non-stick saucepan and heat gently, stirring, until the butter has melted and the sugar has completely dissolved.

3 Bring to a gentle boil and cook for 7 minutes, stirring all the time (to prevent burning), until the mixture thickens and turns a light caramel colour. Pour on to the cooked pastry base and leave until cold.

4 Sprinkle the bananas with lemon juice and arrange in overlapping circles on top of the caramel filling, leaving a gap in the centre. Pipe a swirl of whipped cream in the centre and sprinkle with the grated chocolate.

Cook's Tip
Do not peel and slice the bananas until you are ready to serve or they will become slimy.

Strawberry and Blueberry Tart

This tart works equally well using either autumn or winter fruits as long as there is a riot of colour.

Serves 6 – 8

225g/8oz/2 cups plain
　flour
pinch of salt
75g/3oz/scant ¾ cup
　icing sugar
150g/5oz/generous ½ cup
　unsalted butter
1 egg yolk

For the filling
350g/12oz/1¼ cups
　mascarpone

30ml/2 tbsp icing sugar
few drops of vanilla
　essence
finely grated rind of
　1 orange
450 – 675g/1 – 1½lb/
　4½ cups fresh mixed
　strawberries and
　blueberries
90ml/6 tbsp redcurrant
　jelly
30ml/2 tbsp orange juice

1 Sift the flour, salt and sugar in a bowl. Dice the butter and rub it in until the mixture resembles coarse breadcrumbs. Mix in the egg yolk and 10ml/2 tsp cold water. Gather the dough together, knead lightly, wrap and chill for 1 hour.

2 Preheat the oven to 190°C/375°F/Gas 5. Roll out the pastry and use to line a 25cm/10in fluted flan tin. Prick the base and chill for 15 minutes in the fridge.

3 Line the chilled pastry case with greaseproof paper and baking beans, then bake blind for 15 minutes. Remove the paper and beans and bake for a further 15 minutes, until crisp and golden. Leave to cool in the tin.

4 Beat together the mascarpone, sugar, vanilla essence and orange rind in a mixing bowl until smooth.

5 Remove the pastry case from the tin, then spoon in the filling and pile the fruits on top. Heat the redcurrant jelly with the orange juice until runny, sieve, then brush over the fruit to form a glaze.

Strawberries in Spiced Grape Jelly

This light dessert would be ideal to serve after a rich and filling main course.

Serves 4

*450ml/¾ pint/1¾ cups
  red grape juice
1 cinnamon stick
1 small orange
15ml/1 tbsp gelatine*

*225g/8oz/2 cups
  strawberries, chopped
strawberries and
  shredded orange rind,
  to decorate*

1 Place the grape juice in a saucepan with the cinnamon and thinly pared orange rind. Infuse over a gentle heat for 10 minutes, then remove the cinnamon and orange rind. Sprinkle the squeezed orange juice over the gelatine. Stir into the grape juice to dissolve. Allow to cool until just beginning to set.

2 Stir in the strawberries and then quickly tip the mixture into a 1 litre/1¾ pint/4 cup mould or serving dish. Chill in the fridge until it has set. Dip the mould quickly into hot water and invert on to a serving plate. Decorate with fresh strawberries and shreds of orange rind.

Plum and Port Sorbet

Rather a grown-up sorbet, this one, but you could use fresh still red grape juice in place of the port or wine.

Serves 4

*900g/2lb ripe red plums,
  stoned and halved
75g/3oz/generous ¼ cup
  caster sugar
45ml/3 tbsp water*

*45ml/3 tbsp ruby port or
  red wine
crisp sweet biscuits, to
  serve*

1 Place the plums in a saucepan with the sugar and water. Stir over a gentle heat until the sugar is melted, then cover and simmer gently for about 5 minutes, until the fruit is soft.

2 Turn into a food processor or blender and purée until smooth, then stir in the port or red wine. Cool completely, then tip into a plastic freezer container and freeze until the sorbet is firm around the edges. Process until smooth. Spoon back into the freezer container and freeze until solid.

3 Allow to soften slightly at room temperature for about 15–20 minutes before serving in scoops, with sweet biscuits.

Quick Apricot Blender Whip

This is one of the quickest desserts you could make – and also one of the prettiest.

Serves 4

Drain the juice from 400g/14oz can apricot halves in juice and place the fruit in a blender or food processor with 1 tbsp Grand Marnier or brandy. Process until smooth. Spoon the fruit purée and ¾ cup plain strained yogurt in alternate spoonfuls into four tall glasses or glass dishes, swirling them together slightly to give a marbled effect. Lightly toast 2 tbsp slivered almonds until they are golden. Let them cool slightly and then sprinkle them on top.

Tofu Berry Brulée

This is a lighter variation of a classic dessert. Use any soft fruits that are in season.

Serves 4

225g/8oz/2 cups red
  berry fruits such as
  strawberries,
  raspberries and
  redcurrants

300g/11oz packet silken
  tofu
45ml/3 tbsp icing sugar
65g/2½oz/¼ cup
  demerara sugar

1 Halve or quarter any large strawberries, but leave the smaller ones whole. Mix with the other chosen berries.

2 Place the tofu and icing sugar in a food processor or blender and process until smooth.

3 Stir in the fruits and spoon into a flameproof dish with a 900ml/1½ pint/3¾ cup capacity. Sprinkle the top with enough demerara sugar to cover evenly.

4 Place under a very hot grill until the sugar melts and caramelizes. Chill in the fridge before serving.

Cook's Tip
Choose silken tofu rather than firm tofu as it gives a smoother texture in this type of dish. Firm tofu is better for cooking in chunks.

Emerald Fruit Salad

This vibrant green fruit salad contains a hint of lime and is sweetened with honey.

Serves 4

30ml/2 tbsp lime juice
30ml/2 tbsp clear honey
2 green eating apples,
  cored and sliced
1 ripe Ogen melon, diced

2 kiwi fruit, sliced
1 star fruit, sliced
fresh mint sprigs, to
  decorate

1 Mix together the lime juice and honey in a large bowl, then toss in the apple slices.

2 Stir in the melon, kiwi fruit and star fruit. Place in a glass serving dish and chill in the fridge before serving.

3 Decorate with mint sprigs and serve with yogurt or fromage frais, if you wish.

Cook's Tip
Colour-themed fruit salads are fun to create and easy, given the wide availability of exotic fruits. You could try an orange-coloured salad using cantaloupe melon, apricots, peaches or nectarines, oranges or satsumas, and mango or pawpaw.

Peach and Ginger Pashka

This simpler adaptation of a Russian Easter favourite is made with lighter ingredients than the traditional version.

Serves 4–6

350g/12oz/1½ cups low-fat cottage cheese
2 ripe peaches
120ml/4fl oz/½ cup low-fat natural yogurt
2 pieces stem ginger in syrup, drained and chopped

30ml/2 tbsp stem ginger syrup
2.5ml/½ tsp vanilla essence
peach slices and toasted flaked almonds, to decorate

1   Drain the cottage cheese and rub through a sieve into a bowl. Stone and roughly chop the peaches.

2   Mix together the chopped peaches, cottage cheese, yogurt, ginger, syrup and vanilla essence.

3   Line a new clean flowerpot or a sieve with a piece of clean fine cloth such as muslin.

4   Tip in the cheese mixture, then wrap over the cloth and place a weight on top. Leave over a bowl in a cool place to drain overnight. To serve, unwrap the cloth and invert the pashka on to a plate. Decorate with peach slices and almonds.

Chilled Chocolate Slice

This is a very rich family pudding, but it is also designed to use up the occasional leftover.

Serves 6–8

115g/4oz/½ cup butter, melted
225g/8oz ginger biscuits, finely crushed
50g/2oz stale sponge cake crumbs
60–75ml/4–5 tbsp orange juice
115g/4oz stoned dates

25g/1oz/¼ cup finely chopped nuts
175g/6oz bitter chocolate
300ml/½ pint/1¼ cups whipping cream
grated chocolate and icing sugar, to decorate

1   Mix together the butter and ginger biscuit crumbs, then pack around the sides and base of an 18cm/7in loose-based flan tin. Chill in the fridge while making the filling.

2   Put the cake crumbs into a large bowl with the orange juice and leave to soak. Warm the dates thoroughly, then mash and blend into the cake crumbs along with the nuts.

3   Melt the chocolate with 45–60ml/3–4 tbsp of the cream. Softly whip the rest of the cream, then fold in the melted chocolate mixture.

4   Stir the cream and chocolate mixture into the crumbs and mix well. Pour into the biscuit case, mark into portions and leave to set. Scatter over the grated chocolate and dust with icing sugar. Serve cut in wedges.

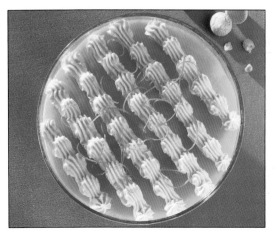

Tangerine Trifle

An unusual variation on a traditional trifle – of course, you can add a little alcohol if you wish.

Serves 4

5 trifle sponges, halved
  lengthways
30ml/2 tbsp apricot jam
15–20 ratafia biscuits
142g/4 3/4oz packet
  tangerine jelly
300g/11oz can mandarin
  oranges, drained,
  reserving juice

600ml/1 pint/2½ cups
  ready-made
  (or home-made)
  custard
whipped cream and
  shreds of orange rind,
  to decorate
caster sugar, for
  sprinkling

1 Spread the halved sponge cakes with apricot conserve and arrange in the base of a deep serving bowl or glass dish. Sprinkle the ratafias over the top.

2 Break up the jelly into a heatproof measuring jug, add the juice from the canned mandarins and dissolve in a saucepan of hot water or in the microwave. Stir until the liquid clears.

3 Make up to 600ml/1 pint/2½ cups with ice cold water, stir well and leave to cool for up to 30 minutes. Scatter the mandarin oranges over the cake and ratafias.

4 Pour the jelly over the mandarin oranges, cake and ratafias and chill in the fridge for 1 hour, or more.

5 When the jelly has set, pour the custard over the top and chill again in the fridge.

6 When ready to serve, pipe the whipped cream over the custard. Wash the orange rind shreds, sprinkle them with caster sugar and use to decorate the trifle.

Blackberry and Apple Romanoff

Rich yet fruity, this dessert is popular with most people and very quick and easy to make.

Serves 6–8

350g/12oz sharp eating
  apples, peeled, cored
  and chopped
40g/1½oz/3 tbsp caster
  sugar
250ml/8fl oz/1 cup
  whipping cream
5ml/1 tsp grated lemon
  rind
90ml/6 tbsp Greek-style
  yogurt

50g/2oz (about 4–6)
  crisp meringues,
  roughly crumbled
225g/8oz/2 cups
  blackberries (fresh
  or frozen)
whipped cream, a few
  blackberries and
  fresh mint leaves,
  to decorate

1 Line a 900ml–1.2 litre/1½–2 pint/4–5 cup pudding basin with clear film. Toss the chopped apples into a saucepan with 1oz/2 tbsp sugar and cook for 2–3 minutes, or until softening. Mash with a fork and leave to cool.

2 Whip the cream and fold in the lemon rind, yogurt, the remaining sugar, apples and meringues.

3 Gently stir in the blackberries, then tip the mixture into the pudding basin and freeze for 1–3 hours.

4 Turn out on to a plate and remove the clear film. Decorate with whirls of whipped cream, blackberries and mint leaves.

Apple and Hazelnut Shortcake

This is a variation on the classic strawberry shortcake and is equally delicious.

Serves 8–10

150g/5oz/generous 1 cup
plain wholemeal flour
50g/2oz/½ cup ground
hazelnuts
50g/2oz/6 tbsp icing
sugar, sifted
150g/5oz/generous 1 cup
unsalted butter
3 sharp eating apples
5ml/1 tsp lemon juice
15–25g/½–1oz/1–2
tbsp caster sugar
15ml/1 tbsp chopped
fresh mint, or 5ml/
1 tsp dried mint
250ml/8fl oz/1 cup
whipping cream
a few drops of vanilla
essence
a few fresh mint leaves
and whole hazelnuts,
to decorate

1 Process the flour, ground hazelnuts and icing sugar with the butter in a food processor in short bursts, until they come together. Bring the dough together, adding a very little iced water if needed. Knead briefly, wrap and chill for 30 minutes.

2 Preheat the oven to 160°C/325°F/Gas 3. Cut the dough in half and roll out each half to an 18cm/7in round. Place on greaseproof paper on baking sheets. Bake for 40 minutes, or until crisp. Allow to cool.

3 Peel, core and chop the apples into a saucepan with the lemon juice. Add sugar to taste; cook for 2–3 minutes, until just soft. Mash the apple gently with the mint; leave to cool.

4 Whip the cream with the vanilla essence. Place one shortbread base on a serving plate. Spread half the apple and half the cream on top.

5 Place the second shortcake on top, then spread over the remaining apple and cream, swirling the top layer of cream gently. Decorate the top with mint leaves and a few whole hazelnuts, then serve at once.

Lemon Cheesecake

A lovely light cream cheese filling is sandwiched between brandy snaps in this tasty dessert.

Serves 8

½ x 142g/4¾ oz packet
lemon jelly
450g/1lb/2 cups low-fat
cream cheese
10ml/2 tsp grated lemon
rind
75–115g/3–4oz/about ½
cup caster sugar
a few drops of vanilla
essence
150ml/¼ pint/⅔ cup
Greek-style yogurt
8 brandy snaps
a few fresh mint leaves
and icing sugar, to
decorate

1 Dissolve the jelly in 45–60ml/3–4 tbsp boiling water in a heatproof measuring jug and, when clear, add sufficient cold water to make up to 150ml/¼ pint/⅔ cup. Chill in the fridge until beginning to thicken. Meanwhile, line a 450g/1lb loaf tin with clear film.

2 Cream the cheese with the lemon rind, sugar and vanilla and beat until light and smooth. Then fold in the thickening lemon jelly and the yogurt. Spoon into the prepared tin and chill until set. Preheat the oven to 160°C/325°F/Gas 3.

3 Place two or three brandy snaps at a time on a baking sheet. Place in the oven for no more than 1 minute, until soft enough to unroll and flatten out completely. Leave on a cold plate or tray to harden again. Repeat with the remaining brandy snaps.

4 To serve, turn the cheesecake out on to a board with the help of the clear film. Cut into eight slices and place one slice on each brandy snap base. Decorate with mint leaves and dust with icing sugar.

Frozen Strawberry Mousse Cake

Children love this cake because it is pink and pretty, and it is just like an ice cream treat.

Serves 4–6

*425g/15oz can
  strawberries in syrup
15ml/1 tbsp powdered
  gelatine
6 trifle sponge cakes
45ml/3 tbsp strawberry
  conserve*

*200ml/7fl oz/scant 1 cup
  crème fraîche
200ml/7fl oz/scant 1 cup
  whipped cream, to
  decorate*

1 Strain the syrup from the strawberries into a large heatproof jug. Sprinkle over the gelatine and stir well. Stand the jug in a saucepan of hot water and stir until the gelatine has dissolved.

2 Leave to cool, then chill in the fridge for just under 1 hour, until beginning to set. Meanwhile, cut the sponge cake in half lengthways and then spread the cut surfaces evenly with the strawberry conserve.

3 Slowly whisk the crème fraîche into the strawberry jelly, then whisk in the canned strawberries. Line a deep 20cm/8in loose-based cake tin with non-stick baking paper.

4 Pour half the strawberry mousse mixture into the tin, arrange the sponge cakes over the surface and then spoon over the remaining mousse mixture, pushing down any sponge cakes which rise up.

5 Freeze for 1–2 hours until firm. Unmould the cake and carefully remove the lining paper. Transfer to a serving plate. Decorate with whirls of cream, a few strawberry leaves and a fresh strawberry, if you have them.

Lemon and Blackberry Soufflé

This tangy dessert is complemented wonderfully by a rich blackberry sauce.

Serves 6

*grated rind of 1 lemon
  and juice of 2 lemons
15ml/1 tbsp powdered
  gelatine
5 size 4 eggs, separated
150g/4oz/1¼ cups caster
  sugar
a few drops of vanilla
  essence
400ml/14fl oz/1⅔ cups
  whipping cream*

For the sauce
*175g/6oz/1½ cups
  blackberries (fresh or
  frozen)
25–40g/1–1½oz/2–3
  tbsp caster sugar
a few fresh blackberries
  and blackberry leaves,
  to decorate*

1 Place the lemon juice in a small saucepan and heat through. Sprinkle on the gelatine and leave to dissolve, or heat further until clear. Allow to cool. Put the lemon rind, egg yolks, sugar and vanilla into a large bowl and whisk until the mixture is very thick, pale and really creamy.

2 Whisk the egg whites until almost stiff. Whip the cream until stiff. Stir the gelatine mixture into the yolks, then fold in the whipped cream and lastly the egg whites. When lightly but thoroughly blended, turn into a 1.5 litre/2½ pint/6 cup soufflé dish and freeze for about 2 hours.

3 To make the sauce, place the blackberries in a pan with the sugar and cook for 4–6 minutes until the juices begin to run and all the sugar has dissolved. Pass through a nylon sieve to remove the seeds, then chill until ready to serve.

4 When the soufflé is almost frozen, scoop or spoon out on to individual plates and serve with the blackberry sauce.

Index

NOTES

Notes

NOTES

NOTES

NOTES

NOTES